# Responsibility to Ensure

# Maritime Cooperation in East Asia

*Series Editors*

Seokwoo Lee (*Inha University Law School*)
Keyuan Zou (*University of Central Lancashire*)

VOLUME 12

The titles published in this series are listed at *brill.com/mcea*

# Responsibility to Ensure

## *Sponsoring States' Environmental Legislation for Deep Seabed Mining and China's Practice*

*By*

Xiangxin Xu

BRILL
NIJHOFF

LEIDEN | BOSTON

Library of Congress Cataloging-in-Publication Data

Names: Xu, Xiangxin, author.
Title: Responsibility to ensure : sponsoring states' environmental legislation for deep seabed mining and China's practice / by Xiangxin Xu.
Description: Leiden ; Boston : Brill Nijhoff, [2021] | Series: Maritime cooperation in East Asia, 2405-934X ; volume 12 | Based on author's thesis (doctoral - Universität Kiel, 2020) issued under title: Environmental Protection and Environmental Regulation with regard to Deep Seabed Mining : From China's Perspective. | Includes bibliographical references and index. | Summary: "In this book, the author highlights and analyzes the sponsoring State's primary responsibility, that is ensuring its sponsored contractors' compliance with environmental obligations under the UNCLOS and related legal instruments by enacting national legislation"– Provided by publisher.
Identifiers: LCCN 2021035063 (print) | LCCN 2021035064 (ebook) | ISBN 9789004472334 (hardback) | ISBN 9789004472341 (ebook)
Subjects: LCSH: Ocean mining–Law and legislation. | Environmental law, International. | Ocean mining–Law and legislation–China. | Law of the sea–China.
Classification: LCC KZA1370 .X8 2021 (print) | LCC KZA1370 (ebook) | DDC 341.4/55–dc23
LC record available at https://lccn.loc.gov/2021035063
LC ebook record available at https://lccn.loc.gov/2021035064

Typeface for the Latin, Greek, and Cyrillic scripts: "Brill". See and download: brill.com/brill-typeface.

ISSN 2405-934X
ISBN 978-90-04-47233-4 (hardback)
ISBN 978-90-04-47234-1 (e-book)



This book is printed on acid-free paper and produced in a sustainable manner.

# Contents

# Acknowledgements

This book, based on my doctoral research at the University of Kiel, Germany, could not have been completed without the support of many people. I would like to express my deep gratitude to my supervisor, Professor Dr. Nele Matz-Lück at the Walther Schücking Institute for International Law (WSI), Kiel University, Germany, for the timely discussion and invaluable suggestions for the entire book. Thanks to her for recommending me to the Rhodes Academy and IFLOS Summer Academy, which provided me a comprehensive understanding of the law of the sea. I am also grateful for her supporting me in my application to the internship at the ISA and ITLOS, from which I gained first-hand insights of the Deep Seabed Mining Regime. I am also grateful to two other professors at the WSI, Professor Dr. Kerstin von der Decken and Professor Dr. Andreas von Arnauld, for their constructive criticisms and suggestions for my thesis during the WSI Ph.D. Seminars.

I offer my particular thanks to Professor Dr. Shaojun Liu at Central South University. Due to his support, I am continuously involved in workshops and projects relating to ISA Draft Exploitation Regulations. I gratefully acknowledge the financial support for my doctoral study provided by the China Scholarship Council (CSC).

Finally, I want to express my special gratitude to my husband, Guokun, for his endless support and love. I also want to thank my parents. Their inspiring encouragement and tireless support made me continuously step forward and achieve my best work.

This book includes all relevant developments and is based on legal instruments as of December 2020.

# Abbreviations

| | |
|---|---|
| ARSIWA | Draft Articles on Responsibility of States for Internationally Wrongful Acts |
| AUD | Australian Dollar |
| BBNJ | Diversity Beyond Areas of National Jurisdiction |
| BGR | Federal Institute for Geosciences and Natural Resources, Germany |
| BPHDC | Beijing Pioneer Hi-Tech Development Corporation |
| CCZ | Clarion-Clipperton Zone |
| CIIC | Cook Islands Investment Corporation |
| CMC | China Minmetals Corporation |
| CMP | China Maritime Police |
| CNY | Chinese Yuan |
| COMRA | China Ocean Mineral Resources R & D Association |
| CPRM | Companhia de Pesquisa de Recursos Minerais S.A., Brazil |
| CPUCH | Convention on the Protection of the Underwater Cultural Heritage |
| CRP | Chatham Rock Phosphate Ltd, New Zealand |
| CZK | Czech Koruna |
| DORD | Deep Ocean Resources Development Co. Ltd., Japan |
| EEZ | Exclusive Economic Zone |
| EIA | Environmental Impact Assessment |
| FLEC | Fisheries Law Enforcement Command at the Chinese Ministry of Agriculture |
| ERC | National People's Congress, China |
| EUR | Euro |
| FC | Finance Committee, ISA |
| FJD | Fijian Dollar |
| GAC | General Administration of Customs, China |
| GBP | Great Britain Pound |
| GIS | Geographic Information System |
| GSR | Global Sea Mineral Resources NV, Belgium |
| ICJ | International Court of Justice |
| ICPC | International Cable Protection Committee |
| IFC | International Finance Corporation |
| Ifremer | Institut français de recherche pour l'exploitation de la mer |
| ILC | International Law Commission |
| IMMS | International Marine Minerals Society |
| IMO | International Maritime Organisation |
| IOM | Interoceanmental Joint Organization |
| ISA | International Seabed Authority |

| | |
|---|---|
| ISO | International Organisation for Standardization |
| ITLOS | International Tribunal for the Law of the Sea |
| IUCN | International Union for the Conservation of Nature |
| JOGMEC | Japan Oil, Gas and Metals National Corporation, Japan |
| JPY | Japanese Yen |
| LOSC | United Nations Convention on the Law of the Sea |
| LTC | Legal and Technical Commission, ISA |
| MAD | Marine Administrative Department under the State Council, China |
| MIDAS | Managing Impacts of Deep-seA reSource exploitation (Research Project) |
| MREL | Marawa Research and Exploration Ltd., Kiribati |
| MSA | Maritime Safety Administration of the Chinese Ministry of Transportation |
| NT EPA | Northern Territory Environment Protection Authority, Australia |
| NORI | Nauru Ocean Resources Inc. |
| NPC | National People's Congress, China |
| NZD | New Zealand Dollar |
| OAA | Ocean Affair Administration, China |
| OMS | Ocean Mineral Singapore Pte. Ltd. |
| OSPAR Convention | Convention for the Protection of the Marine Environment of the North-East Atlantic |
| PCIJ | Permanent Court of International Justice |
| REE | Rare Earth Element |
| RLRF | Pacific-ACP States Regional Legislative and Regulatory Framework for Deep Sea Minerals Exploration and Exploitation |
| ROV | remotely operated vehicle |
| SDC | Seabed Disputes Chamber of the International Tribunal for the Law of the Sea |
| SGD | Singapore Dollar |
| SOA | State Oceanic Administration, China |
| SPC | Secretariat of the Pacific Community |
| TOML | Tonga Offshore Mining Limited |
| TOP | Tongan pa'anga |
| TTR | Trans-Tasman Recourses Ltd, New Zealand |
| UKSRL | UK Seabed Resources Ltd. |
| UNCC | United Nations Compensation Commission |
| UNCLOS III | Third United Nations Law of the Sea Conference |
| UNDRIP | UN Declaration on the Rights of Indigenous People |

| | |
|---|---|
| UN DOALOS | Division for Ocean Affairs and the Law of the Sea at the United Nations |
| UNEP | United Nations Environment Programme |
| UNESCO | United Nations Organization for Education, Science and Culture |
| UNGA | United Nations General Assembly |
| USD | United States Dollar |
| VME | Vulnerable Marine Ecosystem |

# Figures and Tables

## Figures



## Tables

# Treaties and Declarations

## Treaties

Agreement Relating to the Implementation of Part XI of the United Nations Convention on the Law of the Sea of 10 December 1982 (adopted 28 July 1994, entered into force 28 July 1996) 1836 UNTS 3

Basel Protocol on Liability and Compensation for Damage Resulting from Transboundary Movements of Hazardous Wastes and Their Disposal (adopted 10 December 1999, not in force).

Convention for the Protection of the Marine Environment of the North-East Atlantic (adopted 22 September 1992, entered into force 25 March 1998) 2343 UNTS 67 (OSPAR Convention)

Convention on the Protection of the Underwater Cultural Heritage, (adopted 2 November 2001, entered into force 2 January 2009) 41 ILM 40 (2002) (CPUCH)

International Convention Relating to Intervention on the High Seas in Cases of Oil Pollution Casualties (adopted 29 November 1969, entered into force 6 May 1975) 970 UNTS 211

International Convention on Civil Liability for Oil Pollution Damage (adopted 29 November 1969, entered into force 19 June 1975) 973 UNTS 3 (1969 CLC); Protocol to the International Convention on Civil Liability for Oil Pollution Damage, 1969 (adopted 19 November 1976, entered into force 8 April 1981) 1225 UNTS 356; Protocol of 1992 to amend the International Convention on Civil Liability for Oil Pollution Damage, 1969 (adopted 27 November 1992, entered into force 30 May 1996) 1956 UNTS 255 (1992 Protocol)

International Convention on Liability and Compensation for Damage in Connection with the Carriage of Hazardous and Noxious Substances by Sea (adopted 3 May 1996) 35 ILM 1415 (1996) (HNS Convention)

Montreal Protocol on Substances that Deplete the Ozone Layer (adopted 16 September 1987, entered into force 1 January 1989) 1522 UNTS 3, amended 29 June 1990, entered into force 10 August 1992; amended 25 November 1992, entered into force 14 June 1994; amended 17 September 1997, entered into force 10 November 1999; amended 3 December 1999, entered into force 25 February 2002; amended 21 September 2007, entered into force 14 May 2008; amended 15 October 2016, entered into force 1 January 2019

United Nations Convention on the Law of the Sea (adopted 10 December 1982, entered into force 16 November 1994) 1833 UNTS 3

Vienna Convention on the Law of Treaties (adopted 23 May 1969, entered into force 27 January 1980) 1155 UNTS 331

## Declarations

Declaration of the United Nations Conference on the Human Environment (adopted 16 June 1972, UN Doc. A/Conf.48/14/Rev. 1), 11 ILM 1416 (1972) (Stockholm Declaration)
Rio Declaration on Environment and Development (adopted 13 June 1992, UN Doc. A/CONF.151/26 (vol. I)) 31 ILM 874 (1992) (Rio Declaration)
United Nations Declaration on the Rights of Indigenous Peoples (adopted 12 September 2007, A/61/L.67/Annex) (UNDRIP)

# Cases

## Arbitral Awards

*Case Concerning the Difference between New Zealand and France Concerning the Interpretation or Application of Two Agreements, Concluded on 9 July 1986 between the Two States and which Related to the Problems Arising from the Rainbow Warrior Affair, RIAA, 1990, vol. XX*, p. 215.

## ICJ

*Ahmadou Sadio Diallo (Republic of Guinea v. Democratic Republic of the Congo), Compensation, Judgment, I.C.J. Reports 2012*, p. 324

*Corfu Channel case, Judgement of April 9th, 1949, I.C.J. Reports 1949*, p. 4

*Interpretation of the Agreement of 25 March 1951 between the WHO and Egypt, Advisory Opinion, I.C.J Reports 1980*, p. 73

*Legality of the Threat or Use of Nuclear Weapons, Advisory Opinion, I.C.J. Reports 1996*, p. 226

*Pulp Mills on the River Uruguay (Argentina v. Uruguay), Judgment, I.C.J. Reports 2010*, p. 14

*Request for an Examination of the Situation in Accordance with Paragraph 63 of the Court's Judgment of 20 December 1974 in the Nuclear Tests (New Zealand v. France) Case, I.C.J. Reports 1995*, p. 288

## ITLOS

*Southern Bluefin Tuna (New Zealand v. Japan; Australia v. Japan), Provisional Measures, Order of 27 August 1999, ITLOS Reports 1999*, p. 280

*The M/V "Saiga" (No. 2) (Saint Vincent and the Grenadines v. Guinea), Judgement, ITLOS Reports 1999*, p. 10

*MOX Plant (Ireland v. United Kingdom), Provisional Measures, Order of 3 December 2001, ITLOS Reports 2001*, p. 95

*Land Reclamation in and around the Straits of Johor (Malaysia v. Singapore), Provisional Measures, Order of 8 October 2003, ITLOS Reports 2003*, p. 10.

*Responsibilities and Obligations of States with Respect to Activities in the Area, Advisory Opinion, 1 February 2011, ITLOS Reports 2011*, p. 10

## PCIJ

*Factory at Chorzów, Merits, 1928, P.C.I.J., Series A, No. 17*

## ECJ

*Handelskwekerij GJ Bier v. Mines de Potasse d'Alsace, Case 21/76* [1976] *II ECJ Reports*, p. 1735

## ECHR

*Wemhoff v. Germany,* Judgement of 27 June 1968, [1968] ECHR 2

## US

*Re Union Carbide Corporation*, 634 F Supp 842 (1986)
*In re Oil Spill by Amoco Cadiz*, 954 F 2d 1279 (1992)

# Introduction

The discovery of strategic metals (such as cobalt) and metals used in clean energy infrastructure and technologies in the deep seabed (such as manganese, nickel and copper) has led to a surge of interest in mining in the area in the past decade.[1] It has been 19 years since the first six operators started exploration in the International Seabed Area (hereafter the Area)[2] and exploitation is yet to start on a commercial scale.

The current period might be described as a transitional phase between exploration and exploitation as exploitation in the Area is expected to commence in the near future. Concurrent with the increasing interest in deep seabed mining is the potential for increased risk of damage to the marine environment,[3] and how to balance mining and protection of the marine environment is one of the key questions to be addressed before exploitation begins.

The legal regime of deep seabed mining is set out in Part XI and Annex III of the United Nations Convention on the Law of the Sea (hereafter the Convention or the LOSC)[4] and the Agreement Relating to the Implementation of Part XI of the United Nations Convention on the Law of the Sea (hereafter the 1994 Implementing Agreement).[5] Under the LOSC and the 1994 Implementing Agreement, the Area and its resources have been designated the common heritage of mankind[6] with the International Seabed Authority (hereafter the ISA or the Authority) mandated to organize, carry out, and control activities in the Area including protection of the environment.[7] Consequently, any State Party, or state enterprise, natural or juridical person interested in carrying out activities in the Area must apply to the Authority for approval of plans of work

1 Rahul Sharma and Samantha Smith, 'Deep-Sea and the Environment: An Introduction' in Rahul Sharma (eds), *Environmental Issues of Deep-Sea Mining: Impacts, Consequences and Policy Perspectives* (Springer 2019), 3.

2 Status of contracts for exploration and related matters, including information on the periodic review of the implementation of approved plans of work for exploration (ISBA/26/C/4, 17 December 2019), Annex I.

3 Sharma and Smith (n 1) 12–16.

4 United Nations Convention on the Law of the Sea (Montego Bay, 10 December 1982, in force 16 November 1994) 1833 UNTS 3.

5 Agreement Relating to the Implementation of Part XI of the United Nations Convention on the Law of the Sea of 10 December 1982 (adopted 28 July 1994, entered into force 28 July 1996) 1836 UNTS 3.

6 LOSC, article 136.

7 LOSC, article 153(1).

 | DOI:10.1163/9789004472341_002

for activities in the Area.[8] After approval, the plan of work is in the form of a contract and, thus the applicant is known as a contractor.[9] As of 31 December 2019, 30 contracts for exploration had entered into force, of which 18 were for polymetallic nodules, 7 for polymetallic sulphides, and 5 for cobalt-rich ferromanganese crusts.[10] Given that a contractor is the operator of the deep seabed mining activities, whether he carries out environmental obligations under the LOSC and related legal instruments or whether he utilizes the best available technology will determine the degree of environmental protection. Hence, ensuring a contractor's compliance with the LOSC and related legal instruments is one of the most important concerns under the Deep Seabed Mining Regime.

One of the most "interesting"[11] features of the Deep Seabed Mining Regime is the requirement that natural or juridical persons tendering to carry out mining activities in the Area must be either nationals of a State Party or effectively controlled by it or its nationals and also sponsored by such States.[12] The LOSC and 1994 Implementing Agreement, as treaties under international law, just as the Seabed Disputes Chamber indicated, are binding merely upon States Parties rather than binding upon contractors who are entities or individuals.[13] Against this background, the contractors' compliance with the environmental obligations set out in the Convention and 1994 Implementing Agreement might be obtained "through the implementation by the sponsoring States of their obligations under the Convention and related instruments."[14] To this end, the LOSC requires a sponsoring State to adopt laws and regulations and to take administrative measures which are, within its domestic legal framework, reasonably appropriate for securing compliance by its sponsored contractors. This is noted as a sponsoring State's "responsibility to ensure" by the Seabed Disputes Chamber (SDC) of the International Tribunal for the Law of the Sea (ITLOS).[15] By fulfilling the primary obligation, a sponsoring State can be exempted from liability for damage caused by any failure of its sponsored

8 LOSC, article 153(2); Annex III, article 3(1).

9 LOSC, article 153(3).

10 Status of contracts for exploration and related matters (n 2), paragraph 2.

11 Michael W Lodge, 'The Deep Seabed' in Donald Rothwell and others (eds), *The Oxford Handbook of the Law of the Sea* (Oxford University Press 2015), 246.

12 LOSC, article 153(2)(b).

13 *Responsibilities and Obligations of States with Respect to Activities in the Area, Advisory Opinion, 1 February 2011, ITLOS Reports 2011,* p. 10 (SDC Advisory Opinion), paragraph 75.

14 ibid.

15 SDC Advisory Opinion, paragraphs 107–116.

contractor to comply with its obligations.[16] The purpose of doing so is to "ensure that obligations that are binding on States Parties are fulfilled by entities that are subjects of domestic legal systems".[17] In view of this, the effectiveness of a sponsoring State's national legislation for deep seabed mining is crucial to the entire Deep Seabed Mining Regime.

However, the concept of "responsibility to ensure" that motivates a sponsoring State to regulate its sponsored contractor(s) within its legal system seems to be a little problematic and may cause difficulties in practice since the LOSC and 1994 Implementing Agreement do not answer what kind of national legislation is "reasonably appropriate". On the one hand, the LOSC and 1994 Implementing Agreement require a sponsoring State to carry out its primary obligation in due diligence; on the other hand, a sponsoring State is reluctant to place onerous legal burdens on its sponsored contractors, *inter alia*, state-owned enterprises or foreign-funded companies, since it may lead to the losses for this State with negative economic consequences. Hence, a sponsoring State must strike a "reasonably appropriate" balance between its obligation and its interest. Moreover, an interesting but tricky provision, article 21(3), Annex III of the LOSC, has created difficulties for a sponsoring State in the design of its national legislation for deep seabed mining. It stipulates:

> No State Party may impose conditions on a contractor that are inconsistent with Part XI. However, the application by a State Party to contractors sponsored by it, or to ships flying its flag, of environmental or other laws and regulations more stringent than those in the rules, regulations and procedures of the Authority adopted pursuant to article 17, paragraph 2(f), of this Annex shall not be deemed inconsistent with Part XI.

According to article 21(3), Annex III of the LOSC, a sponsoring State may enact national legislation that is more stringent than international regulations. This approach would promote more environmentally-friendly activities with less possibility for adverse impacts on the marine environment during mining activities. It also means a better opportunity of reparation for damage to the environment. However, the sponsoring State must be cautious with the boundary, i.e. the national legislation for deep seabed mining must be consistent with Part XI. The tricky question is how to motivate the sponsoring State to enact more stringent laws and regulations, especially if a state-owned

16 SDC Advisory Opinion, paragraph 119.
17 Lodge (n 11) 248.

enterprise or a foreign-funded company is the contractor. Although the SDC provides some guidance in its Advisory Opinion[18] and the Secretariat of the Pacific Community (SPC) provides a regional model law for the Pacific Island States,[19] no global standards exist for the sponsoring States to follow.

The book aims to find out what "reasonably appropriate" national laws exist under the Deep Seabed Mining Regime with the objective of seeing what role national legislation of sponsoring States can play in marine environmental protection and to what extent it functions in implementing international environmental obligations pertaining to deep seabed mining. Additionally, this book will attempt to find out how much further sponsoring States' national legislation should go than international law, considering that international laws generally use the lowest standards in the event of distinct economic or technical capabilities of developed States or developing States.

This book seeks to analyze the optimal design of the national legislation of a qualified sponsoring State. It should not only explore to what extent international obligations of sponsoring States can be absorbed in its national legislation but also to what degree it can contribute to newly-emerging and immature tools for the environmental protection of the Deep Seabed Mining Regime under development. This book attempts to provide some reference for States Parties that desire guidelines for their national legislation for deep seabed mining in the Area. To this end, the book attempts to answer the following three questions:

(1) What role does a sponsoring State play to ensure its contractor's compliance with its international environmental obligations for activities in the Area?

(2) What should be included in the sponsoring State's national legislation so as to ensure its contractor's compliance with its international environmental obligations for activities in the Area?

(3) How far can a sponsoring State go to ensure its contractor's compliance with its international environmental obligations for activities in the Area?

Based on that discussion, this book will focus on one practical question: To what extent can those measures instruct state practice? Here, China will be used as an example for both particularity and universality. Since 2001, China

18 SDC Advisory Opinion, paragraphs 213–241.

19 SPC, *Pacific-ACP States Regional Legislative and Regulatory Framework for Deep Sea Minerals Exploration and Exploitation* (*RLRF*), Prepared under the SPC-EU EDF 10 Deep Sea Minerals Project (1st edn, July 2012) <https://pacific-data.sprep.org/system/files/PR111.pdf> accessed 8 December 2020.

has sponsored three contractors for five contracts of mineral resource exploration in the Area, covering the three kinds of minerals in the Area, i.e. polymetallic manganese, polymetallic sulphides, and cobalt-rich ferromanganese crust.[20] There is no doubt that China is one of the most important sponsoring States, the contents and effectiveness of whose deep seabed mining legislation have had a decisive influence on global deep seabed protection. Also, China's progress towards environmentally-friendly deep seabed mining is of global interest.

20 The Chinese state-owned enterprise China Ocean Mineral Resources Research and Development Association (COMRA) signed three exploration contracts for polymetallic nodules (entry into force on 22 May 2001, expiry on 21 May 2016, extension to 21 May 2021), polymetallic sulphides (entry into force on 18 November 2011, expiry on 17 November 2026), cobalt-rich ferromanganese crusts (entry into force on 29 April 2014, expiry 28 April 2029) respectively with the ISA; the Chinese state-owned enterprise, China Minmetals Corporation (CMC), signed an exploration contract for polymetallic nodules with the ISA, which entered into force on 12 May 2017 and expires on 11 May 2032; Beijing Pioneer Hi-Tech Development Corporation (BPHDC), signed an exploration contract for polymetallic nodules with the ISA, which entered into force on 18 October 2019 and expires on 17 October 2034. Status of contracts for exploration and related matters (n 2), Annex I.

CHAPTER 1

# Mining Impacts on the Marine Environment and Deep Seabed Mining Regime

## 1 Introduction

The rising demand for minerals or metals, and the decline of land-based mineral resources, has resulted in growing interest in the exploration and exploitation of deep-sea mineral resources from which copper, gold, iron, manganese, lead, zinc, and nickel can be extracted.[1] The United Nations Convention on the Law of the Sea (hereafter the Convention or the LOSC) that entitles all states to explore and exploit minerals in the International Seabed Area (hereafter the Area), with the permission of the International Seabed Authority (hereafter the ISA or the Authority),[2] potentially, provides an exciting opportunity for those states seeking ways to address economic vulnerability and to expand a narrow resource base. In recent years, the annual session of the Authority has witnessed increasing attention to the deep seabed from a range of stakeholders. This is evidenced by increasing numbers of applications for exploration of mineral resources in the Area, the passionate discussion among member States, and by more and more applications for observer status as well as the increasing number of side events. As Secretary-General Michael Lodge said at his inaugural reception, "the fact is that seabed mining is closer to commercial reality now than at any time over the past 25 years."[3]

Although the international community appears to have a high interest in deep seabed mining, scientists show less enthusiasm and caution that

1 For discussions on this account, see Mark Schrope, 'UK Company Pursues Deep-Sea Bonanza' (2013) 495 *Nature* 294; George M Woodwell, 'Curb Deep-Sea Mining Now' (2011) 471 *Nature* 36; 'Digging Deeper' (2010) 3 *Nature Geoscience* 1; Jane Qiu, 'China Outlines Deep-Sea Ambitions' (2010) 466 *Nature*; KS Jayaraman, 'Deep-Sea Nuggets Prove Irresistible to Indian Miners' (2002) 417 *Nature* 212.

2 United Nations Convention on the Law of the Sea (Montego Bay, 10 December 1982, in force 16 November 1994) 1833 UNTS 3, article 140.

3 Secretary-General Michael Lodge hosted his inaugural reception at his residence in Kingston, Jamaica on Friday 3 February 2017, available at <https://www.isa.org.jm/sites/default/files/documents/EN/SG-Stats/reception_speech.pdf> accessed 5 February 2017.

 | DOI:10.1163/9789004472341_003

knowledge of the deep-sea ecosystems is still at an early stage.[4] Owing to the limitation of deep-sea knowledge and scientific uncertainty, large-scale commercial deep seabed mining activities will undoubtedly have a negative impact on the marine environment and ecosystem,[5] likely affecting thousands of square kilometers with ecosystem recovery requiring many decades to millions of years.[6] Certain commentators hold that "full-scale commercial extraction of deep sea minerals must be delayed until the long-term pros and cons of deep seabed mining are scientifically scrutinized and democratically deliberated."[7] However, scientists have not been persuasive enough to stop ongoing interest and attempts in deep seabed mining.

Against this background, a plausible way of mitigating negative impacts on the marine environment would be to establish some mechanisms to manage and control activities relating to exploration and exploitation of mineral resources in the Area. Deep seabed mining is a highly complex process shaped by a broad spectrum of environmental, technical, and social science disciplines in highly different contexts.[8] Environmental regulatory instruments and the synthesis of knowledge across those disciplines play an essential role in instructing and controlling activities in the Area and, as such, play a significant role in marine environmental protection by way of establishing

4 Craig R Smith and others, *Biodiversity, Species Ranges, and Gene Flow in the Abyssal Pacific Nodule Province: Predicting and Managing the Impacts of Deep Seabed Mining* (ISA Technical Study: No. 3) (ISA 2008).

5 For discussions on this account, see Charles L Morgan, Nii Allotey Odunton and Anthony T Jones, 'Synthesis of Environmental Impacts of Deep Seabed Mining' (1999) 17 *Marine Georesources & Geotechnology* 307; Jochen Halfar and Rodney M Fujita, 'ECOLOGY: Danger of Deep-Sea Mining' (2007) 316 *Science* 987; Eva Ramirez-Llodra and others, 'Man and the Last Great Wilderness: Human Impact on the Deep Sea' (2011) 6 *PLoS ONE* e22588; Michelle Allsopp and others, 'Review of the Current State of Development and the Potential for Environmental Impacts of Seabed Mining Operations' [2013] *Greenpeace Research Laboratories Technical Report* (Review) 3; Cindy Lee Van Dover, 'Impacts of Anthropogenic Disturbances at Deep-Sea Hydrothermal Vent Ecosystems: A Review' (2014) 102 *Marine Environmental Research* 59.

6 Adrian G Glover and Craig R Smith, 'The Deep-Sea Floor Ecosystem: Current Status and Prospects of Anthropogenic Change by the Year 2025' (2003) 30 *Environmental Conservation* 219, 219.

7 Rakhyun E Kim, 'Should Deep Seabed Mining Be Allowed?' (2017) 82 *Marine Policy* 134, 136.

8 See *Deep-Seabed Polymetallic Nodule Exploration: Development of Environmental Guidelines* (ISA, Sanya, 1998); SPC, *Deep Sea Minerals: Manganese Nodules, a Physical, Biological, Environmental and Technical Review*, vol 1B (Secretariat of the Pacific Community 2013). An example here is the establishment of an environmental baseline, which is a key element of deep seabed mining, that at least includes biological, chemical, physical, and geochemical aspects.

environmental obligations for actors engaged in deep seabed mining.[9] Those obligations are held by three main actors namely, the Authority which acts as the custodian on behalf of mankind as a whole,[10] contractors who are the mining operators and have the exclusive rights of exploration or exploitation in their contractual area of the Area under the approval of the Authority,[11] and States Parties, especially those who sponsor contractors.[12] Those obligations for actors are presented in existing international instruments relating to the deep seabed mining, such as the LOSC and the *Agreement Relating to the Implementation of Part XI of the United Nations Convention on the Law of the Sea* (1994 Implementing Agreement),[13] the Mining Code adopted by the Authority[14] as well as the Seabed Disputes Chamber of the International Tribunal for the Law of the Sea's (ITLOS) advisory opinion *Responsibilities and Obligations of States Sponsoring Persons and Entities with Respect to Activities in the Area* (SDC Advisory Opinion).[15] Effective implementation of those environmental obligations by these distinct actors is pivotal to avoid or mitigate anthropogenic impacts on the marine space and ecosystems in the process of deep seabed mineral resources exploration or exploitation. Hence, the aim of this chapter is to examine the existing Deep Seabed Mining Regime and to find out whether gaps exist, based on which the direction of development of the Deep Seabed Mining Regime will become clear.

To this end, this chapter will first illustrate likely impacts on the marine environment arising from mining activities in the Area and then present the existing Deep Seabed Mining Regime. Such a description is intended to provide the scientific and legal background of deep seabed mining. It is also necessary to examine the existing Deep Seabed Mining Regime, with a particular focus on

---

9 See 'Recommendations for the Guidance of Contractors for the Assessment of the Possible Environmental Impacts Arising from Exploration for Marine Minerals in the Area' (ISBA/19/LTC/8, 1 March 2013), paragraph 1; AL Clark, J Cook Clark and S Pintz, Towards the Development of a Regulatory Framework for Polymetallic Nodule Exploitation in the Area (ISA Technical Study: No. 11) (ISA, Kingston, 2013), 10–11.

10 Michael W Lodge, 'International Seabed Authority's Regulations on Prospecting and Exploration for Polymetallic Nodules in the Area' (2002) 20 *Journal of Energy & Natural Resources Law* 270, 270.

11 LOSC, Annex III, article 16; LOSC, Annex III, article 3.

12 LOSC, article 153(2).

13 Agreement Relating to the Implementation of Part XI of the United Nations Convention on the Law of the Sea of 10 December 1982 (adopted 28 July 1994, entered into force 28 July 1996) 1836 UNTS 3.

14 For the introduction on this account, see section 3.2.2 of this chapter.

15 *Responsibilities and Obligations of States with Respect to Activities in the Area, Advisory Opinion, 1 February 2011, ITLOS Reports 2011*, p. 10.

the core of this design: the ISA and the system of prospecting, exploration, and exploitation. By examining the ISA-related issues, the merits and demerits of the functions of the ISA in managing the deep seabed mining operators and protecting the marine environment can be determined.

## 2 Deep Seabed Mining and Its Impact on Marine Environment

### 2.1 *Deep Seabed Area in Geography and the Area under International Law*

The deep sea is often defined as the water column and seabed below 200 meters.[16] The oceans have a maximum depth of almost 11000 meters. Eighty-eight per cent of the oceans are deeper than 1000 meters, while 76 per cent are between 3000 and 6000 meters in depth.[17]

The definition of the international deep seabed area in law is distinct from that in geography.[18] The legal meaning of the international deep seabed area stipulated in the LOSC refers to "sea-bed and ocean floor and subsoil thereof, beyond the limits of national jurisdiction".[19] The defining indicator here is not depth, but by "jurisdiction", which refers to seabed areas beyond either 200 nm from the territorial sea baselines, or beyond the outer limits of the outer continental shelf established by coastal States in conformity with article 76 of the LOSC.[20] All the sea-bed and ocean floor and subsoil beyond these limits of national jurisdiction is the international deep seabed area, or "the Area", which constitutes a remarkable 50 per cent of the earth's surface.[21]

However, the LOSC does not offer any definition of the terms "sea-bed", "ocean floor" and "subsoil". The consolidated Glossary by the Technical Aspects of the

16 The unique vertical dimension has led to the conceptual division of the oceanic environment into three main realms or zones, namely the epipelagic (from the surface to 200 m), the mesopelagic (from 200 to 1000 m) and the bathypelagic (from 1000 to 6000 m). The 6000 m lower limit of the bathypelagic realm includes the vast extent of the abyssal plains but excludes the deep trenches, which constitute the hadal realm and extend from 6000 m to the greatest depths. The term "deep-sea" could be loosely used for all habits below the epipelagic zone, ie 200 m. See Peter J Herring, *The Biology of the Deep Ocean* (Oxford University Press 2002), 2.

17 ibid.

18 George K Walker, *Definitions for the Law of the Sea Terms Not Defined by the 1982 Convention* (Martinus Nijhoff Publishers 2012), 103–104.

19 LOSC, article 1(1).

20 Donald Rothwell and Tim Stephens, *The International Law of the Sea* (Hart 2010), 121–123.

21 Michael W Lodge, 'Collaborative Marine Scientific Research on the International Seabed' (2008) 3 *The Journal of Ocean Technology* 30, 30.

Law of the Sea Working Group of the International Hydrographic Organization defines the term "sea-bed" as: "the top of the surface layer of sand, rock, mud or other material lying at the bottom of the sea and immediately above the subsoil".[22] The term "subsoil" means: "all naturally occurring matter lying beneath the sea-bed or deep ocean floor. The subsoil includes residual deposits and minerals as well as the bedrock below."[23] It may be relevant to note that in article 76, the term "deep ocean floor", rather than "sea-bed", is used in reference to the surface layer seaward of the continental rise. It may not be unreasonable to consider that "ocean floor" in article 1 is, in essence, equivalent to "deep ocean floor". The Consolidated Glossary defines "deep ocean floor" as: "the surface lying at the bottom of the deep ocean with its oceanic ridges, beyond the continental shelf margin."[24]

### 2.2 *Three Main Mineral Resources in the Area*

Global interest in the deep seabed began in the 1960s. It does not concern the deep seabed area itself, but rather mineral resources located in the deep seabed. The discovery of tens of millions of tons of polymetallic manganese nodules, found in parts of the seabed, sparked optimistic forecasts of the future economic and strategic benefits of ocean exploitation.[25] Deep seabed mining has even been identified as one of the potential new blue growth sectors by the European Union, and it is deemed as a practical approach to solve supply and demand contradiction.[26] On the one hand, demand had risen due to increasing consumer demand in emerging economies, the development of new technologies that require an increased supply of metals such as copper, and issues

22 Alexander Proelss and others (eds), *United Nations Convention on the Law of the Sea: A Commentary* (CH Beck; Hart; Nomos 2017), 21; UN DOALOS, 'The Law of the Sea, Baselines: An Examination of the Relevant Provisions of the United Nations Convention on the Law of the Sea' (1989) <https://www.un.org/depts/los/doalos_publications/publicationstexts/The%20Law%20of%20the%20Sea_Baselines.pdf> accessed 24 July 2020, Appendix I: Consolidated Glossary of Technical Terms Used in the United Nations Convention on the Law of the Sea, 61.

23 Walker (n 18) 317.

24 UN DOALOS (n 22) 53.

25 Wolfgang Graf Vitzthum, 'International Seabed Area' in *Max Plank Encyclopedia of Public International Law* (2008).

26 ECORYS, 'Blue Growth: Scenarios and Drivers for Sustainable Growth from the Oceans, Seas and Coasts', Third Interim Report under MARE/2010/01 (13 March 2012) <https://webgate.ec.europa.eu/maritimeforum/system/files/Blue_Growth_Third_Interim_Report_130312%20Clean_0.pdf> accessed 24 July 2020, 19.

related to security of supply.[27] On the other hand, the grade of ore from land-based mines continues to decline.[28] Deep seabed mining is an ideal means of easing this situation. However, interest remained at a relatively low level for many years due to a combination of low metal prices, significant engineering challenges, and the legal uncertainty of operating mining activities in the deep seabed.[29] In the current decade, interest has resurged because of technological feasibility.[30]

The main types of mineral deposits of the deep seabed with potential economic value are conventional hydrocarbons (crude oil and natural gas), gas hydrates, placer deposit, phosphorite deposits, evaporate deposit, polymetallic sulphides, polymetallic nodules (manganese nodules), and cobalt-rich ferromanganese crust (cobalt-rich crust).[31] Considering technological feasibility and economic value, the most attractive mineral resources are polymetallic nodules, polymetallic sulphides, cobalt-rich crusts, and phosphorite. Additionally, there is some interest in exploring for metalliferous muds under dense brines in the Red Sea,[32] and, in recent years, the potential for mining deep ocean sediments to recover rare earth elements (REE s) has been suggested.[33]

Nowadays, polymetallic nodules, polymetallic sulphides, and cobalt-rich crust are the three major types of deep seabed minerals in the Area.[34] They have distinct natures, formations, distributions, and exploration and exploitation technologies, and thus will cause different environmental effects in the process of mining. These are explicitly addressed by the ISA Mining Code.[35]

---

27 MIDAS, 'Managing Impacts of Deep Sea Resource Exploitation: Research Highlights', <https://www.eu-midas.net/sites/default/files/downloads/MIDAS_research_highlights_low_res.pdf> accessed 15 June 2020, 1.

28 Guiomar Calvo and others, 'Decreasing Ore Grades in Global Metallic Mining: A Theoretical Issue or a Global Reality?' (2016) 5 *Resources* 36, 36–37.

29 MIDAS (n 27) 1.

30 Rahul Sharma, 'Deep-Sea Mining: Economic, Technical, Technological, and Environmental Considerations for Sustainable Development' (2011) 45 *Marine Technology Society Journal* 28, 38.

31 Stephen E Kesler, *Mineral Resources, Economics, and the Environment* (Macmillan; Maxwell Macmillan Canada; Maxwell Macmillan International 1994), 142.

32 Christine Bertram and others, 'Metalliferous Sediments in the Atlantis II Deep – Assessing the Geological and Economic Resource Potential and Legal Constraints' (2011) 36 *Resources Policy* 315, 317.

33 Yasuhiro Kato and others, 'Deep-Sea Mud in the Pacific Ocean as a Potential Resource for Rare-Earth Elements' (2011) 4 *Nature Geoscience* 535, 535.

34 Report of the Secretary-General of the International Seabed Authority under article 166, paragraph 4, of the United Nations Convention on the Law of the Sea (ISBA/21/A/2, 3 June 2015), paragraph 54.

35 Regarding the introduction of the ISA Mining Code, see section 3.2.2 of this chapter.

### 2.2.1 Polymetallic Nodules

Polymetallic nodules were first discovered in the Kara Sea, in the Arctic Ocean off Siberia. Then they were discovered on the deep seabed in most oceans of the world during the HMS *Challenger* expedition.[36] In fact, they can be found at any depth in all oceans, and even lakes, but the highest concentrations have been found on abyssal plains between 4000 and 6000 meters.[37] Polymetallic nodules are usually half-buried or entirely covered by sediment across the seabed and contain nickel, copper, cobalt, and manganese, among other metals. The composition of specific nodules and their aggregation and abundance on the ocean floor varies substantially. It is noteworthy that not all polymetallic nodule deposits have economic value. Only those, whose abundance exceeds 10 kilograms per square meter, with an average of 15 kg/m$^2$ over areas of several tenths of a square kilometer are of economic interest.[38] Also, not all the nodules are "good nodules" containing sufficiently high concentrations of nickel, copper, manganese, and cobalt. "Good nodules" were defined as averaging at least 1.25–1.5% nickel and 1–1.4% copper, as well as 27–30% manganese and 0.2–0.25% cobalt.[39] According to those standards, there are three areas preferred by potential industrial operators: the center of the north-central Pacific Ocean, the Peru Basin in the south-east Pacific Ocean and the center of the north Indian Ocean.[40] As of 31 December 2019,[41] 18 exploration contracts of polymetallic nodules granted by the ISA are in the Clarion-Clipperton Zone,[42] Central Indian Ocean Basin, and Western Pacific Ocean.

36 ISA, 'Polymetallic Nodules' <https://www.isa.org.jm/files/documents/EN/Brochures/ENG7.pdf> accessed 3 June 2020.

37 ibid.

38 ibid.

39 ibid.

40 ibid.

41 Status of contracts for exploration and related matters (n 2), paragraph 2.

42 The Clarion-Clipperton Zone is located in the eastern central Pacific, to the south and south-east of the Hawaiian Islands. The geographical limits of the management area have been taken to be the area beyond national jurisdiction contained within a box approximately 0°-23°30'N x 115°W-160°W. The Zone is bounded to the north and south by the ENE-WNW trending Clarion and Clipperton Fracture Zones. Its area is approximately 4.5 x 10$^6$ square kilometres (km$^2$). The seafloor in the management area lies mostly between a water depth of 4,000 and 6,000 metres. It is characterized by a number of seamounts, some of which may be fewer than 2,000 metres deep. The widespread seafloor spreading fabric, oriented approximately orthogonal to the trend of the bounding fracture zones, provides a large number of flat-floored valleys, separated by irregular, often discontinuous ridges a few hundred metres high, see Environmental Management Plan for the Clarion-Clipperton Zone (ISBA/17/LTC/7, 13 July 2011), Annex, Figure I.

### 2.2.2 Polymetallic Sulphides

In 1979, scientists discovered the presence of chimney-like formations of dark rock which spewed hot water and fostered a unique ecosystem around them.[43] Moreover, given that these hot waters mixed with the cold surrounding seawater, metal sulphides were precipitated on the chimneys and nearby seabed, in which high concentrations of basic metals (copper, zinc, lead) and especially precious metals (gold, silver) could be extracted.[44] These sulphides accumulate on and below the seafloor. Most deposits are located at the East Pacific Rise, the Southeast Pacific Rise, and the Northeast Pacific Rise, while there are also several deposits at the Mid-Atlantic Ridge and one deposit at the Central Indian Ridge.[45] In the following years, some other deposits were found. Although there is still a paucity of surveys, today, more than 100 deposits of hydrothermal mineralization are known.[46] As of 31 December 2018,[47] seven exploration contracts of polymetallic sulphides granted by the ISA are being executed in the Indian Ocean and the Atlantic Ocean.[48]

### 2.2.3 Cobalt-Rich Ferromanganese Crusts

Oxidized deposits of cobalt-rich ferromanganese crust are found throughout the global oceans on the flanks and summits of seamounts (submarine mountains), ridges, and plateaux, where seafloor currents have swept the ocean floor clear of sediment for millions of years, and thus there is no sediment covering the rock surface.[49] Crusts are usually found at depths of about 440–4000 meters, while the thickest crusts, most abundant in cobalt, are located on out-rim terraces and broad saddles on the summits of seamounts, at depths of 800–2500 meters.[50] The central equatorial Pacific region provides the best

43 ISA, 'Polymetallic Sulphides' <https://isa.org.jm/files/files/documents/eng7.pdf> accessed 15 June 2020.

44 ibid.

45 ibid.

46 ibid.

47 Status of contracts for exploration and related matters (n 2), paragraph 2.

48 They are located in the South-West Indian Ridge conducted by the China Ocean Mineral Resources Research and Development Association, in the Mid-Atlantic Ridge conducted by the Government of the Russian Federation, in the Central Indian Ocean conducted by the Government of the Republic of Korea, in the Mid-Atlantic Ridge conducted by the Institut français de recherche pour l'exploitation de la mer, in the Central Indian Ridge and Southeast Indian Ridge conducted by the Federal Institute for Geosciences and Natural Resources, in the Indian Ocean Ridge conducted by the Government of India, and in the Mid-Atlantic Ridge conducted by the Government of Poland. ibid, Annex I.

49 ISA, 'Cobalt-Rich Crusts' <https://isa.org.jm/files/files/documents/eng9.pdf> accessed 15 June 2020.

50 ibid.

potential for crust mining, especially the exclusive economic zones around Johnston Island and Hawaii, the Marshall Islands, the Federated States of Micronesia, and international waters of the mid-Pacific.[51] Crusts contain a high content of cobalt, up to 1.7%, which are much higher than in land-based ores.[52] They also include other metallic and REEs such as titanium, cerium, nickel, platinum, manganese, phosphorus, thallium, tellurium, zirconium, tungsten, bismuth, and molybdenum. However, whether for purposes of exploration or exploitation, the crusts could be the trickiest one among those three categories of mineral resources in the Area. The physical properties of the crust and the rocks on which they grow are similar, and thus their presence on various rock types makes it difficult to distinguish them from the substrate when using traditional remote sensing techniques. Mining the cobalt-crust is technically much more difficult than mining manganese nodules because nodules sit on a soft-sediment substrate, whereas crusts are weakly to firmly attached to substrate rock.[53] Importantly, it is crucial to recover the crusts without collecting too much substrate, which would substantially dilute the ore quality.[54] As of 31 December 2018,[55] five exploration contracts for cobalt-rich ferromanganese crusts granted by the ISA have been signed in the Pacific Ocean and the Atlantic Ocean.[56]

### 2.3 *Possible Impacts of Mining Activities on the Marine Environment*

It is difficult to deny that intrusion in such a highly sensitive environment through prospecting, exploration, and exploitation may inevitably result in varying degrees of environmental risk. It is widely accepted that environmental risk gradually increases from prospecting, exploration to exploitation. There would be little impact on the marine environment in the stage of prospecting. As far as the exploration phase is concerned, the initial phase would

51 ibid.

52 ibid.

53 ibid.

54 ibid.

55 Status of contracts for exploration and related matters (n 2), paragraph 2.

56 Those exploration contract areas are located in the Western Pacific Ocean, conducted by Japan Oil, Gas and Metals National Corporation (sponsored by Japan); in the Western Pacific Ocean, conducted by the China Ocean Mineral Resources Research and Development Association (sponsored by China); in the Magellan Mountains in the Pacific Ocean, conducted by the Ministry of Natural Resources and Environment of the Russian Federation; in the Rio Grande Rise in the South Atlantic Ocean, conducted by Companhia de Pesquisa de Recursos minerais S.A. (sponsored by Brazil); and in the East of the Northern Mariana Islands in the Pacific Ocean, conducted by the Government of the Republic of Korea. ibid, Annex I.

be non-invasive, relying primarily on remote sensing and standard sampling techniques, whereas the secondary phase, which aims to test collecting systems and processing operations, may cause higher environmental risk than the previous stage.[57] During the process, the large volume of sediment estimated to be re-suspended would be the major influencing factor in environmental impact in the mining area.[58] Godet pointed out that although "effects from precision sampling tools are small in extent and targeted, there can be indirect or accidental effects from this type of sampling".[59] The impacts may change the physical structure of the seabed. Although the scale is smaller than the level of commercial seabed mining operations, it may still have devastating effects on deep-sea ecosystems.[60] More environmental issues will arise during the exploitation phase.

Considerable efforts have been made to examine the degree of impacts of mining activities on the marine environment and methods to minimize that impact as well as the possibility of restoration. Since the 1970s, the United States, Japan, and Germany have conducted several mining tests in the Pacific as well as the Indian Oceans to observe the environmental impacts of the mining system.[61] These experiments are designed to assess the potential impacts by deep-sea mining works, indicating the immediate changes and restoration patterns of environmental conditions in the marine ecosystem. The tests followed the same prototype. Typically, a seabed remotely operated vehicle (ROV) used to collect (nodules) or excavate the deposit (sulphides, crusts) is connected to a vertical transport system to lift the material to the sea surface, where it is collected in a ship or on a platform, de-watered and then transferred to a carrier, and transported to shore for further processing (see Figure 1).[62]

The MIDAS scientific group[63] concluded that the impacts might be categorized as both direct impacts and indirect impacts. The main direct impacts

57 Satya N Nandan, 'Administering the Mineral Resource of the Deep Seabed' in David Freestone, Richard Barnes, and David Ong (eds), *The Law of the Sea: Progress and Prospects* (Oxford University Press 2006), 88.

58 R Sharma, 'Deep-Sea Impact Experiments and their Future Requirements' (2005) 23(4) *Marine Georesources and Geotechnology* 331, 332.

59 L Godet, K Zelnio and C Van Dover, 'Scientists as Stakeholders in Conservation of Hydrothermal Vents' (2011) 25 *Conservation Biology* 214, 221.

60 Allsopp and others (n 5).

61 G P Glasby, 'Deep Seabed Mining: Past Failures and Future Prospects' (2002) 20(2) *Marine Georesources and Geotechnology* 161, 164–170.

62 ECORYS, 'Study to Investigate the State of Knowledge of Deep-sea Ming', Final Report under FWC MARE/2012/06 – SC E1/2013/04 (19 November 2014), 61.

63 The MIDAS project – Managing Impacts of Deep-seA reSource exploitation – was a multidisciplinary research program investigating the environmental impacts of

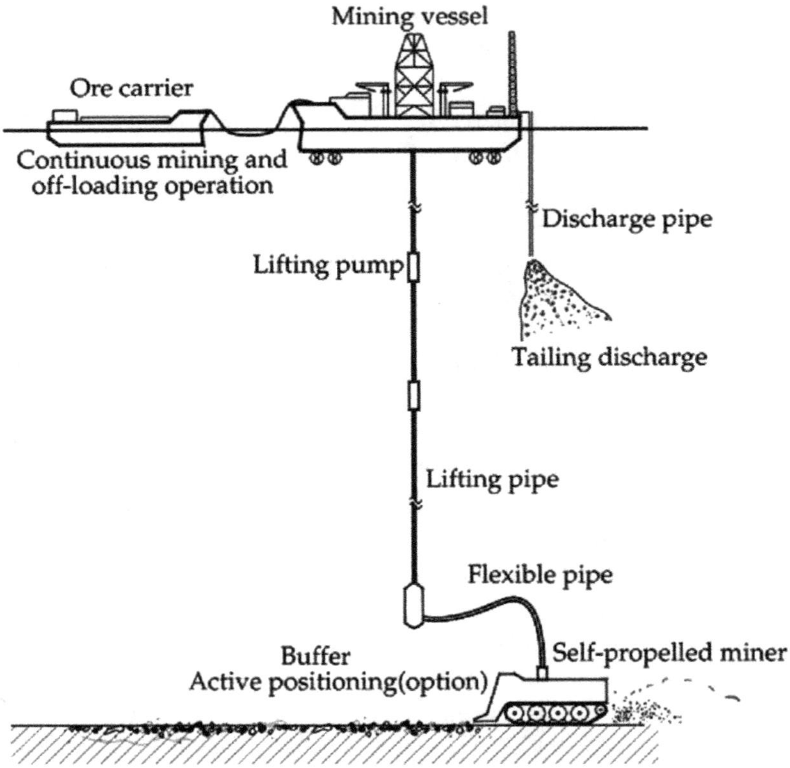


FIGURE 1 Schematic diagram of the integrated deep-sea mining system
SOURCE: LEE M AND OTHERS, 'METAMODEL-BASED MULTIDISCIPLINARY DESIGN OPTIMIZATION OF A DEEP-SEA MANGANESE NODULES TEST MINER' (2012) 2012 JOURNAL OF APPLIED MATHEMATICS 1

of deep seabed mining include: (1) mortality of fauna living on mined substrates; (2) removal of substrate and thus habitat loss; (3) habitat fragmentation; (4) habitat modification (i.e. change of mineral and sediment composition, geomorphology, chemical regimes); and (5) diverse other smaller scale direct impacts. Indirect impacts comprise: (6) the formation of near-seabed

---

extracting mineral and energy resources from the deep-sea environment. This included the exploitation of materials such as polymetallic sulphides, manganese nodules, cobalt-rich ferromanganese crusts, methane hydrates, and the potential for mining of rare earth elements. MIDAS was funded under the European Commission's Framework 7 initiative from November 2013 for a period of 3 years. For details, see <http://www.eu-midas.net> accessed 24 July 2020.

sediment plumes caused by the activity of crawlers and other seabed installations; (7) the returned water plume from dewatering on the vessel, in addition to any leaks along the riser system; (8) the trans-shipment plume when dewatered ores are rewetted for transfer to transport barges; and (9) potential release of toxic substances into the water column and Benthic Boundary Layer by the mining process (for polymetallic sulphides deposits).[64]

Those impacts can also be divided into those affecting the marine environment and benthic impacts. Furthermore, uncertain or unknown impacts also exist, i.e. scientific uncertainty.

### 2.3.1 Mining System's Impacts on the Marine Environment

The mining system's impacts on the marine environment are likely to occur due to the following elements:[65]

i) Underwater Noise. ROVs will inevitably produce noise when they are working in the deep sea. Most species living in the deep sea experience a relatively quiet environment, and the noise generated by the ROVs will substantially increase the ambient sound levels, which will harm those creatures that rely on sensitive acoustic changes for communication and navigation.[66] For example, studies of deep-sea fish have shown that some species appear to communicate through low sound frequencies (<1.2 kHz), whereas other benthic species may use sensitive acoustic systems to detect food up to 100 meters away.[67] Marine mammals, such as whales, that use sound for communication and navigation, provide another example. They may also be affected by vessels and submarine mechanical noise.[68] Moreover, noise travels over large distances (up to 600 km from the site stated by Steiner), potentially resulting in far-field impacts.[69] For instance, there are fears that those noises will

---

64 MIDAS, 'Implications of MIDAS Results for Policy Makers: Recommendations for Future Regulations'<http://eu-midas.net/sites/default/files/downloads/MIDAS_recommendations_for_policy_lowres.pdf> accessed 24 December 2020, 7.

65 Allsopp and others (n 5) 15–16.

66 ibid; see also MB Bashir and others, *A Concept for Seabed Rare Earth Mining in the Eastern South Pacific*, vol 1 (RA Shenoi, PA Wilson and SS Bennett eds, University of Southampton 2012) <https://eprints.soton.ac.uk/349887/> accessed 24 July 2020.

67 ibid; see also Michael Stocker, 'Fish, Mollusks and Other Sea Animals' Use of Sound, and the Impact of Anthropogenic Noise in the Marine Acoustic Environment' (2002) 112 *Journal of the Acoustical Society of America* 2431.

68 Allsopp and others (n 5) 15–16.

69 Richard Steiner, 'Independent Review of the Environmental Impact Statement for the Proposed Nautilus Minerals Solwara 1 Seabed Mining Project, Papua New Guinea' conducted for the Bismarck-Solomon Seas Indigenous Peoples Council (10 January

reduce the volume of fish in certain areas, thus impacting the livelihoods of local peoples.[70]

ii) Underwater Lights. Deep seabed mining activities will increase the level of light in the deep ocean.[71] The benthic environment is dark, and most organisms have adapted to this low-light environment.[72] The eyes of many deep-sea crustaceans have adjusted to the dim light of this depth, and thus they may suffer permanent retinal damage due to changes in light.[73] Light levels that persist for a period of time may damage the organisms and cause them to migrate away from the mining site.[74]

### 2.3.2 Benthic Impacts

Mining collectors, such as ROVs, will cause localized damage, including crushing living organisms, removal of substrate habitat, and disturbance of sediment. The consequences of this damage may be significant.[75] High mortality of sediment-dwelling (infaunal and epifaunal) organisms due to direct removal, burying in side-cast sediment or smothering by resettlement of suspended sediment are widely recognized consequences of using sediment dredge techniques. Similar impacts have been reported in experiments on nodule collection and sediment disturbance.[76]

Manganese nodules, massive seafloor sulphides, and cobalt-rich crust are the three major types of deep seabed minerals.[77] Each are located in the different marine environments and, indeed, form different marine habitats. These

2009) <http://www.deepseaminingoutofourdepth.org/wp-content/uploads/Steiner-Independent-review-DSM1.pdf> accessed 23 July 2020, 5.

70 Allsopp and others (n 5) 15.

71 Environmental Impact Statement, Nautilus Minerals Niugini Limited, Solwara 1 Project, Executive Summary (September 2008).

72 Bashir and others (n 66) 60.

73 Peter J Herring, Edward Gaten and Peter M J Shelton, 'Are Vent Shrimps Blinded by Science?' (1998) 398 *Nature* 116, 116.

74 ibid.

75 Global Ocean Commission, 'Policy Options Paper #5: Strengthening Deep Seabed Mining Regulation' (November 2013) <http://eu-midas.net/sites/default/files/publications/GOC-paper05-seabed-mining.pdf> accessed 24 July 2020, 4.

76 Allsopp and others (n 5) 14; see also H Thiel, 'Deep-sea Environmental Disturbance and Recovery Potential' (1992) 77 *International Review of Hydrobiology* 331; H Bluhm, 'Monitoring Megabenthic Communities in Abyssal Manganese Nodule Sites of the East Pacific Ocean in Association with Commercial Deep-sea Mining?' (1994) 4 *Aquatic Conservation: Marine and Freshwater Ecosystems* 187.

77 Report of the Secretary-General of the International Seabed Authority under article 166, paragraph 4, of the United Nations Convention on the Law of the Sea (ISBA/21/A/2, 3 June 2015), paragraph 54.

include: manganese nodules which take millions of years to form and which support sponges and other marine life;[78] hydrothermal vents which host unique biodiversity;[79] and seamounts which support abundant and rich biodiversity.[80] There are different conservation concerns related to the destruction of these habitats by mining. Consequently, they should be treated in different ways in order to avoid loss of biodiversity and destruction of habitats once mining activities begin.

Manganese nodules collection vehicles will compress and squeeze the sediment and benthic organisms and create a sediment plume, transporting masses of particles over unknown distances.[81] Natural sediments take millions of years to form so these habitats could be completely lost from large areas of seabed. Re-sedimentation from the sediment plume is likely to have a highly significant biological impact, especially on filter-feeding animals.[82]

Hydrothermal vents have a unique community structure, and many animal species in these habitats are protozoa. Mining will thoroughly remove the vent chimneys and will, unavoidably, kill the animals residing there as well.[83] It is still unclear whether the habitat will recover if the vent chimney is rebuilt or whether the animals will return afterward.[84]

Seamounts are prominent features of deep-sea topography and often support high levels of biodiversity and unique biomes including corals and sponges, as well as large numbers of fish. Seamounts are described as underwater oases and appear to be significant habitats for migratory species.[85] Mining near these structures will destroy the corals and sponges that grow on these seamounts. Recent research has shown that recovery time could be as long as decades to centuries.[86]

### 2.3.3 Scientific Uncertainty

In addition to the known adverse impacts on the marine environment that result from mining activities, there are considerable uncertainties that can

---

78 ISA, *A Geological Model of Polymetallic Nodule Deposits in the Clarion-Clipperton Fracture Zone* (ISA Technical Study: No. 6) (ISA 2010), 8.

79 PM Herzig and others, *Polymetallic Massive Sulphide and Cobalt-Rich Ferromanganese Crusts: Status and Prospects* (ISA Technical Study: No. 2) (ISA 2002), 102.

80 ibid, 37.

81 Bluhm (n 76) 188.

82 Allsopp and others (n 5) 3.

83 Herzig and others (n 79), 100.

84 Allsopp and others (n 5) 2.

85 ISA, 'Cobalt-Rich Crusts' (n 49).

86 Allsopp and others (n 5) 3.

influence the management of natural resource systems. Uncertainty is not simply the absence of knowledge, but a situation of inexact, unreliable, and ignorant information.[87] It is defined as being "any departure from the unachievable ideal of complete determinism."[88] According to the nature of uncertainty, it can be divided into two categories, knowledge uncertainty and natural variability, although the terminology used may differ in discrete literature.[89] Knowledge uncertainty is related to aspects, such as, limited and inaccurate data, measurement error, incomplete knowledge, limited understanding, imperfect models, subjective judgement, ambiguities, etc.[90] Natural variability refers to the inherent uncertainty or randomness, due to inherent randomness of nature (the chaotic and unpredictable nature of natural processes), human behavior (discrepancies between what people say and what they actually do), societal variability (the chaotic and unpredictable nature of social, economic, and cultural dynamics), and technological surprise (new developments or breakthroughs in technology or unexpected consequences of technologies).[91] Those uncertainties can be distinguished between the modelers' view of uncertainty and the decision makers' view of uncertainty, which means not all those uncertainties can affect decision-making. Byron Williams is of the view that, at a minimum, four kinds of uncertainties can influence decision-making, i.e. environmental variation (random variability in climate that is largely uncontrollable and possibly unrecognized); partial observability (sampling variation that arises in resource monitoring); partial controllability (the difference between the actions targeted by decision-makers and the actions that are actually implemented); and structural and process uncertainty (a lack of understanding about the structure of biological and ecological relationships that drive resource dynamics).[92] Although different terminologies are used, it is not difficult to conclude the *environmental variation* and the

87 WE Walker and others, 'Defining Uncertainty: A Conceptual Basis for Uncertainty Management in Model-Based Decision Support' (2003) 4 *Integrated Assessment* 5, 8.

88 ibid.

89 Knowledge uncertainty has also been called epistemic uncertainty, subjective uncertainty, or internal uncertainty; Natural variability has also been called aleatory uncertainty, random variability, stochastic variability, objective uncertainty, or external uncertainty. See Gregory Baecher, 'The Nature of Risk in Geotechnical Engineering' (2005) *Post-Mining* 1 <https://www.researchgate.net/publication/255578059_THE_NATURE_OF_RISK_IN_GEOTECHNICAL_ENGINEERING_LA_NATURE_DU_RISQUE_EN_INGENIERIE_GEOTECHNIQUE> accessed 24 July 2019, 6.

90 Walker and others (n 87), 13.

91 ibid, 13–14.

92 Byron K Williams, 'Adaptive Management of Natural Resources – Framework and Issues' (2011) 92 *Journal of Environmental Management* 1346, 1348.

*partial controllability* as natural variability; and conclude the *partial observability* and *structural and process uncertainty* as the knowledge uncertainty. In the context of deep seabed mining, both uncertainties are relevant. Since the deep seabed is the least known area on this planet, there are still considerable knowledge gaps in this respect.[93] An example is provided to show how the scientific uncertainty impacts the decision-making as follows. The operation of mining equipment and the return of dewatered waste may increase the water temperature.[94] Steiner holds that in some cases the seawater temperature increases by as much as 11°C.[95] Deep-sea creatures inhabit a stable temperature environment, so an increase in ambient temperature may have a negative impact on these organisms. However, in practice, little is known about the potential effects of seawater overheating on the growth, metabolism, reproductive success, and survival of deep-sea species.[96] That lack of knowledge will hamper decision-makers in deciding which technical equipment has the least impact on the environment.

Due to the existence of uncertainty, mechanisms, such as the precautionary approach, or adaptive management, need to be used by the policymaker. Likewise, contractors are obliged to apply the precautionary approach in the process of mining in the Area.

### 2.4 *Mitigation Methods for Possible Negative Impacts*

It is not enough to merely draw conclusions regarding the possible impacts of mining. The main purpose of the exercise is to identify mitigation methods for possible negative impacts and to indicate the direction of international and national legislation.

The *mitigation hierarchy* is a tool that guides users towards limiting, as far as possible, the negative impacts of development projects on biodiversity and ecosystem services.[97] It is often used to minimize biodiversity loss in terrestrial mining and offshore oil and gas operations. The mitigation hierarchy includes

---

93 With regard to an overview of the main knowledge gaps in relation to understanding the environment where deep sea minerals occur, see ECORYS, 'Study to Investigate the State of Knowledge of Deep-sea Mining' (n 62) 104–107.

94 ibid.

95 Steiner (n 69) 4.

96 Bashir and others (n 66) 60–61.

97 Jon Ekstrom, Leon Bennun and Robin Mitchell, *A Cross-sector Guide for Implementing the Mitigation Hierarchy* prepared by the Biodiversity Consultancy (Cross Sector Biodiversity Initiative 2015) <http://www.csbi.org.uk/wp-content/uploads/2017/10/CSBI-Mitigation-Hierarchy-Guide.pdf> accessed 24 July 2020.

four sequential steps – *avoidance, minimization, rehabilitation/restoration*, and *offset*.[98]

The first and foremost step of the mitigation hierarchy is *avoidance* under which measures are taken to avoid creating impacts from the outset, such as careful spatial or temporal placement of infrastructure or disturbance. *Avoidance* is often the easiest, cheapest, and most effective way of reducing potential negative impacts, but it requires biodiversity to be considered in the early stages of a project.

In the second step, i.e. *minimization,* measures are taken to reduce the duration, intensity, and extent of impacts that cannot be avoided entirely. Effective *minimization* can eliminate some negative impacts. Examples include measures such as reducing noise and pollution.

In the *rehabilitation/restoration* step, measures are taken to improve degraded or removed ecosystems following exposure to impacts that cannot be avoided or minimized. *Restoration* tries to return an area to the original ecosystem that existed before impacts occurred, whereas *rehabilitation* only aims to restore basic ecological functions and ecosystem services. Typically, the three steps above relating to the mitigation hierarchy are designed to reduce the residual impacts on marine ecosystems and biodiversity as far as possible. Furthermore, the final step *offset*, i.e. in-kind or like-for-like, will also be required to achieve no overall negative impact or a net gain for biodiversity, even after the full application of the former three steps.

However, given that this mechanism is not tailored to deep seabed mining activities, but for overall natural resources management, the four-step mitigation cannot be used in a package. In the deep sea, *restoration* may be unrealistic[99] due to the slow recovery of habitats, i.e. decades to centuries, and the high cost of working in the deep sea.[100] Furthermore, the science of deep-sea benthic *restoration/habitation* is still at the initial stage.[101] *Offset* may be another

98 ibid.

99 It is noteworthy that this opinion is not fully supported by everyone, especially miners. For instance, the Nautilus claims that the "overall effects will be reversible and moderate", see 'Environmental Impact Statement: Solwara 1 Project' (n 71).

100 CL Van Dover and others, 'Ecological Restoration in the Deep Sea: Desiderata' (2014) 44 *Marine Policy* 98, 98–106. See also CL Van Dover and others, 'Biodiversity Loss from Deep-Sea Mining' (2017) 10 *Nature Geoscience* 464, 464.

101 Susanna M Strömberg, Tomas Lundälv and Thomas J Goreau, 'Suitability of Mineral Accretion as a Rehabilitation Method for Cold-Water Coral Reefs' (2010) 395 *Journal of Experimental Marine Biology and Ecology* 153, 153–161.

possible approach,[102] whether in-kind offset or out-of-kind, although it is still questionable in a deep seabed setting as out-of-kind *offset* may bring a violation of the principle of common heritage of mankind in the LOSC due to a transfer of wealth from international waters to national waters.[103] Thus, *avoidance* and *minimization* will be the main mitigation methods against negative impacts on biodiversity and ecosystems arising from mining activities in the deep seabed.[104]

In general, the desire for *avoidance* can be reached through three approaches: *site selection*, *project design*, and *scheduling*. The objective of *site selection* is to avoid areas of high value for biodiversity or ecosystem services through seascape screening before the project starts. Through *project design*, avoidance takes place when selecting the type of infrastructure and choosing construction and operational methods. Impacts may be avoided through *scheduling* by understanding and taking into account seasonal and diurnal patterns of species behavior (e.g. breeding, migration, roosting) and ecosystem functioning (e.g. river flow, tree fruiting patterns, vegetation growth cycle/patterns) as well as the use of natural resources by local communities (e.g. fishing and hunting seasons and locations).[105] As far as deep seabed mining activities are concerned, *site selection* and *project design* can help to mitigate adverse impact through, e.g. collecting environmental data, making an environmental management plan, conducting an environmental impact assessment, and applying best environmental practices, which will have effect when they are deployed in a legal package. In other words, if those elements can be absorbed by the Deep Seabed Mining Regime and can be well implemented and monitored, the negative impact on the marine environment of deep seabed mining activities will be mitigated as far as possible. Therefore, examining the current Deep Seabed Mining Regime and its implementation is meaningful, from which the paucity of the regime will appear.

---

102 Michael W Lodge, Kathleen Segerson and Dale Squires, 'Sharing and Preserving the Resources in the Deep Sea: Challenges for the International Seabed Authority' (2017) 32 *The International Journal of Marine and Coastal Law* 427, 443.

103 Van Dover and others, 'Biodiversity Loss from Deep-Sea Mining' (n 100) 464.

104 ibid.

105 Ekstrom, Bennun and Mitchell (n 97) 26.

## 3 Deep Seabed Mining Regime

The Deep Seabed Mining Regime was established by several international legal instruments. The LOSC and 1994 Implementing Agreement[106] together constructed the basic framework of the Deep Seabed Mining Regime. Within the framework of the LOSC and 1994 Implementing Agreement, the ISA sets rules, regulations, and procedures to regulate prospecting, exploration, and exploitation of marine minerals in the Area, the so-called "Mining Code".[107] The Seabed Disputes Chamber of the International Tribunal for the Law of the Sea's (ITLOS) advisory opinion *Responsibilities and Obligations of States Sponsoring Persons and Entities with Respect to Activities in the Area* (the SDC Advisory Opinion) clarifies the contents of sponsoring States' international environmental obligations and the scope of sponsoring States' liabilities when sponsored persons and entities cause damages in the process of mining in the Area.[108]

### 3.1 *The Historical Development of Deep Seabed Mining Regime*

If attempting to thoroughly understand the current Deep Seabed Mining Regime and even its expected development over the next few years, it will not suffice to consider the final product in isolation. There is the need to also understand the antecedents of the current regime, including its relationship with the competing Reciprocating States regime.

---

106 Pursuant to Annex I, article 2(1), of the 1994 Implementing Agreement, "[t]he provisions of this Agreement and Part XI of LOSC shall be interpreted and applied together as a single instrument. In the event of any inconsistency between these two instruments, the provisions of 1994 implementing agreement shall prevail."

107 The complete set of these regulations will form part of the Mining Code together with recommendations by the Authority's Legal and Technical Commission for the guidance of contractors on the assessment of the environmental impacts of exploration for polymetallic nodules. To date, the Authority has issued Regulations on Prospecting and Exploration for Polymetallic Nodules in the Area (adopted 13 July 2000) which was later updated and adopted 25 July 2013 [Nodules Exploration Regulations]; the Regulations on Prospecting and Exploration for Polymetallic Sulphides in the Area (adopted 7 May 2010) [Sulphides Exploration Regulations] and the Regulations on Prospecting and Exploration for Cobalt-Rich Crusts (adopted 27 July 2012) [Crusts Exploration Regulations]. In these three exploration regulations, there are quite a few provisions that are identical. In this situation, the book calls them the ISA Exploration Regulations as a whole, with specific articles specified.

108 *Responsibilities and Obligations of States with Respect to Activities in the Area, Advisory Opinion, 1 February 2011, ITLOS Reports 2011*, p. 10.

### 3.1.1 Genesis

As mentioned earlier, the first discovery of polymetallic nodules dates back to the end of the nineteenth century, in the Kara Sea, in the Arctic Ocean off Siberia. During the HMS *Challenger* expedition between 1872 and 1876, they were found to occur in most oceans of the world.[109] However, due to their low grade or the configuration of the seabed on which they lay, they were not commercially attractive until the 1950s.[110] During the International Geophysical Year between 1957 and 1958, polymetallic nodules were proved to contain commercially valuable minerals, such as nickel, copper, and cobalt.[111] Serious discussion of the commercial exploitation of the nodules happened in the 1960s and 1970s, given that developments in mining technologies and rising mineral prices made commercial exploitation seem possible and economically feasible. At that time, the seabed beyond the continental shelf was subject to three doctrines,[112] namely, the "exploitability" criterion for the outer limits of the continental shelf,[113] *Res Communis,*[114] and *Res nullius*.[115] No matter which doctrine was adopted, the result was the same. Namely, only a handful of technologically developed States could benefit from mining activities in the deep ocean floor. It was recognized that deep seabed mining is a capital-intensive and formidable technological industry. Developing States, which had insufficient capital and technology, were *de facto* excluded from these activities. More seriously, the common worry was that if unrestricted deep seabed mining were to proceed, the economic advantages to deep seabed mining States

109 ISA, 'Polymetallic Nodules' (n 36).

110 Robin R Churchill and Alan V Lowe, *The Law of the Sea* (3rd edn, Manchester Univeristy Press 1999), 223.

111 P Levy, 'The International Sea-Bed Area', in R J Dupuy and D Vignes (eds), *A Handbook on the New Law of the Sea*, vol 1 (Martinus Nijhoff 1991), 595–602.

112 Churchill and Lowe (n 110) 224–225; Yoshifumi Tanaka, *The International Law of the Sea* (2nd edn, Cambridge University Press 2015), 179.

113 According to this interpretation, the seaward limit of coastal States' continental shelves moved into deeper waters under the "exploitability" criterion enshrined in Article 1 of the 1958 Geneva Convention on the Continental Shelf. It was foreseeable that, eventually, the whole ocean floor would be divided up among coastal States. It would seem to follow that natural resources in the deep seabed would be subject to the sovereign rights of coastal States, according to Yoshifumi Tanaka, ibid.

114 According to this view, the deep seabed is *res communis* and, thus, the ocean beds as well as natural resources would be subject to the freedom of the high seas. Consequently, whereas no State can appropriate the ocean floor, the Area and its resources could be used by any State according to freedom of the high seas.

115 According to this view, the deep seabed as well as its natural resources should be treated as *res nullius*. In this view, mining States would be able to appropriate the ocean floor as well as its natural resources through occupation.

would have similar disadvantages for land-based exporters of the minerals, especially those which were developing States.[116] The consequence could not be accepted by developing States, which were keen to secure a fairer New International Economic Order.[117]

A turning point in this issue was the historic Pardo Speech in 1967. The Maltese Ambassador to the United Nations, Dr. Arvid Pardo, submitted a request for the inclusion of a *note verbal* as a supplementary item on the agenda of the 22nd session of the General Assembly: "Declaration and treaty concerning the reservation exclusively for peaceful purposes of the seabed and ocean floor, underlying the seas beyond the present limits of national jurisdiction, and the use of their resource in the interests of mankind".[118] He called for the deep seabed and its resources to be designated as the "common heritage of mankind".[119] Under the Maltese proposal, neither a State nor any other legal entity has the right to make claims on the seabed or its mineral resources. Pardo's proposal captured the zeitgeist of the late 1960s and quickly gained support.[120] Developing States regarded the common heritage of mankind concept as an integral part of the New International Economic Order that would bring some level of equity to the world economy,[121] and several UNGA resolutions were subsequently adopted to give effect to the Maltese initiative.[122]

This proposal was to be discussed in a newly-established, thirty-five State *ad hoc* committee in 1967,[123] which was replaced in 1968 by the permanent Committee on the Peaceful Uses of the Sea-Bed and the Ocean Floor Beyond

116 Churchill and Lowe (n 110) 223.

117 Tanaka, *The International Law of the Sea* (n 112) 179; Rothwell and Stephens (n 20) 120.

118 UNGA, 'Malta: Request for Inclusion of a Supplementary Item in the Agenda of the Twenty-Second Session' [18 August 1967] GAOR 22nd Session Annexes, Agenda Item 92, 1; see also Rüdiger Wolfrum, 'Common Heritage of Mankind' in *Max Plank Encyclopedia of Public International Law* (2009).

119 UNGA, UN Doc A/C.1. /PV.1516 (1 November 1967), paragraph 13.

120 Edward Duncan Brown, '"Neither Necessary nor Prudent at This Stage": The Regime of Seabed Mining and Its Impact on the Universality of the UN Convention on the Law of the Sea' (1993) 17 *Marine Policy* 81, 81–82.

121 Robert L Friedheim, *Negotiating the New Ocean Regime* (University of South Carolina Press 1993), 221; Roderick C Ogley, 'The Law of the Sea Draft Convention and the New International Economic Order' (1981) 5 *Marine Policy* 240, 240.

122 See, eg A/RES/2340(XXII) (18 December 1967); A/RES/2467(XXIII) (21 December 1968); A/RES/2754(XXIV) (15 December 1969); A/RES/2749(XXV) (17 December 1970); A/RES/2750(XXV) (17 December 1970); A/RES/2881(XXVI) (21 December 1971); A/RES/3029(XXVII) (18 December 1972); A/RES/3067(XXVIII) (16 November 1973); A/RES/3334(XXIX) (17 December 1974); A/RES/3483(XXX) (12 December 1975); A/RES/31/63(XXXI) (10 December 1976).

123 UNGA, UN Doc A/Res/2340(XXII) (18 December 1967).

the Limits of National Jurisdiction. The Committee was tasked with preparing a preliminary study of the legal, technical, scientific, and economic matters relating to the international seabed. The work of the Committee proved to be an important catalyst for UNCLOS III, as it was soon realized that agreement on deep seabed mining could, realistically, be achieved only by simultaneously resolving a complete package of the law of the sea questions, including the interaction of a Deep Seabed Mining Regime with the continental shelf regime.

Before UNCLOS III was convened, the UNGA adopted a series of resolutions on the topic of the deep seabed, of which two are particularly important. The first of these is the 1969 resolution on the "Question of the Reservation Exclusively for Peaceful Purposes of the Sea-Bed and the Ocean Floor, and the Subsoil Thereof, Underlying the High Seas Beyond the Limits of Present National Jurisdiction, and the Use of Their Resources in the Interests of Mankind".[124] This resolution was known as the Moratorium Resolution. It affirmed that the exploitation of the resources of the seabed and ocean floor beyond the limits of national jurisdiction should be carried out for the benefit of mankind as a whole and taking into account the special needs and interests of developing States. This resolution was heavily contested. Although most States accepted the common heritage doctrine in general terms, they were concerned about how it would be given effect and how to ensure investment certainty, as well as how to minimize the chance of confrontation on the high seas.[125] The second important resolution, which followed the Moratorium Resolution in 1970, was the "Declaration of Principles Governing the Sea-Bed and the Ocean Floor, and the Subsoil Thereof, Beyond the Limits of National Jurisdiction" (Declaration of Principles).[126] The Declaration of Principles expanded on the common heritage of humankind concept that had been articulated by Ambassador Pardo:

> The Sea-bed and ocean floor, and the subsoil thereof, beyond the limits of national jurisdiction (hereafter referred to as the area), as well as the resources of the area, are the common heritage of mankind.

This resolution laid the foundation for the Part XI regime: "Although the notion of 'common heritage of mankind' was settled upon as the conceptual framework under which the Area would be governed, the detail of its governance and importantly its customary status increasingly became matters of

124 UNGA, UN Doc A/Res/2574(XXIV) (15 December 1969).

125 Churchill and Lowe (n 110) 227.

126 UNGA, UN Doc A/Res/2749(XXV) (17 December 1970). This resolution attracted 108 votes in favor, none against, and 14 abstentions.

high politics."[127] Numerous developed States disliked the bureaucracy of the institutions established and the alleged deviation from fundamental rules of a market economy.[128] "Even if this was arguably contrary to the Moratorium and Principles Resolutions, the industrialized states did not accept that these declarations had established customary rules, still less peremptory norms from which no derogation is permitted."[129]

### 3.1.2 Co-existing Deep Seabed Mining Regimes: LOSC Regime and the Reciprocating States Regime

The need to resolve the issues concerning deep seabed mining was a major impetus in convening UNCLOS III. However, it was not an easy task to reach an agreement between groups that pursued distinct interests. Nevertheless, despite the disaffection among certain industrial States,[130] UNCLOS III designed an original framework of the Deep Seabed Mining Regime which designates the Area as the "common heritage of mankind."[131] The ISA governs exploration and exploitation of minerals in the Area.[132] All prospective exploration and exploitation activities are required to be sponsored by a State Party to the Convention.[133] In applying for an exploration or exploitation license, an entity submits two broadly similar areas for consideration. If a license is granted, it is the ISA that determines which area will be allotted to the applicant; the second area is reserved for activities by the ISA through the Enterprise or "in association with developing States."[134] However, the Enterprise – the international body that was initially designed to carry out such activities for the benefit of mankind and currently whose functions are performed by the Secretariat – was effectively shelved by the 1994 Agreement.[135] The remaining option was, therefore, for these reserved sites to be exploited by the ISA in association with developing States.

---

127 Duncan French, 'From the Depths: Rich Pickings of Principles of Sustainable Development and General International Law on the Ocean Floor – the Seabed Disputes Chamber's 2011 Advisory Opinion' (2011) 26 *The International Journal of Marine and Coastal Law* 525, 528.

128 ibid.

129 Rothwell and Stephens (n 20) 129.

130 The LOSC was adopted not by consensus, but rather by vote which meant some level of dissent. The voting result was four states against the LOSC, including the United States and 17 states abstained, including the United Kingdom, Belgium, the Federal Republic of Germany, Italy, the Netherlands, the former Soviet Union, and the Eastern bloc states.

131 LOSC, article 136.

132 ibid, article 137(2).

133 ibid, article 157(2)(b).

134 ibid, Annex III, article 8.

135 1994 Implementing Agreement, Annex II, section 2, article 1.

Indeed, before 1994, it was impossible to say that a single regime for deep seabed mining existed. There were, in fact, two alternative regimes, the United Nations regime, based upon the common heritage principle as embodied in the 1982 LOSC, and the Reciprocating States Regime, based upon the principle of the freedom of the high seas and the national legislation of leading industrialized States. The reason for the establishment of the Reciprocating States Regime superficially was the need of an interim regime before entry into force of the LOSC. Indeed, it originated from industrial States' dissatisfaction with the conclusion of UNCLOS III.[136] It is hard to say the LOSC (without Resolution I and II as well as 1994 Implementing Agreement) is a universal agreement because it was adopted not by consensus, but by voting. Those states involved or interested in deep seabed mining did not vote in support of the LOSC, but voted against it or abstained.[137] Consequently, apart from Iceland, all States Parties to the LOSC were developing States.[138] UNCLOS III is not a pure legal conference but embodies quite a lot of political colour. It was a contest of interests between developing countries and industrialized countries. It can be seen from the text of the 1982 LOSC that the developing States won. It dealt mainly with "normal" situations and lacked necessary provisions for the protection of the interests of pioneer mining consortia, predominantly coming from industrialized countries, which had invested heavily in preparation for seabed mining before the adoption of the Convention.[139] In order to solve this problem, UNCLOS III set out special considerations for "pioneer investors" in two resolutions appended to the Final Act of the Conference.[140] Resolution II

136 Just before the tenth session of the UNCLOS III began in 1981, the United States delegation announced that there was to be a wholesale policy review of the negotiating text by the new administration under President Reagan, which identified a range of concerns with Part XI including the preferential treatment for the Enterprise; the mandatory transfer of technology; production limitations to benefit land-based producers; no guaranteed United States representation on the ISA Council; the potential for a Review Conference to adopt amendments binding on the United States without its assent; revenue sharing obligations attaching to contractors; and the absence of protection for preparatory investors. See Satya N Nandan, Michael W Lodge and Shabtai Rosenne, *United Nations Convention on the Law of the Sea, 1982: A Commentary, Volume VI* (Martinus Nijhoff Publishers 2002), 48–49.

137 Tanaka, *The International Law of the Sea* (n 112) 186–187.

138 ibid, 187.

139 Edward Duncan Brown, *Sea-Bed Energy and Minerals: The International Legal Regime. Vol. 2: Sea-Bed Mining* (Martinus Nijhoff Publishers 2001), 5.

140 See Resolution II Governing Preparatory Investment in Pioneer Activities relating to Polymetallic Nodules, paragraph 1(a). Resolution I contained in Annex to the Final Act of the UNCLOS III formally established the Preparatory Commission for the International Seabed Authority and for the International Tribunal for the Law of the Sea. The regime

contained detailed rules involving preparatory investment in pioneer activities relating to polymetallic nodules. A pioneer investor registered under this resolution had the exclusive right to carry out pioneer activities in the pioneer area allocated to it from the date of registration.[141] Resolution II had effect until the entry into force of the LOSC.[142]

In the meantime, some agreements were concluded after 1982 that adopted and amended the operation of Resolution II.[143] The regime was established by "like-minded States",[144] based on their national legislation,[145] most of which followed a similar template. They provided reciprocal recognition of licenses granted for exploration or exploitation of seabed resources by other states, and prohibited exploration or exploitation unless there was such a license.

---

of the pioneer investors is stipulated in the Resolution II contained in Annex I to the Final Act of the UNCLOS III, the intention of which was to "protect the substantial investments already made in the development of seabed mining technology, equipment and expertise". Seven registered pioneer investors were India, France (IFREMER/AFERNOD), Japan (Deep Ocean Resources Development Co. Ltd.), and the State enterprise Yuzhmorgeologiya sponsored by the Soviet Union [now the Russian Federation], the Interoceanmental Joint Organization (IOM), a consortium sponsored by Bulgaria, Cuba, Czechoslovakia [now the Czech Republic and Slovakia], Poland, and the USSR [now the Russian Federation], the China Ocean Mineral Resources Research and Development Association (COMRA), sponsored by the People's Republic of China, and the Government of the Republic of Korea. See Satya N Nandan, Michael W Lodge and Shabtai Rosenne, *The Development of the Regime for Deep Seabed Mining* (International Seabed Authority 2002), 69. With regard to the requirements to be registered as a pioneer investor, see Brown, *Sea-Bed Energy and Minerals* (n 139), chapter 6, section 2.1.

141 Resolution II (n 140), paragraph 6. Concerning Resolution I and II, see Rothwell and Stephens (n 20) 131–132.

142 Resolution II (n 140) stated that "The Third United Nations Conference on the Law of the Sea, … Desirous of making provisions for investments by States and other entities made in a manner compatible with the international regime set forth in Part XI of the Convention and the Annexes relating thereto, before the entry into force of the Convention".

143 They are: Agreement Concerning Interim Arrangements Relating to Polymetallic Nodules of the Deep Sea Bed, made between France, the Federal Republic of Germany, the United Kingdom and the United States, published in September 1982; Draft Memorandum of Understanding on the Settlement of Conflicting Claims with Respect to Seabed Areas, in August 1983; and Provisional Understanding Regarding Deep Seabed Matters between eight industrialized States, ie Belgium, France, the Federal Republic of Germany, Italy, Japan, the Netherlands, the United Kingdom and the United States, in August 1984.

144 Churchill and Lowe (n 110) 232.

145 The United States led the way with its Deep Sea Bed Hard Mineral Resources Act of 1980, followed by the Federal Republic of Germany's Act on the Interim Regulation of Deep Sea Bed Mining in the same year. Then the United Kingdom adopted its Deep Sea Mining (Temporary Provisions) Act in 1981, followed by France. Then Japan adopted its legislation in 1982 and Italy in 1985. The Soviet Union also adopted its legislation in 1982.

The aim of this regime was to attain the comprehensive regulation of deep seabed mining and to avoid potential conflicts arising from overlapping areas of interests to pioneer investors. Those industrialized States declared that the laws and regulations were interim in nature, and without prejudice to Part XI of the LOSC, and in no way an assertion of sovereignty or sovereign rights in the resources of the deep seabed.[146] Indeed, it was difficult to be without prejudice to the LOSC. For instance, no arrangement was made for site-banking, so that the Enterprise or developing States could not access the exploration or exploitation areas which had similar value to the area mined by those industrialized States.[147] Moreover, there was no rush for the parties of the agreements to ratify or access the LOSC, because this regime had solved the problem they cared about and thus they felt no further obligations. That being said, the existence of the Reciprocating States Regime delayed the entry into force of the LOSC.[148] Also, the LOSC would lose its meaning, if those industrialized states that were involved in deep seabed mining did not want to be a part of it.

### 3.1.3 1994 Implementing Agreement and Final Deep Seabed Mining Regime

The co-existence of the LOSC regime and the Reciprocating States Regime appeared to be problematic. On the one hand, the Reciprocating States Regime was criticized by the G-77 and Eastern Europe states because it went against the letter and spirit of the LOSC. On the other hand, there were more and more concerns that the Reciprocating States Regime would impair the unity and universality of the Deep Seabed Mining Regime established in Part XI of the LOSC, especially when the sixtieth instrument of ratification of Guyana was deposited on 16 November 1993, meaning that the LOSC would enter into force in November 1994. It could not be a universal convention if only one developed State participated. It was time to reconsider the Deep Seabed Mining Regime under the LOSC.[149]

Since 1990, two successive Secretaries-General of the United Nations, Javier Pérez de Cuéllar and Boutros Boutros-Ghali, initiated informal consultations in order to resolve the problem of developed States concerning Part XI. In 1993, an informal group of representatives from both developing and developed states was formed to develop a draft UNGA resolution together

146 Brown, '"Neither Necessary nor Prudent at This Stage"' (n 120), 93.

147 ibid, 94.

148 Article 308 of the LOSC provided that it was to enter into force twelve months after the date of deposit of the sixtieth instrument of ratification or accession.

149 Rothwell and Stephens (n 20) 133.

with a draft agreement on the implementation of Part XI of LOSC.[150] This document, known as the "Boat Paper", was discussed and revised heavily and became the basis of the 1994 Implementing Agreement. As a result, the UN General Assembly adopted the Implementing Agreement on 28 July 1994, by a vote of 121 in favour, none against, and seven abstentions. It is worth noting that among those abstentions, only Russia was an industrial State. The conflict between two alternative regimes was finally resolved by the critical 1994 Implementing Agreement, which attempted to reconcile the two competing regimes.

Apart from the Preamble, the 1994 Implementing Agreement is composed of ten articles and an Annex which is divided into nine sections. It would be interpreted and applied together with the Part XI of the LOSC as a single instrument, and in the event of any inconsistency between the two, the provisions of the 1994 Implementing Agreement would prevail.[151] It resolves the outstanding disagreement with the regime of Part XI and also makes significant changes:[152] it takes a functional and cost-effective approach towards the establishment of the institutions under Part XI and the subsidization of the activities of the Enterprise;[153] it provides for a stable environment for investors in deep seabed minerals under a market-oriented regime; it guarantees access to the resources of the seabed to all qualified investors; and it provides for the establishment of a system of taxation that is fair to the seabed miner and from which the international community as a whole may benefit.[154] The specific measures include: 1) removing the provision of production limitation and compulsory technology transfer, improvements of financial terms of contracts, and provisions for assistance from the proceeds of mining to developing land-based producers of minerals whose economies may be affected as a consequence of deep seabed mining;[155] 2) providing for a balance between the powers and functions of the Assembly and Council and establishing a mechanism for decision-making in the Council that enabled all groups to protect their interests;[156] and 3) reviewing the conference.

150 DH Anderson, 'Efforts to Ensure Universal Participation in the UN Convention on the Law of the Sea' (1993) 42 *International and Comparative Law Quarterly* 654.

151 1994 Implementing Agreement, article 2(1).

152 Tanaka, *The International Law of the Sea* (n 112) 188–192.

153 1994 Implementing Agreement, section 2.

154 Nandan, Lodge and Rosenne, *The Development of the Regime for Deep Seabed Mining* (n 140), paragraph 2.

155 ibid.

156 ibid.

Although the LOSC model was substantially modified and far removed from its original design, the essence of the LOSC regime was kept.[157] As Edward Duncan Brown said, the 1994 Implementing Agreement "opened the way for the industrialized States to support the UN Convention regime for sea-bed mining".[158]

### 3.2 *Framework and Principles of the Deep Seabed Mining Regime*

The international community needs a comprehensive Deep Seabed Mining regime to regulate prospecting, exploration, and exploitation of marine minerals in the Area to minimize the damage to the marine environment. Currently, the LOSC and its 1994 Implementing Agreement are, undoubtedly, the most crucial legal framework in this regard. Furthermore, the Mining Code issued by the ISA fills the gaps of the LOSC and sets out specific standards for mining works. The SDC Advisory Opinion, although not legally binding, solves the essential issues regarding sponsoring States' responsibilities and liabilities.

#### 3.2.1 LOSC and Relevant Legal Instruments

The LOSC consists of 17 parts among which broad agreement exists on sixteen of them, but Part XI dealing with the Area once caused significant problems.[159] The 1994 Implementing Agreement helped to resolve the outstanding disagreement by industrialized States to the regime of Part XI, while also making significant changes to it. It was to be interpreted and applied together as a single instrument, and in the event of any inconsistency between the two, the provisions of the 1994 Implementing Agreement would prevail.[160]

---

157 The essential elements governing the Area, namely, the principle of the common heritage of mankind, the non-appropriation of the Area and its natural resources, the use exclusively for peaceful purposes, and the benefit of mankind as a whole, remain intact. Otherwise, the "parallel system" is still intact. See LDM Nelson, 'The New Deep Sea-Bed Mining Regime' (1995) 10 *International Journal of Marine and Coastal Law* 189, 203. In this regard, article 311(6) of the LOSC makes clear that: States Parties agree that there shall be no amendments to the basic principle relating to the common heritage of mankind set forth in article 136 and that they shall not be party to any agreement in derogation thereof.

158 Brown, *Sea-Bed Energy and Minerals* (n 139), 4. Brown held the opinion that the United Nations regime which emerged victorious in 1994 was far from being the original UN Convention model. Rather, it was the UN Convention model as substantially modified by 1994 Implementing Agreement. The model that survived is only "a pale shadow". Although the superficial ideology has been preserved, there has been a marked erosion of the substance of the common heritage regime as originally embodied in the UN Convention.

159 Nandan, Lodge and Rosenne, *The Development of the Regime for Deep Seabed Mining* (n 140), paragraph 2.

160 1994 Implementing Agreement, article 2(1).

Part XI of the LOSC (articles 133 to 191) sets out the regime for the Area and provides the legal framework governing activities in the Area. Part XI, as adjusted by the 1994 Implementing Agreement, must be read together with Annex III (Basic Conditions of Prospecting, Exploration and Exploitation with respect to the resources of the Area) of the Convention, and with Annex IV (Statute of the Enterprise).[161] Related provisions of the Convention include the preamble and articles 1, 82(4), 84(2), 209, 256, 273, 274, 286(3), 287(2), 305, 308(3), (4), and (5), 311(6), 314, 316(5), and 319(2)(a), (b), and (3).[162] Relevant provisions also appear in the Final Act of the Conference, specifically in Resolution I (*Establishment of the Preparatory Commission for the International Sea-Bed Authority and for the International Tribunal for the Law of the Sea*), and Resolution II (*Governing Preparatory Investment in Pioneer Activities relating to Polymetallic Nodules*).[163] Both of these resolutions, which contained, *inter alia*, interim arrangements pending entry into force of the Convention and the establishment of the ISA, were essential elements in the package negotiated in the First Committee at UNCLOS III.[164] Also related to the Deep Seabed Mining Regime under Part XI are the provisions of Annex VI and, in particular, articles 14 and 35 to 40 concerning the establishment and composition of the Seabed Disputes Chamber of the ITLOS.[165]

The LOSC, by its nature, was not intended to contain a comprehensive framework for seabed mining. For instance, neither Part XI dealing with the Area nor Part XII on "Protection and Preservation of the Marine Environment" includes any detailed rules for the protection of the environment in connection with deep seabed mining. Consequently, the ISA was invested with powers to adopt rules and regulations to fill in the gaps in Part XI.[166] In this sense, the Authority has filled the legal framework of the LOSC regarding deep seabed mining.

The "Principles Governing the Area" are set out in section 2, Part XI of the LOSC, arranging from article 136 to article 149. Those provisions are primarily based on the Declaration of Principles adopted by the General Assembly in 1970, with elaboration where necessary or appropriate.[167] The common

161 Nandan, Lodge and Rosenne, *The Development of the Regime for Deep Seabed Mining* (n 140), paragraph 1.

162 ibid.

163 ibid.

164 ibid.

165 ibid.

166 LOSC, article 157.

167 Nandan, Lodge and Rosenne, *The Development of the Regime for Deep Seabed Mining* (n 140), paragraph 38.

heritage of mankind is the overriding principle of the Deep Seabed Mining Regime in the LOSC. This section clarifies the nature of the regime and the types of activities that may be carried out in the Area and the rights and obligations of States and other entities conducting these activities. Most of these articles were accepted early in the negotiations at UNCLOS III, with a focus on the development of general principles.

Many of the principles established in section 2 deal with topics covered in more detail in other provisions of the LOSC, including those concerning responsibility to ensure compliance and liability for damage, the rights and interests of coastal States, the promotion of marine scientific research, the promotion and encouragement of the transfer of technology to developing countries, protection of the marine environment, protection of human life, accommodation of other activities besides seabed mining, the participation of developing States in activities in the Area, and archaeological and historical objects found in the Area.[168]

### 3.2.2 Mining Code of ISA

Since the establishment of the ISA, it has adopted a comprehensive set of rules, regulations, and procedures, within a general legal framework established by the LOSC and the 1994 Implementing Agreement, to regulate prospecting,[169] exploration, and exploitation of marine minerals in the Area, which are to be considered as secondary legislation but nevertheless binding on the States Parties. As of 2019, the ISA has issued three exploration regulations with regard to polymetallic nodules, polymetallic sulphides, and cobalt-rich crusts.[170] The three exploration regulations are almost identical in format, scope, and content, with differences primarily reflecting the different spatial and geological characteristics of the polymetallic nodules, polymetallic sulphides, and cobalt-rich crusts.[171] For ease of reference, these three regulations are cited as the Polymetallic Nodules Regulations, the Polymetallic Sulphides Regulations, and the Cobalt-Rich Crusts Regulations, respectively, and referred to as the ISA Exploration Regulations collectively. The regulations include the forms

168 ibid.

169 The term "activities in the Area" in article 1(3) of the LOSC does not include prospecting, although it is included in the ISA Exploration Regulations.

170 The ISA issued three exploration regulations, see note 107. With regard to the process of negotiating the regulations and their contents, see Michael W Lodge, 'International Seabed Authority's Regulations on Prospecting and Exploration for Polymetallic Nodules in the Area', (2002) 20 *Journal of Energy & Natural Resources Law* 270.

171 Michael Lodge, 'The Deep Seabed' in Donald Rothwell and others (eds), *The Oxford Handbook of the Law of the Sea* (Oxford University Press 2015), 241.

necessary to apply for exploration as well as standard terms of exploration contracts. They also provide further information on the procedure, which applies to the designation of reserved areas[172] and the data and information that must be submitted by an applicant for the purposes of approval of the plan of work for exploration.[173] In addition, the ISA planned to adopt a regulation regarding exploitation issues in 2020, which is currently still under review.[174]

Due to the dynamic and evolutionary nature of mining activities, the LTC is mandated by the ISA Exploration Regulations to issue recommendations of a technical or administrative nature for the guidance of contractors in assisting them to implement the ISA Exploration Regulations.[175] At present, the LTC has issued recommendations regarding the design of training programs, assessment of the possible environmental impacts, reporting the actual and direct exploration expenditure, and the content, format, and structure of annual reports.[176] Unlike "rules, regulations and procedures", recommendations issued by the LTC don't need to be approved by the Council, but they must be reported to the Council. In the event of a recommendation being "inconsistent with the intent and purpose of these Regulations", the LTC must modify or withdraw it.[177] The complete set of these regulations together with recommendations of the LTC forms part of the Mining Code, which regulates all aspects of activities in the Area.[178] It is worth mentioning that although the recommendation is not legally binding, it should be implemented and complied with by the contractor. After all, the LTC that issues the recommendation is also the one that approves the application for exploration and exploitation and determines the extension of the contract. When considering the extension of the

172 Nodules Exploration Regulations, regulations 16 and 17.

173 ibid, regulation 18.

174 Philip PE Weaver and David Billett, 'Environmental Impacts of Nodule, Crust and Sulphide Mining: An Overview' in Rahul Sharma (eds) *Environmental Issues of Deep-Sea Mining: Impacts, Consequences and Policy Perspectives* (Springer 2019), 36.

175 Nodules Exploration Regulations, regulation 39.

176 Recommendations for the guidance of contractors and sponsoring States relating to training programs under plans of work for exploration (ISBA/19/LTC/14); Recommendations for the guidance of contractors for the assessment of the possible environmental impacts arising from exploration for marine minerals in the Area (ISBA/19/LTC/8), which is under review (ISBA/24/C/9); Recommendations for the guidance of contractors for the reporting of actual and direct exploration expenditure (ISBA/21/LTC/11); and Recommendations for the guidance of contractors on the content, format and structure of annual reports (ISBA/21/LTC/15).

177 Lodge, 'The Deep Seabed' (n 171) 242.

178 ibid, 241.

contract, it is impossible for the LTC to ignore a contractor's non-compliance with the recommendations.[179]

### 3.2.3 Advisory Opinion and Prospective Jurisprudence of the ITLOS Seabed Disputes Chamber

On 1 February 2011, the Seabed Disputes Chamber (Seabed Dispute Chamber or the Chamber) of the International Tribunal for the Law of the Sea (ITLOS) unanimously adopted a historic opinion, the *Advisory Opinion on the Responsibilities and Obligations of States Sponsoring Persons and Entities with respect to Activities in the Area* (SDC Advisory Opinion).

#### 3.2.3.1 *SDC Advisory Opinion*

The request for an Advisory Opinion was brought by the Council of the ISA but originated from two small Pacific island developing States, Nauru and Tonga, each applying for approval to obtain contracts to explore for polymetallic nodules to ISA in April 2008 in the reserved area. Like most developing States, neither had the financial and technical capacity to conduct mining activities on their own. Consequently, they sponsored two private entities, namely, Nauru Ocean Resources Inc. and Tonga Offshore Mining Ltd., to undertake exploration activities. However, in May 2009, Nauru and Tonga requested a postponement of their applications. On 1 March 2010, Nauru submitted a proposal to the ISA's Secretary-General seeking an advisory opinion from the Seabed Disputes Chamber regarding the extent of the responsibilities and potential liabilities of sponsoring States. In the proposal, it was stressed:

> its sponsorship of Nauru Ocean Resources Inc. was originally premised on the assumption that Nauru could effectively mitigate (with a high degree of certainty) the potential liabilities or costs arising from its sponsorship.[180]

This was important, as these liabilities or costs could, in some circumstances, far exceed the financial capacities of Nauru (as well as those of many other developing States). Further, Nauru suggested that, if sponsoring States were

---

179 Aline Jaeckel, 'Deep Seabed Mining and Adaptive Management: The Procedural Challenges for the International Seabed Authority' (2016) 70 *Marine Policy* 205, 208.

180 Proposal to seek an advisory opinion from the Seabed Disputes Chamber of the International Tribunal for the Law of the Sea on matters regarding sponsoring State responsibility and liability. Submitted by the delegation of Nauru (ISBA/16/C/6, 5 March 2010).

exposed to potential liabilities for damage caused by activities of the sponsored entity to the Area, Nauru, and other developing States may effectively be precluded from taking part in mining activities, contrary to the purposes and principles of part XI of LOSC.[181]

On 6 May 2010, the Council of the ISA decided to request an advisory opinion, from the Chamber of the ITLOS.[182] This SDC Advisory Opinion answered the following three important questions:

(1) What are the legal responsibilities and obligations of States Parties to the LOS Contention with respect to the sponsorship of activities in the Area in accordance with the LOS Convention, in particular Part XI, and the 1994 Agreement relating to the Implementation of Part XI of the United Nations Convention on the Law of the Sea of 10 December 1982?

(2) What is the extent of liability of a State Party for any failure to comply with the provisions of the LOS Convention, in particular, Part XI, and the 1994 Agreement, by an entity whom it has sponsored under article 153, para 2(b), of the LOS Convention?

(3) What are the necessary and appropriate measures that a sponsoring State must take in order to fulfill its responsibility under the LOS Convention, in particular art 139 and Annex III, and the 1994 Agreement?[183]

It was the first time that the advisory jurisdiction of the Chamber of the ITLOS had been invoked.[184] Unlike a contentious case, the purpose of an advisory opinion is not to solve the disputes between parties, but to "offer legal advice to the organs and institutions requesting the opinion."[185] In other words, it does not legally bind either the requesting entity or any other body or State to take any specific action pursuant to the opinion.[186] Nevertheless, the non-legally binding nature of the advisory opinion does not devalue its importance, since ISA member States are willing to seek advice, especially the sponsoring States, on how to carry out their international responsibility and how to design their national legislation in this regard. Hence, the SDC Advisory Opinion is also an

181 ibid.

182 Decision of the Council of the International Seabed Authority requesting an advisory opinion pursuant to Article 191 of the United Nations Convention on the Law of the Sea (ISBA/16/C/13, 6 May 2010).

183 ibid.

184 Donald K Anton, Robert A Makgill and Cymie R Payne, 'Seabed Mining: Advisory Opinion on Responsibility and Liability' (2011) 41(2) *Environmental Policy and Law* 60, 60.

185 *Legality of the Threat or Use of Nuclear Weapons, Advisory Opinion, I.C.J. Reports 1996*, p. 226, at 236, paragraph 15.

186 Hugh Thirlway, 'Advisory Opinions', in *Max Planck Encyclopedia of Public International Law* (2006).

important part of the Deep Seabed Mining Regime. The analysis of the SDC Advisory Opinion will be given in Chapter 2.[187]

#### 3.2.3.2 *The Seabed Disputes Chamber and Its Prospective Jurisprudence*

More disputes might arise at the exploitation stage in the future because of the complicated and unpredictable situations of exploitation, which might be brought before the Chamber. The prospective jurisprudence of the Chamber will be paramount to the Deep Seabed Mining Regime, although "the decision shall have no binding force except between the parties in respect of that particular case."[188] Nevertheless, the effect of the jurisprudence cannot be underestimated, as Baron Descamps described, "doctrine and jurisprudence no doubt do not create law; but they assist in determining rules which exist."[189] Therefore, it is necessary to introduce the Seabed Disputes Chamber and its jurisdiction.

The Seabed Disputes Chamber is established by virtue of Part XI, section 5, of the LOSC and amplified by Annex VI, article 14 and section 4. The Chamber has jurisdiction in disputes with respect to activities in the Area and is comprised

187 Regarding the analysis of the SDC Advisory Opinion, see David Freestone, 'Responsibilities and Obligations of States Sponsoring Persons and Entities with Respect to Activities in the Area' (2011) 105 *The American Journal of International Law* 755; see also Jianjun Gao, 'The Responsibilities and Obligations of the Sponsoring States Advisory Opinion' (2013) 12 *Chinese Journal of International Law* 771; K Russell LaMotte, 'Introductory Note to the International Tribunal for the Law of the Sea: Responsibilities and Obligations of States Sponsoring Persons and Entities with Respect to Activities in the Area (Request for Advisory Opinion Submitted to the Seabed Disputes Chamber)' (2011) 50 *International Legal Materials* 455; Ximena Hinrichs Oyarce, 'Sponsoring States in the Area: Obligations, Liability and the Role of Developing States' (2018) 95 *Marine Policy* 317; Cymie R Payne, *Seminar on the Outcome of the Advisory Opinion Issued by the Seabed Disputes Chamber of the International Tribunal for the Law of the Sea on 1 February 2011 on the Responsibilities and Obligations of States Sponsoring Activities in the International Seabed Area* (Rochester, NY: Social Science Research Network, 7 April 2011); Rosemary Rayfuse, 'Differentiating the Common? The Responsibilities and Obligations of States Sponsoring Deep Seabed Mining Activities in the Area' (2011) 54 *GYIL* 459; Yoshifumi Tanaka, 'Obligations and Liability of Sponsoring States Concerning Activities in the Area: Reflections on the ITLOS Advisory Opinion of 1 February 2011' (2013) 60 *Netherlands International Law Review* 205; Hui Zhang, 'The Sponsoring State's "Obligation to Ensure" in the Development of the International Seabed Area' (2013) 28 *The International Journal of Marine and Coastal Law* 681.

188 The Statute of the ITLOS, article 33(2).

189 League of Nations. Advisory Committee of Jurists, *Procès-Verbaux of the Proceedings of the Committee, June 16th-July 24th, 1920, with Annexes* (The Hague, Van Langenhuysen 1920), 336.

of 11 judges.[190] The Chamber has compulsory jurisdiction in respect of disputes concerning activities in the Area[191] as well as jurisdiction to give advisory opinions, if requisitioned to do so by the ISA Council or Assembly.[192] While it has not yet decided any contentious cases, as noted above, the Chamber delivered its first Advisory Opinion in 2011.

In reaching its decisions, the Seabed Disputes Chamber is empowered to apply the LOSC as well as the rules, regulations, and procedures adopted by the ISA, the mining contracts, and other rules of international law.[193] The jurisdiction of the Seabed Disputes Chamber can roughly be divided into the following six sub-sections:[194]

(a) Disputes between States Parties concerning the interpretation or application of this Part and the Annexes relating thereto.

In the event of disputes occurring between States Parties, the jurisdiction has two other options. Pursuant to article 188(1), at the request of the parties, disputes may be submitted to either a special Chamber of the ITLOS[195] or to an *ad hoc* Chamber of the Seabed Disputes Chamber,[196] which provides a compromise in the process of negotiation of the Convention.[197] In fact, they also create some flexibility since parties have the right to decide the composition

190 A quorum of seven members is required to constitute the Chamber. Members of the Chamber are selected by the members of the Tribunal every three years and may be selected for a second term. The selection process ensures the representation of the principal legal systems of the world and equitable geographical distribution. The Chamber elects its President from among its members (Statute, article 35). The composition of the Chamber in order of precedence for the period ending 30 September 2023 is as follows: President: Neeru Chadha. Members: José L Jesus; Boualem Bouguetaia; Jin-Hyun Paik; Alonso Gómez-Robledo; Óscar Cabello Sarubbi; Kriangsak Kittichaisaree; Roman Kolodkin; Liesbeth Lijnzaad; Jielong Duan; Kathy-Ann Brown.

191 LOSC, articles 187, 287(2).

192 LOSC, article 191.

193 LOSC, article 293; Annex VI, article 38.

194 LOSC, article 187.

195 The Tribunal may form such chambers, composed of three or more of its elected members, as it considers necessary for dealing with particular categories of disputes. The Tribunal shall form a chamber for dealing with a particular dispute submitted to it if the parties so request. The composition of such a chamber shall be determined by the Tribunal with the approval of the parties.

196 An *ad hoc* chamber is composed of three members of the Seabed Disputes Chamber. The composition of the *ad hoc* chamber is determined by the Seabed Disputes Chamber with the approval of the parties to the dispute. Members of the *ad hoc* chamber may not be in the service of, or nationals of, any of the parties.

197 With regard to distinct views regarding the *ad hoc* chambers, see Nandan, Lodge and Rosenne, *United Nations Convention on the Law of the Sea, 1982: A Commentary, Volume VI* (n 136), 625.

of the Chamber. However, no special chamber or *ad hoc* chamber has been created in the context of article 187 to date.[198]

(b) Disputes between a State Party and the Authority.
These disputes concern:
- acts or omissions of the Authority or of a State Party alleged to be in violation of this Part or the Annexes relating thereto or of rules, regulations and procedures of the Authority adopted in accordance therewith; or
- acts of the Authority alleged to be in excess of jurisdiction or a misuse of power;

(c) Disputes between parties to a contract, being States Parties, the Authority or the Enterprise, state enterprises and natural or juridical persons referred to in article 153, paragraph 2(b).
These disputes concern:
- the interpretation or application of a relevant contract or a plan of work; or
- acts or omissions of a party to the contract relating to activities in the Area and directed to the other party or directly affecting its legitimate interests.

It is important to note that in the case of contractual disputes, the jurisdiction of the Chamber is not exclusive, since article 188(2) provides other options. Pursuant to article 188(2), at the request of any party to it, such a dispute will be submitted to binding commercial arbitration, unless the parties otherwise agree. However, the commercial arbitral tribunal has no jurisdiction to decide any question of interpretation of the Convention. Under this situation, that question must be referred to the Seabed Disputes Chamber for a ruling and the award of the arbitral tribunal shall be in conformity with the ruling of the Seabed Disputes Chamber.

(d) Disputes between the Authority and a prospective contractor
These disputes concern the refusal of a contract or a legal issue arising in the negotiation of the contract. The prospective contractor must have been sponsored by a State as provided in article 153, paragraph 2(b), and has duly fulfilled the conditions referred to in Annex III, article 4, paragraph 6, and article 13, paragraph 2.

(e) Disputes between the Authority and a State Party, a state enterprise or a natural or juridical person sponsored by a State Party as provided for

198 Proelss and others (n 22), 1266.

in article 153, paragraph 2(b), where it is alleged that the Authority has incurred liability as provided in Annex III, article 22.

These disputes may arise due to wrongful acts of the Secretary-General and the staff of the ISA. For instance, in the event that a staff member or a former staff member of the ISA discloses "any industrial secret, proprietary data which are transferred to the Authority … or any other confidential information coming to their knowledge by reason of their employment with the Authority".[199]

(f) Any other disputes for which the jurisdiction of the Chamber is specifically provided in this Convention.

This situation at least includes cases concerning:[200]

- the suspension of a State Party from the exercise of its rights and privileges as a member of the Authority for gross and persistent violation of the provisions in Part XI;[201]
- disapproval of a plan of work;[202] and
- prescription of provisional measures.[203]

Furthermore, there may be some disputes concerning activities in the Area that may not be included in the scenarios of this article. The potential situations of conflicts may be: 1) conflicts between two contractors; 2) disputes between a contractor and other sea users, such as the International Cable Protection Committee (ICPC); and 3) the claims against a sponsoring State or a contractor about compensation. These disputes, based on the specific circumstances, may resort to the full tribunal of the ITLOS or other international or domestic courts.

However, pursuant to article 189 of the LOSC, the Chamber has no jurisdiction to review the discretionary powers of the ISA directly. Thus, the Chamber cannot "pronounce itself on the question of whether any rules, regulations, and procedures of the Authority are in conformity with this Convention, nor declare invalid any such rules, regulations and procedures."[204] In other words, the Chamber is not able to control the law-making functions of the ISA through judicial review. Instead, its jurisdiction is confined to deciding individual cases.[205]

---

199 P Chandrasekhara Rao and Philippe Gautier, *The International Tribunal for the Law of the Sea: Law, Practice and Procedure* (Edward Elgar Pub 2018), 124; LOSC, article 168(2).

200 ibid, 125.

201 LOSC, article 185(2).

202 1994 Implementing Agreement, Annex, section 3(12).

203 LOSC, article 290(5).

204 LOSC, article 189.

205 LOSC, article 189.

### 3.3 *The System of the Prospecting, Exploration, and Exploitation of Mineral Resources in the Area*

It is difficult to deny that "mining" is the core concern of the Deep Seabed Mining Regime. Generally speaking, there are three stages of mining, namely, prospecting, exploration, and exploitation.[206] Prospecting, as general research for deposits of deep seabed minerals, can be conducted without exclusive rights by any State after submitting notification to ISA.[207] Exploration is a process of intensively and systematically analyzing mineral deposits, taking into account all appropriate factors before exploitation. It should be noted that the State which intends to explore the mineral deposits in the Area must apply to the ISA for approval of plans of work for exploration.[208] After permission has been granted, it has the exclusive right for exploration within the approved area. Exploitation is the recovery, for commercial purposes, of deep seabed minerals in the Area, and the extraction of the minerals from that place is the substantial and intractable phase.[209] Indeed, up to now, no exploitation practice has taken place as yet in the Area. Nevertheless, it is important to note that exploitation practice has already occurred in seabed areas within national jurisdictions, which provides important experiences for the international community to better understand their processes and the potential impact on the marine environment.[210] Indeed, increasing numbers of exploration activities are taking place in the seabed areas within national jurisdictions.[211] A range of mining operations happens at relatively shallow water depths (up to 140 m), including diamond commercial seabed mining operations offshore in Namibia

206 LOSC, Annex III, articles 2, 3.

207 LOSC, Annex III, article 2. Nodules Exploration Regulations, regulation 1(3)(e); Sulphides Exploration Regulations, regulation 1(3)(e); Crusts Exploration Regulations, regulation 1(3)(e).

208 Nodules Exploration Regulations, regulation 1(3)(c); Sulphides Exploration Regulations, regulation 1(3)(c); Crusts Exploration Regulations, regulation 1(3)(c).

209 Nodules Exploration Regulations, regulation 1(3)(b); Sulphides Exploration Regulations, regulation 1(3)(b); Crusts Exploration Regulations, regulation 1(3)(b).

210 Canadian firm Nautilus Minerals has been granted a 20-year license by the Papua New Guinea government to commence the Solwara 1 project, the world's first commercial deep seabed mining operation. It indicated the initiation of production will start by the first half of 2019. In addition, in 2017, the Ministry of Economy, Trade and Industry (METI) and the Japan Oil, Gas and Metals National Corporation (JOGMEC) conducted and succeeded in the world's first pilot test of excavating and ore lifting for polymetallic sulphides approximately 1,600 m below sea level near Okinawa Prefecture.

211 Nautilus Minerals of Canada, for example, currently holds more than 100 active prospecting licenses in Tonga, Fiji, Solomon Islands, and Vanuatu as well as a seafloor mining concession in Papua New Guinea. See Global Ocean Commission (n 75), 2.

and South Africa.[212] Exploration is also taking place in the Red Sea (Atlantis II Deep basin), Japan (Okinawa Trough, Izu-Bonin volcanic arc), New Zealand (iron sands off the North Island, Kermadec Trench, Chatham Rise), Namibia (phosphorite/phosphates), Italy (Ionian Sea), and Western Australia.[213] Notably, Namibia proposes to dredge phosphate enriched sediments off Walvis Bay at depths of 180–300 m.[214]

The LOSC created a system of exploration and exploitation of the resources of the Area. Activities may be carried out by: i) the Enterprise, ii) States Parties, iii) state enterprises, iv) natural or juridical persons that possess the nationality of States Parties or are effectively controlled by them or their nationals, when sponsored by such States, or v) any group of the foregoing,[215] provided that each entity follows procedures and meets the qualification standards set forth in the provisions of Part XI and Annex III of the LOSC, the 1994 Implementing Agreement and the rules, regulations, and procedures of the ISA. In order to access the system, any prospective contractor, including the Enterprise, is required to submit an application for approval of a plan of work for activities in the Area.[216] Once approved by the ISA, the plan of work will be in the form of a contract between the Authority and the applicant, except for applications made by the Enterprise.[217]

### 3.3.1 Prospecting

Prospecting, as aforementioned, is the first stage of deep seabed mining, with relatively few limitations. It is considered general research for deep seabed mineral resources, similar to marine scientific research. As defined in the ISA Exploration Regulations,[218] it refers to "the search for deposits of polymetallic nodules/polymetallic sulphides/cobalt crusts in the Area, including estimation of the composition, sizes, and distributions of deposits of polymetallic nodules/polymetallic sulphides/cobalt crusts and their economic values,

212 NT EPA, *Interim Report: Seabed Mining in the Northern Territory* (NT EPA, November 2012), 20.

213 See Global Ocean Commission (n 75), 2.

214 J Midgley and Associates, *Environmental Impact Assessment for the Proposed Dredging of Phosphate Enriched Sediments from Marine License Area No. 170,* Prepared for Namibian Marine Phosphate (Pty) Ltd. (January 2012).

215 Nandan, Lodge and Rosenne, *United Nations Convention on the Law of the Sea, 1982* (n 136), 311.

216 LOSC, article 153(3), and Annex III, article 3(3).

217 LOSC, Annex III, article 3(5).

218 The ISA Exploration Regulations mentioned in this book refer to all three exploration regulations adopted by the ISA, see note 107.

without any exclusive rights."[219] The LOSC does not provide too many details concerning prospecting, except for article 2, Annex III. In this article, it is said that prospecting is essentially free and encouraged by the ISA, requiring a satisfactorily written undertaking by the proposed prospector of complying with the LOSC and the relevant rules, regulations, and procedures of the LOSC with regard to cooperation in the training programs and the protection of the marine environment.[220] In fact, prospecting is excluded from "activities in the Area" by the article 1(3) of the LOSC, although prospecting is included in the ISA Exploration Regulations, according to which the proposed prospector shall notify the ISA of the approximate areas of prospecting. It should be noted that the ISA does not confer any exclusive rights to proposed prospectors, which means there may be several prospectors simultaneously working in the same areas.[221] The ISA Exploration Regulations offer further detail concerning notification of prospecting, protection, and preservation of the marine environment during prospecting and the annual report.[222] It is worth noting that prospecting may not be undertaken if there is substantial evidence of risk of serious environmental harm within an area covered by an approved plan of work for exploration, in a reserved area, or in an area which the Council has disapproved for exploitation for environmental reasons.[223] It also provides for the prospectors' obligation of notifying the ISA regarding objects of an archaeological or historical nature.[224]

It is noteworthy that prospecting is not a necessary procedure before exploration and exploitation. Indeed, in practice, all other operators, apart from the Federal Institute for Geosciences and Natural Resources of the Federal Republic of Germany (BGR) that is sponsored by Germany, prefer to prospect the deep seabed minerals by way of marine scientific research, rather than "prospecting" as stipulated in the LOSC. Technologically speaking, identical results can be reached by either marine scientific research or prospecting and distinctions between the two are difficult to identify. However, from a legal perspective, they are entirely different, as the latter is managed and controlled

219 Nodules Exploration Regulations, regulation 1(3)(e); Sulphides Exploration Regulations, regulation 1(3)(e); Crusts Exploration Regulations, regulation 1(3)(e).

220 LOSC, Annex III, article 2, paragraph 1(b).

221 LOSC, Annex III, article 2(1)(c); article 2(2).

222 Nodules Exploration Regulations, regulations 2–7; Sulphides Exploration Regulations, regulations 2–7; Crusts Exploration Regulations, regulations 2–7.

223 Nodules Exploration Regulations, regulation 2(3); Sulphides Exploration Regulations, regulation 2(3); Crusts Exploration Regulations, regulation 2(3).

224 Nodules Exploration Regulations, regulation 8; Sulphides Exploration Regulations, regulation 8; Crusts Exploration Regulations, regulation 8.

by the ISA, while the former is subject to the high sea regime, although marine scientific research in the Area shall have some special concerns, for instance, it shall be carried out for the benefit of mankind as a whole.[225] Compared with prospecting, marine scientific research is much freer and not constrained by any international organization, which means users need not notify, report, and be verified by any organization. Moreover, due to non-exclusive rights conferred in prospecting, there are few conflicts among users.[226] Therefore, marine scientific research, rather than prospecting, is chosen at this stage. In this situation, the ISA may feel powerless to oversee the activities by way of marine scientific research.

### 3.3.2 Exploration

#### 3.3.2.1 *Sponsorship and Parallel System*

Activities in the Area are to be carried out by the Enterprise, States Parties, state enterprises, or natural or juridical persons possessing the nationality of States Parties or effectively controlled by them, or any combination of these in accordance with the LOSC and the ISA Exploration Regulations.[227] Each applicant, apart from the State Party and the Enterprise, must be sponsored by a State Party of which the applicant is a national, or by the state by which it is effectively controlled.[228] Moreover, an applicant must meet the relevant qualification requirements.[229] However, it does not mean each potential applicant who fulfills those criteria can take for granted the sponsorship from the state of which he or she is a national or effectively controlled by the state or its nationals. In fact, "the grant of sponsorship is made at the discretion of a Member State".[230]

Pursuant to the Nodules Exploration Regulations, any application for exploration for polymetallic nodules by an applicant must cover an area "sufficiently

225 LOSC, article 143(1).

226 In exploration stage, the contractor is given exclusive rights to specific resources in the specific area if the application is approved. Thus, to obtain the exclusive rights and avoid conflicts with other potential applicants, the likely resources users prefer to apply for the ISA and obtain the legal rights. In contrast, due to the lack of these exclusive rights, it is not necessary for the potential resources users to secure their prospecting.

227 LOSC, article 153(2); Annex III, articles 3 and 4; Nodules Exploration Regulations, regulation 9; Sulphides Exploration Regulations, regulation 9; Crusts Exploration Regulations, regulation 9.

228 LOSC, Annex III, article 4; Nodules Exploration Regulations, regulation 11; Sulphides Exploration Regulations, regulation 11; Crusts Exploration Regulations, regulation 11.

229 LOSC, Annex III, article 4; Nodules Exploration Regulations, regulation 12; Sulphides Exploration Regulations, regulation 13; Crusts Exploration Regulations, regulation 13.

230 Proelss and others (n 22), 2141.

large and of sufficient estimated commercial value to allow two mining operations" and must indicate how this area is to be divided into two parts.[231] If a license is granted, the ISA determines which area will be allotted to the applicant; the second area is reserved for activities by the ISA through the Enterprise or "in association with developing States."[232] However, the Enterprise – the international body that was originally designed to carry out such activities for the benefit of mankind and currently whose functions are performed by the Secretariat – was effectively shelved by the 1994 Implementing Agreement, since it stipulates that the functions of the Enterprise shall be performed by the Secretariat of the ISA until it begins to operate independently.[233]

#### 3.3.2.2 *Approval of Plans of Work and Contracts*

According to article 153(3) of the LOSC, activities in the Area shall be carried out in keeping with a formal written plan of work, which must be approved by the Council in accordance with the LTC's recommendation. The plan of work shall be in the form of a contract, which shall be provided for the security of tenure, meaning that the contract shall not be revised, suspended, or terminated except in the following situations.[234] The contract shall enter into negotiations to revise it when it is rendered inequitable or it is impracticable or impossible to achieve the objectives set out in the contract or Part XI.[235] Furthermore, the contract cannot be revised until the parties agree with it.[236] The suspension or termination of the contract may occur when: 1) the contractor's activities may result in serious, persistent, and willful violations of the fundamental terms of the contract, Part XI and the rules, regulations and procedures of the ISA, regardless of warnings by the ISA; or 2) the contractor has failed to comply with a final binding decision of the dispute settlement body applicable to him.[237] It is noteworthy that it cannot happen until the contractor exhausts the judicial remedies.[238]

The proposed plans of work are taken up in the order in which they are received,[239] and should include operational requirements and financial contributions.[240] The ISA Exploration Regulations provide more details about

231 Nodules Exploration Regulations, regulation 15.
232 LOSC, Annex III, article 8.
233 1994 Implementing Agreement, Annex, section 2(1).
234 LOSC, article 153(3) and (6).
235 LOSC, Annex III, article 19(1).
236 LOSC, Annex III, article 19(2).
237 LOSC, Annex III, article 18(1).
238 LOSC, Annex III, article 18(3).
239 LOSC, Annex III, article 6(3).
240 ibid.

the operational requirements and financial capabilities.[241] The ongoing Draft Exploitation Regulation, due to high risks and complexity of exploitation, requires more information at this stage.[242] In principle, if the proposed plans of work conform to those requirements, the Authority shall approve them. In fact, although regulation 23 of the Sulphides Exploration Regulations provide the details for the consideration of the application by the LTC, its decision-making is still mysterious due to "insufficient" transparency.[243]

#### 3.3.2.3 *Protection and Preservation of the Marine Environment*

The protection and preservation of the marine environment is always an important concern of the LOSC, as well as for Part XI. However, the LOSC does not shed sufficient light on this topic. On this point, the section on the protection of the marine environment of the ISA Exploration Regulations introduces some innovations which have the potential to significantly develop the legal regime for the Area .[244] Regulation 31 requires the ISA, sponsoring States, and contractors to take measures to protect and preserve the marine environment in accordance with the precautionary approach as reflected in Principle 15 of the 1992 Rio Declaration on Environment and Development.[245] This provision buffers the LOSC as the precautionary approach was not an accepted principle of international law at the time of its preparation. In furtherance thereof, the protection of the marine environment is an issue that has been integrated into the provisions on prospecting and exploration for the resources covered by the regulations.

More detailed obligations, with respect to the marine environment, are imposed upon entities wishing to conduct exploration activities for mineral resources in the Area. When submitting plans of work for exploration activities, applicants are required to include *inter alia* a preliminary assessment of

---

241 Sulphides Exploration Regulations, regulations 13, 20 and 23.

242 The ISA Draft Exploitation Regulations (March 2019) require the applicant to provide relevant data and information, a mining workplan, a financial plan, an Environmental Impact Statement, an Emergency Response and Contingency Plan, a Healthy and Safety Plan, a Training Plan, a Closure Plan, and an application prepared fee. ISA Draft Exploitation Regulations (March 2019), regulation 7.

243 Jeff A Ardron, Henry A Ruhl and Daniel OB Jones, 'Incorporating Transparency into the Governance of Deep-Seabed Mining in the Area beyond National Jurisdiction' (2018) 89 *Marine Policy* 58, 59.

244 ISA Exploration Regulations, part V.

245 Regarding the legal status and implications of the precautionary principle, see P Birnie, A Boyle, and C Redgwell, *International Law and the Environment* (3rd edn, Oxford University Press 2009), 159–164.

the possible impact of the proposed exploration activities on the marine environment, as well as a description of a program for oceanographic and environmental baseline studies which would allow an assessment of the potential environmental impact of the proposed exploration activities once they have commenced.[246] Contractors are also required to monitor their environmental impacts during exploration and to take "necessary measures to prevent, reduce and control pollution and other hazards to the marine environment arising from its activities in the Area as far as reasonably possible, applying a precautionary approach and best environmental practices."[247] Such measures are vital given that there is still a relative lack of understanding about deep seabed ecosystems and how mining may affect them.[248]

To protect marine habitats, Greenpeace is calling for the implementation of a global network of marine reserves which would protect at least 40% of the world's oceans, particularly vulnerable areas such as seamounts and hydrothermal vents.[249] Similarly, the LTC recommended the establishment of nine areas of particular environmental interest in the Clarion-Clipperton Zone.[250]

These actions to protect the deep seabed environment are essential developments in the legal system related to the Area. They establish an environmental protection system in the Area to clarify the contractor's environmental obligations and empower the ISA to effectively respond to pollution emergencies while ensuring that the polluter bears the cost of remedial measures. However, given that scientists are only just beginning to appreciate the complexities of deep seabed ecosystems, it may be that the mandate of the ISA is already broader than it is commonly believed and is capable of playing a significant role in regulating this aspect of deep seabed activities in the future.[251] Then, whether the Authority has sufficient capacity to enforce these regulations and ensure that contractors comply with these regulations will be crucial.

---

246 ISA Exploration Regulations, regulation 20(1)(b).

247 Nodules Exploration Regulations, regulation 31(5); Sulphides Exploration Regulations,regulation 33(5); Crusts Exploration Regulations, regulation 33(5).

248 Biodiversity, Species Range and Gene Flow in the Abyssal Pacific Nodule Province: Predicting and Managing the Impacts of Deep Seabed Mining (ISBA/14/C/2, 14 February 2008).

249 Allsopp and others (n 5).

250 Environmental Management Plan for the Clarion-Clipperton Zone (ISBA/17/LTC/7, 13 July 2011).

251 T Scovazzi, 'Mining, Protection of the Environment, Scientific Research and Bioprospecting; Some considerations on the Role of the International Seabed Authority' (2004) 19 *The International Journal of Marine and Coastal Law* 383, 383.

### 3.3.3 Ongoing Drafting of Exploitation Regulations

It is now the transition period from the exploration stage to the exploitation stage. Six of those exploration contracts expired in 2016 and another in 2017. All those contractors applied for and were granted five-year extensions.[252] Moreover, they were "invited" to come into the exploitation stage afterward.[253] However, contractors are reluctant to participate in exploitation if the exploitation regulations are not in place, as it means they may face unknown risks, such as unpredictable obligations or investment losses.

Against this background, the Council, at its seventeenth session in 2011, requested the Secretariat to prepare a strategic work plan for the formulation of the regulations for mining of deep-sea minerals in the Area.[254] During its nineteenth session in 2013, the LTC began consideration of the issues relating to proposed regulations for exploitation of polymetallic nodules in the Area.[255] The ISA began the process of developing regulations for exploitation of mineral resources in the Area in 2014, and has been gradually making progress.[256] In February 2014, the ISA published the *Developing Financial Terms for*

252 Status of contracts for exploration and related matters (n 2), Annex I.

253 See eg Decision of the Council of the International Seabed Authority relating to an application by the China Ocean Mineral Resources Research and Development Association for extension of a contract for exploration for polymetallic nodules between the China Ocean Mineral Resources Research and Development Association and the Authority (ISBA/22/C/24, 18 July 2016).

254 Statement of the President of the Council of the International Seabed Authority on the work of the Council during the seventeenth session (ISBA/17/C/21, 21 July 2011).

255 Summary report of the Chair of the Legal and Technical Commission on the work of the Commission during the nineteenth session of the International Seabed Authority (ISBA/19/C/14, 9 July 2013).

256 The ongoing Exploitation Regulations may have different drafts in the meantime, which have an impact on specific sections of the book. This book includes relevant developments and is based on legal instruments as of August 2020. The following workshops directly related to the development of specific areas of the Exploitation Code were held: Workshop on Mineral Exploitation in the Area (Singapore 16–17 June 2015); Workshop on the Deep Seabed Mining Payment Regime Workshop (San Diego, 17–18 May 2016); Workshop on Environmental Assessment and Management for Exploitation of Minerals in the Area (Surfer's Paradise, 23–26 May 2016); Workshop on Enhancing Stakeholder Participation and Transparency in the ISA Process (Ocho Rios, Jamaica, 16 July 2016); Workshop Towards and ISA Environmental Management Strategy for the Area (20–24 March 2017, Berlin, Germany); Deep Seabed Mining – Payment Regime Workshop (PRW) #3 (Singapore 19–21 April 2017); Workshop on the Draft Regulations for the Exploitation of Mineral Resources in the Area: Policy, Legal and Institutional Considerations (London, 12–13 February 2018). The Secretariat has also issued the following Discussion Papers: Discussion Paper 1- Dispute Resolution Considerations Arising Under the Proposed New Exploitation Regulations (April 2016); Discussion Paper 2- Data and Information Management Considerations Arising Under the Proposed New

*Deep Sea Mining Exploitation*, a comparable study of mining industry fiscal regimes.[257] Later, in March, the ISA launched a Stakeholder Survey aimed at soliciting relevant information for the development of a regulatory framework for the exploitation of minerals in the Area from members of the Authority and current and future stakeholders.[258] The Stakeholder Survey was the first in a series of stakeholder engagements introduced by the ISA to begin the development of a regulatory framework. At the very beginning, the ISA chose to make the Exploitation Regulations by way of "building blocks", due to the complexity of exploitation legislation.[259] The blocks were designed in three parts. In addition to the *First Working Draft of the Regulations and Standard Contract Terms on Exploitation for Mineral Resources in the Area* launched by the ISA in February 2016,[260] two other sets of regulations, namely "Environmental Regulations" and "Seabed Mining Directorate Regulations" were published.[261] The "Environmental Regulations" came out in January 2017. The "Seabed Mining Directorate Regulations" were not published as expected.[262] Later on, instead of the "building blocks" approach, the ISA improved and integrated all the contents into one draft, called the *Draft Regulations on Exploitation of Mineral Resources in the Area,*[263] to "establish a more concise, consolidated,

Exploration Regulations (April 2016); Discussion Paper 3- Developing a Communications and Engagement Strategy for the International Seabed Authority to Ensure Active Stakeholder Participation in the Development of a Minerals Exploitation Code (April 2016); Discussion Paper 4- Enforcement and Liability Challenges for Environmental Regulation of Deep Seabed Mining (June 2016); Discussion Paper 5- The Implementation of the Precautionary Approach by the International Seabed Authority (March 2017). Concerning the contents of those documents, see <https://www.isa.org.jm/mining-code/discussion-papers> accessed 29 July 2020.

257 ISA, 'Making the Most of Deep Seabed Mineral Resources- Developing Financial Terms for Deep Sea Mining Exploitation' (2014) <https://www.isa.org.jm/files/documents/EN/Regs/FinTerms2014.pdf> accessed 29 December 2020.

258 Regarding details of Stakeholder Survey of 2014, see <https://www.isa.org.jm/survey/stakeholder-survey-march-2014> accessed 29 July 2020.

259 Aline Jaeckel, 'Current Legal Developments: International Seabed Authority' (2016) 31 *The International Journal of Marine and Coastal Law* 706, 707.

260 First Working Draft of the Regulations and Standard Contract Terms on Exploitation for Mineral Resources in the Area launched by the ISA (February 2016) <https://www.isa.org.jm/files/documents/EN/Regs/DraftExpl/Draft_ExplReg_SCT.pdf> accessed 29 July 2020.

261 ibid, paragraphs 9–11.

262 A Discussion Paper on the Development and Drafting of Regulations on Exploitation for Mineral Resources in the Area- Environmental Matters (January 2017).

263 Draft Regulations on Exploitation of Mineral Resources in the Area (ISBA/23/LTC/CRP.3*, 8 August 2017).

streamlined and structured framework for regulation of exploitation activities, whilst also avoiding duplication and inevitable inconsistencies and ambiguities arising from multiple regulatory instruments".[264] Subsequently, three updated versions of draft exploitation regulations were released.[265] The ISA Exploitation Regulations are being prepared and can be expected in the near future.

### 3.4 *The ISA*

It is impossible to introduce the Deep Seabed Mining Regime without mentioning the custodian of this regime, i.e. the ISA. It is no exaggeration to say that without the ISA, the entire international seabed system would not be operational.

The ISA, an intergovernmental organization with international legal personality,[266] was established on 16 November 1994, upon the entry into force of the LOSC. It is one of three new and autonomous international institutions established by the LOSC, headquartered in Kingston, Jamaica.[267] States Parties to the LOSC are, *ipso facto,* Members of the ISA,[268] yet it should be noted that states which are willing to become a Member of the ISA do not need to be a party to 1994 Implementing Agreement. As of 25 July 2017, there were 168 members[269] of the ISA; as of 27 July 2019, the ISA has 90 observers.[270]

---

264 Draft Regulations on Exploitation of Mineral Resources in the Area. Note by the Secretariat (ISBA/23/LTC/6, 5 July 2017), paragraph 4.

265 Draft Regulations on Exploitation of Mineral Resources in the Area (ISBA/24/LTC/WP.1, 30 April 2018); Draft Regulations on Exploitation of Mineral Resources in the Area (ISBA/24/LTC/WP.1/Rev.1, 9 July 2018); Draft Regulations on Exploitation of Mineral Resources in the Area (ISBA/25/C/WP.1, 25 March 2019).

266 LOSC, article 176.

267 The others being the International Tribunal for the Law of the Sea (ITLOS), and the Commission on the Limits of the Continental Shelf (CLCS). It is not part of the UN system, but in practice it is closely related to its origins and day-to-day operations.

268 LOSC, article 156(2).

269 Concerning the list of members, see <https://www.isa.org.jm/member-states> accessed 27 July 2020. Indeed, the ISA had a broader membership initially, as any state which had signed the 1994 Implementing Agreement or which had consented to its adoption in General Assembly were eligible for provisional membership of the ISA. 1994 Implementing Agreement, Annex, section 1, paragraph12. For example, the United States was initially one of provisional member of the ISA. However, all provisional membership expired on 16 November 1998. See James Harrison, *Making the Law of the Sea: A Study in the Development of International Law* (Cambridge University Press 2011), 117.

270 Observers incorporate states, intergovernmental, organizations, and NGO s. Concerning the list of the observers, see <https://www.isa.org.jm/observers> accessed 27 July 2020.

The ISA is mandated to organize and control activities in the Area, particularly with a view to administering the resources of the Area on behalf of mankind as a whole.[271] In other words, "the ISA acts as a trustee for administering a common good, which has been vested on mankind as a whole".[272] Furthermore, the ISA was considered as "the international organization which bears the main responsibility to realize a just and equitable economic order on the oceans and seas".[273] Therefore, as the "centralized organ"[274] of the Deep Seabed Mining Regime, the ISA's structure, powers, and functions as well as its decision-making process requires in-depth examination.

### 3.4.1 Powers and Functions of the ISA

The ISA is the core of the design of the Deep Seabed Mining Regime and also the institutional element of the common heritage of mankind.[275] The nature and powers of the ISA were one of the most controversial issues at UNCLOS III. Developing States took the view that the ISA should have far-reaching powers to regulate deep seabed mining activities, whereas the industrialized States perceived it as a more skeletal institution that works as a registry.[276] The fact is that the ISA functions as far more than a registry.

The powers and functions of the ISA are expressly conferred and delimited in the LOSC and the 1994 Implementing Agreement.[277] As already noted, the core function of the ISA is to organize and control activities in the Area, particularly with a view to administering the resources of the Area.[278] In this regard, the jurisdiction of the ISA is exclusive, which means no State or entities or natural and juridical persons can engage in activities in the Area without the

271 The LOSC, article 157; 1994 Implementing Agreement, Annex, section 1, paragraph1.

272 Oyarce (n 187) 318. On this particular matter see also Marie Bourrel, Torsten Thiele and Duncan Currie, 'The Common of Heritage of Mankind as a Means to Assess and Advance Equity in Deep Sea Mining' (2018) 95 *Marine Policy* 311.

273 Tullio Scovazzi, 'The Concept of Common Heritage of Mankind and the Genetic Resources of the Seabed beyond the Limits of National Jurisdiction' (2007) 14 *Agenda Internacional* 11, 16.

274 Tanaka, 'Obligations and Liability of Sponsoring States Concerning Activities in the Area' (n 187) 207.

275 Aline L Jaeckel, *The International Seabed Authority and the Precautionary Principle: Balancing Deep Seabed Mineral Mining and Marine Environmental Protection* (Brill Nijhoff 2017), 88.

276 AV Lowe, The International Seabed: A Legacy of Mistrust (1981) 5 *Marine Policy* 205, 205.

277 LOSC, article 157(2).

278 LOSC, article 157(1).

approval of the ISA.[279] The scope of this core function of the ISA can be summarized in three points.

First, spatial scope (*ratione loci*) of the core function of the ISA.[280] The ISA's mandate is spatially limited to the deep seabed outside areas of national jurisdiction which are referred to in the LOSC as the "Area". The "Area" is defined in the Convention as "the seabed and ocean floor and subsoil thereof, beyond the limits of national jurisdiction".[281] According to article 135 of the LOSC, the ISA's mandate shall not affect the legal status of the waters superjacent to the Area or that of the air space above those waters.

Second, is the material scope (*ratione materiae*) of the core function of the ISA.[282] It is necessary to clarify that the ISA does not govern everything in the Area, but only those activities concerning deep seabed minerals beyond national jurisdiction. The term 'activities in the Area' refers to all activities of exploration for, and exploitation of, the mineral resources of the Area.[283] Additionally, the ISA has "incidental powers"[284] as are implicit in and necessary to exercise its powers and functions with respect to activities in the Area by virtue of article 157(2). Nevertheless, these incidental powers are not unlimited. They are limited to mineral resources; the ISA can, for example, have no role in regulating genetic resources. Other uses of the Area, such as deep-sea fishing,[285] laying submarine pipelines and cable,[286] marine scientific research unconnected with the deep seabed mineral resources,[287] are beyond the mandate of the ISA.

Third, personal scope. Activities in the Area are to be carried out by the Enterprise, and in association with the Authority by States Parties, or state enterprises or natural or juridical persons, or any group of the foregoing.[288] Those applicants must undertake:[289]

---

279 FH Paolillo, 'Institutional Arrangements', in RJ Dupuy and D Vignes (eds), *A Handbook on the New Law of the Sea*, vol 1 (Martinus Nijhoff 1991), 706.

280 ibid, 720.

281 LOSC, article 1(1).

282 Paolillo (n 279) 718.

283 LOSC, article 1(1).

284 "Incidental powers" are those unwritten powers necessary for an international organization to effectively implement such powers and functions as are expressly conferred upon it. See Nandan, Lodge and Rosenne, *United Nations Convention on the Law of the Sea, 1982* (n 136), 360–361.

285 LOSC, articles 87(1); article 116.

286 LOSC, article 112.

287 LOSC, article 143(2); article 256.

288 LOSC, article 153(2).

289 LOSC, Annex III, article 4(6).

(a) to accept as enforceable and comply with the applicable obligations created by the provisions of Part XI, the rules, regulations, and procedures of the Authority, the decisions of the organs of the Authority and terms of his contracts with the Authority;
(b) to accept control by the Authority of activities in the Area, as authorized by this Convention;
(c) to provide the Authority with a written assurance that his obligations under the contract will be fulfilled in good faith; and
(d) to comply with the provisions on the transfer of technology set forth in article 5 of this Annex.[290]

It can be seen that anyone who is willing to apply for an exploration or exploitation contract must be subject to the ISA, including natural persons. Thus, this is an exception in international law, which is concerned mainly with regulating behavior by States and international organizations. At this point, it can be said that the ISA has a supranational jurisdiction.[291]

Apart from the aforementioned core function, the ISA has other related functions, such as, to promote and encourage the conduct of marine scientific research in the Area and to coordinate and disseminate the results of such research and to take the necessary measures for the protection of the flora and fauna of the marine environment from activities in the Area.[292] Other tasks of the ISA relate to: the distribution of certain revenues from the continental shelf beyond 200 miles from baselines;[293] providing assistance to developing countries which suffer serious adverse effects from activities in the Area; and the review of, and proposed amendments to, certain provisions in Part XI. Also, the ISA has specific functions in relation to "prospecting", as well as the distribution of benefits from activities in the Area.

In order to fulfill these functions, the LOSC conferred on the ISA two pivotal categories of mandates. The first was legislative power under article 17(1) of Annex III:

> The Authority shall adopt and uniformly apply rules, regulations, and procedures in accordance with article 160, paragraph 2(f)(ii), and article 162, paragraph 2(o)(ii), for the exercise of its functions as set forth

290 According to the 1994 Implementing Agreement, Annex, section 5, paragraph 2, "[t]he provisions [regarding "transfer of technology"] of Annex III, article 5, of the Convention shall not apply".

291 Tanaka, *The International Law of the Sea* (n 112) 184.

292 LOSC, articles 143 and 145.

293 LOSC, article 82(4).

> in Part XI on, *inter alia*, the following matters: (a) administrative procedures relating to prospecting, exploration, and exploitation in the Area; (b) operations; ... (c) financial matters; ... (d) implementation of decisions taken pursuant to article 151(10) and article164(2)(d).[294]

In addition, the ISA is also mandated to adopt appropriate rules concerning protection of the marine environment,[295] protection of human life,[296] installations used for carrying out activities in the Area,[297] the equitable financial and other economic benefits derived from activities in the Area, and the payments and contributions made pursuant to article 82,[298] especially those relating to prospecting, exploration, and exploitation in the Area.[299] As James Harrison points out:

> Part XI of LOSC was never intended to provide a comprehensive legal code including every aspect of the regulation of the Area. Rather, it was aimed to gradually develop Deep Seabed Regime with the expanding of knowledge, while the ISA is given legislative mandate to make rules and regulations to fill gaps in the framework left by the Law of the Sea Convention.[300]

The second one is the contract-related power, i.e. the mandate of granting a mining contract, monitoring, and enforceable power. The ISA manages and controls the operators by the contract. The following sections will specify how the ISA plays its role, by presenting the structure of the ISA, decision-making of the ISA, and enforcement by the ISA.

### 3.4.2 Structure of ISA

The principal organs of the ISA are the Assembly, the Council, and the Secretariat (headed by a Secretary-General). In addition, there is a Finance Committee (FC), elected by the Assembly, and a Legal and Technical Commission (LTC),

---

294 LOSC, Annex III, article 17(1). Yoshifumi Tanaka, 'Protection of Community Interests in International Law: The Case of the Law of the Sea' (2011) 15 *Max Planck Yearbook of United Nations Law Online* 329, 344.

295 LOSC, article 145.

296 LOSC, article 146.

297 LOSC, article 147(2)(a).

298 LOSC, article 160(2)(f)(i).

299 LOSC, article 160(2)(f)(ii) and162(2)(o)(ii).

300 Harrison (n 269) 116.

which is a subsidiary organ of the Council. The Convention also provides for an Economic Planning Commission with advisory functions concerning economic planning, the functions of which are to be performed by the LTC until the Council decides otherwise or until the approval of the first plan of work for exploitation.

In addition to the three principal organs, the ISA has its operational organ: the Enterprise,[301] which is to function independently and to conduct mining in joint ventures or even directly alongside other mining enterprises, if this is commercially sound.[302] The Enterprise conducts its initial operations through joint ventures.

#### 3.4.2.1 *The Assembly*

The Assembly is "considered to be the supreme organ of the Authority", to which the other principal organs are accountable as specifically provided for in the LOSC.[303] It meets in regular annual sessions[304] to execute the power to establish (in collaboration with the Council) "general policies" in conformity with the relevant provisions of the LOSC.[305] In addition, it has specific powers and functions laid down in article 160(2) of the LOSC.

There are relatively few meetings of the Assembly. In addition to elections for the Council, Finance Committee, and Secretary-General and the debate on the Secretary-General's annual report, meetings tend to be largely a formality to provide an occasion for general statements about the ISA's work.[306] Decisions on any matter for which the Council also has the competence or on any administrative, budgetary, or financial matter shall be based on the recommendations of the Council. If the Assembly does not accept the recommendations of the Council on any matter, it shall return the matter to the Council for further consideration.[307] Decisions of the Assembly (and the Council) having financial or budgetary implications shall be based on the recommendations of the FC.[308]

---

301 1994 Implementing Agreement, Annex, section 2(1).

302 1994 Implementing Agreement, Annex, section 2(2).

303 LOSC, article 160.

304 Otherwise, if decided by the Assembly, or convened by the Secretary-General at the request of the Council or of a majority of the members of the ISA, the Assembly shall meet in special sessions. See LOSC, article 159(2).

305 LOSC, article 160(1); 1994 Implementing Agreement, Annex, section 3(1).

306 Michael C Wood, 'The International Seabed Authority: Fifth to Twelfth Sessions (1999–2006)' (2007) 11 *Max Planck Yearbook of United Nations Law* 47, 62.

307 1994 Implementing Agreement, Annex, section 3(4).

308 ibid.

#### 3.4.2.2 *The Council*

The Council is the "executive organ" of the ISA. The Council is the most important organ which, as a decision-making body of the ISA, has the power to establish "specific policies" in conformity with the LOSC and the "general policies" established by the Assembly.[309] In addition, it has the specific powers and functions set out in article 162(2) of the LOSC.

Due to its importance, the composition of the membership is very delicate: the 36 members of the Council are to be elected by the Assembly from five interested groups:

(a) Four members from among those States Parties which, during the last five years for which statistics are available, have either consumed more than 2 per cent in value terms of total world consumption or have had net imports of more than 2 per cent in value terms of total world imports of the commodities produced from the categories of minerals to be derived from the Area, provided that the four members shall include one State from the Eastern European region having the largest economy in that region in terms of gross domestic product and the State, on the date of entry into force of the Convention, having the largest economy in terms of gross domestic product, if such States wish to be represented in this group;

(b) Four members from among the eight States Parties which have the largest investments in preparation for and the conduct of activities in the Area, either directly or through their nationals;

(c) Four members from among States Parties, which on the basis of production in areas under their jurisdiction, are major net exporters of the categories of minerals to be derived from the Area, including at least two developing States whose exports of such minerals have a substantial bearing upon their economies;

(d) Six members from among developing States Parties, representing special interests. The special interests to be represented shall include those of States with large populations, States which are land-locked or geographically disadvantaged, island States, States which are major importers of the categories of minerals to be derived from the Area, States which are potential producers for such minerals, and least developed States;

(e) Eighteen members elected according to the principle of ensuring an equitable geographical distribution of seats in the Council as a whole,

309 LOSC, article 162(1).

provided that each geographical region shall have at least one member elected under this subparagraph. For this purpose, the geographical regions should be Africa, Asia, Eastern European, Latin America, and the Caribbean and Western Europe and Others.[310]

Decision-making in the Council is intended to ensure the protection of the special interests, especially those represented by Groups A, B, and C. As a general rule decision-making should be by consensus.[311] If all efforts to reach a consensus are exhausted, decisions on questions of procedure shall be taken by a majority of the members present and voting. In practice, the Council has always acted by consensus.

#### 3.4.2.2.1 The Economic Planning Commission

The Economic Planning Commission was envisaged under article 163 as a subsidiary organ to the Council, responsible for: 1) proposing measures to implement decisions relating to activities in the Area; 2) reviewing trends of and factors affecting supply, demand, and prices of materials which may be derived from the Area; 3) examining any situation arising from exploitation of resources in the Area likely to lead to adverse effects on developing countries' economies; and 4) proposing the establishment of an economic assistance fund designed to finance assistance to developing land-based producer States affected by deep seabed mining.[312]

The Economic Planning Commission is not currently operational as a result of the 1994 Implementing Agreement, since it provides that "[t]he functions

310 The composition of the Council was originally provided in article 161(1) of the LOSC which has been replaced by a revised provision in paragraph 15, section 3 of the Annex to the 1994 Implementing Agreement. Regarding the composition of the Council of the International Seabed Authority (1996–2000), see <https://www.isa.org.jm/authority/council/members> accessed 12 August 2020.

311 1994 Implementing Agreement, Annex, section 3(2).

312 LOSC, article 164(2). The fourth function of the Economic Planning Commission stipulated by article 164(2)(d) is affected by the 1994 Implementing Agreement, which substantially modified article 151. The wording of article 164(2)(d) is "propose to the Council for submission to the Assembly, as provided in article 151, paragraph 10, a system of compensation or other measures of economic adjustment assistance for developing States which suffer adverse effects caused by activities in the Area. The Commission shall make the recommendations to the Council that are necessary for the application of the system or other measures adopted by the Assembly in specific cases." However, the 1994 Implementing Agreement, Annex, section 7, no longer foresees the establishment of "a system of compensation" but rather the establishment of "an economic assistance fund". See Nandan, Lodge and Rosenne, *United Nations Convention on the Law of the Sea, 1982* (n 136), 468.

of the Economic Planning Commission shall be performed by the Legal and Technical Commission until such time as the Council decides otherwise or until the approval of the first plan of work for exploitation".[313]

#### 3.4.2.2.2 The Legal and Technical Commission

The Legal and Technical Commission (LTC) which is one of two sub-ordinary organs of the Council, was initially composed of 15 persons elected by the Council from among candidates nominated by States.[314] The members are to have appropriate technical or legal qualifications.[315] Due to increasing interest in deep seabed mining, although controversial, the LTC is continuously expanding, taking advantage of the flexibility allowed by the LOSC.[316] Since 2016, the LTC has had a membership of 30. After intense discussions and careful study, the Council decided to manage the membership of the LTC based on the nominations in the year before the election. That is also a general practice in most of the independent expert bodies elected by the States Members of the United Nations.[317] Admittedly, with the worldwide increasing interest in deep seabed mining, the workload of the LTC has mushroomed in recent years.[318] However, there is no evidence that enlarging the scale of the LTC will result in increased efficiency.[319] On the contrary, given that the LTC makes decision principally by consensus, it is becoming more or more difficult to reach an agreement because of the large membership. Hence, the LTC should focus on the equitable geographical representation and balance of expertise.[320] Alternatively, the Review Committee, which is established based on article 154 of the LOSC recommends that the LTC, "should be encouraged to continue its practice of setting up working groups dealing with particular areas of expertise. In this context, the establishment of a working group dealing with environmental issues should be considered".[321]

313 1994 Implementing Agreement, Annex, section 1(4).

314 LOSC, article 163(2).

315 Members of the Legal and Technical Commission shall have appropriate qualifications such as those relevant to exploration for and exploitation and processing of mineral resources, oceanology, protection of the marine environment, or economic or legal matters relating to ocean mining and related fields of expertise.

316 LOSC, article 163(2).

317 Election of members of the Legal and Technical Commission, Report of the Secretary-General (ISBA/23/C/2, 11 November 2016), paragraph 25.

318 ibid, paragraph 4.

319 ibid, paragraph 23.

320 ibid, paragraph 24.

321 Letter dated 3 February 2017 from the Chair of the Committee established by the Assembly to carry out a periodic review of the international regime of the Area pursuant to article

The reason why the LTC has attracted so much attention is that the LTC's role in Deep Seabed Mining Regime is of vital importance. The LTC's main tasks have been to prepare draft mining regulations for adoption by the Council and the Assembly, as well as guidelines; to consider draft plans of work (contracts) with mining contractors; and to consider annual reports from the contractors. Due to the "closed door" nature of the LTC – only LTC members can participate in meetings and Secretariat staff can observe –, the decision-making process is under challenge. The lack of transparency and public participation has been a bone of contention.

#### 3.4.2.3 *The Finance Committee*

The FC is composed of 15 persons elected by the Assembly.[322] The members of the FC are elected based on the need for equitable geographical distribution and the representation of special interests. The special interests are: i) Group A, B, C and D of the Council shall each have at least one member; and ii) until the ISA becomes self-financing, the five largest financial contributors to the administrative budget are entitled to be represented on the FC.[323] But no two members of the FC shall be nationals of the same State Party.[324] The members of the Committee serve in their individual capacity, for a five-year term. They are eligible for re-election "for a further term".[325] Decisions of the FC on questions of procedure are taken by a majority of members present and voting, and decisions on questions of substance must be taken by consensus.[326] The FC, which meets for between two and four days each session, depending on the amount of work to be done, has in practice taken all decisions by consensus (as it is legally required to do for questions of substance).

The primary functions of the FC are to recommend to the Council and the Assembly the budget and the scale of assessment, as well as to make recommendations on all other financial matters. Annex section 9(7) of the 1994 Implementing Agreement lists those matters on which decisions of the Council and the Assembly must take into account or be based upon the recommendations of the Committee.

---

154 of the United Nations Convention on the Law of the Sea to the Secretary-General of the International Seabed Authority (ISBA/23/A/3, 8 February 2017), recommendation 14.

322 1994 Implementing Agreement, Annex, section 9(1).

323 1994 Implementing Agreement, Annex, section 9(3).

324 1994 Implementing Agreement, Annex, section 9(2).

325 1994 Implementing Agreement, Annex, section 9(4).

326 1994 Implementing Agreement, Annex, section 9(8).

#### 3.4.2.4 *The Secretariat and Secretary-General*

The Secretariat has the responsibility for the administration of the ISA and for maintaining contacts with other international and non-governmental organizations. Its main functions include:

- Providing support to the Secretary-General in fulfilling the functions entrusted to him or her under UNCLOS and the 1994 Agreement and in implementing the mandates provided by member States;
- Producing reports and other documents containing information, analyses, historical background, research findings, policy suggestions, etc., that facilitate the deliberations and decision-making by the other principal organs and their subsidiary bodies;
- Providing secretariat services to the other principal organs and their subsidiary bodies and providing meeting services (translation, interpretation, and reporting services) to the other principal organs, in accordance with the policies adopted by the Assembly;
- Producing publications, information bulletins and analytical studies and disseminating information on the activities and decisions of ISA;
- Organizing and servicing expert group meetings, seminars and workshops;
- Implementing the work programmes and policies laid down by the other principal organs and their subsidiary bodies;
- Ensuring compliance with plans of work for exploration and exploitation approved in the form of contracts;
- Performing the functions of the Enterprise as specified in Section 2 of the Annex to the 1994 Agreement until such time as the Enterprise begins to operate independently.[327]

In accordance with the LOSC, "the Secretariat of the Authority shall comprise a Secretary-General and such staff as the Authority may require." The Secretary-General is the chief administrative officer of the ISA. He or she is elected for four years by the Assembly from among candidates proposed by the Council. Satya N. Nandan (Fiji) was elected the first Secretary-General in 1996. His successor, Nii Allotey Odunton (Ghana) took over on 1 January 2009 and served two consecutive terms.[328] Mr. Michael W. Lodge of the United Kingdom was elected as Secretary-General on 21 July 2016 at the Authority's 22nd Session at its headquarters in Kingston for a 4-year term beginning as of 1 January 2017.[329]

---

327 ISA, 'the Secretariat' <https://www.isa.org.jm/secretariat> accessed 29 July 2020.

328 Jaeckel, 'Current Legal Developments: International Seabed Authority' (n 259) 712.

329 Decision of the Assembly of the International Seabed Authority concerning the appointment of the Secretary-General of the International Seabed Authority (ISBA/22/A/10, 21 July 2016).

The Secretariat is organized on a cost-effective basis. It has 38 staff members (the number changes due to personnel changes) consisting of experts (appropriately qualified scientists), and legal, administrative, and support staff. The Secretariat is currently organized into four functional units, i.e. Executive Office of the Secretary-General; Office of Environmental Management and Mineral Resources; Office of Legal Affairs, and Office of Administration and Management.

The Executive Office of the Secretary-General (EOSG) supervises and coordinates the work of the Secretariat in the implementation of policies, external relations, protocol matters, liaison, and representation of the Authority. The EOSG also supervises the work of the Contract Management Unit which was created to better serve the contractors by promoting better communication between relevant work units in the Secretariat and maintaining a list of Permanent Representatives and persons accredited to the Authority.

The Office of Environmental Management and Mineral Resources was established to provide scientific and technical input for the development of rules, regulations, and procedures for activities within the Area. The office is also responsible for the development and maintenance of information technology facilities to support the needs of the Authority and the central data repository resources of the international seabed area and endeavours to promote and encourage the conduct of marine scientific research in the Area, producing and distributing publications on the work of the Authority and monitoring trends and developments of deep seabed mining activities relating to the prospecting and exploration of the Area including areas reserved for the Authority.[330]

The Office of Legal Affairs is the central legal service of the Secretariat and provides legal advice to the Secretary-General, the Secretariat, and the other principal organs of the Authority and their subsidiary bodies. It represents the Secretary-General in legal conferences and judicial proceedings. The Office of Legal Affairs is also responsible for the Satya N. Nandan Library, the official documentation of the Authority and for managing the provision of conference services for sessions of the Authority.

The Office for Administrative Services provides general administrative and management support to the Secretariat. Its functions include financial management and control, preparation of proposed budgets, assessment of

330 ISA, 'Office of Environmental Management and Mineral Resources', <https://www.isa.org.jm/secretariat> accessed 29 July 2020.

contributions of member States, recruitment of staff and contractors, procurement of goods and services, personnel management, and security.[331]

The work of the Secretariat is essential because it is the foundation of the other organs' work. The efficiency and effective coordination of the Secretariat will determine whether the next job can proceed smoothly. Therefore, it is not difficult to imagine that for such a small international organization of around 40 staff, it is extremely challenging to carry out the excessive workload, such as preparing materials for various departments, holding seminars, and coordinating the management of contractors. Also, the expertise of the staff is one of the elements determining the quality of work. As the Review Committee recommends, "[t]he Secretary-General should be requested to keep under review the required skills and available expertise within the secretariat and to make adjustments when necessary."[332]

#### 3.4.2.5 *The Enterprise*

Article 170(1) of the LOSC envisaged the establishment of the "Enterprise", which would be 'the organ of the Authority which shall carry out activities in the Area directly', under the so-called 'parallel system', under which mining was to be carried out by States and companies on the one hand, and by the Enterprise on the other. However, under the 1994 Implementing Agreement the Secretariat is to perform the functions of the Enterprise until the Enterprise begins to operate independently of the Secretariat.[333] The 1994 Implementing Agreement further provides that the Enterprise shall conduct its initial deep seabed mining operations through joint ventures and that upon certain eventualities, "the Council shall take up the issue of the functioning of the Enterprise independently of the Secretariat of the Authority. If joint-venture operations with the Enterprise accord with sound commercial principles, the Council shall issue a directive … providing for such independent functioning".[334] The Enterprise was designed to be the Authority's mining arm, but as a result of the 1994 Implementing Agreement it was not established as an independent entity. Surprisingly, in October 2012, the ISA received a proposal to develop a

331 ISA, 'Office for Administrative Service', <https://www.isa.org.jm/secretariat> accessed 29 July 2020.

332 Letter dated 3 February 2017 from the Chair of the Committee established by the Assembly to carry out a periodic review of the international regime of the Area pursuant to article 154 of the United Nations Convention on the Law of the Sea to the Secretary-General of the International Seabed Authority (ISBA/23/A/3, 8 February 2017), recommendation 11.

333 1994 Implementing Agreement, Annex, section 2(1) (a)-(h).

334 1994 Implementing Agreement, Annex, section 2(2).

joint venture with the Enterprise, submitted by Nautilus Minerals Inc. (a private company incorporated in Canada).[335] But the Council concluded that it was premature for the Enterprise to function independently.[336] It requested a further study of the legal, technical, and financial implications for the operation of the Enterprise.[337]

### 3.4.3 The Decision-making of the ISA

The decision-making regime is stipulated in the Annex, section 3 of the 1994 Implementing Agreement. To safeguard the interests of all states, the decision-making procedure of the ISA is complicated and relates to the three principal organs of the ISA. Generally, "decision-making in the organs of the Authority should be by consensus".[338] If a consensus cannot be achieved, the organ may have to fall back on a majority vote.[339] Among the organs of the ISA, the Council and the LTC play the most important roles in decision-making.

#### 3.4.3.1 *An Overriding Principle: Consensus*

In practice, three kinds of decisions are predominantly applied by an international organization: consensus, majority voting, and weighted voting. Moreover, decision-making in some international organizations is subject to special arrangements, such as multiple-veto systems and fast-track procedures.[340] Majority voting is the most common decision-making rule among

---

335 Proposal for a Joint Venture Operation with the Enterprise. Report by the Interim Director-General of the Enterprise (ISBA/19/C/4, 20 March 2013).

336 Statement of the President of the Council of the International Seabed Authority on the work of the Council during the nineteenth session (ISBA/19/C/18, 24 July 2013), paragraph 16(a).

337 Regarding the legal, technical, and financial implications for the operation of the Enterprise, see Considerations relating to a proposal by Nautilus Minerals Inc. for a Joint Venture Operation with the Enterprise (ISBA/19/C/6, 4 April 2013); see also ISA, 'A Study Related to Issues on the Operationalization of the Enterprise-Legal, Technical and Financial Implications for the International Seabed Authority and for States Parties to the United Nations Convention on the Law of the Sea' (Technical Report 1/2019, 13 June 2019), Prepared By Edwin Egede, Mati Pal and Eden Charles, <https://isa.org.jm/files/files/documents/enterprise_study.pdf> accessed 29 December 2020.

338 1994 Implementing Agreement, Annex, section 3(2).

339 1994 Implementing Agreement, Annex, section 3(3) and (5).

340 Thomas Sommerer and Jonas Tallberg, *Decision-Making in International Organizations: Actors, Preferences, and Institutions*, Annual Convention of the International Studies Association, Atlanta, March, 16–19 2016, <https://papers.ssrn.com/abstract=3059444> accessed 18 May 2020.

international organizations, while consensus and weighted voting take the second and third places, respectively.[341]

The organs of the ISA adopt *consensus* as the general rule of the decision-making, since the provisions of the LOSC "go some way towards safeguarding the interests of the various constituencies concerned with sea-bed mining."[342] As Robin R. Churchill notes, "broadly speaking, the more important a decision is for sea-bed mining interests, the more it is insulated from simple majority decision-making within the Authority."[343]

Consensus does not mean every member has to agree with the specific proposal to reach a decision but implies the absence of formal objection.[344] To facilitate the achievement of consensus, the LOSC designed some procedural devices to defer a vote,[345] providing a "cooling off" period, during which a compromise may be sought on divisive issues.[346]

As a general rule, decision-making in all organs of the ISA should be by consensus, except for the election of the Secretary-General and (on one occasion, in 1998) the adoption of the scale of assessment for contributions to the budget.

#### 3.4.3.2 *A Supplementary Approach: Voting*

The LOSC also takes into consideration the eventuality that no consensus might be reached. A majority of the members of the ISA constitutes a quorum.[347] If all efforts to reach consensus have been exhausted, decisions on questions of procedure shall be taken by a majority of the members present and voting, and decisions on questions of substance by a 2/3 majority,[348] provided that such decisions are not opposed by a majority in any one of the four 'Chambers' in the Council (each group of States elected under Groups A, B, C, is treated as a chamber and the developing States elected to Groups D and E are treated as a single chamber) .[349] That design of Coucil chambers is to prevent "simple majorities in the Authority from overriding the interests of

341 Daniel J Blake and Autumn Lockwood Payton, 'Balancing Design Objectives: Analyzing New Data on Voting Rules in Intergovernmental Organizations' (2015) 10 *The Review of International Organizations* 377, 395.

342 Churchill and Lowe (n 110) 245.

343 ibid.

344 ibid.

345 LOSC, article 159(9) and (10).

346 Churchill and Lowe (n 110) 245.

347 LOSC, article 159(5).

348 1994 Implementing Agreement, Annex, section 3(3).

349 1994 Implementing Agreement, Annex, section 3(5) and (9).

the special groups."[350] However, poor attendance at the Assembly is a recurring problem. The absence of a quorum may hamper decision-making by the Assembly and Council if any delegation raises the matter, as happened at the time of the adoption of the scale of assessments in 1998.

#### 3.4.3.3 *Two Powerful Organs: The Council and the LTC*

In fact, almost all critical decisions of the ISA are made by the Council and the LTC. After the fundamental change in wording by the 1994 Implementing Agreement that "the general policies of the Authority shall be established by the Assembly in collaboration with the Council",[351] and "if the Assembly does not accept the recommendation of the Council on any matter, it shall return the matter to the Council for further consideration".[352] Furthermore, the decision concerning any rules, regulations, or procedures relating to prospecting, exploration, and exploitation in the Area and the financial management and internal administration of the Authority which have been adopted by the Council is provisionally valid, pending the approval of the Assembly and resubmission to the Council for further consideration under the situation of the Assembly rejecting the recommendations of the Council.[353] Those provisions give the Council a pivotal role in the formation and implementation of ISA policy. The Assembly can do no more than refuse to confirm decisions on these matters taken by other organs.[354] Likewise, the LTC works as the Council's "brain". The Council makes decisions based on the LTC's recommendations. In practice, the LTC's recommendations are rarely denied by the Council. With an "overwhelming workload and inadequate time",[355] the LTC has been holding two meetings annually since 2013.[356]

### 3.4.4 Oversight and Enforceable Power of the ISA

Article 153(3) explicitly stipulates that "activities in the Area shall be carried out in accordance with a formal written plan of work drawn up in accordance

---

350 Churchill and Lowe (n 110) 245.

351 1994 Implementing Agreement, Annex, section 3(1).

352 1994 Implementing Agreement, Annex, section 3(4).

353 LOSC, article 162(2)(o)(ii).

354 Churchill and Lowe (n 110) 245.

355 Statement of the President of the Council of the International Seabed Authority on the work of the Council during the nineteenth session (ISBA/19/C/18, 24 July 2013), paragraph 9.

356 Summary report of the Chair of the Legal and Technical Commission on the work of the Commission during the eighteenth session of the International Seabed Authority (ISBA/18/C/20, 20 July 2012), paragraph 27.

with Annex III and approved by the Council after review by the Legal and Technical Commission." Article 153(4) further provides that the ISA "shall exercise such control over activities in the Area" and secures compliance with the relevant part of the LOSC, the rules, regulations, and procedures of the ISA and the approved plan of work. In order to reach such control and security of compliance, the ISA "shall have the right to take at any time any measures provided for under this Part"[357] and specifically "have the right to inspect all installations in the Area used in connection with activities in the Area".[358] With regard to "any measures" the ISA shall take, the ISA only requests the contractors to submit an annual report and modify the plan of work every five years.[359] Regarding the inspections, the organs of the ISA have discrete responsibilities, i.e. the Council shall "establish appropriate mechanisms for directing and supervising a staff of inspectors";[360] the LTC is responsible for making such recommendations.[361] It is noteworthy that the ISA, as of now, has not carried out any inspection activities.

The enforceable power of the ISA is related to its oversight mandate. Annex III, article 18 describes the enforcement jurisdiction of the ISA, which includes three categories of penalties (warning, monetary penalty, suspend or terminate a contract). The LOSC strictly stipulates two circumstances under which the ISA has competence to suspend or terminate a contract: (a) the contractor's operations result in serious, persistent, and willful violations of the fundamental terms of the contract, Part XI and the rules, regulations, and procedures of the ISA; and (b) the contractor has failed to comply with a final binding decision of the dispute settlement body on it.[362] The ISA Exploration Regulations further develop this article by specifying the competent organ for imposing penalties (Council) and by adding a third circumstance in which a contract may be suspended or terminated.[363] The third circumstance refers to the contractor's bad financial situation, i.e. it

> becomes insolvent or commits an act of bankruptcy or enters into any agreement for composition with its creditors or goes into liquidation or receivership, whether compulsory or voluntary, or petitions or applies to

357 LOSC, article 153(5).
358 ibid.
359 Sulphides Exploration Regulations, regulation 30.
360 LOSC, article 162(2)(z).
361 LOSC, articles 165(2)(m).
362 LOSC, Annex III, article 18(1).
363 ISA Exploration Regulations, Annex IV, section 21.1.

> any tribunal for the appointment of a receiver or a trustee or receiver for itself or commences any proceedings relating to itself under any bankruptcy, insolvency or readjustment of debt law, whether now or hereafter in effect, other than for the purpose of reconstruction.[364]

Not all cases of non-compliance, but only violation of "fundamental terms", can result in the suspension or termination of a contract. In case of other violations, the ISA may impose monetary penalties in proportion to the seriousness of non-compliance.[365] As Gwénäelle Le Gurun said, "grave penalties such as suspension and even more termination of a contract will be imposed as a last resort, as the ultimate point of an escalation process, in case of very grave and repeated violations by a contractor of its essential contractual undertakings."[366] Also, even if one of these three circumstances does occur, the Council "may", but not "shall", suspend or terminate this contract.[367] Suspension or termination may be substituted by monetary penalties under the discretion of the ISA.[368] In any case, no penalty may be executed until the contractor has had the possibility to exhaust the judicial remedies available under Part XI, section 5, of the LOSC.[369] The ISA's enforceable competence is highly restricted by those provisions.

### 3.5 *Observations on the Current Deep Seabed Mining Regime*

It is vital to note that contractors are first in line in influencing the marine environment. They are the direct operators of deep seabed mining. However, in traditional international law, States and international organizations are the subjects of international law, whereas contractors, as individuals, are not and thus not subject to the LOSC.[370] Notwithstanding, this situation has changed considerably in the last several decades and the individual today is qualified

364 ISA Exploration Regulations, Annex IV, section 21.1(c).
365 LOSC, Annex III, article 18(2).
366 Proelss and others (n 22), 2253.
367 LOSC, Annex III, article 18(1); ISA Exploration Regulations, Annex IV, section 21.1.
368 LOSC, Annex III, article 18(2).
369 LOSC, Annex III, article 18(3).
370 This opinion is explicitly express in ITLOS SDC Advisory Opinion, paragraph 75. It provides: "The purpose of requiring the sponsorship of applicants for contracts for the exploration and exploitation of the resources of the Area is to achieve the result that the obligations set out in the Convention, a treaty under international law which binds only States Parties thereto, are complied with only entities that are subjects of domestic legal systems."

as a "partial" subject of international law.[371] While the LOSC is enshrined as the "Constitution for the Oceans"[372] with the Part XI being an "exceptionally precise, detailed instrument closer in appearance to a commercial contract or concession than to an international treaty"[373] in setting out the Deep Seabed Mining Regime and protecting the marine environment, a substantial gap remains. The LOSC and 1994 Implementing Agreement, as treaties under international law, just like the Seabed Disputes Chamber mentioned, are merely binding upon States Parties, rather than upon contractors who are entities or individuals.[374] Therefore, the environmental protection regime faces the tough task of implementing existing environmental obligations.

To solve those problems, the LOSC established the notion of "sponsorship", which means natural or juridical persons intending to carry out mining activities in the Area must be either nationals of a State Party or effectively controlled by it or its nationals and in the meanwhile sponsored by such States. It is a key and fundamental tool to ensure the contractors' compliance with the environmental obligations set out in the Convention. The SDC Advisory Opinion outlines specific approaches to ensure the contractors' compliance:

> This result is obtained through the provisions of the Authority's Regulations that apply to such entities and through the implementation by the sponsoring States of their obligations under the Convention and related instruments.[375]

Two approaches are outlined for regulating contractors' behavior: one is the Authority's Regulations which apply to contractors; the other is the function of sponsoring States' national legislation, specifically, sponsoring States' domestic laws, regulations, and administrative measures in relation to deep seabed mining activities. As to the former approach, obvious imperfections exist. As is known, the international organization has limited mechanisms to enforce compliance, such as persuasion, incentives, disincentives, force, and legally

---

371 Christian Walter, 'Subjects of International Law' in *Max Plank Encyclopedia of Public International Law* (2007).

372 T B Koh, 'A Constitution for the Oceans', in United Nations, *The Law of the Sea: United Nations Convention on the Law of the Sea with Index and Final Act of the Third United Nations Conference on the Law of the Sea* (United Nations 1983), xxxiii-xxxvii; see also Nico Schrijver, *Development without Destruction: The UN and Global Resource Management* (Indiana University Press 2010), 218.

373 Churchill and Lowe (n 110) 18.

374 SDC Advisory Opinion, paragraph 75.

375 SDC Advisory Opinion, paragraph 75.

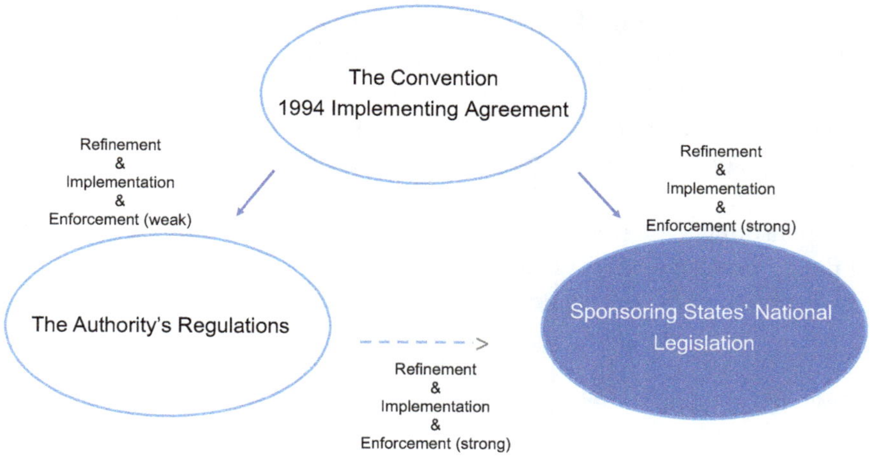


FIGURE 2 Implementation of contractors' environmental obligations in the deep seabed mining regime

binding sanctions.[376] Consequently, the Authority does have limited means of applying sanctions in the face of violations of their obligations by contractors. These include written warnings, monetary penalties, suspension, or termination of contracts. However, it should be noted that suspension and termination of contracts are very serious penalties that are only appropriate in the event of a serious violation of the fundamental terms of the contract, Part XI of the Convention, the 1994 Implementing Agreement and the rules, regulations, and procedures of the Authority. The Authority may be silent on minor violations or other non-compliance on the part of the contractors. If after letters of warning the contractors do not cease their violations of obligations or their non-compliant activities, the Authority has limited means of enforcing compliance. This issue is addressed by article 153(4), of the Convention which stipulates that the States Parties shall assist the Authority to ensure contractors' compliance because States Parties or sponsoring States have the power of enforcement within their domestic legal systems. In this regard, both the former and the latter approaches for regulating contractors eventually refer to States Parties or sponsoring States (see Figure 2).

Indeed, the major problem of the current Deep Seabed Mining Regime is not the lack of a legal framework at the international level but the incomplete

376 Volker Röben, 'The Enforcement Authority of International Institutions' in Armin von Bogdandy and others (eds), *The Exercise of Public Authority by International Institutions*, vol 210 (Springer 2010), 837.

implementation and weak enforcement of relevant instruments among contractors. The relevant national legislation of sponsoring States could contribute to better implementation of international environmental obligations and stronger supervision and more rigorous penalties for contractors in cases of non-compliance. The legislation of the sponsoring State is an essential and necessary part of the entire Deep Seabed Mining Regime. The legislation of the sponsoring State is advantageous for the validation and implementation of the international system at the domestic level and can even make up for the shortcomings of the international system in managing contractors.

## 4 Conclusion

Deep seabed mining activities in the Area will inevitably cause some environmental consequence and even damage. Thus, avoiding and mitigating adverse impacts on the marine environment should always be a priority among mining-related issues. Among actors participating in mining activities, the contractor, as the operator of deep seabed mining activities, is usually in the first position to exercise control over the source of potential damage and, consequently, may most effectively prevent damage. However, under current Deep Seabed Mining Regime, which is constructed by the LOSC, 1994 Implementing Agreement and Mining Code, a noticeable imperfection is that the contractor, as an individual, is not subject to international law and thus not subject to the LOSC. Furthermore, the ISA, which is mandated to organize and control activities in the Area on behalf of mankind as a whole, particularly in relation to administering the resources of the Area, has limited monitoring capacity when the contractors conduct mining activities in the Area as well as limited enforceable power if the contractors fail to comply with provisions of the Deep Seabed Mining Regime.

To solve those problems, the LOSC established the notion of "sponsorship", which means natural or juridical persons tending to carry on mining activities in the Area must be either nationals of a State Party or effectively controlled by it or its nationals and in the meanwhile sponsored by such States. Derived from this notion, as the Seabed Disputes Chamber of ITLOS indicated, the State has the primary obligation, i.e. responsibility to ensure the compliance of its sponsored contractor with its obligations in the LOSC, and one of those direct obligations is to assist the ISA in realizing effective control and management of contractors. Through this design, the sponsoring State serves as a bridge between the Deep Seabed Mining Regime and contractors. As a sovereign State, a sponsoring State has a variety of ways to monitor its sponsored contractor and enforce compliance. This design seems to solve problems in theory; however, there are still several problems in practice. For instance, the LOSC does not provide any standards or parameters to guide sponsoring States on how to fulfil the primary obligation and direct obligation. Moreover, as far as a sponsoring State is concerned, the sponsored contractors are either state-owned entities or significant investors of the State, so the sponsoring State might be reluctant to rigorously regulate the sponsored contractors as the country may risk suffering economic losses if it does so.

In this context, this chapter concludes that a sponsoring State must play an important role in assisting the ISA to realize effective control and management of contractors, *inter alia*, in monitoring and enforcement. However, the challenge is to find out why a sponsoring State carries certain obligations and what is involved. To this end, the objectives of the next chapter will be to outline the legal basis and reasons of the obligations of the sponsoring State, followed by the exploration of the substantial question, i.e. what must the sponsoring States do to assist the ISA, that is, what are the standards of "responsibility to ensure"? Finally, what consequences the sponsoring States will face, i.e. liability issues, if they fail to carry out their primary and direct obligations will be examined as well.

CHAPTER 2

# Responsibility to Ensure

***Primary Obligation of a Sponsoring State***

## 1 Introduction

As presented in chapter 1, deep seabed mining is characterized by potential commercial benefits as well as environmental risks and uncertainties. These require a sound and well-established Deep Seabed Mining Regime to regulate the behavior of each actor, especially the contractor, with the aim of mitigating anthropogenic impacts on the marine environment when he conducts mining activities in the Area. It is recognized that, under the ISA-centralized Deep Seabed Mining Regime, the ISA is a weak custodian in its management of contractor incompliance with its environmental obligations as the ISA has limited monitoring and enforcement powers. The assistance of sponsoring States is invaluable in this situation as a sovereign State has a variety of means by which to enforce the compliance of its sponsored contractor, which is either a national or is controlled by nationals. Thus, the sponsoring State has a role in environmental protection. The LOSC also explicitly indicates that States Parties have the responsibility to ensure that their sponsored contractors' activities in the Area conform to Part XI of the LOSC.[1] The LOSC also indicates that States Parties shall assist the ISA in ensuring such compliance.[2] However, the position of the sponsoring State is complex as the sponsored contractors are either state-owned entities or important investors in the State, so it could be difficult for the sponsoring State to rigorously regulate the sponsored contractors as the loss of investments might result in analogical economic losses. In this context, it is necessary to determine the legal basis and conditions under which the sponsoring State could regulate sponsored contractors. Theoretically, "assisting the ISA" is an obligation of member States, and thus a sponsoring State shall do it based on the *Pacta Sunt Servanda* Principle[3] which is inherent in

1 LOSC, article 139(1).

2 LOSC, article 153(4).

3 Vienna Convention on the Law of Treaties (Vienna, 23 May 1969, in force 27 January 1980) 1155 UNTS 331, article 26. *Pacta Sunt Servanda* is the fundamental principle of treaty law, which means treaties are binding upon the parties to them and must be performed in good faith, stated by article 26 of the Vienna Convention on the Law of Treaties. For the discussion regarding the principle of *Pacta Sunt Servanda*, see H Wehberg, 'Pacta Sunt Servanda'

 | DOI:10.1163/9789004472341_004

the concept of the common heritage of mankind and sponsorship. This will be further discussed in section 3 of this chapter. Moreover, a sponsoring State will entail liability if it is in breach of its obligation.

The substantial question is: What can the sponsoring States do to fulfill their obligations and assist the ISA? In other words, what are the specific obligations of sponsoring States in their efforts to assist the ISA? Furthermore, what consequences will the sponsoring States face if they fail to carry out those obligations or if damages result from wrongful acts of their sponsored contractors? If a consequence involves financial compensation that might be beyond a State's financial capacity, it would exclude a number of States, *inter alia,* developing States, from deep seabed mining activities. On 6 May 2010, the Council of the ISA decided to request an advisory opinion at the request of a small Pacific island developing State, Nauru, from the Seabed Disputes Chamber of the International Tribunal for the Law of the Sea (the Seabed Disputes Chamber).[4] This advisory opinion, *Responsibilities and Obligations of States Sponsoring Persons and Entities with Respect to Activities in the Area* (the SDC Advisory Opinion),[5] clarifies the extent of sponsoring States' international environmental obligations and the scope of sponsoring States' liabilities for damages during the process of mining in the Area as well as the necessary and appropriate measures that a sponsoring State must take in order to fulfill its responsibility. The responses to three questions posed by the ISA Council are instructive.[6]

---

(1959) 53 *American Journal of International Law* 775; II Lukashuk, 'The Principle Pacta Sunt Servanda and the Nature of Obligation Under International Law' (1989) 83 *American Journal of International Law* 513; Daniel Davison-Vecchione, 'Beyond the Forms of Faith: Pacta Sunt Servanda and Loyalty' (2015) 16 *German Law Journal* 1163.

4 Proposal to Seek an Advisory Opinion from the Seabed Disputes Chamber of the International Tribunal for the Law of the Sea on Matters Regarding Sponsoring State Responsibility and Liability, submitted by the delegation of Nauru (ISBA/16/C/6, 5 March 2010).

5 *Responsibilities and Obligations of States with Respect to Activities in the Area, Advisory Opinion, 1 February 2011, ITLOS Reports 2011,* p. 10.

6 Decision of the Council of the International Seabed Authority Requesting an Advisory Opinion Pursuant to Article 191 of the United Nations Convention on the Law of the Sea (ISBA/16/C/13, 6 May 2010). The three questions are: 1. What are the legal responsibilities and obligations of States Parties to the LOS Contention with respect to the sponsorship of activities in the Area in accordance with the LOS Convention, in particular Part XI, and the 1994 Agreement relating to the Implementation of Part XI of the United Nations Convention on the Law of the Sea of 10 December 1982? 2. What is the extent of liability of a State Party for any failure to comply with the provisions of the LOS Contention, in particular Part XI, and the 1994 Agreement, by an entity whom it has sponsored under article 153, paragraph 2(b), of the LOS Convention? 3. What are the necessary and appropriate measures that a sponsoring State must take in order to fulfill its responsibility under the LOS Convention, in particular article 139 and annex III, and the 1994 Agreement?

In this "historic"[7] Advisory Opinion, the Seabed Disputes Chamber points out that "the obligation to ensure compliance by sponsored contractors with the terms of the contract and the obligations set out in the Convention and related instruments" ("responsibility to ensure") is a sponsoring State's primary obligation, that is, what sponsoring States are obliged to do under the LOSC.[8]

This chapter focuses on the issues that relate to sponsoring States, rather than contractors and attempts to provide the rationale for the concept of "responsibility to ensure" and related issues. It begins with an analysis of the legal genesis of the sponsoring States' primary obligation – "responsibility to ensure" – and then presents details and implementing parameters, i.e. "of conduct" and "of due diligence", which are to be embodied in the laws, regulations, and administrative measures within the domestic legal system of the sponsoring States. The national legislation of sponsoring States must be "reasonably appropriate" and the implication of "reasonably appropriate" national legislation will be presented as well. Finally, the consequences of a State's failure to carry out its obligation, i.e. liability, will be explored.

## 2 Terminology: Responsibility and Liability

Before going to the substantive part of this chapter, it is necessary to clarify two confusing but significant terms: responsibility and liability. International responsibility was studied as a discrete subject in the late 19th century.[9] However, international law is not consistent in the use of the terms "responsibility" and "liability". Through long-term development, the modern framework of state responsibility and liability has now been codified in three works of the International Law Commission (ILC), i.e. the *Draft Articles on Responsibility of States for Internationally Wrongful Acts* (ARSIWA), the *Articles on Prevention of Transboundary Harm from Hazardous Activities*, and the *Principles on the Allocation of Loss in the Case of Transboundary Harm Arising Out of Hazardous Activities*.[10] The first instrument focuses on issues of "responsibility", while the

7 David Freestone, 'Responsibilities and Obligations of States Sponsoring Persons and Entities with Respect to Activities in the Area' (2011) 105 *The American Journal of International Law* 755, 755.

8 SDC Advisory Opinion, paragraph 108.

9 James Crawford, *State Responsibility: The General Part* (Cambridge University Press 2013), 3.

10 ILC, *Articles on Responsibility of States for Internationally Wrongful Acts*, printed in 'Report of the International Law Commission on its Fifty-third session', UN Doc A/56/10 (2001), 26–143; ILC, *Articles on Prevention of Transboundary Harm from Hazardous Activities*, printed in 'Report of the International Law Commission on its Fifty-third

last two instruments focus on issues of "liability".[11] The ARSIWA indicates that "every internationally wrongful act of a State entails the international responsibility of that State."[12] The internationally wrongful act refers to a State's conduct – an action or omission – which is attributable to the State under international law, and constitutes a breach of an international obligation of the State.[13] In this context, the difference between the two terms is not categorical, and "responsibility" and "liability" bear the same meaning.[14] However, responsibility is concerned with "acts which are unlawful under international law, whereas [liability] is concerned with activities which *prima facie* are not, but which might give rise to harm in operations for which (absent due diligence) responsibility/liability might rise."[15]

Under the LOSC, several articles that include the terms "responsibility" and "liability" relating to the Deep Seabed Mining Regime do not seem to have exactly the same meaning as in the works of the ILC and do not correspond to each other as well. Those articles citing "responsibility" and "liability" include article 139(1) and (2) ("States Parties shall have the responsibility to ensure"), article 235(1) ("States are responsible for the fulfilment"), Annex III, article 4(4) ("States shall ... have the responsibility to ensure"), article 235(3) ("States shall cooperate ... the further development of international law relating to responsibility and liability ..."), Annex III, article 22 ("responsibility or liability for any damage") and article 304 ("responsibility and liability for damage").

In article 139, article 235(1), and Annex III, article 4(4), the term "responsibility" means "obligation", which is distinct from the meaning in the ILC Articles on State Responsibility.[16] In article 235(3), Annex III, article 22, and article 304, the term "responsibility" is similar in meaning to that in the ARSIWA, which means the consequences of a breach of the primary obligation.[17] Hence,

session', UN Doc A/56/10 (2001), 146–170; ILC, *Principles on the Allocation of Loss in the Case of Transboundary Harm Arising Out of Hazardous Activities*, printed in 'Report of the International Law Commission on its Fifty-eight session', UN Doc A/61/10 (2006), 101–182.

11 Concerning the history of these three instruments, see Alan Boyle, 'Liability for Injurious Consequences of Acts not Prohibited by International Law' in James Crawford, Alain Pellet, and Simon Olleson (eds), *The Law of International responsibility* (Oxford University Press 2010), 95–97.

12 ARSIWA, article 1.

13 ARSIWA, article 2. Analysis as to the elements of internationally wrongful act, see ARSIWA, commentaries to article 2; see also Rüdiger Wolfrum, 'Internationally Wrongful Acts' in *Encyclopedia of Disputes Installment 10* (Elsevier 1987).

14 Crawford (n 9), 63.

15 Crawford (n 9), 63, reproduced from ILC Ybk 2001/II(2), 150.

16 SDC Advisory Opinion, paragraphs 65–66.

17 ibid.

"responsibility to ensure" and "obligation to ensure" share the same meaning in the context of the Deep Seabed Mining Regime. To conform with the wording of the LOSC, this book uses "responsibility to ensure" to refer to the primary obligation of the sponsoring State. But, beyond that, to avoid confusion, this book will use "obligation", rather than "responsibility". Likewise, this book will use "liability", not "State responsibility" to refer to the consequences of a breach of obligations as the indication of the SDC Advisory Opinion,[18] although the term "responsibility" in article 235(3), Annex III, article 22, and article 304 has the same implication.

## 3 The Legal Genesis of Responsibilities of Sponsoring States

### 3.1 *Common Heritage of Mankind*

Article 136 of the LOSC explicitly provides that "the Area and its resources are the common heritage of mankind", a concept viewed as the main innovation of the LOSC.[19] The conceptual framework of governance of the Area is based on the concept of the "common heritage of mankind".[20]

Although there is no express definition of the "controversial legal concept"[21] "common heritage of mankind" in the LOSC, its meaning "can be derived from other provisions of Part XI, in particular, the general principles governing the

18 SDC Advisory Opinion, paragraph 70.

19 Tullio Scovazzi, 'The Seabed Beyond the Limits of National Jurisdiction: General and Institutional Aspects' in Alex G Oude Elferink and Erik J Molenaar (eds), *The International Legal Regime of Areas beyond National Jurisdiction: Current and Future Developments* (Brill Academic Publishers 2010), 43–60.

20 Duncan French, 'From the Depths: Rich Pickings of Principles of Sustainable Development and General International Law on the Ocean Floor – the Seabed Disputes Chamber's 2011 Advisory Opinion', (2011) 26 *The International Journal of Marine and Coastal Law* 525, 528. For discussion on how the common heritage of mankind was implemented in the LOSC, see Alfredo C Robles, Jr, 'The 1994 Agreement on Deep Seabed Mining: Universality vs. the Common Heritage of Humanity' (1996) 12 *World Bulletin* 20, 61.

21 Prue Taylor, 'The Concept of the Common Heritage of Mankind' in Douglas Fisher (eds), *Research Handbook on Fundamental Concepts of Environmental Law* (Edward Elgar Publishing 2016), 306; Egede argued "Undoubtedly, ideological, political and economic interests of the various States play a key role in the divergent interpretations of CHM. However, it is suggested that divergence in culture perspectives cannot be ignored in explaining why certain States, including those from Africa, were more inclined to interpret the CHM as incorporating the idea of common property rather than mere common management." See Edwin Egede, *Africa and the Deep Seabed Regime: Politics and International Law of the Common Heritage of Mankind* (Springer 2011), 61–64.

Area set out in section 2 [of the Part XI of the LOSC]".[22] Yoshifumi Tanaka concludes that three legal elements contribute to the concept of "common heritage of mankind" in the LOSC.[23] The first element is the non-appropriation of the Area or its natural resources. That means that no State may claim or exercise sovereignty or sovereign rights over the Area or its resources which are vested in mankind as a whole and the rights of those resources may not be alienated.[24] The second element is related to the "benefit of mankind". Activities in the Area shall be carried out for the benefit of mankind as a whole, regardless of the geographical location of States.[25] The ISA is called on to provide for the equitable sharing of financial and other economic benefits derived from activities in the Area through any appropriate mechanism, on a non-discriminatory basis, in accordance with article 160, paragraph 2(f)(i).[26] The third element is related to the peaceful use of the Area as stipulated in article 141 of the LOSC.

The second element should be given careful consideration. The "common heritage" is not only a statement of common ownership of resources by all States on a non-discriminatory basis, but it also includes obligations to be met by those States.[27] Those obligations emphatically incorporate "protection of the natural environment" by all States as concluded by Noyes[28] and thus "States have a responsibility to protect the marine environment from harmful effects that may be caused by activities in the Area".[29]

22 Satya N Nandan, Micheal W Lodge and Shabtai Rosenne, *United Nations Convention on the Law of the Sea, 1982: A Commentary, Volume VI* (Martinus Nijhoff Publishers 2002), 99. Those articles includes article 137(1)(2), article 140(1)(2), article 141 and article 145.

23 Yoshifumi Tanaka, *The International Law of the Sea* (2nd edn, Cambridge University Press 2015), 180–181.

24 LOSC, article 137(1) and (2).

25 LOSC, article 140(1).

26 LOSC, article 140(2).

27 Cymie R Payne, 'Seminar on the Outcome of the Advisory Opinion Issued by the Seabed Disputes Chamber of the International Tribunal for the Law of the Sea on 1 February 2011 on the Responsibilities and Obligations of States Sponsoring Activities in the International Seabed Area' (7 April 2011) <https://papers.ssrn.com/sol3/papers.cfm?abstract_id=1815604> accessed 24 June 2020.

28 John E Noyes concludes that the following elements are associated with the common heritage of mankind: a prohibition of acquisition of, or exercise of sovereignty over, the area or resources in question; the vesting of rights to the resources in question in humankind as a whole; reservation of the area in question for peaceful purposes; protection of the natural environment; an equitable sharing of benefits associated with the exploitation of the resources in question, paying particular attention to the interests and needs of developing states; and governance via a common management regime. See John E Noyes, 'The Common Heritage of Mankind: Past, Present, and Future' (2012) 40 *Denver Journal of International Law and Policy* 447, 450–451.

29 Nandan, Lodge and Rosenne (n 22) 99.

Sponsoring States are those States Parties of the LOSC which carry out special functions, and thus they carry out, *ipso facto,* obligations of States Parties, including protecting the marine environment during mining operations in the Area. The SDC Advisory Opinion explains how the common heritage status of the Area shapes the role of the sponsoring State:

> The role of the sponsoring State, as set out in the Convention, contributes to the realization of the common interest of all States in the proper application of the principle of the common heritage of mankind which requires faithful compliance with the obligations set out in Part XI. The common-interest role of the sponsoring State is further confirmed by its obligation, set out in article 153, paragraph 4, of the Convention, to 'assist' the Authority, which, as stated in article 137, paragraph 2, of the Convention, acts on behalf of mankind.[30]

Thus, each member State, whether developed or developing, has the responsibility to protect the common interests. Surely, that implies assisting the ISA to regulate the contractors in order to avoid damage to the marine environment and ensure that sponsored contractors comply with those regulations.

### 3.2 *Sponsorship*

It must be emphasized that contractors, as non-state actors, are not subject to international law, and therefore, not subject to the LOSC and related instruments[31] which outline measures for the preservation and protection of the marine environment during the mining process. To tackle the "traditional weakness",[32] the LOSC made use of the mechanism – sponsorship – under which state enterprises or natural or juridical persons intending to explore or exploit resources in the Area must meet two requirements simultaneously. First, they must be nationals of States Parties or be effectively controlled by a States Party

30 SDC Advisory Opinion, paragraph 76.

31 SDC Advisory Opinion, paragraph 75. The responsibilities of the private sector and how to encourage them to comply with international standards by good behavior have been at the forefront of recent discussions on corporate social responsibility, as is shown by the 2011 Report of the Special Representative of the Secretary-General on the issue of human rights and transnational corporations and other business enterprises: 'Guiding Principles on Business and Human Rights: Implementing the United Nations "Protect, Respect and Remedy" Framework' (A/HRC/17/31, 21 March 2011).

32 Peter Holcombe Henley, 'Minerals and Mechanisms: The Legal Significance of the Notion of the Common Heritage of Mankind in the Advisory Opinion of the Seabed Disputes Chamber' (2011) 12 *Melbourne Journal of International Law* 373, 382.

or its nationals. Second, they shall be sponsored by those States Parties.[33] The requirement of sponsorship ensures a direct link between the entity seeking to undertake activities in the Area and the State which has legal obligations under the LOSC. By this means private entities can also be brought within the framework of the international rule of law.[34] Under the regime of sponsorship, sponsoring States shall "adopt laws and regulations and take administrative measures which are, within the framework of its legal system, reasonably appropriate for securing compliance" by the entities.[35] The inclusion of sponsorship serves to achieve the goal of ensuring entities comply with the obligations set out in the LOSC and related instruments by way of transferring them from international convention to States Parties' national legislation.[36] In the context of deep seabed mining, the sponsoring State's national legislation is crucial, charged, as it is, with implementing the environmental obligations in order to ensure the compliance of sponsored contractors and thus protect and preserve the marine environment from the adverse consequences of mining operations. In this regard, as the Seabed Disputes Chamber indicated, the role of the sponsoring State in the realization of the common interest of all States in the proper application of the principle of the common heritage of mankind should be highlighted.[37] This strategy benefits both from the strong enforceable power of domestic jurisdiction and retains the advantage of international regulation as a management tool of a common resource.[38]

As far as sponsoring States are concerned, the functions of legislation relating to deep seabed mining in the Area are twofold. First, it is a reflection of the *Pacta Sunt Servanda* Principle. The Convention requests States Parties ensure a sponsored contractor's compliance with the terms of its contract and its obligations under the Convention by way of adopting laws and regulations and taking administrative measures within the framework of its national legal system.[39] Laying down national deep seabed mining legal instruments means that sponsoring States are required to carry out their international obligations under the Convention. If a State does not act in conformity with what is required of it by an obligation, it constitutes "a breach of an international obligation" according to the ARSIWA,[40] which may further lead to "an internationally wrongful act of

33 LOSC, article 153(2).
34 French (n 20) 530.
35 LOSC, Annex III, article 4(4).
36 SDC Advisory Opinion, paragraph 75.
37 SDC Advisory Opinion, paragraph 76.
38 Henley (n 32) 382.
39 The LOSC, Annex III, article 4(4).
40 ARSIWA, article 12.

a State".[41] Since "every internationally wrongful act of a State entails the [liability] of that State",[42] the State which fails to assume its international obligation will bear liability. Second, it also has the function of exempting the sponsoring State from liability for damage caused by the sponsored contractor.[43] Pursuant to the Convention, States Parties shall bear liabilities for damages arising from their failure to carry out obligations. Meanwhile, the Convention provides that sponsoring States which have adopted necessary and appropriate measures shall not be liable for the damage caused by contractors. This means that a sponsoring State can be exempted from liability as long as it adopts the necessary and appropriate measures to ensure its sponsored contractor's compliance with international obligations. There is no doubt that this stipulation gives the sponsoring State the impetus to take action. However, with regard to the explanation of "necessary and appropriate measures", the Convention refers to article 153(4) and Annex III, article 4(4), instead of providing an explicit explanation. Those two provisions do not, in fact, contain an explanation of "necessary and appropriate measures", but indicate that "necessary and appropriate measures" at least include laws and regulations and administrative measures as to activities in the Area adopted by sponsoring States, and those legal instruments should be "reasonably appropriate".[44] However, the Convention is silent on a precise definition of "reasonably appropriate". This issue will be discussed in the following section.

## 4 Sponsoring State's Primary Responsibility and Its Implementation

In the SDC Advisory Opinion, the primary legal obligation of a sponsoring State is the so-called "responsibility to ensure", which is revealed in article 139(1), article 153(4), and Annex III, article 4(4). The first provision reads:

> States Parties shall have the responsibility to ensure that activities in the Area, whether carried out by States Parties or state enterprises or natural or juridical persons which possess the nationality of States Parties or are

41 ARSIWA, article 2.

42 ARSIWA, article 1. As indicated in the part of introduction of this study, the term "liability" in the Deep Seabed Mining Regime and the term "international responsibility" of the ARSIWA shared the same meaning, to avoid confusion, this study uses the term "liability" referring to the result of breaching an international obligation.

43 SDC Advisory Opinion, paragraph 119.

44 SDC Advisory Opinion, paragraph 120.

> effectively controlled by them or their nationals, shall be carried out in conformity with this Part.

Furthermore, under Annex III, article 4(4), sponsoring States are obliged to make laws and regulations and administrative measures within their systems, to ensure their sponsored contractors' compliance pursuant to article 139, which reads:

> The sponsoring State or States shall, pursuant to article 139, have the responsibility to ensure, within their legal systems, that a contractor so sponsored shall carry out activities in the Area in conformity with the terms of its contract and its obligations under this Convention. A sponsoring State shall not, however, be liable for damage caused by any failure of a contractor sponsored by it to comply with its obligations if that State Party has adopted laws and regulations and taken administrative measures which are, within the framework of its legal system, reasonably appropriate for securing compliance by persons under its jurisdiction.

Although "responsibility to ensure" is mentioned several times in the Convention, no definition is provided.[45] The absence of an explicit explanation for "responsibility to ensure" impedes the efforts of sponsoring States in carrying out this primary obligation in practice. Given the significance of the phrase "responsibility to ensure", its meaning should be thoroughly discussed.

### 4.1 *The Implications of the Concept "Responsibility to Ensure"*

The term "responsibility to ensure" implies that the sponsoring State must ensure that the "activities in the Area" conducted by its sponsored contractor(s) comply with the rules governing the contractor(s). In other words, to identify the concept which the "responsibility to ensure" entails, three important elements need to be clarified, namely, the meaning of "to ensure", the scope of "activities in the Area", and the rules with which a contractor must comply. The first element makes a connection between the conduct of private persons or entities which is not attributable to the State and the application of the international law. The second element indicates which activities the sponsoring State should regulate within its domestic legal system, while the third

45 Those provisions which expressly mentions "responsibility to ensure" are in article 139(2) and Annex III, article 4(4).

element clarifies the legal instruments the sponsoring State could cite when it considers its relevant national legislation.

First, "responsibility to ensure" does not mean that a sponsoring State must scrutinize every act of its sponsored contractors in every case,[46] neither does it mean that the sponsoring State is liable for all negative impacts on the marine environment by sponsored contractors when it conducts seabed mining activities.[47] " 'Responsibility to ensure' aims to establish a mechanism through which the rules of the Convention concerning activities in the Area become effective for sponsored contractors which find their legal basis in domestic law."[48] Hence, a sponsoring State is required to exercise "regulatory diligence",[49] i.e. adopting "laws and regulations and taken administrative measures" for securing compliance by the contractor. If such laws, regulations, and administrative measures are "reasonably appropriate", it implies that the sponsoring State has achieved the aim of "to ensure". That being said, "to ensure" is an obligation of the conduct of the sponsoring State. The obligation of conduct will be further clarified in section 4.2.

The scope of "activities in the Area" is defined generally in article 1(1)(3) of the LOSC as "all activities of exploration for, and exploitation of, the resources of the Area". However, there is an inconsistency between the LOSC and the ISA Exploration Regulations in the specifics of defining the scope of "activities in the Area". The ISA Exploration Regulations are broader in scope of than that in the LOSC. The ISA Exploration Regulations includes processing and transportation, while the description in the LOSC does not. The Seabed Disputes Chamber pointed out that the ISA Regulations are subordinate to the LOSC, which means they should be interpreted in conformity with it to ensure consistency with the LOSC.[50]

In light of the above, the SDC Advisory Opinion differentiates between those processes that take place on land and on the high seas and those under the ocean when determining "activities in the Area." For instance, "processing", through which metals are extracted from minerals that are conducted on land, and, the movement of material, "transportation", from the high seas to various points on land, should not be perceived as "activities in the Area".[51]

46 SDC Advisory Opinion, paragraph 110.

47 LOSC, Annex III, article 4(4).

48 Yoshifumi Tanaka, 'Obligations and Liability of Sponsoring States Concerning Activities in the Area: Reflections on the ITLOS Advisory Opinion of 1 February 2011' (2013) 60 *Netherlands International Law Review* 205, 209.

49 French (n 20) 539.

50 SDC Advisory Opinion, paragraph 93.

51 SDC Advisory Opinion, paragraphs 95 and 96.

The processes conducted in the ocean, which include water evacuation and disposal of the material of "processing" and "transportation" of material from the seabed to the surface when directly connected with extraction and lifting, are understood to be "activities in the Area".[52] Therefore, according to the SDC Advisory Opinion, the expression "activities in the Area" in the context of exploration and exploitation involve: The recovery of minerals from the seabed and lifting them to the water surface. Specifically, it includes:

- drilling, dredging, coring, and excavation;[53]
- disposal, dumping and discharge into the marine environment of sediment, wastes or other effluents;
- construction and operation or maintenance of installations, pipelines and other devices related to such activities;[54]
- water evacuation and disposal of the material of "Processing"; and
- transportation within that part of the high seas, directly connected to extraction and lifting.

Finally, the Seabed Disputes Chamber also determines the rules with which a contractor should comply. They not only include Part XI of the LOSC and Annexes III and IV of the LOSC, but also incorporate the rules, regulations, and procedures of the ISA. Since the ISA is mandated to develop details under the framework of the LOSC, it is taken for granted that its rules, regulations, and procedures are part of the LOSC.[55] In addition, "the terms of its contract and its obligations"[56] and "the plans of work approved in accordance with paragraph 3"[57] are also included. The contents of the aforementioned legal instruments must be obeyed by the contractors and thus need to be integrated into the sponsoring State's national legislation.

### 4.2 *Implementing "Responsibility to Ensure" as an Obligation of Conduct with High Standards*

Theoretically, the obligations of a State can be divided into two categories: obligations of result and obligations of conduct. The Seabed Disputes Chamber is

52 ibid. See also Rosemary Rayfuse, 'Differentiating the Common? The Responsibilities and Obligations of States Sponsoring Deep Seabed Mining Activities in the Area' (2011) 54 *GYIL* 459, 480.

53 The evacuation of water from the minerals and the preliminary separation of materials of no commercial interest, including their disposal at sea, are deemed to be covered by the expression "activities in the Area".

54 SDC Advisory Opinion, paragraph 87.

55 SDC Advisory Opinion, paragraphs 103–106.

56 LOSC, Annex III, article 4(4).

57 LOSC, article 153(4).

of the view that a sponsoring State's "responsibility to ensure" is an obligation "of conduct" and not "of result".[58] Thus, it is required to differentiate between the two categories so that the instruction of implementing the "responsibility to ensure" by a certain conduct can be achieved.

Rüdiger Wolfrum provided the definitions of the obligation of the result as follows: "Obligations of result have been described above as those where States have to achieve a specific factual situation the prescription of which may be either prohibitive or commanding."[59] One typical example of the obligation of the result is taken from the Montreal Protocol on Substances that Deplete the Ozone Layer, which stipulates that after 1 January 2010, the calculated level of production of certain controlled substances should not exceed zero.[60] Wolfrum also provided the definition of the obligation of conduct: "Obligations of conduct have been defined as those where the State concerned is required to undertake a particular action and in general of procedure nature."[61] It can be concluded that the obligation of result refers to a concrete result, whatever efforts and stages a State makes, while obligations of conduct do not focus on a concrete result, by contrast, it focuses on a State's show of particular efforts and establishment of a particular procedure or practice.

In the context of deep seabed mining, there are two implications of "responsibility to ensure" as an obligation of conduct. First, as the Seabed Disputes Chamber pointed out "it is not an obligation to achieve, in each and every case, the result that the sponsored contractor complies with the obligations above".[62] It merely requires a sponsoring State to make certain efforts which aim to achieve the result that its sponsored contractor complies with its relevant environmental obligations. The positive efforts on the domestic level include "the executive measures taken to conform to the international obligation but also whether legislative acts or even decisions of the judiciary are in conformity with the international obligation".[63] The Seabed Disputes

58 SDC Advisory Opinion, paragraph 110.

59 Rüdiger Wolfrum, 'Obligation of Result Versus Obligation of Conduct: Some Thoughts About the Implementation of International Obligations' in Mahnoush H Arsanjani, Jacob Cogan, Robert Sloane, and Siegfried Wiessner (eds), *Looking to the Future* (Brill 2010), 369.

60 Montreal Protocol on Substances that Deplete the Ozone Layer (Montreal, 16 September 1987, in force 1 January 1989) 1522 UNTS 3, amended or adjusted in 1990 (London), 1991 (Nairobi), 1992 (Copenhagen), 1993 (Bangkok), 1995 (Vienna), 1997 (Montreal), 1998 (Australia), 1999 (Beijing) and 2016 (Kigali), article 2.

61 Wolfrum (n 59) 373.

62 SDC Advisory Opinion, paragraph 110.

63 Wolfrum (n 59) 376.

Chamber specifically indicates the "certain efforts" refer to "necessary and appropriate measures to secure effective compliance".[64] This is further clarified as "adopted laws and regulations and taken administrative measures which are, within the framework of its legal system".[65] Thus, in the context of deep seabed mining, the proof of a sponsoring State carrying out its obligation of conduct is that it adopts a certain type of legislation within its domestic legal system.

When undertaking this particular action, specific measures, such as legislative models and hierarchy are at the discretion of sponsoring State. Several options in this field will be provided in section 2 of chapter 3. There has been limited discussion regarding "administrative measures". According to the description in the SDC Advisory Opinion,[66] it could be reasoned that such administrative measures include: "institutional capabilities such as an identified regulatory body, with monitoring and enforcement functions and access to appropriate personnel, equipment and other technical capacity to implement them."[67] Furthermore, it is necessary "to compare the conduct prescribed with the actual conduct undertaken",[68] which is an effective way to check whether a sponsoring State fulfills the requirements of the obligation of conduct. If the indicated action or omission is inconsistent with the conduct requested, then the obligation is violated.[69]

Second, the actions taken by a sponsoring State should be of a 'high standard', according to the SDC Advisory Opinion, in which it indicates: "it is an obligation to deploy adequate means, to exercise best possible efforts, to do the utmost, to obtain this result." There is no question that words such as "adequate", "best possible efforts", and "utmost" imply a high standard. Yet, a high standard does not mean infinitely high. The measure of the standard of a sponsoring State's diligence is "due diligence". To measure whether a sponsoring State conducts due diligence, the prerequisite is to specify the standard of due diligence.[70]

---

64 SDC Advisory Opinion, paragraph 119.

65 ibid.

66 LOSC, Annex III, art 4(4).

67 Hannah Lily, *Sponsoring State Approaches to Liability Regimes for Environmental Damage Caused by Seabed Mining*, Liability Issues for Deep Seabed Mining Series, Paper No.3 (December 2018).

68 Wolfrum (n 59) 375.

69 ibid.

70 N Matz-Lück and E van Doorn, 'Due Diligence Obligations and the Protection of the Marine Environment' (2017) 42 *L'Observateur des Nations Unies* 169, 183.

### 4.3 *Implementing "Responsibility to Ensure" "of Due Diligence"*

Principally, a State does not bear responsibility for the behavior of natural or legal persons within its jurisdiction, but due diligence applies in the context that the State is expected to exclusively control private persons in its sphere when (or in case) international law is breached by such private persons.[71] The obligation of due diligence does not mean a State is required to guarantee a particular result; rather it is expected to "take the necessary, diligent steps towards that end".[72] This is echoed by the Seabed Disputes Chamber in its Advisory Opinion by stating that sponsoring States are not requested to achieve the result in each and every case, rather, they should "deploy adequate means, to exercise best possible efforts, to do the utmost, to obtain this result."[73]

Hence, it can be concluded that the obligations of due diligence and obligations of conduct are connected. The Seabed Disputes Chamber highlights this opinion by citing the Judgement of the International Court of Justice (ICJ) in the *Pulp Mills on the River Uruguay*:

> An obligation to adopt regulatory or administrative measures ... and to enforce them is an obligation of conduct. Both parties are therefore called upon, under article 36 [of the Statute of the River Uruguay], to exercise due diligence in acting through the [Uruguay River] Commission for the necessary measures to preserve the ecological balance of the river.[74]

Moreover, the Seabed Disputes Chamber also quoted this judgement to illuminate the relationship between "obligation to ensure" and obligation of due diligence, by citing: "It is an obligation which entails not only the adoption of appropriate rules and measures but also a certain level of vigilance in their enforcement and the exercise of administrative control ... such as the monitoring of activities."[75]

With the development of international law, the application of due diligence has broadened with different implications, albeit mostly identical in various fields. After the no harm principle, the application of due diligence extended to the environment of the global commons. In the context of deep seabed

---

71 Timo Koivurova, 'Due Diligence' in *Max Planck Encyclopedia of Public International Law* (2010).

72 ibid.

73 SDC Advisory Opinion, paragraph 110.

74 *Pulp Mills on the River Uruguay (Argentina v. Uruguay), Judgment, I.C.J. Reports 2010, p. 14,* at 77, paragraph 187.

75 ibid, paragraph 197.

mining, it still presents its obvious implications, but with new characteristics. Complying with direct obligations which are concluded by the Seabed Disputes Chamber can be seen to be relevant in meeting the due diligence "obligation to ensure".[76] Hence, examining direct obligation can also provide a reference to the understanding of "obligation to ensure".

### 4.3.1 Character of Due Diligence

#### 4.3.1.1 *Variable Concept*

It is unarguable that due diligence is a dynamic concept. As the Seabed Disputes Chamber noted, due diligence:

> is variable, which means measures are considered as sufficiently diligent at a certain moment but as oppositely at another moment, or measures taken in exploration phase are considered sufficiently diligent but not diligent enough in exploitation phase.[77]

Additionally, the Seabed Disputes Chamber also pointed out that "different kinds of minerals ... may require a different standard of diligence."[78] It can be concluded that in the context of deep seabed mining in the Area there are at least three layers for the "variable" due diligence. First, due to the continuous gaining of new insights or new information and constant improvement of technology, the standards of "damage" keep changing. When the situation changes, utilization of "old" technology may not be able to achieve the purpose of protecting the environment. In this circumstance, a sponsoring State has the responsibility to make new standards or urge the contractor to update its technology. If it does not do so, then the sponsoring State cannot be seen to have carried out its "due diligence" obligation.

Second, the levels of risk at different stages of mining may be different. As presented in chapter 1, there are generally three stages of deep seabed mining. Risks increase from prospecting to exploitation, hence, it is necessary to differentiate the requirements and obligations for the different stages. Similarly, if domestic legislation does not reflect any differentiation in obligations at distinct stages, then it would also be difficult to consider that the requirement of "due diligence" has been fulfilled.

---

76 SDC Advisory Opinion, paragraph 123. In SDC Advisory Opinion, both wording "obligation to ensure" and "responsibility to ensure" are used with the same meaning. This study also follows the SDC Advisory Opinion's example.

77 SDC Advisory Opinion, paragraph 117.

78 ibid.

Third, as also presented in chapter 1, risks vary in relation to various types of mineral resources. This is supported by scientists who hold the view that no "one regulation fits all"![79] The sponsoring States need to take note of this point as well.

#### 4.3.1.2 *Due Diligence and Developing States*

Although general provisions exist that activities in the Area shall take into particular consideration the interests and needs of developing States[80] and the SDC Advisory Opinion originates from the concerns of the small island developing State (Nauru) regarding the responsibilities and liabilities of sponsoring States, it does not mean that the responsibilities and liabilities of developing States will be reduced or lowered. The Seabed Disputes Chamber "rejected the idea of a two-tiered model of responsibility and liability based solely on the economic development status of States."[81] As the Seabed Disputes Chamber recognized, all sponsoring States, whether developing or developed, have the same obligations in light of activities in the Area, including obligations with regard to the protection of the marine environment. Specifically, all sponsoring States must carry out high standards of due diligence to apply a precautionary approach, best environmental practices, and to undertake effective environmental impact assessment.[82] Indeed, encouraging developing States' participation in international seabed mining activities cannot be at the expense of environmental benefits, as evidenced in the Preamble of the LOSC: "desirability of establishing through this Convention, … will promote … the study, protection and preservation of the marine environment."[83] The Seabed Disputes Chamber further consolidated its view in two aspects. First, the LOSC explicitly grants preference to developing States in a specific field in the provisions, such as reserved area, capacity-building, and others.[84] Among

79 Sven Peterson, 'Characteristics and Resource Potential of Seafloor Mineral Occurrences in the Deep Sea' presented in the workshop *Environmental Standards for Deep Seabed Mining* (Tromsø, Norway, 8–9 May 2015).

80 LOSC, article 140(1) and article 148.

81 Rayfuse (n 52) 474.

82 SDC Advisory Opinion, paragraphs 159–161.

83 LOSC, Preamble, paragraph 4.

84 Those provisions which expressly provide a preference to developing States are in: 1. LOSC, Annex III, articles 8 and 9 (granting a preference to developing States that wish to engage in mining in areas of the deep seabed reserved for the Authority); 2. LOSC, article 143(3) (the obligation of States to promote international cooperation in marine scientific research in the Area in order to ensure that programs are developed "for the benefit of developing States"); 3. 1994 Implementing Agreement, the Annex, section 5 and LOSC, article 144(1) (the obligation of the Authority and of States Parties to promote the transfer of technology to developing States); 4. LOSC, article 144(2) and section 5 of the Annex

those provisions, none expressly calls for the provision of special treatment for developing States in light of responsibilities or the liability of the sponsoring States. Hence, the Seabed Disputes Chamber concludes that "the general provisions concerning the responsibilities and liability of the sponsoring State apply equally to all sponsoring States, whether developing or developed".[85] Second, the situation of sponsoring States "of convenience" may appear due to preferential treatment given to developing States. Developed countries may exploit this situation by setting up companies in a developing State to pursue sponsorship from the developing State and thus benefit from less onerous regulations and controls imposed by those developing States. These tendencies have appeared in the context of shipping and high seas fisheries, with so-called "flags of convenience", and have induced tricky problems, such as illegal, unreported, and unregulated fishing.[86] Analogically, sponsoring States "of convenience" would "jeopardize uniform application of the highest standards of protection of the marine environment, the safe development of activities in the Area and protection of the common heritage of mankind".[87] In summary, there is no plan to provide different treatment for developing States and developed States on the issues of the sponsoring States' responsibility and liability in the LOSC, including the obligation of "due diligence".

### 4.3.2 Elements of Due Diligence

In addition to "responsibility to ensure", the Seabed Disputes Chamber also details direct obligations of sponsoring States on the basis of the LOSC, the 1994 Implementing Agreement and ISA Exploration Regulations.[88] Those direct obligations are:

to the 1994 Agreement (to provide training opportunities for personnel from developing States); 5. LOSC, article 152 (in the permission granted to the Authority in the exercise of its powers and functions to give special consideration to developing States, notwithstanding the rule against discrimination); 6. LOSC, articles 160(2)(f)(i), and 162(2)(o)(i) (the obligation of the Council to take "into particular consideration the interests and needs of developing States" in recommending and approving, respectively, rules regulations and procedures on the equitable sharing of financial and other benefits derived from activities in the Area).

85 SDC Advisory Opinion, paragraph 158.

86 Regarding this issue, see Rosemary Gail Rayfuse, *Non-Flag State Enforcement in High Seas Fisheries* (Martinus Nijhoff Publishers 2004).

87 SDC Advisory Opinion, paragraph 159.

88 When the SDC Advisory Opinion adopted in 2011, Cobalt-Rich Regulations was not yet adopted, and thus the Seabed Disputes Chamber only make reference to Nodule Regulations and Sulphides Regulations.

> the obligation to assist the Authority in the exercise of control over activities in the Area; the obligation to apply a precautionary approach; the obligation to apply best environmental practices; the obligation to take measures to ensure the provision of guarantees in the event of an emergency order by the Authority for protection of the marine environment; the obligation to ensure the availability of recourse for compensation in respect of damage caused by pollution; and the obligation to conduct environmental impact assessments.[89]

Implementation of the primary obligation, i.e. the due diligence obligation to ensure, is described by the Seabed Disputes Chamber as, "compliance with these obligations can also be seen as a relevant factor in meeting the due diligence 'obligation to ensure' and that the said obligations are in most cases couched as obligations to ensure compliance with specific rules".[90] Hence, in order to meet the due diligence obligation, the direct obligations have to be complied with.[91] Direct obligations are "integral aspects of the general obligation of due diligence".[92] Moreover, it "enriches due diligence and highlights the integrated and over-arching nature of the obligation."[93] They can be "viewed as a minimum checklist to be fulfilled by the sponsoring State. As such, they provide the starting point for implementation."[94] Therefore, they can be treated as elements of due diligence, but are not exhaustive, which is useful in the process of its implementation. Importantly, the Seabed Disputes Chamber stressed that those obligations are mentioned only as examples.[95] It will be not sufficient to meet the due diligence if the sponsoring State adopts them "*pro forma* without accompanying administrative measures and control".[96]

#### 4.3.2.1 *Implement the Precautionary Approach*

In the Deep Seabed Mining Regime, although it does not appear explicitly in Part XI of the LOSC, the precautionary approach (also used as the "precautionary

89 SDC Advisory Opinion, paragraph 122.

90 SDC Advisory Opinion, paragraph 123.

91 Jianjun Gao, 'The Responsibilities and Obligations of the Sponsoring States Advisory Opinion' (2013) 12 *Chinese Journal of International Law* 771, 779.

92 French (n 20) 547.

93 ibid.

94 Elana Geddis, 'The Due Diligence Obligation of a Sponsoring State: A Framework for Implementation' in Myron H Nordquist, John Norton Moore and Ronan Long (eds), *International Marine Economy: Law and Policy* (Brill 2017), 253.

95 SDC Advisory Opinion, paragraph 236.

96 Geddis (n 94) 253.

principle" in certain circumstances)[97] is adopted by the ISA Exploration Regulations as an obligation of all three actors of mining activities in the Area, including the sponsoring State.[98] Further, the Seabed Disputes Chamber highlighted the "implicit" link between the due diligence obligation and the precautionary approach by citing the *Southern Bluefin Tuna Cases*[99] and Principle 15 of the 1992 Rio Declaration on Environment and Development.[100] It was summarized as one of the direct obligations of sponsoring States and stated that sponsoring States must apply a precautionary approach as an integral part of their due diligence obligations "in situations where scientific evidence concerning the scope and potential negative impact of the activity in question is insufficient but where there are plausible indications of potential risks."[101] That is echoed by Duncan French: "it would seem logical, regardless of legal formality, to incorporate the precautionary approach within 'due diligence' ".[102]

As noted in section 2.3, chapter 1, there are many environmental risks and "undetected"[103] environmental results which may arise from mining activities in the Area due to absence of comprehensive knowledge of the deep

---

97 Aline Jaeckel concludes the difference between two concepts "precautionary approach" and "precautionary principle" is mainly a "semantic squabble". There are no substantive differences between commitments to apply "precautionary approach" and "precautionary principle". One possible distinction is that "approach" is viewed as allowing for more flexibility and comprising socio-economic considerations, such as the cost-effectiveness of any measures. See Aline L. Jaeckel, *The International Seabed Authority and the Precautionary Principle: Balancing Deep Seabed Mineral Mining and Marine Environmental Protection* (Brill Nijhoff 2017), 21–22; See also Nicolas De Sadeleer, *Environmental Principles: From Political Slogans to Legal Rules* (Oxford University Press, 2002), 92; Rosie Cooney, 'A Long and Winding Road? Precaution from Principle to Practice in Biodiversity Conservation' in Elizabeth Fisher, Judith Jones, and René von Schomberg (eds), *Implementing the Precautionary Principle: Perspectives And Prospects* (Edward Elgar Publishing, 2006), 224; Arie Trouwborst, 'The Precautionary Principle in General International Law: Combating the Babylonian Confusion' (2007) 16 *Review of European Community & International Environmental Law* 185; Simon Marr, *The Precautionary Principle in the Law of the Sea: Modern Decision Making in International Law* (Martinus Nijhoff Publishers 2003), 17.

98 See eg ISA Polymetallic Nodules Exploration Regulations, regulation 31(2).

99 SDC Advisory Opinion, paragraph 132. *Southern Bluefin Tuna (New Zealand v. Japan; Australia v. Japan), Provisional Measures, Order of 27 August 1999, ITLOS Reports 1999, p. 280,* at 296, paragraphs 77, 79 and 80.

100 Rio Declaration on Environment and Development (adopted 13 June 1992, UN Doc. A/CONF.151/26 (vol. I)) 31 ILM 874 (1992) (Rio Declaration).

101 SDC Advisory Opinion, paragraph 131.

102 French (n 20) 548.

103 Adrian G Glover and Craig R Smith, 'The Deep-Sea Floor Ecosystem: Current Status and Prospects of Anthropogenic Change by the Year 2025' (2003) 30 *Environmental Conservation* 219, 237.

sea. However, lack of full scientific certainty cannot be used as a reason for postponing cost-effective measures to prevent environmental degradation. This is endorsed in Principle 15 of the 1992 Rio Declaration on Environment and Development, which encourages the application of the precautionary approach.[104] Craig R. Smith provides an accurate summary indicating why the application of the precautionary approach is important:

> Anthropogenic impacts in the deep sea have substantially outstripped the predictive abilities of scientists, and this situation will worsen with the accelerated human exploitation of the deep ocean. Environmental protection in the deep sea, perhaps more than in any other habitat, will require the application of the 'precautionary principle', in which reasonable conservation measures are implemented prior to detailed scientific understanding of the ecosystem.[105]

The precautionary approach requires an assessment of possible harm that is considered unacceptable, and the implementation of interventions proportionate (with specific regard to cost) to the desired level of protection and the magnitude of that possible harm. Science can estimate a risk level within a certain range of error but cannot tell us what level of risk is socially acceptable. Decisions made by applying the precautionary approach, therefore, cannot appeal solely to scientific or technical information for justification but must also align with social norms and values about what harm is considered acceptable.

The doctrine of the precautionary approach is incrementally applied by the international judiciary and arbitration. For example, precautionary language appears several times in ICJ cases. It is first raised in New Zealand's 1995 request concerning French nuclear testing.[106] *Pulp Mills on the River Uruguay* in 2010 also invoked the precautionary principle.[107] Moreover, the Seabed Disputes Chamber even holds the view of that "this has initiated a trend towards making this approach part of the customary international

---

104 ibid.

105 Craig R Smith and others, 'The Near Future of the Deep-Sea Floor Ecosystems', in Nicholas VC Polunin (eds), *Aquatic Ecosystems: Trends and Global Prospects* (Cambridge University Press 2008), 349.

106 *Request for an Examination of the Situation in Accordance with Paragraph 63 of the Court's Judgment of 20 December 1974 in the Nuclear Tests (New Zealand v. France) Case, I.C.J. Reports 1995, p. 288.*

107 *Pulp Mills on the River Uruguay (Argentina v. Uruguay) (n 74).*

law",[108] although different voices are raised regarding the radical view of the Seabed Disputes Chamber.

Then, we come back to this concept itself. The precautionary approach aims to provide guidance in the development and application of international environmental law where there is scientific uncertainty. However, this "over-regulation and limiting human activity" approach is not used only where scientific uncertainty exists.

Although it can be used "without full evidence", this does not mean an absence of evidence. It may be applied where there is adequate available data that significant environmental damage is occurring or will occur. Although a few international treaties recognize the precautionary approach, some provisions seem to be very cautious and limited. For example, the *International Convention Relating to Intervention on the High Seas in Cases of Oil Pollution Casualties*, concluded in 1969, was one of the earliest treaties to recognize the limitations of the precautionary approach. It said, taking account of "the extent and probability of imminent damage if those measures are not taken".[109] Even where justified, application of the precautionary approach should be prudent. Some issues need to be carefully considered, such as, 1) how much caution should be applied; 2) where is the line between acceptable and unacceptable risks, and 3) what degree of certainty is required to determine this acceptability.

In conclusion, the function of the precautionary approach as an environmental management tool should be highlighted, but it cannot be overstated. It should be without prejudice to provisions in LOSC and avoid abuse. Although it is adopted by the ISA Exploration Regulations as an obligation of the sponsoring State and contractor, its application still needs development in practice. Its application should be, first, justified, including fulfilling trigger requirements. Second, it should confirm how much caution should be taken and demonstrate due regard to other sea users.

#### 4.3.2.2 *Apply Best Environmental Practices*

"Best environmental practices" is an obligation borne jointly by sponsoring States and contractors. The Seabed Disputes Chamber observed that "best environmental practices" are required by the ISA regulations and the standard clauses for exploration contracts.[110] That a sponsoring State applies "best

108 SDC Advisory Opinion, paragraph 135.

109 International Convention relating to Intervention on the High Seas in cases of Oil Pollution Casualties (adopted 29 November 1969, entered into force 6 May 1975) 970 UNTS 211.

110 See eg ISA Sulphides Exploration Regulations, regulation 33(2) and Annex 4, section 5.1.

environmental practices" in light of the advancement of the scientific knowledge can be seen as evidence of carrying out its obligation of due diligence.[111]

In fact, the original version of the first ISA exploration regulation, i.e. Nodules Exploration Regulations, adopted the terminology "best available technology", rather than "best environmental practices".[112] The terminology "best environmental practices" was first adopted by the Sulphides Exploration Regulations and then applied to Cobalt-rich Crust Exploration Regulations and later modified in the Nodules Exploration Regulations. The express requirement for "best environmental practices" under the regulations and standard clauses is a broader concept than "best available technology." The latter appears to be limited by what is technologically achievable, while a survey of the former in a variety of international instruments shows that it requires the application of the most appropriate combination of environmental control measures and strategies.[113]

The Seabed Disputes Chamber did not provide a clear definition of the concept of best environmental practice, whilst the ISA Draft Exploitation Regulations (January 2017) do provide a dedicated definition of the term "best environmental practices", specifically, "… the application of the most appropriate combination of environmental control measures and strategies, [including Best Available Techniques]".[114] As this term explicitly incorporates the term "best available techniques", which is also provided for in schedule 1 of that draft, it is necessary to read these two terms together in order to determine the full nature and scope of the term above. "Best available techniques" is defined as:

> … the latest stage of development, state of the art processes, of facilities or of methods of operation that indicate the practical suitability of a particular measure for the prevention, reduction and control of pollution

---

111 SDC Advisory Opinion, paragraph 136.

112 Decision of the Assembly of the International Seabed Authority regarding the amendments to the Regulations on Prospecting and Exploration for Polymetallic Nodules in the Area (ISBA/19/A/9, 25 July 2013).

113 Donald K Anton, Robert A Makgill and Cymie R Payne, 'Seabed Mining: Advisory Opinion on Responsibility and Liability' (2011) 41 *Environmental Policy and Law* 60, 63; see also Use of the terms *best available techniques, best environmental practice* and related concepts in international environmental instrument, Expert Group on best available techniques, best environmental practice (UNEP/POPS/EGB.1/INF/3, 29 January 2003).

114 A Discussion Paper on the development and drafting of Regulations on Exploitation for Mineral Resources in the Area- Environmental Matters (January 2017) <https://www.isa.org.jm/files/documents/EN/Regs/DraftExpl/DP-EnvRegsDraft25117.pdf> accessed 24 June 2020.

> and the protection of the Marine Environment from the harmful effects of Exploitation Activities.

This definition was slightly modified by the ISA Draft Exploitation Regulations (July 2018), which read: "'Best Environmental Practices' means the application of the most appropriate combination of environmental control measures and strategies, taking into account the criteria set out in the applicable Guidelines."[115] This definition was further developed by the Draft Exploitation Regulations (March 2019) (Schedule, Use of terms and scope): "the application of the most appropriate combination of environmental control measures and strategies, that will change with time in the light of improved knowledge, understanding or technology, taking into account the guidance set out in the applicable Guidelines."[116] This might indicate that the ISA will provide specific guidelines to support the implementation of the best environmental practices.

Every State has its unique economic and technological situation. The sponsoring State plays an indispensable role in the application of "best environmental practices", since in comparison with the ISA, the sponsoring State can judge whether the measure adopted by the contractor is "best" or not within the capability of this State. If a sponsoring State could act accordingly, it would demonstrate irrefutable proof of having carried out its due diligence obligation.

#### 4.3.2.3 *Conduct Environmental Impact Assessments*

Due diligence will require a State to inform itself of the environmental consequences of any potential environmentally harmful activities it proposes, and the duties of notification and consultation further require that this information be shared with potentially affected states.[117] There is no doubt that the environmental impact assessment (EIA) is one of the central mechanisms used by states to acquire knowledge as to the environmental consequences of their actions. This is commonly defined as "the process of identifying, predicting, evaluating and mitigating the biophysical, social, and other relevant effects of development proposals prior to major decisions being taken and commitments made".[118] The

115 Draft Regulations on Exploitation of Mineral Resources in the Area (ISBA/24/LTC/WP.1/Rev.1, 9 July 2018).

116 Draft Regulations on Exploitation of Mineral Resources in the Area (ISB/25/C/WP.1, 22 March 2019).

117 Neil Craik, *The International Law of Environmental Impact Assessment: Process, Substance and Integration* (Cambridge University Press 2008), 120.

118 IAIA and IEA, 'Principles of Environmental Impact Assessment Best Practice' (1999) <https://www.iaia.org/uploads/pdf/principlesEA_1.pdf> accessed 24 June 2020.

primary purpose of the EIA process is to encourage the consideration of environmental issues in planning and decision making and to arrive at actions which are ultimately more environmentally compatible.[119] EIAs address foreseeability by requiring project proponents to comprehensively analyze the likely impacts of proposed activities and address the reasonableness of the activities undertaken through the requirement to look at the feasibility of alternatives to the proposal.[120] As Niel Craik pointed out, "EIA implements a state's due diligence obligation to inform itself of the environmental effects of proposed activities."[121]

The 1994 Implementing Agreement explicitly sets out that it is a contractor's obligation to conduct an EIA.[122] The ISA has indicated that some exploration activities, such as dredging or testing of collection systems, require prior EIA.[123] The ISA Exploration Regulations further establish the direct obligation of a sponsoring State to ensure such compliance by the sponsored contractor with this obligation.[124] The Seabed Disputes Chamber indicates that ensuring that a potential contractor undertakes such an assessment prior to the submission of an application for a plan of work to the ISA can "be read as a relevant factor for meeting the sponsoring State's due diligence obligation."[125] That requires a sponsoring State to use "appropriate means to ensure that the contractor complies with its obligation to conduct an environmental impact assessment".[126]

However, although the Seabed Disputes Chamber recognized that the obligation to conduct an EIA is a general obligation under customary international law by citing the ICJ Judgment in *Pulp Mills on the River Uruguay*,[127] it does not provide the details as to the minimum requirements that a sponsoring State needs to satisfy, which leaves some challenges for a sponsoring State in establishing its domestic legislation.

---

119 Anji Reddy Mareddy, *Environmental Impact Assessment: Theory and Practice* (Elsevier/ BH, Butterworth-Heinemann, an imprint of Elsevier 2017), 1.

120 Craik (n 117) 64.

121 ibid, 65.

122 1994 Implementing Agreement, Annex, section 1(7).

123 See eg ISA Polymetallic Nodules Exploration Regulations, Annex IV, section 5.2(a).

124 ISA Polymetallic Nodules Exploration Regulations, regulation 31(6); ISA Sulphides Exploration Regulations, regulation 33(6); and ISA Cobalt-rich Curst Exploration Regulations, regulation 33(6).

125 SDC Advisory Opinion, paragraph142.

126 ibid.

127 *Pulp Mills on the River Uruguay* (*Argentina v. Uruguay*) (n 74), at 83, paragraph 204.

### 4.3.2.4 *Guarantees in the Event of an Emergency Order by the Authority for Protection of the Marine Environment*

In the process of mining, there may be an incident which causes or poses a threat of serious harm to the marine environment. In this case, the Council may issue emergency orders, as reasonably necessary, to prevent, contain, and minimize serious harm or the threat of serious harm to the marine environment. Those emergency orders may require the contractor to suspend or adjust its operations to reach the aim. Alternatively, the Council shall take actions by itself or through arrangements with others in the case of a contractor's incompliance with an emergency order. To enable the Council to immediately undertake the practical measures to prevent, contain, and minimize the serious harm or threat of serious harm to the marine environment, the contractor is required to provide a guarantee of its financial and technical capabilities to comply promptly with emergency orders or to assure that the Council can take such emergency measures. However, if a contractor does not offer such guarantees, a sponsoring State should assist the ISA to ensure that the sponsored contractor provide such guarantees.[128] The ISA's Exploration Regulations stipulate,

> the sponsoring State or States shall, in response to a request by the Secretary-General and pursuant to articles 139 and 235 of the Convention, take necessary measures to ensure that the contractor provides such a guarantee or shall take measures to ensure that assistance is provided to the Authority in the discharge of its responsibilities under paragraph 7.[129]

The Seabed Disputes Chamber considers this a direct obligation of a sponsoring State. This obligation only arises if the sponsored entity or person has not provided the ISA with a guarantee of its financial and technical capability to comply with emergency orders. A sponsoring State must have arrangements to ensure the contractor's guarantee within its domestic legal system. Doing so is one proof that a sponsoring State has carried out its due diligence obligation. Thus, a sponsoring State has to check its sponsored contractor's financial and technical capability not only to confirm it can carry out the mining activities but also to ensure it has the capability to comply with emergency orders.

128 Nodules Exploration Regulations, regulation 33. Also, Sulphides Exploration Regulations and Crusts Exploration Regulations contain a similar provision, regulation 35.

129 Nodules Exploration Regulations, regulation 33(8). Also, Sulphides Exploration Regulations and Crusts Exploration Regulations contain a similar provision, regulation 35(8).

#### 4.3.2.5 *Ensure Availability of Adequate Reparation*

Article 235 of the LOSC requires that "States shall ensure that recourse is available in accordance with their legal systems for prompt and adequate compensation or other relief in respect of damage caused by pollution of the marine environment by natural or juridical persons under their jurisdiction."[130] The Seabed Disputes Chamber indicates that the sponsoring State is required to adopt laws and regulations to ensure that recourse is available in the sponsoring State's legal system for prompt and adequate compensation or other relief, which is also another direct obligation of a sponsoring State.[131]

This design, which is reflected in Principle 13 of the Rio Declaration on Environment and Development, is the foundational design of any liability regime and is in line with the general requirements for restitution under the law of liability.[132] In the context of deep seabed mining, ensuring prompt and adequate compensation may require that a sponsoring State has an arrangement of adjudication, which means the case can be brought before its domestic courts after the damage happens. Also, a domestic liability regime should be in place so that victims can be compensated. Last, but not least, a sponsoring State may establish a national fund from which a victim could obtain compensation in the event of inadequate or delayed compensation. Those actions can be seen as carrying out the direct obligation as well as a factor of carrying out the due diligence obligation.

### 4.4 *"Reasonably Appropriate" Implementing "Responsibility to Ensure"*

In addition to carrying out the "responsibility to ensure" of due diligence and of conduct, the Seabed Disputes Chamber indicates that a sponsoring State is required to take measures within its legal system. The applicable standard is that the measures must be "reasonably appropriate".[133] On this point, the Seabed Disputes Chamber provides some reference when it answered the third question, i.e. the necessary and appropriate measures that a sponsoring State must take. Although it is not comprehensive and systematic, the Seabed Disputes Chamber gave some specific examples. For instance, 1) financial viability and technical capacity of sponsored contractors; 2) conditions for issuing a certificate of sponsorship; and 3) penalties for non-compliance by such contractors. They may also include the establishment of enforcement mechanisms for active supervision of activities of the sponsored contractor and for

130 LOSC, article 235(2).
131 SDC Advisory Opinion, paragraph 139.
132 ARSIWA, article 35.
133 SDC Advisory Opinion, paragraph 120.

co-ordination between the activities of the sponsoring State and those of the ISA.[134]

Those States which do not have such legislation will be required to introduce new laws or amending existing laws to provide the necessary rules, regulations, and procedures. However, the SDC Advisory Opinion stresses that enacting laws, *per se,* is not sufficient to satisfy a sponsoring State's obligations. Administrative implementation and oversight are also needed. To further clarify, the Seabed Disputes Chamber quotes the ICJ judgment in *Pulp Mills on the River Uruguay* indicating that this consists of "not only the adoption of appropriate rules and measures but also a certain level of vigilance in their enforcement and the exercise of administrative control applicable to public and private operators, such as the monitoring of activities undertaken by such operators. ..."[135]

Furthermore, some principles which are enshrined in the LOSC and relevant legal instruments are also useful to understand the implication of "reasonably appropriate". They are probably not necessary to explicitly appear in legal texts of sponsoring State's national legislation. However, they must be borne in mind by the national legislators as guiding principles in the process of legislating and instructing the formation and development of national legislation. Those principles include, but are not limited to, good faith, minimum standards of stringency, as well as review.

### 4.4.1 Good Faith

The primary legislative principle that sponsoring States should follow is *good faith*. According to article 136 of the LOSC, the Area and its resources are the common heritage of mankind. Article 137 further elaborates that "no State shall claim or exercise sovereignty or sovereign rights over any part of the Area, nor shall any State or natural or juridical person appropriate any part thereof". As noted in the SDC Advisory Opinion, "the sponsoring State does not have absolute discretion with respect to the adoption of laws and regulations and the taking of administrative measures. It must act in *good faith*, taking the various options into account in a manner that is reasonable, relevant and conducive to the benefit of mankind as a whole".[136] That being said, granting exclusive exploration or exploitation rights to a certain contractor merely represents that the contractor has exclusive exploration or exploitation rights of a particular category of resources in a certain area. It does not involve other

134 SDC Advisory Opinion, paragraphs 212–241.

135 *Pulp Mills on the River Uruguay* (*Argentina v. Uruguay*) (n 74), at 69, paragraph 197.

136 SDC Advisory Opinion, paragraph 230.

types of resources, nor does it affect other users of the sea. The exclusive exploration or exploitation rights enjoyed by a contractor are only those conditionally exercised by it under the authority of the ISA, and they must be exercised within the limits of the authority to take due account of the common interests and conduct in *good faith*. *Good faith* plays an eminent role in the international community as a subjective legal fact, an objectivizing legal standard, and a general principle of law.[137] Without good faith, social relations would be doomed to fail. It has manifold expressions and concretizations, such as *pacta sunt servanda*, estoppel, acquiescence, equity, and prohibition of abuse of rights.[138] In this context, *good faith* can be explained as the prohibition of abuse of rights.[139] Furthermore, rights and obligations being interdependent, where the exercise of a right would impinge on an obligation assumed, that right must be exercised reasonably and in good faith. Thus, the doctrine of the prohibition of abuse of rights, "while protecting the legitimate interests of the owner of the right, imposes such limitations upon the right as will render its exercise compatible with that party's treaty obligations, or, in other words, with the legitimate interests of the other contracting party".[140]

In order to express the purpose of *good faith*, at least the following points should be considered to different degrees in sponsoring States' deep seabed national legislation: 1) strict requirements of access to a license for exploration and exploitation activities in the Area; 2) clear provisions regarding environmental obligations of a contractor as well as monitoring its compliance together with enforceable measures to obey those obligations; 3) a contractor's rights and the guarantee of those rights; 4) due consideration to social-cultural impacts in the mining area; and 5) due regard to other sea users and cumulative impacts. The inability of a State to demonstrate those requirements would be seen as an act of bad faith or a failure of due diligence. Then, even if the

137 With regard to three meanings of *good faith* in public international law, see Robert Kolb, *Good Faith in International Law* (Hart Publishing 2017), 15–28.

138 Andreas R Ziegler and Jorun Baumgartner, 'Good Faith as a General Principle of (International) Law' in Andrew D Mitchell, M Sornarajah, and Tania Voon (eds) *Good Faith and International Economic Law* (Oxford University Press 2015), 9–36.

139 With regard to doctrine of the prohibition of abuse of rights and its relationship with good faith, see Kolb (n 137), 133–147; and Alexandre Kiss, 'Abuse of Rights' in *Max Planck Encyclopedia of Public International Law* (2006).

140 Bin Cheng, *General Principles of Law as Applied by International Courts and Tribunals* (Cambridge University Press 2006), 129; see also Bin Cheng and Georg Schwarzenberger, *General Principles of Law as Applied by International Courts and Tribunals* (Stevens and Sons 1953); Markus Kotzur, 'Good Faith (*Bona fide*)' in *Max Planck Encyclopedia of Public International* (2009).

State has national legislation for activities in the Area, it would not be considered to have fulfilled its due diligence obligations.

### 4.4.2 Minimum Standard of Stringency

The LOSC, Annex III, article 21(3) empowers sponsoring States within their national legal frameworks to impose more stringent conditions on its sponsored contractors than Part XI of the LOSC in terms of environmental issues by stating,

> No State Party may impose conditions on a contractor that are inconsistent with Part XI. However, the application by a State Party to contractors sponsored by it, or to ships flying its flag, of environmental or other laws and regulations more stringent than those in the rules, regulations and procedures of the Authority adopted pursuant to article 17, paragraph 2(f), of this Annex shall not be deemed inconsistent with Part XI.

It was made clear in the SDC Advisory Opinion that the relevant provisions of the ISA regulations should be regarded as the minimum standards for environmental protection provisions and that the domestic legislation of the sponsoring State would be more stringent than that of the ISA.[141]

"*Minimum standard of stringency*", being a legislative principle, is based on two considerations. First, considering the differences in the economic, technical, social, and natural environment of distinct States, it is virtually impossible for international conventions and regulations to set identical and stringent environmental standards for all its member States, as those standards may be achieved only by high-level financial or technological support. Those high standards may exist in name only, if they are unachievable, especially to certain States with low-level financial or technological capacity. On this basis, international law and international regulations work as a minimum standard, in keeping with which sponsoring States could make in-depth and detailed provisions of the reasonable and appropriate concrete expression in accordance with their own actual situations. Second, environmental issues should be a top priority for human concern, as the ICJ noted in its advisory opinion: "the environment is not an abstraction but represents the living space, the quality of life and the very health of human beings, including generations unborn."[142] The environment is an organic whole, and the air, water, climate,

141 SDC Advisory Opinion, paragraph 240.

142 *Legality of the Threat or Use of Nuclear Weapons, Advisory Opinion, I.C.J. Reports 1996*, p. 226, at 241, paragraph 29.

soil, animals, plants, and even the entire natural ecosystem are connected with the well-being of mankind as a whole. From this point of view, every country has to use strict standards to minimize environmental risks.

Therefore, in the process of legislation, especially on environmental issues, the minimum standards of the provisions of the LOSC and the ISA regulations should be adhered to, regardless of the sponsoring States' individual wealth or capacity. For the understanding of "stringency", there are two approaches in this respect. First, sponsoring States could adopt higher (e.g. amount of monetary sanction. This method is usually applied to quantifiable indicators) or stricter (e.g. liability of the contractor) standards than that at the international level. Second, sponsoring States could provide more details at the national level. Given that there are quite a few non-quantifiable indicators at the international level, providing details seems to be a more common method. For example, conducting the EIA is an international environmental obligation of a contractor. The ISA Environmental Regulation Draft plans to provide a template for an EIA.[143] If a sponsoring State required extra information in addition to that prescribed in the aforementioned template, it can be seen as "more stringent than that of the ISA".

#### 4.4.3 Kept Under Review

In addition to good faith and minimum standards of stringency, keeping sponsoring States' national legislation updated is another paramount principle. International law is not static. The Seabed Disputes Chamber indicated that the LOSC ensures that the Deep Seabed Mining Regime will be influenced by developments in international law generally, which demonstrates the Seabed Disputes Chamber's inclination towards a "living tree" approach to interpretation.[144] Especially in the field of deep seabed mining, technology changes rapidly and something considered environmentally friendly in one period may prove harmful to the environment in the next. Thus, the relevant international laws and regulations are expected to develop. Accordingly, sponsoring States'

143 A Discussion Paper on the development and drafting of Regulations on Exploitation for Mineral Resources in the Area (Environmental Matters) (n 114).

144 Henley (n 32) 379. The concept of interpreting a convention or statute as a "living tree", which is a progressive interpreting approach that takes changing times and usages into account, was famously articulated by Lord Sankey in *Edwards v Attorney-General of Canada* [1930] AC 124 with respect to the Constitution of Canada, where he stated that the Constitution was "a living tree capable of growth and expansion within its natural limits": at 136. Ian Brownlie refers to this interpretative practice as an 'evolutionary' or 'teleological' approach which has 'many pitfalls', see Ian Brownlie, *Principles of Public International Law* (7th edn, Oxford University Press 2008), 635–636.

national legislation must make timely adjustments. As the Seabed Disputes Chamber pointed out "the national measures, once adopted, may not be appropriate in perpetuity … that such measures should be kept under review so as to ensure that they meet current standards and that the contractor meets its obligations effectively without detriment to the common heritage of mankind".[145] Failure to review and update the domestic law cannot be considered "reasonable and appropriate", nor could it be considered that the sponsoring State had fulfilled its "due diligence" obligations.

The principle of "kept under review" should be understood from two perspectives. On the one hand, sponsoring States must keep pace with the development of the ISA regulations. When the ISA adopts new regulations or amends existing regulations, the sponsoring State shall react accordingly, by at least meeting the minimum standard of ISA regulations. On the other hand, even if there is no update of ISA regulations, the sponsoring States shall proactively and regularly (for example, every five years) review their legislation. The power to review national legislation should be given to the legislative agency of the sponsoring State. The sponsoring States should also have to amend their legislation as new information becomes available or good industry practices and best environmental practices are updated, which is also a requirement of the "due diligence" obligation indicated in section 4.3.1.2 of this chapter.

## 5 Liability of the Sponsoring State

International liability for environmental damage is premised upon a breach of an international legal obligation established by treaty, or by a rule of customary international law, or possibly under general principles of international law.[146] Thus, a violation of "responsibility to ensure" entails liability.[147] Not only that, if a sponsoring State fails to carry out its legal responsibility and obligations under customary international law, whether or not damage occurs, the sponsoring State has to bear liabilities. Liability of sponsoring States proved to be the most serious concern of every sponsoring State, especially developing States, since infinite and unpredictable liability would be a barrier to their participation in mining activities in the Area. This section roughly depicts a comprehensive picture of the liability regime for deep

145 SDC Advisory Opinion, paragraph 222.

146 Philippe Sands and others, *Principles of International Environmental Law* (3rd edn, Cambridge University Press 2012), 705.

147 SDC Advisory Opinion, paragraph 109.

seabed mining, without which it will be difficult to sort out the liability of the sponsoring State. Then, it will focus on the liability of a sponsoring State under the framework of the LOSC. Afterwards, corollaries for success to carry out the "responsibility to ensure" and for failure to carry out the "responsibility to ensure" will be presented, respectively. Finally, liability gaps under the existing liability regime will be identified and possible solutions to close the gaps will be provided.

### 5.1 *Basic Architecture of Liability in the Deep Seabed Mining Regime*

There are a variety of actors involved, either directly or indirectly, in activities in the Area, such as the contractor (including sub-contractors), the sponsoring State, and the ISA. Any damage will inevitably lead to issues of channeling liability, which is a matter of clarifying who is liable for the damage caused by a particular activity and to what extent.

Liability for activities in the Area is addressed by the Convention (mainly article 139, and articles 4 and 22 of Annex III, secondarily articles 235 and 304), the ISA Exploration Regulations, and the standard contract provisions. Although the ISA is mandated to develop rules, regulations and procedures for the Deep Seabed Mining Regime, as far as existing regulations are concerned, it hasn't made a breakthrough contribution to the liability regime. Relevant provisions in the ISA Exploration Regulations and Standard Contract only make reference to the Convention without going further or beyond the existing contents under the LOSC when it addresses responsibility and liability.[148] Hence, the main clues for what constitutes liability for activities in the Area exist in the LOSC.

The liability of contractors and the ISA is addressed in article 22, Annex III of the LOSC:

> The contractor shall have responsibility or liability for any damage arising out of wrongful acts in the conduct of its operations, account being taken of contributory acts or omissions by the Authority. Similarly, the Authority shall have responsibility or liability for any damage arising out of wrongful acts in the exercise of its powers and functions, including violations under article 168, paragraph 2, account being taken of contributory acts or omissions by the contractor. Liability in every case shall be for the actual amount of damage.

148 See eg ISA Nodules Exploration Regulations, regulation 30; Annex IV, section 16.

In the view of the Seabed Disputes Chamber, this provision reflects the distribution of liability for deep seabed mining activities between the contractor, the ISA and the Sponsoring State.[149] It further deduces that "the main liability for a wrongful act committed in the conduct of the contractor's operations or in the exercise of the ISA's powers and functions rests with the contractor and the ISA, respectively, rather than with the sponsoring State", since "no reference is made in this provision to the liability of sponsoring States" and these liabilities are common to and not joint and several with the sponsoring State.[150] The ordinary posture of international law is first to look to a responsible private operator or contractor for compensation for harm caused that is not the result of a wrongful act attributable to the state.[151] This is also the case of the Deep Seabed Mining Regime. However, it does not mean that there is no liability for the sponsoring State. Liability for the sponsoring State is addressed in article 139(2) and Annex III, article 4(4). Article 139(2) of the LOSC reads:

> Without prejudice to the rules of international law and Annex III, article 22, damage caused by the failure of a State Party or international organization to carry out its responsibilities under this Part shall entail liability; States Parties or international organizations acting together shall bear joint and several liability. A State Party shall not however be liable for damage caused by any failure to comply with this Part by a person whom it has sponsored under article 153, paragraph 2(b), if the State Party has taken all necessary and appropriate measures to secure effective compliance under article 153, paragraph 4 and Annex III, article 4, paragraph 4.

While Annex III, article 4, paragraph 4 further provides:

> A sponsoring State shall not, however, be liable for damage caused by any failure of a contractor sponsored by it to comply with its obligations if that State Party has adopted laws and regulations and take administrative

149 SDC Advisory Opinion, paragraph 200.

150 ibid.

151 See Gunther Doeker and Thomas Gehring, 'Private or International Liability for Transnational Environmental Damage – The Precedent of Conventional Liability Regimes' (1990) 2 *Journal of Environmental Law* 1; ILC, Survey of liability regimes relevant to the topic of international liability for injurious consequences arising out of acts not prohibited by international law (international liability in case of loss from transboundary harm arising out of hazardous activities) – Prepared by the Secretariat (24 June 2004) U.N. Doc. A/CN.4/543, paragraphs 340–386.

> measures which are, within the framework of its legal system, reasonably appropriate for securing compliance by persons under its jurisdiction.

It can be concluded from the abovementioned provisions that the liability of the sponsoring State arises from its failure to meet its obligation to "ensure" compliance by the sponsored contractor and also relates to its sponsored contractor's behavior. However, not every violation of an obligation by a sponsored contractor automatically gives rise to the liability of the sponsoring State.[152] Where damages arise from the failure of a sponsored contractor to comply with its obligation, the sponsoring State is only liable if that failure relates to its own lack of due diligence.[153] The liability of the contractor and the sponsoring State are similar. As a consequence, the sponsoring State is not responsible for residual damages flowing from a contractor's wrongdoing, but rather only for damages that arise from its failure to exercise due diligence. If the contractor has already paid for the actual amount of damage, there is no need for a sponsoring State to compensate.[154] That is different from joint and several liability by which full compensation can be claimed from all or any of attributors.[155]

The abovementioned articles establish the main structure of the liability regime for activities in the Area. In addition, article 304 of the LOSC supplements the existing architecture by stating:

> The provisions of this Convention regarding responsibility and liability for damage are without prejudice to the application of existing rules and the development of further rules regarding responsibility and liability under international law.

On this point, the Seabed Disputes Chamber refers to rules under customary law, especially in light of the ARSIWA.[156] It further points out that it refers not

152 SDC Advisory Opinion, paragraph 109. See also Legal Working Group on Liability, *Legal Liability for Environmental Harm: Synthesis and Overview*, Liability Issues for Deep Seabed Mining Series, Paper No.1 (July 2018), 6.

153 LOSC, article 139(2).

154 SDC Advisory Opinion, paragraph 202.

155 See John E Noyes and Brian D Smith, 'State Responsibility and the Principle of Joint and Several Liability' (1988) 13 *Yale Journal of International Law* 225.

156 SDC Advisory Opinion, paragraph 169. Seabed Disputes Chamber states that several articles of ARSIWA are considered to reflect customary international law. It cited it not only in the SDC Advisory Opinion but also the former case. For instance, *The M/V "Saiga" (No. 2) (Saint Vincent and the Grenadines v. Guinea), Judgement, ITLOS Reports 1999*, p. 10, at 65, paragraphs 169–171. But some commentators criticized the ITLOS's direct utilization of ARSIWA. For instance, Louise de la Fayette, 'ITLOS and the Saga of the Saiga: Peaceful

only to "existing international law rules on responsibility and liability, but also to the development of further rules."[157] This article "opens the liability regimes for deep seabed mining to new developments in international law."[158]

### 5.2 *Conditions of Liability of the Sponsoring State under the LOSC*

As mentioned above, a sponsoring State's liability is a fault-based liability, rather than strict liability, and thus there is no residual liability of sponsoring States.[159] That being said, as the Seabed Disputes Chamber indicated, only when three requirements are met at the same time is the sponsoring State liable. They read: i) a sponsoring State, in an act or an omission, fails to carry out their responsibility, whatever primary obligations or direct obligations; ii) the damage occurs, including the damage to the Area, its resources or marine environment; and iii) a proven causal link exists between failure and damage.[160]

#### 5.2.1 Failure to Carry Out Its Obligations under the Convention

Article 139(2) indicates that the first requirement leading to sponsoring State's liability, that is, where the sponsoring State fails to carry out its obligations under the LOSC. These obligations include both due diligence obligations, discussed in section 4 of this chapter, and direct obligations presented in section 4.3.2. Under this requirement, the sponsoring State must take all necessary and appropriate measures to secure effective compliance of its sponsored contractor. According to the Seabed Disputes Chamber, "necessary and appropriate measures" could be further explained as "reasonably appropriate" "laws and regulations and … administrative measures". Specifically, a sponsoring State could make reference to section 4 of this chapter in theory and make reference to chapter 3 in practice if it is willing to carry out its "responsibility to ensure". It is worth noting that this book only attempts to analyze the formats and contents of "reasonably appropriate" "laws and regulations and … administrative measures" referred to by the LOSC and provides a toolbox for the sponsoring State which intends to carry out its "responsibility to ensure" and establish legislation and administrative measures to govern activities in the Area. Simply following the recommendations of this book does not provide incontestable evidence that a sponsoring State has carried out its "responsibility to ensure".

---

Settlement of a Law of the Sea Dispute' (2000) 15 *The International Journal of Marine and Coastal Law* 355, 388–391.

157 SDC Advisory Opinion, paragraph 211.

158 ibid.

159 SDC Advisory Opinion, paragraph 204.

160 SDC Advisory Opinion, paragraphs 172–184.

After all, due diligence is not a static concept. A sponsoring State which does not have any "laws and regulations and take administrative measures" for activities in the Area cannot be seen as carrying out its obligations under the LOSC since due diligence is an obligation "of conduct" as well.

#### 5.2.2 Occurrence of Damage

The second requirement leading to a sponsoring State's liability is the occurrence of damage. However, the LOSC does not specify what constitutes damage. The ISA Draft Exploitation Regulations (July 2018) indicate that it includes damage to the marine environment.[161] According to Sands, damage could be explained as "pure environmental damage" (damage to environment and its resources) and "consequential environmental damage" (consequential damage to people and property).[162] Although there is no specific wording, there is no doubt that damage is included to persons and property as a result of seabed mining activities, since the claim was related to persons and property damage resulting from changes to the environment.[163]

In the context of deep seabed mining, more attention needs to be paid to "pure environmental damage". Neither the LOSC nor ISA Exploration Regulations specify what constitutes environmental damage. Existing liability agreements have taken different approaches to what constitutes environmental damage.[164] A narrow definition of environmental damage is limited to damage to natural resources alone (air, water, soil, fauna and flora, and their interaction); a more extensive approach includes damage to the natural resources and property that form part of the cultural heritage; the most extensive definition includes landscape and environmental features.[165] The UNEP Working Group suggested that environmental damage could relate to 'impairment of the environment', which may be defined as: A change which has a measurable adverse impact on the quality of a particular environment of any of its components including its use and non-use values and its ability to support and sustain an acceptable quality of life and a viable ecological balance.[166]

161 Draft Regulations on Exploitation of Mineral Resources in the Area (n 115), Annex X, section 7.

162 Sands and others (n 146) 715.

163 ibid, 328.

164 For an introduction on this account, see Ruth Mackenzie, *Liability for Environmental Harm from Deep Seabed Mining Activities: Defining Environmental Damage*, Liability Issues for Deep Seabed Mining Series, Paper No.8 (February 2019), 2–11.

165 Sands and others (n 146) 706.

166 See UNEP, Training Manual on International Environmental Law (Division of Policy Development and Law, United Nations Environment Programme 2006), 52.

Regarding the potential categories of damage in the context of deep seabed mining, the Seabed Disputes Chamber observed that "[i]t may be envisaged that the damage in question would include damage to the Area and its resources constituting the common heritage of mankind, and damage to the marine environment."[167] The Seabed Disputes Chamber categorized the damage into "damage to the Area and its resources" and "damage to the environment". The ISA Draft Exploitation Regulations define the "[m]arine [e]nvironment" as including "the physical, chemical, geological and biological and genetic components, conditions and factors which interact and determine the productivity, state, condition and quality and connectivity of the marine ecosystem(s), the waters of the seas and oceans and the airspace above those waters, as well as the seabed and ocean floor and subsoil thereof."[168] The Seabed Disputes Chamber treated the "damage to the Area and its resources" as a single category, independent from "damage to the environment". Indeed, it may be difficult to separate them. The definition of the marine environment in the ISA Draft Exploitation Regulations states that "the Area and its mineral resources" constitute part of the "marine environment" of the Area.[169] In addition, the "marine environment" also comprises "genetic components", "marine ecosystem" and "waters", which are consistent with environmental impacts of deep seabed mining indicated in section 2.3 of the chapter 1. Mining activities might impact the seabed, the resources, the ecosystem, and also might impact the water column. It will not only impact the Area, but also areas under national jurisdiction. Capturing "various components and the complexity of the marine ecosystem" seems to present "significant challenges in terms of the assessment and possible restoration or reinstatement of components of the environment."[170]

In considering the above, Ruth Mackenzie identifies types of damage in the context of deep seabed mining in the Area as follows:

- damage to persons and property occurring as a result of seabed mining activities in the Area, including loss arising as a result of environmental damage caused by seabed mining activities;
- damage to the marine environment of the Area, including damage to living resources of the Area;
- damage to the Area and its resources constituting the CHM;

167 SDC Advisory Opinion, paragraph 179.

168 Draft Regulations on Exploitation of Mineral Resources in the Area (n 115), Schedule 1, Use of Terms and Scope.

169 Mackenzie (n 164) 15.

170 ibid, 14.

– damage to living resources in the water column above the Area (i.e., in the high seas); and
– damage to the marine environment and natural resources outside the Area (i.e., in areas under national jurisdiction).[171]

While this is an appropriate description of damage in accordance with the definition of the ISA Draft Exploitation Regulations, it is very broad. It must be carefully considered how it would relate to the rules applicable in those maritime zones, especially the consideration, in due course, of the relationship between the Deep Seabed Mining Regime and any new instrument that may be adopted in addressing marine biological diversity of the Area beyond national jurisdiction.[172]

#### 5.2.3 A Causal Link between Failure and Damage

The first two requirements are indicated by article 139(2) of the LOSC, whereas the Seabed Disputes Chamber comments there must be a causal link between the two requirements that result in the liability of the sponsoring State. In international law, the common situation is that the actions of private actors are not directly attributable to States unless the State empowers the private actor to act as a State organ[173] or the actions conducted by private actors are acknowledged by the State.[174] Therefore, if liability due to damage arises from the action of a private actor is attributable to a State, there must be evidence that there is a causal link between the failure and the damage. The lack of causal link between failure and damage frees the State from liability.

### 5.3 *Corollaries: Reparation or Exemption of Liability*

In the event that damage occurs, whether or not the State has carried out its "responsibility to ensure", there are two distinct results: reparation or exemption of liability.

#### 5.3.1 Reparation

A corollary of meeting the three requirements of liability for the sponsoring State may be reparation. As the famous dictum of the Permanent Court

171 ibid, 13–14.

172 ibid, 14. For instance, the ongoing Intergovernmental Conference on an international legally binding instrument under the United Nations Convention on the Law of the Sea on the conservation and sustainable use of marine biological diversity of areas beyond national jurisdiction (BBNJ) <https://www.un.org/bbnj/> accessed 24 June 2020.

173 ARSIWA, article 5.

174 ARSIWA, article 11.

of International Justice said, "it is a principle of international law, and even a general conception of law, that any breach of an engagement involves an obligation to make reparation".[175] Furthermore, providing for a full reparation is part of customary international law, which was first concluded in *Factory at Chorzów*.[176] The approaches of reparation are now reflected in the ARSIWA, which envisage that reparation for an injury caused by an internationally wrongful act shall take the form of restitution,[177] compensation,[178] and satisfaction, either singly or in combination.[179] Reparation for injuries arising from activities in the Area may make some reference from it.

#### 5.3.1.1 *Restitution*

With regard to restitution or *restitutio in integrum*, the precondition is to collect sufficient baseline data prior to the occurrence of damage, without which it will be difficult to protect or rehabilitate the ecological system. Baseline data collection could be the responsibility of either the sponsoring State or the contractor, or even as a joint effort. In practice, the contractor would be a valuable operator of data collection. Indeed, even if baseline data collection is tackled, there is still an insurmountable scientific problem. As stated in section 2.4 of chapter 1, the nature of impacts of deep seabed mining activities on the marine environment may render restoration or reinstatement of the environment unrealistic, although some opposing voices exist. In this sense, preventative measures and emergency plans are more efficient than restitution, as stated in section 2.4 of chapter 1, *avoidance* and *minimum* are efficient mitigating measures.

#### 5.3.1.2 *Compensation*

Whilst all pollution or human activity having adverse effects might give rise to environmental damage, it is unlikely that all environmental damage results in liability. There are no agreed upon international standards that establish a threshold for environmental damage that triggers liability and allows claims

---

175 *Factory at Chorzów, Merits, 1928, P.C.I.J., Series A, No. 17*, at 29.

176 ibid.

177 Restitution is aimed at re-establishing the situation that existed before the wrongful act was committed, provided and to the extent that it is not materially impossible and does 'not involve a burden out of all proportion to the benefit deriving from restitution instead of compensation'. ARSIWA, article 35.

178 ARSIWA, article 36. Compensation is to be provided for damage that is not made good by restitution and should cover 'any financially assessable damage including loss of profits insofar as it is established'.

179 ARSIWA, article 34.

to be brought.[180] What constitutes compensable damage should be the first important element which needs to be illuminated in this part, as Akiho Shibata observed, "the concept of damage sets the parameters for monetary compensation."[181] According to the existing liability regime in other areas, compensation for damage to the marine environment in the context of deep seabed mining not only includes damage to the marine environment, *per se,* but also includes the costs of restoration or reinstatement, offset and reasonable preventative measures or response measures.[182] The United Nations Compensation Commission (UNCC) also gives examples of costs of reasonable monitoring and assessment of the environmental damage, damage to public health, or medical screening,[183] which is also applicable to deep seabed mining.

The Seabed Disputes Chamber provided some clues regarding forms and amounts of compensation. It pointed out that the selection of the forms depends on "both the actual damage and the technical feasibility of restoring the situation to the *status quo ante*".[184] It is helpful to state at this point that damage could be divided into two categories: the damage that can be monetarily valued and calculated (e.g. damage to people and property, or damage to mineral resources or living resources such as fishes) and non-economic values associated with the environmental damage (or pure environmental damage or pure ecological loss).[185] For the former category, monetary compensation for losses incurred may be applicable. There is no explicit reference in the LOSC about the amount of compensation by sponsoring States. It only provides that, as far as the ISA and the contractor are concerned, "liability in every case shall be for the actual amount of damage."[186] The Seabed Disputes Chamber analogizes that "the provisions ..., are equally valid with regard to the liability of the

180 Sands and others (n 145) 708.

181 Akiho Shibata, 'A New Dimension in International Liability Regimes' in Akiho Shibata (eds), *International Liability Regime for Biodiversity Damage: The Nagoya-Kuala Lumpur Supplementary Protocol* (Routledge 2014), 36.

182 Mackenzie (n 164) 13.

183 UNCC, 'Decision taken by the Governing Council of the United Nations Compensation Commission during its third session, at 18th meeting, held on 28 November 1991, as revised at the 24th meeting held on 16 March 1992: Criteria for Additional Categories of Claims' (17 March 1992) S/AC.26/1991/7/Rev.1, paragraph 35.

184 SDC Advisory Opinion, paragraph 197.

185 Michael Bowman, 'Biodiversity, Intrinsic Value, and the Definition and Valuation of Environmental Harm' in Michael Bowman and Alan Boyle (eds), *Environmental Damage in International and Comparative Law: Problems of Definition and Valuation* (Oxford University Press 2002), 42.

186 LOSC, Annex III, article 22.

sponsoring State."[187] In most cases, it can be simply measured by looking at market prices, although there are some problem areas for valuation in the context of environmental damage assessment.[188] For instance, it may be possible to ascribe economic value to the loss of mineral resources on the basis of some form of commercial valuation.[189] Moreover, in the case of other high levels of transboundary damage, compensation of operators is usually limited to a fixed amount, with other economic measures, such as environmental bonds or insurance, for the guarantee or establishment of a compensation fund.[190]

In addition to economic loss, there is still pure environmental damage. The UNCC found that there was "no justification for the contention that general international law precludes compensation for pure environmental damage."[191] This idea was echoed and supported by the ILC in its Commentary to Draft Principle 2, although it admitted that "such damage is difficult to quantify."[192] The measurement of pure environmental damage may be done on the basis of an abstract quantification calculated in accordance with a theoretical model, or on the costs of measures of restoration, or on some other basis?[193] For the other liability regime, the damage that cannot be economically assessed or valued is compensated for by way of restoration or offset.[194] However, as presented in section 2.4 of chapter 1, it is unrealistic to restore and offset for

---

187 SDC Advisory Opinion, paragraph 195.

188 Those problem areas for valuation are the robustness of value estimates, the aggregation procedure, the transferability of estimates, ethical issues, and property right allocations, see Nick Hanley, 'The Economic Value of Environmental Damage' in Michael Bowman and Alan Boyle (eds), *Environmental Damage in International and Comparative Law: Problems of Definition and Valuation* (Oxford University Press 2002), 35–39.

189 Mackenzie (n 164) 15.

190 See Guifang (Julia) Xue, *The Use of Compensation Funds, Insurance and Other Financial Security in Environmental Liability Schemes*, Liability Issues for Deep Seabed Mining Series, Paper No.6 (February 2019).

191 UNCC, 'Report and Recommendations Made by the Panel of Commissioners concerning the Fifth Instalment of "F4" Claims' (30 June 2005) UN Doc S/AC.26/2005/10, paragraph 55.

192 ILC, *Principles on the Allocation of Loss in the Case of Transboundary Harm Arising Out of Hazardous Activities*, printed in 'Report of the International Law Commission on its Fifty-eight session' (1 May-9 June and 3 July-11 August 2006) UN Doc A/61/10 (2006), 101–182.

193 See Philippe Sands and Richard B Stewart, 'Valuation of Environmental Damage – US and International Law Approaches' (1996) 5 *Review of European Community and International Environmental Law* 290; Bowman and Boyle (n 188); Mark Wilde, *Civil Liability for Environmental Damage: A Comparative Analysis of Law and Policy in Europe and the United States* (Kluwer Law International 2002); Linda B Burlington, 'Valuing Natural Resource Damages: A Transatlantic Lesson' (2004) 6 *Environmental Law Review* 77.

194 Mackenzie (n 164) 14–15.

damage in the context of deep seabed mining. Hence, using a theoretical model seems to be a possible solution. Moreover, in the Ahmadou Sadio Diallo case, the ICJ observed that quantification of compensation for non-material injury rests on equitable considerations and awarded compensation on this basis.[195] Although this case did not involve environmental damage, it may still suggest possible solutions.

Given that the Area is the common heritage of mankind, in addition to monetary compensation, other ways of compensating for damage to the environment need to be developed where restoration and offset are deemed to be of no real value. In this regard, preventing and minimizing environmental damage should be of utmost significance, as they are effective ways to mitigate environmental damage.

#### 5.3.1.3 *Satisfaction*

Satisfaction is to be provided if the injury cannot be made good by restitution or compensation, for example by an acknowledgment of the breach, an expression of regret, or a formal apology.[196] It should be highlighted that satisfaction is not a standard form of reparation. It is required only in the situation where those two forms have not provided full reparation.[197]

Satisfaction is usually used for an injury that is symbolic in nature. It is usually used in the case of a breach of an obligation of the State, regardless of producing substantial consequences or damage. Compensation can typically be used to offset injuries that can be financially measured, whereas satisfaction is commonly used to make good for injuries that cannot be financially measured. As stated in the *Rainbow Warrior Arbitration*, "[satisfaction] relates particularly to the case of moral or legal damage done directly to the State".[198] Typical applications for satisfaction include: insults to the symbols of the State, such as the national flag, violations of sovereignty or territorial integrity, attacks on ships or aircraft, ill-treatment of or deliberate attacks on heads of State or Government or diplomatic or consular representatives or other protected persons, and violations of the premises of embassies or consulates or of the

---

195 *Ahmadou Sadio Diallo (Republic of Guinea v. Democratic Republic of the Congo), Compensation, Judgment, I.C.J. Reports 2012, p. 324*, at 334, paragraph 24.

196 ARSIWA, article 37(1) and (2).

197 ARSIWA, commentary to article 37, paragraph 1.

198 *Case concerning the difference between New Zealand and France concerning the interpretation or application of two agreements, concluded on 9 July 1986 between the two States and which related to the problems arising from the Rainbow Warrior Affair (Rainbow Warrior Arbitration), RIAA, 1990, vol. XX*, p. 215, at 272–273, paragraph 122.

residences of members of the mission.[199] In addition, satisfaction can be used in combination with other forms of reparation. For example, in the *Rainbow Warrior Arbitration* case, in addition to compensation, France was required to give a "formal and unqualified apology" to New Zealand for the sinking of Greenpeace's vessel in Auckland Harbor.[200]

Article 37(2) of the ARSIWA illustrates several modalities of satisfaction, such as an acknowledgement of the breach, and expression of regret, a formal apology. However, it does not exhaust all the possibilities. ARSIWA further indicates that "appropriate modality" also includes due inquiry into the causes of an accident resulting in harm or injury, a trust fund to manage compensation payments in the interests of the beneficiaries, disciplinary or penal action against the individuals whose conduct caused the internationally wrongful act, or the award of symbolic damages for non-pecuniary injury, assurances, or guarantees of non-repetition.[201] Furthermore, the most common modality of satisfaction is a declaration of the wrongfulness of the act by a competent court or tribunal. For example, in the *Corfu Channel* case, it said:

> to ensure respect for international law, of which it is the organ, the Court must declare that the action of the British Navy constituted a violation of Albanian sovereignty. This declaration is in accordance with the request made by Albania through her Counsel, and is in itself appropriate satisfaction.[202]

Furthermore, article 37(3) of the ARSIWA places limitations on satisfaction, which require both the proportionality of satisfaction to the injury and no humiliation to the responsible State.

In the context of the injury arising from activities in the Area, satisfaction may apply in the situation of damage not being compensable or in the event of a sponsoring State's failure to carry out its obligations but no damage occurs.[203]

### 5.3.2 Exemption of Liability

The LOSC also provides exemptions for the sponsoring State from liability. As the Seabed Disputes Chamber presents in the Advisory Opinion, sponsoring States' national legislations have two functions. First, they have the function

199 ARSIWA, commentary to article 37, paragraph 4.
200 *Rainbow Warrior Arbitration* (n 198), at 224, paragraph 12.
201 ARSIWA, commentary to article 37, paragraph 5.
202 *Corfu Channel case, Judgement of April 9th, 1949, I.C.J. Reports 1949, p. 4,* at 35.
203 See section 5.4 of this chapter.

of ensuring compliance by the contractor with its obligations. Second, they also have the function of exempting the sponsoring States from liability for damage caused by the contractor,[204] which is stipulated in article 139(2) of the LOSC, that a State "shall not however be liable for damage", if it has taken "all necessary and appropriate measures to secure effective compliance". This is an exemption clause for the sponsoring States. However, the relationship between the two functions, as such, was not elaborated upon since the Seabed Disputes Chamber did not clearly state the requirements for complying with due diligence obligations and obtaining the benefit of the exemption.[205]

Theoretically, if a sponsoring State makes a reasonable and appropriate gesture to regulate its sponsored contractor with due diligence as analyzed in section 4, it can be exempted from liability even though the damage happened as a result of its sponsored contractor's wrongful acts. Those two elements are interconnected. First, the sponsoring State shall carry out the responsibilities and obligations to ensure a sponsored contractor's compliance with its obligations, especially arising from the abovementioned international legal instruments with regard to deep seabed mining, by way of national legislation. Further, it is "inherent in the 'due diligence' obligation of the sponsoring State to ensure that the obligations of a sponsored contractor are made enforceable".[206] By so doing, the sponsoring State will not be liable although damage might arise from the contractor's mining activities. Thus, if a sponsoring State is willing to structure sound domestic legislation, those obligations must be identified and then integrated into the national legislation, with accompanying enforceable measures.

### 5.4 *Liability Gaps and Possible Solutions*

The LOSC rules out strict liability for sponsoring States. However, it does leave a "liability gap" in at least four instances: i) where a State takes all necessary and/or appropriate measures required by international law and the blameless actions of the contractor nevertheless cause environmental harm;[207] ii) where a State takes the requisite necessary and/or appropriate measures and the private operator is blameworthy, but insolvent or its assets are beyond the reach of the sponsoring State;[208] iii) where the sponsoring State has failed to take the required measures but there has been no damage;[209] and iv) where the

204 SDC Advisory Opinion, paragraph 217.
205 Henley (n 32) 387.
206 SDC Advisory Opinion, paragraph 239.
207 SDC Advisory Opinion, paragraph 178.
208 SDC Advisory Opinion, paragraph 203.
209 SDC Advisory Opinion, paragraph 178.

sponsoring State has failed to take the required measures but there is no causal link with the environmental harm.[210] Obviously, this listing of liability gaps is not exhaustive. New issues, including liability gaps, will emerge at the more complicated exploitation phase. In any case, these gaps can be divided into two general categories in terms of whether the sponsoring State has fulfilled its "responsibility to ensure". The first two instances may be seen in the context where a State carries out its "responsibility to ensure" and damage occurs but is not attributed to the State. The second two instances are in the event that a State fails to carry out its "responsibility to ensure" whether it leads to damage or not. Indeed, no matter which of the above situations occurs they cannot be attributed to the State, since they do not meet all three requirements of liability of the sponsoring State, as discussed in section 5.2 of this chapter. Situations in liability gap category one lack the first requirement (failure to carry out its obligation under the LOSC), whereas situations in liability gap category two lack either the second requirement (occurrence of damage) or the third requirement (a causal link between such failure and damage). The question in such cases is, since the sponsoring States do not bear residual liability, who should be liable for those gaps? The residual liability of States when an operator or contractor is unable to or shielded from providing compensation, however, has not yet become a regular feature of these liability conventions.[211] The following sections will discuss these two categories of liability gaps, respectively.

### 5.4.1 Liability Gaps Category One

In liability gaps category one, the State carries out its "responsibility to ensure" and thus it can exempt itself from liability under the LOSC as indicated in section 5.3.2 of this chapter. In this situation, damage occurs due to a contractor's blameworthy or blameless acts. In the event that the contractor is insolvent or otherwise unable to repay, both of these circumstances lead to the same result: the damage is unclaimed.

A solution proposed by the Seabed Disputes Chamber to deal with this circumstance is the establishment of a fund to compensate for the damages that contractors are unable to cover.[212] Utilizing a compensation fund to pay for the

210 SDC Advisory Opinion, paragraph 203.

211 A notable exception moving in this direction is article 15, Basel Protocol on Liability and Compensation for Damage Resulting from Transboundary Movements of Hazardous Wastes and Their Disposal, Decision V/29 and Annex III, Report of the Fifth Meeting of the Conference of the Parties to the Basel Convention, UN Doc UNEP/CHW.1/WG/1/9/2 (10 December 1999) (not in force).

212 SDC Advisory Opinion, paragraph 205.

loss not covered is not the creation of the ISA. Since the 20th century, as the number of transnational activities at sea has increased, the risk of environmental damage caused by these activities has also increased. In response to this situation, many compensation funds have been established, serving as remedial measures and even preventive measures to damage arising from those transnational activities. Currently, international compensation regimes exist in the fields of oil and bunker fuel pollution, hazardous and noxious substances pollution, nuclear damage, and environmental issues in the Antarctic.[213] The ongoing draft of ISA Exploitation Regulations adopted the idea suggested by the Seabed Disputes Chamber. In the latest version, the contents of the Environmental Compensation Fund (formerly Environmental Liability Trust Fund prior to 2019 version) are stipulated in part IV, section 5, draft regulations 54–56.[214] In fact, the LOSC provides a solid legal basis for the establishment of a compensation fund. For instance, article 235(3) of the LOSC makes a reference to a compensation fund as a means of ensuring "prompt and adequate compensation", which provides the legitimacy for the establishment of a compensation fund. The necessity of liability and compensation for the victims of pollution and other environmental damage was also stressed in Principle 22 of the Stockholm Declaration of the United Nations Conference on the Human Environment[215] and Principle 13 of the Rio Declaration on Environment and Development.[216]

The ISA Draft Exploitation takes the compensation fund into account and provides the main purposes of the trust fund in regulation 55. The primary objectives of the Fund will include:

(a) The implementation of any necessary measures designed to prevent, limit or remediate any damage to the Area arising from activities in

213 For introduction of existing compensation fund, see Xue (n 190), 2–11.

214 The provisions as to the Environmental Compensation Fund emerges at the first time in the version in January 2017, although it had already been taken into account by the ISA's initiate actions. Concerning initiate actions, see *Developing a Regulatory Framework for Mineral Exploitations in the Area* in 2015, <https://ran-s3.s3.amazonaws.com/isa.org.jm/s3fs-public/documents/EN/Survey/Report-2015.pdf> *This link is broken. accessed 20 February 2020. In the latest version, the contents of the Environmental Compensation Fund are stipulated on Part IV, section 5, draft regulations 54–56. Indeed, although stipulated in different draft regulations due to different versions, there is no material modification of the contents of the Environmental Compensation Fund from the initial version to the latest version.

215 Report of the United Nations Conference on the Human Environment, Stockholm, 5–16 June 1972, A/Conf.48/14/Corr. 1, 11 ILM 1416 (1972).

216 Rio Declaration on Environment and Development (n 100).

the Area, the costs of which cannot be recovered from a Contractor or sponsoring State, as the case may be;

(b) The promotion of research into methods of marine mining engineering and practice by which environmental damage or impairment resulting from exploitation activities in the Area may be reduced;

(c) Education and training programmes in relation to the protection of the marine environment;

(d) The funding of research into Best Available Techniques for the restoration and rehabilitation of the Area; and

(e) The restoration and rehabilitation of the Area when technically and economically feasible and supported by Best Available Scientific Evidence.[217]

How a compensation fund would be adequately financed is no doubt one of the most critical issues and also one of the most thorny. Draft regulation 56 stipulates the resources of the Environmental Compensation Fund as follows:

(a) the prescribed percentage of fees paid to the ISA;

(b) the prescribed percentage of penalties to the ISA;

(c) the prescribed percentage of amounts recovered by the ISA because of a violation of an exploitation contract;

(d) any monies paid into the Fund at the direction of the Council, based on recommendations of the Finance Committee; and

(e) any income received by the Fund from the investment of monies belonging to the fund.[218]

Despite the recognition of the need to establish a compensation fund, draft regulations 55 and 56 have caused much controversy.[219] According to stakeholders' responses submitted to the Secretariat by 19 November 2018, most comments focus on two main aspects: 1) the purpose of the fund; and 2) the

---

217 Draft Regulations on Exploitation of Mineral Resources in the Area (ISBA/25/C/WP.1, 25 March 2019), draft regulation 55.

218 Draft Regulations on Exploitation of Mineral Resources in the Area (n 217), draft regulation 56.

219 The Secretariat has received 42 submissions to the draft regulations, with 17 submissions relating to the Environmental Compensation Fund. The list of submission and contents of response, see website: <https://www.isa.org.jm/files/files/documents/comments_0.pdf> accessed 20 December 2020. The submissions mentioning the Environmental Compensation Fund include the African Group (regional groups), Australia, Belgium, Chile, China, Germany, Italy, Jamaica, Japan, Nauru, Singapore, Tonga, UK (member States), Deep Sea Conservation Coalition (E-NGO), Center for Polar and Deep Ocean Development, Deep Ocean Stewardship Initiative, EU ATLAS Horizon 2020 Project (Academic/Scientific).

operation of the fund. Skeptics of regulation 55 hold the view that this compensation fund should focus on addressing compensation for liability gaps consistent with the opinion of the Seabed Disputes Chamber, whereas the current overbroad purposes may dilute the core objective of the fund and may not provide sufficient funding in the case of environmental damage.[220]

With regard to draft regulation 56, those funding resources can be divided into three categories. First, extracting monies from a certain percentage of expected income of the ISA, such as fees, penalties, or liquidated damages, will be the basis of the Environmental Compensation Fund. Second is that monies are paid into the Fund at the direction of the Council. Incomes earned from the investment of monies belonging to the fund will be the third category of funding sources. Two observations may be made. First, no additional contributions are expected in this design, whether voluntary or compulsory. Second, although there is no extra contribution, the majority of the funding will be, *de facto,* from contractors, since fees, penalties, or liquidated damages are all generated by contractors. It has been suggested that compulsory contributions should be made to the Environmental Compensation Fund to ensure stability and predictability. However, it was felt that it would not be fair for only contractors to be required to pay compulsory contributions although they are the principal contributors to the risk of deep seabed mining activities. The duty to contribute should be related to the degree of risk attached to mining activities.[221] However, it is not easy to identify *ex ante* the kind of activities that contribute to the loss, and the only alternative then is for the government to pay for it either directly or by financing a compensation fund.[222] Therefore, sponsoring States should make contributions to this compensation fund. Furthermore, sponsoring States could be contributing to the risks as well due to their failures to carry out their responsibilities to ensure that sponsored contractors comply with environmental obligations, which is also one of the justifications for sponsoring States to be contributors.

Although the necessity and importance of the existence of the Environmental Compensation Fund are unquestionable, there are still many

---

220 See eg China's response to the ISA Draft Exploitation Regulations (July 2018), submitted on 28 September 2018, <https://www.isa.org.jm/files/documents/EN/Regs/2018/Comments/China.pdf> accessed 20 February 2020; DOSI's response to the ISA Draft Exploitation Regulations (July 2018), submitted on 30 September 2018, <https://www.isa.org.jm/files/documents/EN/Regs/2018/Comments/DOSI.pdf> accessed 20 February 2020.

221 MG Faure and T Hartlief, 'Compensation Funds versus Liability and Insurance for Remedying Environmental Damage' (1996) 5 *Review of European Community & International Environmental Law* 321, 324.

222 ibid.

practical difficulties in the actual establishment process. The significant challenges facing the existing compensation funds include unwillingness of compulsory contributors to make contributions, the lack of universal adherence of States to the idea of creating such collective compensation arrangements, difficulties in assessing reasonable costs of mitigation, restoration, and reinstatement of environmental damage.[223] Those difficulties may arise with the operation of Environmental Compensation Fund as well, in which sources of contributions might be on the top of the list.

### 5.4.2 Liability Gaps Category Two

Liability gaps category two refers to situations in which a State fails to carry out its "responsibility to ensure". Consequently, a damage occurs, but no causal link is established between the act and result; or there is no damage at all. This section will, from two mutually independent perspectives, analyze a State's failure to carry out its "responsibility to ensure" and measures to deal with damages. The reason why there are two independent perspectives is, under the second category, regardless of whether or not there is damage, it cannot be attributed to the State. Hence, the measures of dealing with damage is a separate issue.

This category of liability gaps is solved by the Seabed Disputes Chamber in the "without prejudice" clause of the SDC Advisory Opinion, which describes the relationship between the LOSC and international law by stating that, "a gap in liability which might occur in such a situation cannot be closed by having recourse to liability of the sponsoring State under customary international law."[224] As the LOSC stipulates, provisions of the LOSC regarding responsibility and liability for damage are without prejudice to the application of those in existing rules and the development of further rules.[225] This means that under customary international law, a sponsoring State may be liable if it breaches its obligation where no damage has been caused.[226] It seems to follow that even if a sponsoring State is not liable under the Deep Seabed Mining Regime of the LOSC, it may still be liable at the customary law level.[227]

223 Ilias Bantekas, 'Trust Funds' in *Max Planck Encyclopedia of Public International Law* (2010).

224 SDC Advisory Opinion, paragraph 209.

225 LOSC, articles 139(2) and 304.

226 Robin Churchill, 'Dispute Settlement in the Law of the Sea: Survey for 2011' (2012) 27 *International Journal of Marine and Coastal Law* 517, 533.

227 Tanaka (n 48) 220.

Indeed, although occurrence of damage is a necessary requirement of attribution to the sponsoring State under the LOSC, damage is not a necessity for attribution of liability to a State under customary international law. A State may be held liable under customary international law even if no material damage results from its failure to meet its international obligations, which was explicitly presented in the *Rainbow Warrior Arbitration*[228] and ARSIWA. In the situation of no special treaty regime or lacking specific provisions in relevant treaty, ARSIWA can be cited, as they are default rules.[229] Pursuant to ARSIWA, damage is not a prerequisite for a State's wrongful act which will invoke liability of that State. The only two elements that constitute a wrongful act on the part of a State are breach of obligations and attribution.[230] In this category of liability gaps, as long as the sponsoring State fails to carry out "responsibility to ensure", it will undoubtedly entail liability.

The question, then, is, what is the State liable for if there is no damage? As Niel Craik notes, "While it is clear that international law will hold a state liable for damages that arise out of activities undertaken without due diligence, it is less clear what the consequences are for failing to exercise due diligence in the absence of environmental damage."[231] He further pointed out:

> [t]he better view is that due diligence give rise to a separate duty on states to take measures to prevent harm. Failure to take such measures does not render the proposed activity unlawful *per se*, but the affected state has the right to insist that the State of origin comply with its due diligence obligations.[232]

In the context of deep seabed mining, the absence of national legislation regulating the sponsored contractor's behavior in the Area means potential environmental harm to the Area. In this situation, States Parties should have a right to request the sponsoring State to have national legislation for activities in the Area in place before the mining activities conducted by the sponsored contractor commence.

---

228 *Rainbow Warrior Arbitration* (n 198), at 267, paragraph 110.

229 Anne Van Aaken, 'Shared Responsibility in International Law: A Political Economy Analysis', in André Nollkaemper and Dov Jacobs (eds), *Distribution of Responsibilities in International Law* (Cambridge University Press 2015), 158.

230 ARSIWA, articles 1 and 2.

231 Craik (n 117) 66.

232 ibid.

## 6 Conclusion

The Area and its resources are the common heritage of mankind, which is not only a statement of common ownership of resources by all states on a non-discriminatory basis, but it also includes obligations distributed to all states. Hence, under the notion of "common heritage", "responsibility to ensure" is an international obligation a sponsoring State shall abide by. Carrying out that obligation is a reflection of the *Pacta Sunt Servanda* Principle for a sponsoring State. Moreover, abiding by that obligation also has the function of exempting the sponsoring State from liability deriving from damage caused by its sponsored contractors. The aforementioned reasons lay a legal foundation for a sponsoring State to carry out its primary obligation.

The "responsibility to ensure" concludes that the sponsoring State must ensure that the "activities in the Area" conducted by its sponsored contractor comply with the rules to which they refer. The SDC Advisory Opinion indicates "it is an obligation to deploy adequate means, to exercise best possible efforts, to do the utmost, to obtain this result." Hence, "responsibility to ensure" is an obligation of conduct and of "due diligence". In the context of deep seabed mining, proof of a sponsoring State carrying out its obligation of conduct is that it adopts a certain type of legislation within its domestic legal system. When undertaking this particular action, specific types of measures, such as legislative models and hierarchy is under the discretion of the sponsoring State. A sponsoring State shall "reasonably appropriate" such legislation. The standard of care is "due diligence". Due diligence is a variable concept with the differences of technology development, mining stage, and mining category. When implementing the due diligence obligation to ensure, a sponsoring State can make reference to direct obligations concluded by the Seabed Disputes Chamber, including implementing a precautionary approach, applying best environmental practices, conduct EIAS, provide guarantees in the event of an emergency order by the Authority for protection of the marine environment, and ensure the availability of adequate reparation. In addition, some guiding principles must be borne in mind by the national legislators that will instruct the formation and development of national legislation. Those principles include, but are not limited to, good faith, a minimum standard of stringency, as well as review.

A sponsoring State is one of the actors which may entail liability in the Deep Seabed Mining Regime. The LOSC rules out the strict liability of the sponsoring State as indicated by the Seabed Disputes Chamber. Hence, only when three requirements are met at the same time is the sponsoring State liable: i)

A sponsoring State, in an act or an omission, fails to carry out its responsibility, whatever primary obligations or direct obligations; ii) The damage occurs, including the damage to the Area, its resources or marine environment; and iii) A proven causal link between failure and damage. When the three requirements are met at the same time, a sponsoring State has to make reparation in the event that its sponsored contractors are unable to make reparation for the damage. Liabilities of the sponsoring State and contractor are parallel. But, if a sponsoring State has carried out its "responsibility to ensure" and direct obligations, it can be exempted from liability, regardless of any damage that may occur. Moreover, the large-scale cumulative effects (global warming, ocean acidification, and fisheries) may occur and other ocean users (shipping and fisheries, etc.) may exist, which may jointly lead to the final environmental results.[233] Those circumstances need to be considered when channeling begins. Even if state liability is in some manner limited for damages caused by a sponsored entity as a result of its breaches of Part XI of the Convention, a State's broader responsibility will remain. That being said, the sponsoring State still needs to carry out its responsibility under general international law, in addition to that under the LOSC. As the Seabed Disputes Chamber pointed out, those rules in international law supplement the rules regarding sponsoring States' liabilities articulated in the LOSC.[234] Despite any limits that exist under these provisions, States have comprehensive and detailed obligations established by a large number of treaties and customary international law to protect and preserve the marine environment in a host of different ways.[235] It is important to recognize that the issues raised represent only a narrow aspect of the broader responsibility of this part of the country. A breach of these wide-ranging obligations caused by deep seabed mining that is attributable to

233 ISA, Environmental Assessment and Management for Exploitation of Minerals in the Area: Report of an international Workshop convened by the Griffith University Law School in collaboration with the International Seabed Authority in Queensland, Australia, 23–26 May 2016 (ISA Technical Study: No. 16) (ISA 2017), 17.

234 SDC Advisory Opinion, paragraph 171.

235 Some of these obligations beyond the Convention, such as prescribing measures relating to exchange of information, monitoring risk, and pollution prevention based on the requirements "co-operation" and "prudence and caution" are confirmed by ITLOS's jurisprudence in *MOX Plant (Ireland v. United Kingdom), Provisional Measures, Order of 3 December 2001, ITLOS Reports 2001*, p. 95; also in *Land Reclamation in and around the Straits of Johor (Malaysia v. Singapore), Provisional Measures, Order of 8 October 2003, ITLOS Reports 2003*, p. 10. See Alan Boyle, 'The Environmental Jurisprudence of the International Tribunal for the Law of the Sea' (2007) 22 *The International Journal of Marine and Coastal Law* 369.

the State is a wrongful act for which a State is responsible under international law and for which the State must make reparations.

This chapter thoroughly examined the legal genesis of "responsibility to ensure", the meaning of "responsibility to ensure" and the consequences of a failure to carry out that obligation. The next chapter will discuss the substantial question of how a sponsoring State reflects the "responsibility to ensure" within its domestic legal system.

CHAPTER 3

# Key Elements of "Reasonably Appropriate" Sponsoring States' Environmental Legislation for Deep Seabed Mining in the Area

## 1 Introduction

As argued in earlier chapters, contractors who assume numerous obligations in mining activities cannot be subject to international law, thus whether, or how, sponsoring States carry out their responsibility to ensure their sponsored contractors' compliance, namely, how they display those obligations with "necessary and appropriate measures" within their domestic legal system, is of importance to protect the marine environment from adverse consequences in the process of exploration and exploitation of mineral resources in the Area.

The ISA is concerned about the development of its member States' national legislation in relation to exploration and exploitation of mineral resources in the Area. Thus, the Council, in 2011, invited sponsoring States and other members of the ISA to provide information on relevant national laws, regulations, and administrative measures to the Secretariat of the ISA.[1] Based on the information provided by States, the Secretariat established an online database that is updated as new information is received.[2] As at 20 May 2020, the following 33 States had provided information on or the texts of relevant national legislation: Belgium, Brazil, China, Cook Islands, Cuba, Czech Republic, Dominican Republic, Fiji, France, Georgia, Germany, Guyana, India, Japan, Kiribati, Micronesia (Federated States of), Mexico, Montenegro, Nauru, Netherlands, New Zealand, Nigeria, Niue, Oman, Republic of Korea, Russian Federation, Singapore, Sudan, Tonga, Tuvalu, the United Kingdom, the United States, and Zambia. Submissions had also been received from the Pacific Community.[3]

1 Decision of the Council of the International Seabed Authority (ISBA/17/C/20, 21 July 2011), paragraph 3.

2 Database on National Legislation with Respect to Activities in the Area, available at: <https://www.isa.org.jm/national-legislation-database> accessed 5 August 2020.

3 Laws, regulations and administrative measures adopted by sponsoring States and other members of the International Seabed Authority with respect to the activities in the Area, and related matters, including a comparative study of existing national legislation (ISBA/26/C/19, 22 May 2020), paragraph 5.

 | DOI:10.1163/9789004472341_005

The information in the database does not show Georgia and Guyana having national legislation for activities in the Area. Cuba, India, Mexico, Montenegro, Nigeria, Niue, Omen, Sudan, and Zambia, although submitting the national legislation relating to terrestrial mining, marine time zone, and/or marine environmental protection, do not have national legislation directly relating to activities in the Area. Brazil, Cook Islands, Cuba, Dominic Republic, Netherlands, Republic of Korea, and the Russian Federation are in the process of reviewing, amending, or adopting their national legislation in relation to the activities in the Area.[4]

Those States which have national legislation relating to activities in the Area can be divided into three groups according to "the timing of their promulgation and against some benchmark events".[5] The first group comprises those States which adopted national legislation for activities in the Area under the Reciprocating States Regime, including the United States, Germany, the United Kingdom, France, Japan, and Italy;[6] the second group comprises those States which adopted national legislation for activities in the Area after the entry into force of the Convention and before the adoption of the SDC Advisory Opinion, and include Russia, Germany, New Zealand, and the Czech Republic; the third group comprises States which adopted national legislation for activities in the Area after the adoption of the SDC Advisory Opinion, and include Belgium, Fiji, United Kingdom, Tonga, Tuvalu, China, Kiribati, and France (see Table 1).[7] It is important to note that since the Reciprocating States Regime is a product of a special historical period, with the entry into force of the Convention, reciprocating States, such as Germany, Belgium, France, and the United Kingdom, began to amend or adopt new legislation to adapt to the Convention. Also, after another benchmark – the SDC Advisory Opinion – some States amended their legislation, adapting to the instructions and requirements of the SDC Advisory Opinion, such as Russia.

In 2017, the Assembly invited the sponsoring States to review their respective national legislation to control activities by their sponsored contractor,

4 Comparative Study of the Existing National Legislation on Deep Seabed Mining (Unedited Advanced Text) <https://isa.org.jm/files/files/documents/compstudy-nld.pdf> accessed 5 August 2020, paragraph 11.

5 ibid, paragraph 12.

6 With regard to the Reciprocating States Regime, see section 3.1.2 of chapter 1.

7 Comparative Study of the Existing National Legislation on Deep Seabed Mining (n 4), paragraphs 13–15.

TABLE 1 National legislation relating to activities in the area

| Group | State | Legislation |
|---|---|---|
| Reciprocating States Regime (1980s) | Germany | Act of Interim Regulation of Deep Seabed Mining 1980; amended 1982 |
| | United Kingdom | Deep Seabed Mining (Temporary Provisions) Act 1981 |
| | France | Law on the Exploration and Exploitation of the Mineral Resources of the Deep Seabed 1981 |
| | Japan | Law on Interim Measures for Deep Sea-Bed Mining 1982 ("Japan Law") |
| | Italy | Regulations on the Exploration and Exploitation of the Mineral Resources of the Deep Sea-bed 1985 |
| After Entry into Force of the Convention (1994–2011) | Russian Federation | Russian Federation Decree of the President No. 2099 of 22 November 1994 on the activities of Russian physical and legal entities related to the exploration and development of the mineral resources of the seabed outside the continental shelf ("Russian Federation Decree of the President") and<br>Government Decree No. 410 of 25 April 1995 on the procedure of activities of Russian physical and legal entities related to the development of mineral resources of the seabed outside the continental shelf ("Russian Federation Government Decree") |
| | Germany | Germany Seabed Mining Act of 6 June 1995, amended by article 74 of the Act of 8 December 2010 ("Germany Act") |
| | New Zealand | New Zealand United Nations Convention on the Law of the Sea Act 1996 ("New Zealand Act") |
| | Czech Republic | Czech Republic Act No. 158/2000 of 18 May 2000 on Prospecting, Exploration for and exploitation of Mineral Resources from the Seabed beyond the limits of National Jurisdiction ("Czech Republic Act") |

TABLE 1 National legislation relating to activities in the area (*cont.*)

| Group | State | Legislation |
|---|---|---|
| Post Advisory Opinion Period (2011-) | Belgium | Belgium Act on prospecting and exploration for and exploitation of, resources of the seabed and ocean floor and subsoil thereof, beyond the limits of national jurisdiction, adopted on 17 August 2013 ("Belgium Act") |
| | Fiji | Fiji International Seabed Mineral Management Decree 2013 ("Fiji Decree") |
| | United Kingdom | United Kingdom Deep Sea Mining (Temporary Provision) Act 1981, as amended by the Deep Seabed Mining Act 2014, which entered into force on 14 July 2014 ("the United Kingdom Act") |
| | Tonga | Tonga Seabed Minerals Act 2014 ("Tonga Act") |
| | Tuvalu | Tuvalu Seabed Minerals Act 2014 ("Tuvalu Act") |
| | Federated States of Micronesia | Seabed Resources Act of 2014 ("Micronesia Act") |
| | Singapore | Singapore Deep Seabed Mining Act 2015 ("Singapore Act") |
| | Nauru | Nauru International Seabed Minerals Act 2015 ("Nauru Act") |
| | China | Deep Seabed Area Resource Exploration and Exploitation Law of the People's Republic of China (adopted 26 February 2016) ("China's Deep Seabed Law") |
| | Kiribati | Kiribati Seabed Mineral Act 2017 ("Kiribati Act") |
| | France | France Ordinance No. 2016–1687 of 8 December 2016 relating to the maritime areas under the sovereignty or jurisdiction of the Republic of France ("France Ordinance") |

SOURCE: THE INFORMATION IS FROM THE NATIONAL LEGISLATION DATABASE, AVAILABLE AT: HTTPS://WWW.ISA.ORG.JM/NATIONAL-LEGISLATION-DATABASE. SEE ALSO COMPARATIVE STUDY OF THE EXISTING NATIONAL LEGISLATION ON DEEP SEABED MINING, AVAILABLE AT: HTTPS://WWW.ISA.ORG.JM/FILES/FILES/DOCUMENTS/COMPSTUDY-NLD.PDF. THE UNION OF SOVIET SOCIALIST REPUBLICS AND UNITED STATES HAVE NATIONAL LEGISLATION ON MINING ACTIVITIES BEYOND NATIONAL JURISDICTION DURING THE PERIOD OF THE RECIPROCATING STATES REGIME. FOR THE PURPOSE OF THE CHAPTER, THEY ARE NOT INCLUDED IN THIS FORM.

drawing on the SDC Advisory Opinion.[8] The Assembly also requested the Secretary-General to provide the Council with a comparative study of the existing national legislation with a view to derive common elements therefrom.[9] It is titled *Comparative Study of the Existing National Legislation on Deep Seabed Mining* (ISA Comparative Study, completed and released in 2019).[10] These efforts indicate that sponsoring States' national legislation is recognized for its important role in addressing environmental problems caused by activities in the Area. However, although sponsoring States' national legislation is imperative and necessary to preserve and protect the marine environment and pending seabed mining activities, no standards or guidelines as to the instruction and evaluation of the sponsoring State's national legislation exist.

As at 31 December 2019, the ISA's 30 exploration contracts comprised 21 ISA contractors (including seven contractors who hold more than one contract each).[11] They are sponsored by 20 different sponsoring States, including one contract (held by Interoceanmetal Joint Organization, known as "IOM") sponsored by a consortium of six States, and nine sponsoring States who hold more than one sponsorship: China has sponsored five contracts; Russia has sponsored four contracts; Korea has sponsored two contracts and one pending contract; Japan, France, India, Germany, and the United Kingdom have each sponsored two contracts; Poland has sponsored one contract as part of the IOM consortium and one other pending contract; Belgium, Tonga, Nauru, Singapore, Kiribati, the Cook Islands, and Brazil have each sponsored one contract; Bulgaria, the Czech Republic, Cuba, Slovakia [and Poland] have each sponsored the IOM consortium contract.[12]

8 Decision of the Assembly relating to the final report on the first periodic review of the international regime of the Area pursuant to article 154 of the United Nations Convention on the Law of the Sea (ISBA/23/A/13, 18 August 2017), section B.

9 Decision of the Assembly relating to the final report on the first periodic review of the international regime of the Area pursuant to article 154 of the United Nations Convention on the Law of the Sea (n 8), section E, paragraph 3.

10 Comparative Study of the Existing National Legislation on Deep Seabed Mining (n 4).

11 Contractors who hold more than one contract are the Russian Government (Polymetallic Sulphides, Cobalt-rich Crusts); the Korean Government (Polymetallic Nodules, Polymetallic Sulphides, Cobalt-rich Crusts); COMRA, sponsored by China (Polymetallic Nodules, Polymetallic Sulphides, Cobalt-rich Crusts); Ifremer, sponsored by France (Polymetallic Nodules, Polymetallic Sulphides); the Indian Government (Polymetallic Nodules, Polymetallic Sulphides); BGR sponsored by Germany (Polymetallic Nodules, Polymetallic Sulphides); and UKSRL (two for Polymetallic Nodules). See Status of contracts for exploration and related matters, including information on the periodic review of the implementation of approved plans of work for exploration (ISBA/26/C/4, 17 December 2019).

12 ibid.

The current status among the 20 sponsoring States in relation to national legislation is as follows. Twelve States have relevant national legislation on activities in the Area. Among the eight sponsoring States who do not have relevant national legislation, the situation is that the governments of Korea and India are contractors, rather than an entity that needs sponsorship, and thus whether there is need for a relevant national legislation is a "moot point".[13] There are still six sponsoring States which do not have national legislation on activities in the Area (see Table 2).[14] It is a fact that a considerable number of States would like to follow the principle of incorporating elements of international treaties or customary international law into their national legislation. However, those instruments do not provide precise guidance for their application on the national plane.[15] The lack of guidance, to some extent, results in varying quality and slow progress of sponsoring State's national legislation for exploration and exploitation of mineral resources in the Area.

The ISA Comparative Study does not describe in what ways and to what extent domestic legislation can play a role. The author of this book is of the view that there is a minimal line and an optimal line for sponsoring State's national legislation. Attaining the minimal line requires a sponsoring State to abide by the basic requirements of the LOSC and SDC Advisory Opinion, whereas reaching the optimal line means the sponsoring State tries its best to establish more stringent standards than the requirements of the LOSC according to its capabilities. The legal base is article 21, Annex III of the LOSC, indicating that the sponsoring State can adopt more stringent regulations than the ISA.

In keeping with the nature of sponsored contractors, sponsoring States provide sponsorship for three main categories of contractors: state-owned enterprises (such as COMRA sponsored by China), domestic private enterprises (such as GRS sponsored by Belgium) and enterprises composed of foreign investment (such as NORI sponsored by Nauru). The different characteristics of contractors impact the national legislation of sponsoring States. For instance, legislation of small island developing States (such as Kiribati, Nauru, Tonga, and Tuvalu), which have a lot of similarities, focus on attracting and

---

13 Hannah Lily, *Sponsoring State Approaches to Liability Regimes for Environmental Damage Caused by Seabed Mining*, Liability Issues for Deep Seabed Mining Series, Paper No.3 (December 2018), 5.

14 ibid.

15 Ian Brownlie, *Principles of Public International Law* (7th edn, Oxford University Press 2008), 47–49.

TABLE 2 Sponsoring states and status of their national legislation

| State | Contractor | Location | Resource | Start date | National legislation? |
|---|---|---|---|---|---|
| Poland | IOM | CCZ | Nodules | 2001 | No |
| | Government | Mid-Atlantic | SMS | 2018 | |
| Russia | IOM | CCZ | Nodules | 2001 | Yes[a] |
| | Yuzhmorgeologiya | CCZ | Nodules | 2001 | |
| | Government | Mid-Atlantic | SMS | 2012 | |
| | Government | Pacific Ocean | Crusts | 2015 | |
| Bulgaria | IOM | CCZ | Nodules | 2001 | No |
| Cuba | IOM | CCZ | Nodules | 2001 | No |
| Czech Republic | IOM | CCZ | Nodules | 2001 | Yes |
| Slovakia | IOM | CCZ | Nodules | 2001 | No |
| Korea | Government | CCZ | Nodules | 2001 | No |
| | Government | Central Indian | SMS | 2014 | |
| | Government | Pacific | Crusts | 2018 | |
| China | COMRA | CCZ | Nodules | 2001 | Yes |
| | COMRA | SW Indian | SMS | 2011 | |
| | COMRA | W Pacific | Crusts | 2014 | |
| | CMC | CCZ | Nodules | 2017 | |
| | Hi-Tech | W Pacific | Nodules | 2019 | |
| Japan | DORD | CCZ | Nodules | 2001 | Yes |
| | JOGMEC | W Pacific | Crusts | 2014 | |
| France | Ifremer | CCZ | Nodules | 2001 | Yes |
| | Ifremer | Mid-Atlantic | SMS | 2014 | |
| India | Government | Central Indian | Nodules | 2002 | No |
| | Government | Central Indian | SMS | 2016 | |
| Germany | BGR | CCZ | Nodules | 2006 | Yes |
| | BGR | Indian | SMS | 2015 | |
| Nauru | NORI | CCZ | Nodules | 2011 | Yes |
| Tonga | TOML | CCZ | Nodules | 2012 | Yes |
| Belgium | GSR | CCZ | Nodules | 2013 | Yes |
| United Kingdom | UKSRL | CCZ | Nodules | 2013 | Yes |
| | UKSRL | CCZ | Nodules | 2016 | |
| Kiribati | MREL | CCZ | Nodules | 2015 | Yes |
| Singapore | OMS | CCZ | Nodules | 2015 | Yes |
| Brazil | CPRM | S Atlantic | Crusts | 2015 | No |

TABLE 2 Sponsoring states and status of their national legislation (*cont.*)

| State | Contractor | Location | Resource | Start date | National legislation? |
|---|---|---|---|---|---|
| Cook Islands | CIIC | CCZ | Nodules | 2016 | No |

SOURCE: HANNAH LILY, SPONSORING STATE APPROACHES TO LIABILITY REGIMES FOR ENVIRONMENTAL DAMAGE CAUSED BY SEABED MINING, LIABILITY ISSUES FOR DEEP SEABED MINING SERIES, PAPER NO.3 (DECEMBER 2018), 4. INFORMATION IS UPDATED BASED ON STATUS OF CONTRACTS FOR EXPLORATION AND RELATED MATTERS, INCLUDING INFORMATION ON THE PERIODIC REVIEW OF THE IMPLEMENTATION OF APPROVED PLANS OF WORK FOR EXPLORATION (ISBA/26/C/4, 17 DECEMBER 2019)

[a] Russian Note Verbale, available at: <https://www.isa.org.jm/files/documents/EN/NatLeg/Russia/rus.pdf> accessed 25 December 2020.

ensuring robust foreign investment.[16] In addition, those States which belong to the common law system or the civil law system will also generate differences in national legislation. It is, therefore, unrealistic to provide a one-for-all template.

Consequently, the aim of this chapter is not to provide a uniform template for sponsoring States' national legislation for activities in the Area. Rather, it has the modest objective of presenting the possible, but not exhaustive, elements of sponsoring States' environmental legislation in relation to the exploration and exploitation of mineral resources in the Area and in doing so to explore a model of "reasonably appropriate" measures to fulfill the sponsoring State's primary obligation of "responsibility to ensure". This chapter also attempts to present how and to what extent a sponsoring State could play a role in application, oversight, and liability. Chapter 2 attempted to explain the theory behind the "responsibility to ensure" concept, whereas chapter 3 explores the "responsibility to ensure" in practice. The overall objective of this chapter is to provide a toolbox, from which a sponsoring State could tailor a "reasonably appropriate" national legislation and fulfil its "responsibility to ensure". To this end, this chapter will, mainly, examine the national legislations of Belgium, the

16 The similarities of national legislation of the small islands developing States also result from the utilization of same template. See SPC, *Pacific-ACP States Regional Legislative and Regulatory Framework for Deep Sea Minerals Exploration and Exploitation* (*RLRF*), Prepared under the SPC-EU EDF 10 Deep Sea Minerals Project (1st edn, July 2012) <https://pacific-data.sprep.org/system/files/PR111.pdf> accessed 8 August 2020, Annex 2.

Czech Republic, Fiji, Germany, Japan, Kiribati, Nauru, New Zealand, Singapore, Tonga, Tuvalu, and the United Kingdom. Russia and France are not included in this list because Russia's specific law is currently being drafted, and France's legislation contains only one provision. Nevertheless, they will be mentioned if necessary. China's national legislation will be systematically introduced and examined in chapter 4 and thus not considered in this chapter unless absolutely required.

## 2 Preliminary Issues

Before discussing substantive elements of sponsoring States' national legislation with regard to deep seabed mining in the Area, it will be instructive to examine several preliminary issues in advance, such as objectives and legislative models.

### 2.1 *Objectives*

The objective of the legislation is the primary content of statutory law. It not only sets the tone of the law but also decides the content of the law. The objective of the legislation is closely related to the definition, the scope of application, obligations, and liabilities of the legislation. All these elements, collectively, construct a law. The national legislation of all 12 States Parties incorporates the objective, albeit with distinct expressions and contents.[17] For the purpose of meeting the sponsoring State's "responsibility to ensure", three aspects are suggested for inclusion in the objectives of the legislation.

i) The legislation is suggested to expressly indicate the objective of implementation of international obligations of contractors in the LOSC, the 1994 Implementing Agreement, the procedures, rules, and regulations of the ISA in relation to activities in the Area, and the contract. For example, one of the purposes of the Germany Act is "to ensure compliance with the obligations of the Federal Republic of Germany deriving from Part XI of the Convention, its Annex III, the Implementing Agreement and the rules and regulations issued by the Authority".[18]

ii) It is suggested that the legislation describes the objective of regulating the sponsored contractors' activities in the Area. For instance, the wording might

17 On this account, see Comparative Study of the Existing National Legislation on Deep Seabed Mining (n 4), paragraph 23.

18 Germany Act, section 1(1)(1).

be "to regulate the exploration for and exploitation of resources in the Area by persons sponsored by Singapore under the Convention and the Agreement".[19]

iii) It is suggested that the legislation articulates the objective of the protection of marine environment. For instance, the Singapore Act provides that the purpose of this Act is "to ensure the effective protection of the marine environment against any harmful effects of those activities"[20]; the Germany Act indicates that the purpose of the Act is "to take precautions against hazards deriving from prospecting and activities in the Area for life, health or the assets of third parties".[21]

Those three objectives reflect the sponsoring State's willingness to play a role in "assisting the ISA" and attempts to ensure its sponsored contractors' compliance with the LOSC, the procedures, rules, and regulations of the ISA in relation to activities in the Area, and their contracts. In addition, the sponsoring State adapts the objectives of the legislation in accordance with its own interests and without prejudice to the common interests, by including tailored objectives such as, "to provide a stable, transparent and predictable regulatory environment for investors",[22] "to secure optimum benefits, long term-economic growth and sustainable development",[23] "to ensure the safety of workers in seabed mining and of the operational facilities for seabed mining",[24] or "to promote resources investigation and marine scientific research".[25]

### 2.2 *Selection of Legislative Models*

In addition to objectives, selection of legislative forms or models for sponsoring States' environmental legislation for deep seabed mining within their legal framework is another important issue. As stipulated in the LOSC, a sponsoring State can make "laws, regulations and administrative measures" to carry out its primary responsibility. This implies that the LOSC allows the sponsoring State the discretion to decide what kind of legislative forms and models it wishes to choose.[26]

Sponsoring States have different options in deciding on the most appropriate legislative model. Each State can determine the model of legislation in

19 Singapore Act, article 3(a).
20 Singapore Act, article 3(b).
21 Germany Act, section 1(1)(3).
22 Nauru Act, article 5(d).
23 Nauru Act, article 5(e).
24 Germany Act, section 1(1)(2).
25 China Law, article 1.
26 See section 4 of chapter 2.

accordance with its individual situation. Options include a single, comprehensive legal instrument or a set of legal instruments. In the case of the latter, it is recommended that the instrument comprise a primary legislation which should provide a comprehensive framework and secondary legislation to provide operational details, such as regulations, rules, or guidelines. For example, China's legislation for activities in the Area is composed of one law which establishes a framework for regulating its sponsored contractors' activities in the Area and three administrative regulations that provide operational details, respectively, in licensing, sample management and data management.[27]

Generally speaking, there are two main legislative models. One is to merge the contents of deep seabed mining in the Area into one of the existing congeneric national laws; the other is to establish a new legal instrument specializing in deep seabed mining in the Area within its overarching legal framework. With regard to special cases of deep seabed mining, certain sponsoring States are inclined to use the sponsorship agreement between the sponsoring State and its sponsored contractor as a means of national legislation. This method is frowned upon by the SDC Advisory Opinion, which will be discussed at end of this section.

### 2.2.1 Addressing Environmental Issues of Deep Seabed Mining in the Area within a Broader National Legislation

In a number of cases, mining-related legislation or law-of-the-sea-related legislation has been incorporated into a sponsoring State's domestic legal system.

27 Permanent Mission of China, *Note Verbale from the Permanent Mission of the People's Republic of China to the International Seabed Authority*, No. (18)-4 (26 April 2018), available at: <https://www.isa.org.jm/files/documents/EN/NatLeg/China/China-1a.pdf> accessed 5 December 2020. For an introduction on this account, see section 3 of chapter 4. See also Xiangxin Xu, Guobin Zhang and Guifang (Julia) Xue, 'China's Deep Seabed Law: Towards "Reasonably Appropriate" Environmental Legislation for Exploration and Exploitation of Deep Sea Minerals in the Area' (2017) *Asian Yearbook of International Law* 183; Jiancai Jin and Guobin Zhang, 'Chapter 9: The Forthcoming Breakthrough: China's Legislation on Activities in the Deep Seabed Area' in Myron H. Nordquist, John Norton Moore, and Ronán Long (eds), *International Marine Economy* (Brill Nijhoff 2017), 235; Hao Shen, 'International Deep Seabed Mining and China's Legislative Commitment to Marine Environmental Protection Regional Focus and Controversies' (2017) 10 *Journal of East Asia and International Law* 489; Guobin Zhang and Pai Zheng, 'A New Step Forward: Review of China's 2016 Legislation on International Seabed Area Exploration and Exploitation' (2016) 73 *Marine Policy* 244; Nengye Liu and Rakhyun E Kim, 'Current Legal Developments: China's New Law on Exploration and Exploitation of Resources in the International Seabed Area of 2016' (2016) 31 *The International Journal of Marine and Coastal Law* 691.

However, those legislations are set up to regulate terrestrial mining, deep seabed mining within national jurisdiction, or even broader law of the sea issues, rather than a specific piece of deep seabed mining legislation applicable to mining activities in the areas beyond national jurisdiction. In such cases, it is more likely that existing mining-related legislation is amended, supplanted, or supplemented so as to include specific reference to deep-sea mining. Making a seabed mining law for activities both within and beyond national jurisdiction is also one of the options. Typical examples are the Seabed Mineral Acts for Tonga, Tuvalu, and Kiribati. Alternatively, all activities in the Area may be addressed under a broad legislation on law of the sea. For instance, the France Ordinance is an ordinance relating to all maritime spaces under its sovereignty or jurisdiction, in which chapter X entitled "the International Seabed Area" is composed of an article consisting of three paragraphs dealing with activities in the Area.

Addressing deep seabed mining in the Area within a broader national legislation has at least three interconnected advantages. First, the process of modification or combination is obviously much easier than that of making a new legal instrument. Amending the contents of an existing legislation by adding some new content requires less work. Second, this approach minimizes cross-sectoral inconsistency, regulatory gaps, and overlaps. Third, fewer legislative instruments facilitate efficient and timely decision-making. However, due to the specialty of deep seabed mining, the remote location of the Area as well as the dual-track administration between the ISA and sponsoring States' governments, it is difficult to tackle all the problems in one package. Therefore, it should be noted that despite its merits, this approach is not the best way to protect the marine environment.

Nevertheless, this type of legislation may be efficiently applied to States that already have legislation relating to exploration and exploitation of mineral resources within national jurisdiction and those States whose legislative capacity is limited and whose budgets are unable to support independent legislation. A possible example is the Cook Islands, which has legal instruments regulating seabed mining activities within its national jurisdiction.[28] It is

28 In 2009, the Cook Islands adopted its Seabed Minerals Act 2009, which was amended in 2015 by Seabed Minerals (Amendment) Act 2015, and also promulgated its Seabed Minerals (Prospecting and Exploration) Regulations 2015; these instruments regulate the management of the seabed minerals within national jurisdiction of the Cook Islands. Currently the Cook Islands is reviewing the Seabed Minerals Act and Regulations. See Comparative Study of the Existing National Legislation on Deep Seabed Mining (n 4), paragraph 11.

suggested to amend and merge activities in the Area into its existing national legislation.

### 2.2.2 Establishing a Specific Deep Seabed Mining Law for Activities in the Area

Admittedly, deep seabed mining and terrestrial mining both extract minerals from ores, so the technique and governance share common elements. Indeed, the operation and management of deep seabed mining draws on experience of terrestrial mining in many respects. However, that does not mean they should be confused. In fact, their discrete characteristics are more pronounced than their commonalities.

It was seen in chapter 1 that the deep-sea environment is intensely different from that on land. Deep seabed mineral resources are located in a different environment and thus form distinct marine habitats and host a unique biodiversity. They should, thus, be treated differently in order to avoid loss of biodiversity and destruction of habitats once seabed mining activities begin. Furthermore, from a legal perspective, deep seabed mining in the Area happens in "the Area", which is not only geographically remote from sponsoring States but also beyond the jurisdiction of sponsoring States. That is to say, in addition to the sponsoring State, there is another regulator, the ISA, controlling and managing activities in the Area. This implies that legislation on deep seabed mining in the Area will be different from that for terrestrial mining. The legislation on deep seabed mining in the Area not only has to adopt provisions from the international level into the national level to "assist the ISA" to regulate contractors but also to try to avoid unnecessary duplication within the ISA. Moreover, the geographical remoteness of the location, makes it much more difficult to monitor deep seabed mining activities than terrestrial mining activities. Therefore, much stricter mechanisms or special mechanisms should be implemented to monitor deep seabed mining activities and to react promptly once an emergency situation happens.

Thus, if conditions permit, the sponsoring States are encouraged to establish law specific to deep seabed mining in the Area. This would not only facilitate more streamlined management by taking full account of the particularity of deep-sea mining activities but would also be more user-friendly for contractors to operate. In addition, taking full account of the particularity of deep-sea mining activities and instituting special management mechanisms is a manifestation of "due diligence". Indeed, making a specific law is the most popular choice of sponsoring States that have pieces of legislation on activities in the Area (exceptions are France, Tonga, and Kiribati).

### 2.2.3 Contractual Arrangement

Because of the sponsorship regime,[29] a contractual arrangement may be established between a sponsoring State and the contractor to specify the sponsorship and respective responsibilities and obligations. A popular opinion is for contractual arrangements, such as a sponsoring agreement or a project agreement, to have a similar function with corresponding legislation through which the State can regulate and supervise the contractors' activities and subsequently ensure their compliance with international environmental obligations, actually playing the same role with specific legislation in deep seabed mining. Consequently, proponents of this opinion believe that those sponsoring States who have already signed a sponsoring agreement with a sponsored contractor do not need deep seabed mining legislation.

Nauru, a proponent of such an arrangement, once declared that enacting legislation, specifically in deep seabed mining was too costly and a kind of waste of limited government resources.[30] The primary reason provided was that many States may sponsor only one contractor, as is, indeed, the situation in most of the Area.[31] Moreover, deep seabed mining legislation seems to have no other use to those States that do not have an offshore industry or a mining and resource sector. In short, it would be unwise to enact legislation to regulate merely one contractor. Rather, a project agreement or other contractual arrangement instead of legislation may be an efficient and more cost-effective mechanism.

However, the Seabed Disputes Chamber expressly denied Nauru's proposal in its Advisory Opinion by stating that, in accordance with the LOSC, the measures taken by a sponsoring State should be by way of laws and regulations and administrative measures,[32] not a contractual arrangement. The reason

29 With regard to sponsorship regime, please see chapter 2.

30 Statement by the Republic of Nauru regarding the questions submitted to the Seabed Disputes Chamber for an advisory opinion on the responsibilities and obligations of States sponsoring entities with respect to activities in the international seabed area (5 August 2010) <https://www.itlos.org/securedl/sdl-eyJ0eXAiOiJKV1QiLCJhbGciOiJIUzI1NiJ9.eyJpYXQiOjE2MT-k1Nzc1OTAsImV4cCI6MTYxOTY2NzU5MCwidXNlciI6MCwiZ3JvdXBzIjpbMCwtMV-0sImZpbGUiOiJmaWxlYWRtaW5cL2lobG9zXC9kb2N1bWVudHNcL2Nhc2VzXC9jYX-NlX25vXzE3XC9DMTdfV3JpdHRlbl9TdGF0ZW1lbnRfTmF1cnUucGRmIiwicGFnZSI6M-TA5fQ.FTTjHOxiWyDuqSyoUl6MkoxQwICzw1yJ855URBuTA9Y/C17_Written_Statement_Nauru.pdf> accessed 5 December 2020, paragraph 26.

31 Among the twenty sponsoring States, ten of them sponsor only one contractor. They are Bulgaria, Cuba, Czech Republic, Nauru, Tonga, Belgium, Kiribati, Singapore, Brazil, and the Cook Islands. See Figure 2 of this chapter; see also Status of contracts for exploration and related matters, including information on the periodic review of the implementation of approved plans of work for exploration (ISBA/26/C/4, 17 December 2019).

32 LOSC, Annex III, article 4(4).

why not taking a contractual arrangement as "a law, a rule or an administrative measure" is obvious since it lacks transparency. As the Seabed Disputes Chamber illustrated, "a sponsorship agreement may not be publicly available and, in fact, may not be required at all".[33] So it is difficult to verify whether a sponsoring State is carrying out its obligations. Therefore, a contractual arrangement cannot be seen as a form of "laws and regulations and administrative measures".

It is noteworthy that the past decade has witnessed a soaring interest in deep seabed mineral resources. It can be predicted that there will be more and more States sponsoring more than one contractor in the future with the rising demand for minerals or metals and the decline in land-based mineral resources. Thus, it is worth investing in deep seabed mining legislation for sponsoring States to establish a good market order.

## 3 Components of Environmental Legislation

One of the characteristics of the Deep Seabed Mining Regime is that it is a two-track governance regime, in which the ISA is the main regulator and a sponsoring State is obliged to assist the ISA to ensure its sponsored contractor's compliance with environmental obligations. Thus, the task of the sponsoring State is to endeavour to assist the ISA to achieve its objectives for protecting environmental resources and addressing potential degradation. The objectives of the ISA's mandate in marine environmental protection are: (i) reducing the likelihood and magnitude of environmental damage in a cost-effective (least-cost) way;[34] and (ii) providing funds for response, possible restoration, and compensation.[35] As far as the task of assisting the ISA is concerned, two

33 Annex III of the LOSC and the ISA Exploration Regulations contain no requirement that a sponsorship agreement, if any, between the sponsoring States and the contractor should be submitted to the ISA or made publicly available. The only requirement is the submission of a certificate of sponsorship issued by the sponsoring State, regulation 11(3)(f), of the ISA Exploration Regulations, in which the sponsoring State declares that it "assumes responsibility in accordance with article 139, article 153(4) and Annex III, article 4(4), of the UNCLOS". See SDC Advisory Opinion, paragraph 225.

34 Cost-effective or least-cost conservation within the context of the mitigation hierarchy's four steps (avoidance, minimization, restoration/rehabilitation, and offset) can lead to greater overall conservation given limited funds for conservation. See section 2.4 of chapter 1.

35 Michael W Lodge, Kathleen Segerson and Dale Squires, 'Sharing and Preserving the Resources in the Deep Sea: Challenges for the International Seabed Authority' (2017) 32 *The International Journal of Marine and Coastal Law* 427, 443.

extreme scenarios should be avoided. First, a sponsoring State's national legislation should not simply be a copy of the LOSC and ISA regulations. Second, a pure domestic law without consideration of the relevant contents of international law is also not the right approach and would breach international obligations. These two scenarios cannot be deemed to be carrying out "responsibility to ensure".

To assist the ISA to fulfill its objectives of environmental protection, the sponsoring State should bring its national legislation to a certain standard. This standard can be divided into the minimal standard and the optimal standard. The minimum standard represents the minimum requirements that the sponsoring State's legislation needs to meet. Failure to meet the minimum standard means that the sponsoring State has not fulfilled its "responsibility to ensure". The optimal standard could be: 1) the sponsoring State, apart from meeting the minimum requirements, explores in which aspects it can also play a role according to its national conditions and capabilities to assist the ISA in achieving its objectives; or 2) the sponsoring State, based on the minimum requirements, can adopt more stringent requirements for the most significant extent.

Regarding the minimal standard, the sponsoring State could cite the SDC Advisory Opinion. It does not set out specific standards to which a contractor must adhere but focuses on the obligations of the sponsoring State in ensuring compliance by the sponsored contractor with its commitments and characterizes it as due diligence. That clearly presents the Seabed Disputes Chamber's expectation of sponsoring States to regulate all stages of activities in the Area.[36] Likewise, the Seabed Disputes Chamber "has set a reasonably clear benchmark of what it expects of sponsoring States" to undertake regulatory behavior to meet the due diligence obligation.[37] "Responsibility to ensure" does not require sponsoring States to seek to achieve the "result" of "ensure" but rather the "conduct" of that, namely, conduct of taking measures within its legal system to outline the expectations of due diligence. An effective approach of doing so is to set clear parameters and to avoid ambiguity in sponsoring States' national legislation. "To establish whether a State has complied with its obligations of conduct, it is necessary to compare the conduct prescribed with the actual conduct undertaken. When the action or omission noted does not conform with the conduct specifically required there is a breach of the obligation in

36 Duncan French, 'From the Depths: Rich Pickings of Principles of Sustainable Development and General International Law on the Ocean Floor – the Seabed Disputes Chamber's 2011 Advisory Opinion' (2011) 26 *The International Journal of Marine and Coastal Law* 525, 540.

37 French (n 37) 542.

question."[38] In order to reach the minimal line, the following three points must be ensured. First, obligations and requirements that a contractor should comply[39] should be presented in the national legislation; Second, the contractor's behavior needs to be monitored, which requires mechanisms for monitoring in the sponsoring State's national legislation; and third, the national legislation must establish mechanisms for recourse, such as access to domestic courts, enforcement of decisions of international courts or tribunals, and providing funds for response and compensation. All aforementioned components have a direct impact on the marine environment, and thus should be set as mandatory components, and expressly incorporated into the sponsoring State's national legislation. Mandatory components are, at a minimum: (i) Licensing regime; (ii) Environmental duties and obligations of the contractor; (iii) Rights of the contractor; and (iv) Monitoring and enforcement.

The optimal line standard is what the sponsoring State explores to reduce the likelihood and magnitude of environmental damage in a cost-effective way in its national legislation according to its capability. For instance, in the application phase, the sponsoring States should introduce mechanisms to ensure the applicant's financial and technological capability or consider how to instruct and incentivize the contractor to operationalize its obligations, as embodied in the precautionary approach. This attempt should be represented in the entire process of the mining activities.

A sponsoring State's national legislation must reach the minimal line and seek to approach to the optimal line. The difference between the two lines is not the components included in the national legislation, but the degree of endeavour and effort to take more specific and stringent requirements than the international standard.

### 3.1 *Thresholds of Accessing to Mining in the Area*

The key requirement of a sponsoring State's national legislation should be that deep seabed mining activities beyond the national jurisdiction, even if approved by the ISA, cannot be conducted until national approval or permission in the form of a license or a sponsorship agreement is received. No matter what formality a sponsoring State takes (signing a sponsorship agreement or granting a mining license), the essence is identical. The license regime is provided as an example.

---

38 Rüdiger Wolfrum, 'Obligation of Result Versus Obligation of Conduct: Some Thoughts About the Implementation Of International Obligations', in Mahnoush H Arsanjani and others (eds), *Looking to the Future* (Brill 2010), 375.

39 SDC Advisory Opinion, paragraphs 103–106.

Domestic legislation should establish a regulatory agency with responsibility for granting licenses and thus given the mandate to scrutinize applications for access to mining activities in the Area. This would ensure the legitimacy of the agency and its actions.[40] Simultaneously, there should be specific and clear standards guiding the application process for potential applicants. National legislation, first and foremost, needs to outline a clear description of the activities that may be licensed. Second, the criteria to be met by entities to qualify for a license and procedures to be followed should be specified. Last, but not least, the substantive qualifications of applicants need to be presented. The regulatory agency will assess the license application based on pre-established criteria.

Apart from guidelines for licenses, the agency should have operational parameters and performance standards, such as baseline data collection requirements, a timetable, and data retention, which can be followed by the license-holder. Additionally, the license-holder should be required to report on his performance annually.[41] Those who breach the provisions of the licensing regime will be subject to appropriate sanctions, including revocation of the license.

### 3.1.1 Categories of Licensing

The contents of an application to conduct seabed mining activities, and the licenses granted, are likely to vary in keeping with the different activities proposed and their potential impacts. This is because, as presented in section 4.3.1.1 of chapter 2, due diligence is a variable concept, and the level of due diligence is different for each distinct stage of seabed mining. For example, "Prospecting is usually less likely to cause damage than exploration, which similarly has fewer risks attached than exploitation."[42] The ISA differentiates the applications for each accordingly. Thus, it is suggested that the sponsoring State follow the ISA's example in the arrangement of the legislation and differentiate the licensing requirements and processes, around the different phases of seabed mining activities. Japan, Kiribati, New Zealand, Singapore, Tonga, Tuvalu, and the United Kingdom differentiate the distinct category of license in their national legislation.[43]

---

40 Details regarding the establishment and power and functions of the regulatory agency will be provided in section 4.2 of this chapter.

41 Details regarding monitoring will be provided in section 3.4 of this chapter.

42 French (n 37) 540–554; SDC Advisory Opinion, paragraph 117.

43 Comparative Study of the Existing National Legislation on Deep Seabed Mining (n 4), paragraph 40.

### 3.1.2 Qualified Applicants

The criteria for applicants to qualify for a license should be clarified in the national legislation of the sponsoring State. The LOSC outlines the major criteria for applicants: "States Parties, state enterprises or natural or juridical persons which possess the nationality of States Parties or are effectively controlled by them or their nationals" and simultaneously sponsored by States Parties can carry out mining activities in association with the Authority.[44]

The most important requirement for applicants, whether they are an enterprise or a natural or legal person, is that they must be nationals of or controlled by a State Party, which is also the essence of sponsorship. Thus, in a sponsoring State's national legislation, the applicants who want to access to deep seabed mining activities must be controllable. The specific requirements of being "controllable" may vary according to the individual situation of the sponsoring State. Nationality is an easy parameter. Most States, such as Belgium, China, Czech Republic, Fiji, Japan, Kiribati, Nauru, New Zealand, Singapore, Tonga, and Tuvalu, adopt "nationality" or registration in those States as a necessary requirement to apply for a license.[45] By contrast, only Belgium and Germany include "effective control" as a criterion of the applicant.[46] Obviously, the criterion of "nationality" is easy to check, whereas the criterion of "effective control" is difficult to check since there is no explicit definition in the LOSC and any other relevant legal instruments. At first glance, taking "nationality" as a criterion of the applicants seems to be a very effective way to control applicants. However, this approach ignores a situation where an applicant is registered in a developing State yet remains a wholly-owned subsidiary of an experienced mining company in a developed State.[47] Such an entity may repatriate profits to the parent company. Under this situation, the sponsoring State must be very careful about the controllability of such an entity despite nationality or registration. Article 9 of the 2006 draft articles on diplomatic protection of the ILC addresses this situation:

> For the purposes of the diplomatic protection of a corporation, the State of nationality means the State under whose law the corporation was

---

44 LOSC, article 153(2)(b). Enterprise is not discussed in this chapter.

45 Comparative Study of the Existing National Legislation on Deep Seabed Mining (n 4), paragraph 33.

46 ibid.

47 Examples can be found in Issues related to the sponsorship of contracts for exploration in the Area, monopolization, effective control and related matters (ISBA/22/LTC/13, 21 June 2016), paragraph 6.

> incorporated. However, when the corporation is controlled by nationals of another State or States and has no substantial business activities in the State of incorporation, and the seat of management and the financial control of the corporation are both located in another State, that State shall be regarded as the State of nationality.[48]

In respect of diplomatic protection not suitable to the Deep Seabed Mining Regime, this article reminds the sponsoring State that:

> if the veil cannot be lifted, the sponsoring State will not be in a position to exercise its effective control over the parent company and may not be able to comply with its due diligence obligations and direct obligations as a sponsoring State by virtue of the Convention and its related instruments.[49]

Regarding the definition of "effective control", the LTC is of the view that the definition of "effective control" needs to be clarified but it falls "under the competence of the State that exercises it" and it "is left to municipal law".[50] That being said, the sponsoring State which utilizes this criterion is obliged to clarify this concept. Rojas and Phillips propose two interpretations of "effective control" from the analysis of comparative legal sources and of the way in which ISA organs have treated the issue: an economic approach (control or influence over the entity) or a regulatory approach (jurisdiction of incorporation).[51] The economic control approach considers factors such as ownership of a majority of the applicant's shares; ownership of a majority of the applicant's capital; holding a majority of the applicant's voting rights; holding the right to elect a majority of the applicant's board of directors or equivalent body; having an influence over the applicant sufficient to determine its decisions; or any combination or variation of the above.[52] Under the regulatory control approach,

48 International Law Commission, *Draft Articles on Diplomatic Protection*, printed in 'Report of the International Law Commission on its Fifty-eight session', UN Doc A/61/10 (2006), 16–100, article 9.

49 Analysis of regulation 11.2 of the Regulations on Prospecting and Exploration for Polymetallic Nodules and Polymetallic Sulphides in the Area (ISBA/20/LTC/10, 5 June 2014), paragraph 17.

50 ibid, paragraph 21.

51 Andrés Sebastián Rojas and Freedom-Kai Phillips, *Effective Control and Deep Seabed Mining: Toward a Definition*, Liability Issues for Deep Seabed Mining Series, Paper No.7 (February 2019), 9.

52 ibid.

the LTC notes that nationality, "combined with the undertakings given as a sponsoring State" can be sufficient.[53] It should be pointed out that these two approaches are not mutually exclusive. On the contrary, the sponsoring State can combine the two approaches to different degrees according to the actual situation.

### 3.1.3 Approaches to Accessing a License

Application and tendering are two possible options through which a sponsoring State may provide access to a mining license in the Area.

#### 3.1.3.1 *Application*

The application route is the approach that almost all the States have chosen to issue a license or permission for sponsorship for activities in the Area.[54] Entities wanting to conduct deep seabed mining activities in the Area and are potentially qualified may submit applications to the sponsoring State's relevant regulatory agency. The process recommended follows.

After receiving an application, in keeping with the ISA's model, the regulatory agency should issue a general public notification that an application has been made, without disclosing the exact coordinates of the prospecting or exploration area. This would assist public understanding and inform other deep seabed mining operators which sites are already under application.

It is strongly recommended that the criteria by which an applicant is selected is clearly set out so as to avoid the risk of corrupt decision-making, especially when competing applications are received for the same area. Several approaches could be used in this situation, such as, "first come, first considered" or a simple assessment of the best-qualified applicants. The latter method should seek the opinions of an expert group which should prudently assess applications according to requirements in section 3.1.4 of this chapter. In any event, the regulatory agency should make decisions for granting licenses.

#### 3.1.3.2 *Tendering*

International tender is an established and transparent way of attracting a credible international company to express its interest in exploring or exploiting deep seabed minerals in the Area. This method is used by some Pacific Islands States that have exploration or exploitation practices for deep sea

53 Analysis of regulation 11.2 of the Regulations on Prospecting and Exploration for Polymetallic Nodules and Polymetallic Sulphides in the Area (n 50), paragraph 22.

54 Comparative Study of the Existing National Legislation on Deep Seabed Mining (n 4), paragraph 39.

mineral resources within its national jurisdiction. For instance, the Kiribati Act stipulates that the Kiribati's Seabed Minerals Secretariat may invite applications for a license to conduct seabed mining activities in an area of Kiribati's Continental Shelf by way of a public tender.[55] The precondition is that there should be a system to indicate which area could apply. The Government of Kiribati utilizes a map-based Geographic Information System (GIS) system to identify which sites are already under application or license, which sites are available for applications, and which sites are protected. Therefore, the State announces and publicizes opportunities to open up these areas, allowing time for the expression of interest. The regulatory agency then reviews and scores these tenders based on predetermined criteria, and finally selects an operator from among the applicants. Tendering legislation or mining legislation provides a clear guide on the selection criteria for tendering.[56]

So far, no State has applied this approach to activities in the Area. Indeed, it is questionable whether a State is entitled to seek potential applicants who are willing to explore or exploit in the Area through tendering. After all, the potential contract area is beyond a State's ownership.

#### 3.1.4 Key Requirements of Application

Regardless of whether the tendering or application system is used, the sponsoring State has the responsibility to duly assess applicants to ensure that they are capable of following "good industry practice" and respond promptly to environmental incidents as well as being able to provide prompt and adequate compensation if necessary. This is important to ensure sponsored contractor's compliance and protection of the marine environment.

The ISA outlines the criteria for accessibility in its regulations. The ISA Draft Exploitation Regulations (March 2019) require the applicant to provide relevant data and information, a mining work plan, a financial plan, an environmental impact statement, an emergency response and contingency plan, a health and safety plan, a training plan, a closure plan, and an application fee.[57] The LTC assesses the eligibility, financial capability, technical capability of the applicant, and technical achievability, economic viability, and effectiveness of

55 Kiribati Act, article 56(1).

56 Tearinaki Tanielu, 'Establishment of A National Regulatory Framework for the Exploration and Exploitation of Deep Sea Minerals: A Case Study for Kiribati' (United Nations-Nippon Foundation of Japan Fellowship Programme, December 2013) <https://www.un.org/Depts/los/nippon/unnff_programme_home/fellows_pages/fellows_papers/Tanielu_1314_Kir.pdf> accessed 8 August 2020, 81–82.

57 Draft Exploitation Regulations (March 2019), regulation 7.

the environmental protection strategies of the proposed plan of work.[58] The exploration application is less complicated. It focuses on the financial and technical capabilities of the applicant and the proposed plan of work.[59] A license for prospecting only requires the submission of notification to the ISA.[60]

Indeed, as indicated in chapter 1, the LTC is the organ that is mandated to approve plans of work and applications, and thus it scrutinizes all documents provided. It is unnecessary for the sponsoring State's regulatory agency to repeat all the work done by the ISA. At the national level, the sponsoring State should focus on areas within its jurisdiction. This section does not examine all the requirements of an application but discusses some areas in which sponsoring States can play a role.

#### 3.1.4.1 *Financial Capabilities*

The financial capability of the applicant is an important factor considered by the LTC when approving an application. It determines whether an applicant has the capacity to consistently use best available technology in the process of mining, whether it is capable of committing or raising sufficient financial resources to cover the costs of the mining activities, monitoring plan, and closure plan, whether it can promptly and effectively deal with emergencies or damages, and whether it can afford insurance products.[61]

The SDC Advisory Opinion highlights that financial viability and technical capacity of sponsored contractors are necessary components of the domestic law of sponsoring States.[62] However, merging this requirement into domestic law is problematic due to the lack of off-the-shelf quantitative standards. The LOSC does not set out specific standards for the financial and technical capabilities of the applicant, albeit that Annex III, article 4(4) of LOSC stipulates that qualification standards shall relate to such capabilities. Based on this instruction, the ISA Exploration Regulations further developed standards in which provisions do not quantify financial standards. Instead, it requires discrete financial information according to the nature of the firms.[63] To be specific, a State or a State enterprise merely provides a statement by the State

58 Draft Exploitation Regulations (March 2019), regulation 13.

59 Nodules Exploration Regulations, regulation 12; Sulphides Exploration Regulations, regulation 13; Crusts Exploration Regulations, regulation 13.

60 Nodules Exploration Regulations, regulation 3; Sulphides Exploration Regulations, regulation 3; Crusts Exploration Regulations, regulation 3.

61 Draft Exploitation Regulations (March 2019), regulation 13(2).

62 Advisory Opinion, paragraph 234.

63 Nodules Exploration Regulations, regulation 12(4)-(7); Sulphides Exploration Regulations, regulation 13(3) and (4); Crusts Exploration Regulations, regulation 13(3)-(6).

or the sponsoring State certifying the applicant's financial capacity; members of the private sector must provide audited financial statements for three years, certified by a duly qualified firm of public accountants in conformity with internationally accepted accounting principles. Borrowing for supporting approval of a plan of work for exploration is permitted if detailed information, such as the amount, the repayment period, and the interest rate is submitted.[64]

Since the ISA Regulations shifted the burden of checking an enterprise's financial capability to the sponsoring State (in case of a state enterprise as an applicant), the sponsoring State should have several mechanisms to ensure it. The sponsoring State can also check the financial capability of private enterprises, as it has a clear understanding of the national economic level and enterprise strength under its control. Hence, the legislation of a sponsoring State must be designed to set specific financial standards for applicants. These might include a minimum amount of operating capital, appropriate insurance, or other certification of financial responsibility, undertakings that relevant industry standards are adhered to by the operator. It is worth mentioning that the relevant national legislation of Germany and Japan requires the applicant to submit credibility records as one means of ensuring the applicant's financial capability.[65] Importantly, it is suggested for the sponsoring State to check the sponsored contractor's financial situation regularly even after issuing a license, by reviewing its audit reporting, to ensure a contractor's continued financial capability of carrying out mining activities. Once the contractor's financial capability is found to have a significant problem, appropriate measures should be taken, including terminating the contractor's license, if deemed necessary.

#### 3.1.4.2 *Technological Capabilities, Equipment and Personnel*

The contractor is the operator of the mining activities and thus its technical capabilities directly influence the marine environment and ecosystem. Take manganese nodules as an example, high technology means less sediment disturbance in the process of exploration and exploitation and better re-sedimentation afterwards, which is likely to have a highly significant biological impact, especially on filter-feeding animals.[66] Technological capacity is

---

64 ibid.

65 Germany Act, section 4(6)2(a); Mining Act of Japan, article 29(ii)(iii). It should be noted that there are two relevant Acts in Japan: Act on Interim Measures for Deep Seabed Mining (Japan Law) and Mining Act (Mining Act of Japan).

66 A manganese nodules collector vehicle will compress and squeeze the sediment and benthic organism and create a sediment plume, transporting masses of particles over unknown distances. Natural sediment themselves take millions of years to form so these habitats could be completely lost from large areas of seabed. Re-sedimentation from

vital to the prudent stewardship of the marine ecosystem and thus crucial in the assessment of applicants. The ISA Draft Exploitation Regulations (March 2019) stipulate the requirements of an applicant's technological capability. Regulation 13 provides:

> In considering the technical capability of an applicant, the Commission shall determine in accordance with the Guidelines whether the applicant has or will have:
>
> (a) The *necessary technical and operational capability* to carry out the proposed Plan of Work in accordance with Good Industry Practice using appropriately qualified and adequately supervised personnel;
> (b) The *technology and procedures necessary to comply with* the terms of the Environmental Management and Monitoring Plan [(EMMP)] and the Closure Plan, including the *technical capability to monitor* key environmental parameters and *to modify* management and operating procedures when appropriate;
> (c) *Established the necessary risk assessment and risk management systems to effectively implement* the proposed Plan of Work in accordance with Good Industry Practice, Best Available Techniques and Best Environmental Practices and these regulations, including the technology and procedures to meet health, safety and environmental requirements for the activities proposed in the Plan of Work;
> (d) The *capability to respond effectively* to Incidents, in accordance with the Emergency Response and Contingency Plan; and
> (e) The *capability to utilize and apply Best Available Techniques*.[67] [emphasis added]

National legislation should reflect these requirements of technical capability. The most important aspect is the technology that the applicant acquires, including the technology at the time of application and the potential to apply advanced technology. Execution of the plan of work, EMMP, and the closure plan requires a certain degree of technical ability, the standard of which is the capability to meet the good industry practice, best available techniques, and

the sediment plume is likely to have a highly significant biological impact, especially on filter-feeding animals. See H Bluhm, 'Monitoring Megabenthic Communities in Abyssal Manganese Nodule Sites of the East Pacific Ocean in Association with Commercial Deep-sea Mining' (1994) 4 *Aquatic Conservation: Marine and Freshwater Ecosystems* 187, 188.

67 Draft Exploitation Regulations (March 2019), regulation 13(3).

best environmental practices.[68] At the time of application, the applicant must have the appropriate technical skills as well as the potential to make adjustments as the standards of good industry practice changes. In addition to the technology, *per se*, financial capability and the expertise of personnel are also fundamental to being able to meet the standards of good industry practice. Personnel are essential as people are operators of equipment and technologies. All the staff should be systematically trained.

Sponsoring States' legislation should require applicants to provide evidence of technological capabilities. For instance, a general description of the applicant's previous experience, knowledge, skills, technical qualifications, expertise, equipment, and methods is the main reference of technical capacity. The Czech Republic Act gives an example in this regard. It sets a specific provision regarding the expertise of personnel.[69] Article 6 of the Czech Republic Act provides that expertise shall mean:

(a) Completed university education, specialization in geology or mining, and three years of experience in geological surveying or mining mineral raw materials;

---

68 These terminologies are frequently mentioned in the context of deep seabed mining. They are defined in the Use of terms and scope, Draft Exploitation Regulations (March 2019). "Good Industry Practice" means the exercise of that degree of skill, diligence, prudence, and foresight which would reasonably and ordinarily be expected to be applied by a skilled and experienced person engaged in the marine mining industry and other related extractive industries worldwide. "Best Available Techniques" means the latest stage of development, and state-of-the-art processes, of facilities or of methods of operation that indicate the practical suitability of a particular measure for the prevention, reduction, and control of pollution and the protection of the Marine Environment from the harmful effects of Exploitation activities, taking into account the guidance set out in the applicable Guidelines. "Best Environmental Practices" means the application of the most appropriate combination of environmental control measures and strategies that will change with time in the light of improved knowledge, understanding, or technology, taking into account the guidance set out in the applicable Guidelines. As Leonardus Gerber and Renee Grogan conclude that "[u]ltimately, GIP reflects the process by which outcomes are achieved. Alternatively put, BEP establishes the process by which inputs (baseline environmental values, engineering technology) would be described, processes determined with reference to specific triggers to ensure environmental protection at all times, and outputs monitored. The implementation of BEP processes therefore contributes to GIP, by allowing proponents to (within the framework of the particular BEP described) adapt their management strategies to achieve the best outcome for the industry and the environment." See Leonardus J. Gerber and Renee L. Grogan, 'Challenges of Operationalising Good Industry Practice and Best Environmental Practice in Deep Seabed Mining Regulation' (2020) 114 *Marine Policy* 103257.

69 Czech Republic Act, article 6.

(b) Demonstrable knowledge of either the English or the French language at the level of state language examination; and
(c) Demonstrable knowledge of the provisions hereof; [Part I, XI, XII and XV of the LOSC; Annex III to V; the Implementing Agreement; and mandatory regulations of the ISA];
(d) Experience in prospecting or in activities in the Area of at least one year's duration, at least one month of which should be in maritime activities; maritime experience can be replaced by successful graduation from a special course organized by the International Ocean Institute or successful graduation from a training programme organized by the Authority.[70]

The Czech Republic Act further provides that the expertise outlined under (b) and (c) shall be demonstrated by a certificate issued by the Ministry of Industry and Trade of the Czech Republic.[71] The Czech Republic provides very specific requirements according to its actual situation, such as the certificate of expertise. From this point of view, the Czech Republic can be said to have fulfilled the obligation of due diligence in examining expertise of personnel because it sets clear, reasonable, and appropriate criteria in this regard. It is suggested that other sponsoring States follow this example in their legislation. Moreover, evidence or undertakings as to the seaworthiness, manning, equipment, and navigation of those vessels should be reflected in the legislation as well.[72]

#### 3.1.4.3 *Environmental Performance Guarantee and Compulsory Insurance*

It is likely that a growing number of States will use *command-and-control regulation* as the primary approach for environmental protection and will use *economic instruments* as supplementation.[73] Therefore, apart from the aforementioned command-and-control requirements (requirements of application in domestic law), economic instruments are also necessary. In the context of deep seabed mining, the Environmental Performance Guarantee and compulsory

70 Czech Republic Act, article 6(1).
71 Czech Republic Act, article 6(2).
72 SPC, *RLRF* (n 17), paragraph 14.19.
73 The principles and rules of international environmental law established by treaty and other sources of international law are applied to a range of regulatory techniques. These can broadly be divided into two types: traditional forms of direct regulation (frequently referred to as "command-and-control"), and techniques that make use of economic incentives (referred to as "economic instruments"). See Philippe Sands and others, *Principles of International Environmental Law* (3rd edn, Cambridge University Press 2012), 121.

insurance are useful economic instruments, which need to be paid before the commencement of any activities in the Area.

An environmental bond or financial guarantee, which are used to supervise a contractor's performance by way of repayment or forfeiture of such deposit, taking into account the contractors' compliance or non-compliance with obligations, may be required from the contractor upfront. Those moneys will be returned (with accrued interest) if the contractor complies with its obligations. It is worth noting that the financial guarantee is merely designed as a "Decommissioning Guarantee" for "post-mining activities" based on regulation 26(2) of the Draft Exploitation Regulations.

Since the function of the environmental bonds or financial guarantee is to urge the contractor to assume its environmental obligations, it is necessary to consider to whom those deposits should be paid to achieve this goal more effectively – The ISA or sponsoring State? The Draft Exploitation Regulations (March 2019) instruct that such a financial guarantee (Environmental Performance Guarantee) should be given to the ISA.[74] It can be judged from section 13 of the standard clauses for exploitation contract that the ISA treats Environmental Performance Guarantee as one of the means of enforcement. However, in practice, this guarantee, if charged by the sponsoring State, can also achieve this goal. When the ISA finds a contractor's incompliance with those obligations under section 13(1) of standard clauses for exploitation contract, it may notify the sponsoring State to deduct or forfeit the deposit because the sponsoring State has an obligation to assist the ISA and not *vice versa*. If the sponsoring State finds the contractor non-compliant, it has no power to order the ISA to do so. Another benefit of handing over the guarantee to the sponsoring State is that this power of forfeiture can act as an incentive for the sponsoring State to monitor the contractor at all stages. Besides, assuming the responsibilities without the economic tools is not fair to sponsoring States who are directly responsible for the contractors' performance. Therefore, giving the sponsoring State the management of the Environmental Performance Guarantee would enhance its ability to better monitor the sponsored contractor's performance.

Regardless of who receives the Environmental Performance Guarantee and in spite of the provisions of regulation 26 which have solved some problems, there are still other questions to be clarified relating to that mechanism. For example, how is "failure to comply with obligations" measured? Is non-compliance determined by virtue of conducts of non-compliance or

74 Draft Exploitation Regulations, regulation 26(1).

consequences arising from such non-compliance? Does forfeiture apply to non-compliance with regard to one obligation or several obligations?

Insurance is another economic instrument which benefits both contractors and victims. Article 235(3) of the LOSC suggests taking the compulsory insurance as a means to assure prompt and adequate compensation.[75] Section 16(5), Annex IV, of the Exploration Regulations embodies article 235(3), providing that "the contractor shall maintain appropriate insurance policies with internationally recognized carriers, in accordance with generally accepted international maritime practice."[76] Regulation 36 of the Draft Exploitation Regulations (March 2019) expressly treats the compulsory insurance as an obligation of the contractor and provides more details in this regard. Also, the ISA indicates that they are reviewing the issue of insurance.[77] At this point, the sponsoring State can assist the ISA by incorporating compulsory insurance into its domestic legislation and making it one of the conditions for granting a license.

### 3.2 *Environmental Duties and Obligations of a Contractor*

In order to ensure the sponsored contractor's compliance with international environmental obligations and environmental duties, the obligations of a contractor should be explicitly presented in the sponsoring State's national legislation. Such legislation should aim to incorporate all the relevant international legal obligations comprehensively. First, powers, duties, and functions under national deep seabed mining legislation, including environmental duties and obligations of a contractor, must always be consistent with the LOSC and other rules of international law not incompatible with the LOSC.[78] They should include:

- General duty to protect and preserve the marine environment and rare or fragile ecosystems and habitats;
- Duty to prevent, reduce, and control pollution from seabed activities or caused by ships or by the dumping of waste and other matter at sea;

75 LOSC, article 235(3).

76 Nodules Exploration Regulations, Annex IV, section 16.5; Sulphides Exploration Regulations, Annex IV, section 16.5; Crusts Exploration Regulations, Annex IV, section 16.5.

77 Draft Regulations on Exploitation of Mineral Resources in the Area, Note by the Legal and Technical Commission (ISBA/25/C/18, 27 March 2019), paragraph 25.

78 ISA, *Environmental Management Needs for Exploration and Exploitation of Deep Sea Minerals: Report of a Workshop held by The International Seabed Authority in collaboration with the Government of Fiji and the SOPAC Division of the Secretariat of the Pacific Community (SPC) in Nadi, Fiji, from 29 November to 2 December 2011* (ISA Technical Study: No. 10) (ISA 2012), 29–30.

- Duty to follow other marine environmental conventions applicable to ships concluded under the auspices of the International Maritime Organisation (IMO);
- Duty to prevent transboundary harm;
- Prior environmental impact assessment of activities likely to cause significant harm;
- Duty to take measures for ensuring safety at sea;
- Duties not to interfere with rights and freedoms of other States, such as the installation of submarine pipelines and cables, and marine scientific research; and ongoing monitoring of environmental impacts.[79]

Furthermore, some other key international legal obligations such as the duty to conserve biodiversity need to be incorporated into national legislation as well.[80]

Second, duties and obligations of a contractor under national deep seabed mining legislation should also be consistent with the ISA rules, procedures, and regulations. As of now, the important obligations of a contractor included in the ISA Exploration Regulations are:

- Include environmental information with application;[81]
- Take necessary measures to prevent, reduce, and control pollution and other hazards to the marine environment, applying a precautionary approach and best environmental practice;[82]
- Cooperate with the Authority in the establishment and implementation of monitoring and evaluation programs;[83]
- Gather environmental baseline data and establish baselines, taking account of any recommendations issued by the LTC;[84] and
- Report annually to the Authority.[85]

Moreover, the ISA Exploitation Regulations are underway. The existing exploitation draft version increased the contractor's obligations. Additional

---

79 ibid.

80 ibid.

81 Nodules Exploration Regulations, regulation 18(1)(b); Sulphides Exploration Regulations, regulation 20(1)(b); Crusts Exploration Regulations, regulation 20(1)(b).

82 Nodules Exploration Regulations, regulation 31(5); Sulphides Exploration Regulations, regulation 33(5); Crusts Exploration Regulations, regulation 33(5).

83 Nodules Exploration Regulations, regulation 31(6); Sulphides Exploration Regulations, regulation 33(6); Crusts Exploration Regulations, regulation 33(6).

84 Nodules Exploration Regulations, regulation 32(1); Sulphides Exploration Regulations, regulation 34(1); Crusts Exploration Regulations, regulation 34(1).

85 Nodules Exploration Regulations, Annex IV, section 10; Sulphides Exploration Regulations, Annex IV, section 10; Crusts Exploration Regulations, Annex IV, section 10.

obligations of contractors[86] include: reasonable regard for other activities in the marine environment;[87] preventing, responding and notifying to incidents;[88] notifying and protecting human remains and objects and sites of an archaeological or historical nature,[89] and a training commitment.[90]

If a sponsoring State's national legislation can incorporate the aforementioned obligations, it would be seen as one of the signals to carry out the obligation of due diligence, at least at this moment. Due diligence is a variable concept which needs to be developed in tandem with the Deep Seabed Mining Regime updates or emergence of new technology. What the sponsoring States need to consider is how to deploy and implement those obligations at the national level. The aforementioned obligations can be divided into two categories: general ones (such as the duty to protect and preserve the marine environment and rare or fragile ecosystems) and specific ones (such as the precautionary approach and best environmental practice). Two different approaches can be used by a sponsoring State to deploy these accordingly.

Incorporation of the general obligations into domestic law could be achieved by an overriding principle in the legislation, by adopting the example of Germany. The German Act specifies in section 1 that:

> (1) The purpose of this Act is, to ensure compliance with the obligations of the Federal Republic of Germany Deriving from Part of the Convention, its Annex, the Implementing Agreement and the rules and regulations issued by the Authority … (2) The provisions of the Convention, of the Implementing Agreement and the rules and regulations issued by the Authority shall govern the rights to the Area, to its resources and to minerals extracted from it. (3) For prospectors and contractors, the provisions of this Act and of the ordinances issued on the basis of Section 7 shall also apply in addition to the provisions of the Convention, of the Implementing Agreement, to the rules and regulations and instructions of the Authority and the stipulations contained in the contracts concluded by them with the Authority.[91]

86 Those contents have already been mentioned in the ISA Exploration Regulations, but not under the title "Rights and obligations of Contractors". The ongoing Exploitation Regulations expressively incorporate them under the title "Rights and obligations of Contractors", see eg Draft Exploitation Regulations (March 2019), part III.

87 Draft Exploitation Regulations (March 2019), regulation 31.

88 Draft Exploitation Regulations (March 2019), regulations 33 and 34.

89 Draft Exploitation Regulations (March 2019), regulation 35.

90 Draft Exploitation Regulations (March 2019), regulation 37.

91 Germany Act, section 1.

However, such a high-level statement about interpretation should not, of course, replace careful consideration of the relevant international obligations during the drafting process.[92]

Those relatively "specific" obligations are indeed either abstract (such as the precautionary approach and best environmental practice) or difficult to operationalize due to the lack of specific standards (such as baseline data collection and EIA). As Aline Jaeckel notes, "the challenge lies in translating the abstract obligation … into meaningful practical actions."[93] This part does not solve all the tricky issues. Instead, this section attempts to analyze to what extent and how some essential obligations can be implemented through the sponsoring State's national legislation. Some obligations, such as the precautionary approach, best environmental practice, and EIA, were already discussed in chapter 2 and will be addressed in this section again. Discourse in chapter 2 justifies them as elements of due diligence, whereas discourse in this part tends to focus on their operationalization in national legislation.

### 3.2.1 Baseline Data Collection

"Environmental Baseline" means the starting point (a certain date or state) against which the changes in the condition of a variable or a set of variables are measured.[94] Further, it can be used to evaluate actual impacts and predict potential environment risks. Not only that, the function of adequate environmental baseline data cannot be substituted, even though some environmental management tools, such as adaptive management, are applied in the context of scientific uncertainty.[95] It also demonstrates whether an applicant has adequate and comprehensive knowledge to start mining activities, *inter alia*, exploitation activities. The importance of environmental baseline data for the assessment of the potential environmental impact of a mining project, measurement of changes in the process of mining activities, and then to avoid or minimize impacts on marine environment is unquestionable.

---

92 SPC, *RLRF* (n 17), paragraph 7.2.

93 Aline Jaeckel, 'The Implementation of Precautionary Approach by the International Seabed Authority', Discussion Paper No. 5 (March 2017), 1.

94 A Discussion Paper on the development and drafting of Regulations on Exploitation for Mineral Resources in the Area (Environmental Matters) <https://www.isa.org.jm/files/documents/EN/Regs/DraftExpl/DP-EnvRegsDraft25117.pdf> accessed 8 August 2020, 96.

95 Adaptive management cannot compensate for a lack of baseline environmental data or inadequate modelling. Ministry for the Environment, *New Zealand's experiences with adaptive management for seabed mining projects: A submission to the International Seabed Authority to support the development of a regulatory framework for the exploitation of seabed minerals* (Ministry for the Environment 2016), 20.

Two questions need further interrogation here. First, what constitutes "good" or "adequate" environmental baseline data? A number of instruments noted that insufficient data should be avoided. However, the word "insufficient" needs further consideration. In practice, marine environment data is continuously "insufficient" due to environmental variation, partial observability, and structural uncertainty. It is strongly recommended to give a definition and establish a threshold for insufficient data here, if not, the applicants cannot implement it. Second, to what extent do those standards need to be specific? The Pew Charitable Trusts Code Project provides some reference. It said that "good baselines" are required to:

- Identify the existence and location of internationally and regionally recognized marine protected areas, other areas of special interest, other contractor license areas and, where appropriate, Vulnerable Marine Ecosystems (VMEs);
- resolve seasonal variation, inter-annual variation, and other relevant, potentially episodic and extreme, events;
- assess potential ore and sediment toxicity;
- determine existing levels of nutrient loading and pollution at sites;
- determine the nature, magnitude and extent of existing impacts / modifications to the area (e.g. from fishing, climatic change);
- allow the locations, size, number and spacing of impact reference areas and preservation reference areas to be determined including buffer zones;
- establish the broad geomorphology of the contractor license area;
- establish characteristics of the benthic and pelagic species in the area which may be affected [species present / biodiversity, population sizes and biomass of species, distribution of species and populations in space and time, ecosystem functioning, ecosystem services], including data on connectivity and affected ecosystems;
- Determine alien/invasive species present in the area;
- establish marine mammal and fish populations which may be affected;
- establish currents, tides, eddies and other oceanographic data sufficient to assess potential effects;
- establish the physical and chemical composition of the sediment which may be affected; and
- establish societal values placed on the area and its resources.[96]

---

96 Pew Charitable Trusts, First Report of the Code Project: Developing ISA Environmental Regulations (1st edn, 19 July 2017) <https://www.pewtrusts.org/-/media/assets/2017/08/first-report-of-the-code-project-developing-international-seabed-authority-environmental-regulations.pdf> accessed 8 August 2020, 46.

At the national level, it is suggested that the sponsoring State incorporate procedural standards of data collection into its national legislation and also introduce consequences for any contractor failing to do so. Regarding the sufficiency of data, sponsoring States' national legislation could cite the aforementioned Pew Charitable Trusts Code Project in creating their own specific standards for environmental baseline data collection.

### 3.2.2 Conducting the Environmental Impact Assessment

From the legal perspective, the EIA is a general obligation under customary international law. In the Deep Seabed Mining Regime, a contractor has the obligation of conducting the EIA. In the SDC Advisory Opinion, the Chamber recognizes that the sponsoring State is under a due diligence obligation to ensure that a potential contractor undertakes such an assessment prior to the submission of an application for a plan of work to the ISA. Furthermore, the ISA has indicated that some exploration activities, such as testing of collection systems, require prior EIA[97] and an environmental monitoring program[98] is needed during and after the specific activity. Prior EIA, which assesses impact at the initial stage, should form part of the application for a license for review by the regulatory agency of sponsoring States. This is required to inform the State's decision as to whether the deep seabed mining activity can proceed and whether the State could approve sponsorship to this applicant.

An EIA assists with identifying potential adverse environmental (including social and economic) impacts and developing tailored mitigation strategies. Warner comments that the threshold of approving or rejecting a plan of work is whether the applicant demonstrates an effective system to protect the marine environment from the harmful effects of mining activities, which requires an applicant to engage in a very thorough identification of the risks and uncertainties of the proposed mining activities for the marine environment of the Area and to propose plans to address these risks and uncertainties.[99] Implementing this threshold requires an applicant to conduct an EIA.[100] Through the EIA, the contractor can also operationalize several of its key obligations, such as

97 Nodules Exploration Regulations, regulation 18(1)(b); Sulphides Exploration Regulations, regulation 20(1)(b); Crusts Exploration Regulations, regulation 20(1)(b).

98 Nodules Exploration Regulations, Annex IV, sections 5.4 and 5.5; Sulphides Exploration Regulations, Annex IV, sections 5.4 and 5.5; Crusts Exploration Regulations, Annex IV, sections 5.4 and 5.5.

99 Robin Warner, 'International Environmental Law Principles Relevant to Exploitation Activity in the Area' (2020) 114 *Marine Policy* 103503.

100 ibid.

applying the precautionary approach.[101] An EIA is not a single report, but part of a wider process, with a number of general activities that include: screening to determine if an EIA is required; scoping to identify the issues and impacts; impact analysis to identify and predict effects of the proposal; mitigation and impact management to establish measures to manage impacts; preparation of the report to document all the issues and measures; review process; and decision-making to approve, reject, or modify the proposal.[102]

The sponsoring States' national legislation may wish to specify the particular format of the EIA required for each seabed mining activity. In this regard, it may be relevant to note that, in 2002, the LTC issued Recommendations for the Guidance of the Contractors for the Assessment of the Possible Environmental Impacts arising from Exploration for Polymetallic Nodules in the Area.[103] The Recommendations specified activities which required a prior EIA as well as an environmental monitoring program.[104] Given that the scope and content of an EIA often remains obscure and entails the risk of creating disputes with regard to the quality of the EIA,[105] the Recommendations will be useful to specify the contents of EIAs. Currently, the ISA is also preparing a template to be included in the new exploitation regulations.[106]

Sponsoring States could make reference to, or adopt, those templates in their national instruments. It is expected that certain sponsoring States already have in place EIA requirements and laws. In keeping with this, the legislation of deep seabed mining in the Area could cite existing national legislation and requirements and processes. Alternatively, the existing EIA requirements can be embedded in sponsoring States' national legislation as to deep seabed mining in the Area. However, they may also need to be amended accordingly to ensure that mining activities in the Area and their likely effects are appropriately covered.

---

101 Jennifer M Durden and others, 'Environmental Impact Assessment Process for Deep-Sea Mining in "the Area"' (2018) 87 *Marine Policy* 194, 194.

102 ISA, *Towards an ISA Environmental Management Strategy for the Area: Report of an International Workshop convened by the German Environment Agency (UBA), the German Federal Institute for Geosciences and Natural Resources (BGR), and the Secretariat of the International Seabed Authority (ISA) in Berlin, Germany, 20–24 March 2017* (ISA Technical Study: No. 17)(ISA 2017), 54.

103 Recommendations for the guidance of the contractors for the assessment of the possible environmental impacts arising from exploration for polymetallic nodules in the Area (ISBA/7/LTC/1/Rev.1, 13 February 2002).

104 ibid, paragraph 10.

105 Neil Craik, *The International Law of Environmental Impact Assessment: Process, Substance and Integration* (Cambridge University Press 2008), 89.

106 Draft Exploitation Regulations (March 2019), Annex IV, Environmental Impact Statement.

In addition, the appropriate qualifications of persons undertaking the preparation of EIAs needs discussion. The model that is increasingly used by terrestrial mining is to provide pre-selected expert personnel and company pools, from which operators must choose, to prepare the EIA.[107] Legislation on deep seabed mining in the Area may follow this example.

In any case, the EIA should be accurate and realistic. An EIA provides fundamental information on environmental impact and lays the basis on which mitigation measures are generated. Inaccurate basic information will cause unpredictable consequences. For example, in the Deepwater Horizon Oil Spill case, the estimates of harm used by BP and accepted by the regulators were far less damaging than the events that actually occurred and no "worst case" scenario was considered. Similarly, the Japanese planners apparently failed to account for the possibility of earthquakes and tsunamis as severe as those that actually occurred.[108]

Given the dynamism of the environment and the situation in the deep seabed technology is consistently being updated, the assessment of the impact of mining activities on environment should also be a continuous and iterative process, namely EIAs should be conducted in every stage of the mining process. It should not be terminated with the success of the application. Prior EIAs existing for the current ISA Exploration Regulations are "only a portion of a robust EIA process".[109] An EIA must be performed not just at the preliminary stage of a project but at several key points, and it must be site specific. Omitting an EIA at crucial points may cause serious environmental consequences.

In the current international Deep Seabed Mining Regime, there are no requirements for conducting any EIA other than at the preliminary stage. The large cost of an EIA is an obvious reason. However, a sponsoring State could make arrangements in keeping with its financial capability and require its sponsored contractor to conduct EIAs at several crucial points. That would also provide proof that a sponsoring State assumes the obligation of due diligence and takes on much stricter standards than the international level.

---

107 SPC, *RLRF* (n 17), paragraph 18.1.

108 Cymie R Payne, *Seminar on the Outcome of the Advisory Opinion Issued by the Seabed Disputes Chamber of the International Tribunal for the Law of the Sea on 1 February 2011 on the Responsibilities and Obligations of States Sponsoring Activities in the International Seabed Area* (Rochester, NY: Social Science Research Network, 7 April 2011).

109 Durden and others (n 102) 195.

### 3.2.3 Application of the Precautionary Approach

The precautionary approach has emerged as an accepted principle of environmental governance and management.[110] As presented in the section 4.3.2.1 of chapter 2, it provides guidance in responding to uncertainty. Numerous studies, guidelines, policy documents, and international instruments have offered distinct interpretations as to what its implementation entails.[111] Under the Deep Seabed Mining Regime, it is not only an obligation of the ISA and sponsoring States, but also an obligation of the contractor. Although most scholars study this issue with a special view to decision-making, they can provide some guidance on the actions of sponsoring States and contractors.

Aline Jaeckel identifies three dimensions in the implementation of the precautionary approach: the procedural dimension (decision-making process), institutional dimension (the ISA's capacity and competencies to provide for precautionary decision-making, facilitate risk assessment and risk management, adopt protective measures, and ensure their monitoring and enforcement), and the taking of protective measures.[112] To reach the goal of finding measures that are both *effective* in reaching the conservation objective and also *proportionate* to it,[113] the contractor is helpful at the following two levels. First, at the overall level, the contractor is vital for conducting research, "particularly scientific and economic research that contributes to a better understanding of the long-term options available".[114] Second, at the project level, it is very helpful for environmental protection if the contractor can identify the uncertainties inherent in its plan of work and EIA, and to demonstrate to what extent and how these certainties are addressed, although it is not a requirement of the application under the LOSC and existing ISA regulations. In this regard, the government of a sponsoring State may motivate the contractor to

---

110 Rosie Cooney, *The Precautionary Principle in Biodiversity Conservation and Natural Resource Management: An Issue Paper for Policy-Makers, Researchers and Practitioners* (IUCN 2004), 1.

111 Jaeckel, 'The Implementation of Precautionary Approach by the International Seabed Authority' (n 94) 2. For a detailed discussion, see Arie Trouwborst, *Precautionary Rights and Duties of States* (Martinus Nijhoff 2006), chapters 7-9.

112 Aline L Jaeckel, *The International Seabed Authority and the Precautionary Principle - Balancing Deep Seabed Mineral Mining and Marine Environmental Protection* (Brill 2017), chapter 2.

113 Jaeckel, 'The Implementation of Precautionary Approach by the International Seabed Authority' (n 94) 4.

114 Ellen Hey, 'The Precautionary Concept in Environmental Policy and Law: Institutionalizing Caution' (1992) 4 *Georgetown International Environmental Law Review* 303, 311.

become involved in the marine scientific research by way of policy advocacy or financial allocation.

However, the precautionary approach cannot be applied based merely on data from contractors. It needs collective action. It would be prudent for the ISA to create a holistic design for the operationalization of the precautionary approach, including regulations and guidelines which contractors could follow.

### 3.2.4 Best Environmental Practices

As mentioned in section 4.3.2.2 of chapter 2, the definition of best environmental practices is provided by the Draft Exploitation Regulations (March 2019): "the application of the most appropriate combination of environmental control measures and strategies, that will change with time in the light of improved knowledge, understanding or technology, taking into account the guidance set out in the applicable Guidelines."[115] Under this definition, applying the obligation of best environmental practices requires the sponsoring States and contractors to review the relevance of environmental measures considering technological, economic, and social elements, and applying the most appropriate measures in the light of technological and scientific advances, which also provide an evolutionary standard of due diligence.[116]

In fact, the Draft Exploitation Regulations (March 2019) borrowed the definition of best environmental practices from the *Convention for the Protection of the Marine Environment of the North-East Atlantic* (the 'OSPAR Convention').[117] Lessons might be learnt from Appendix 1, paragraph 6 of the OSPAR Convention, which provides a range of measures which could be selected based on specific cases. They are:

---

115 Draft Exploitation Regulations (March 2019), Schedule, Use of terms and scope.

116 Yoshifumi Tanaka, 'Obligations and Liability of Sponsoring States Concerning Activities in the Area: Reflections on the ITLOS Advisory Opinion of 1 February 2011' (2013) 60 *Netherlands International Law Review* 205, 211.

117 The Convention for the Protection of the Marine Environment of the North-East Atlantic (the 'OSPAR Convention') was opened for signature at the Ministerial Meeting of the Oslo and Paris Commissions in Paris on 22 September 1992. It was adopted together with a Final Declaration and an Action Plan. The Convention has been signed and ratified by all of the Contracting Parties to the original Oslo or Paris Conventions (Belgium, Denmark, the European Union, Finland, France, Germany, Iceland, Ireland, the Netherlands, Norway, Portugal, Spain, Sweden, and the United Kingdom) along with Luxembourg and Switzerland.

(a) the provision of information and education to the public and to users about the environmental consequences of choice of particular activities and choice of products, their use and ultimate disposal;
(b) the development and application of codes of good environmental practice which cover all aspect of the activity in the product's life;
(c) the mandatory application of labels informing users of environmental risks related to a product, its use and ultimate disposal;
(d) saving resources, including energy;
(e) making collection and disposal systems available to the public;
(f) avoiding the use of hazardous substances or products and the generation of hazardous waste;
(g) recycling, recovery and re-use;
(h) the application of economic instruments to activities, products or groups of products; and
(i) establishing a system of licensing, involving a range of restrictions or a ban.[118]

Most of these elements are relevant to deep seabed mining activities. Element (b) requires special attention. Quite a lot of codes or guidelines are, purportedly, aimed at guiding contractors, such as the International Finance Corporation (IFC) Performance Standards,[119] the family of International Organization for Standardization (ISO) standards,[120] and the International Marine Mineral Society.[121] As of now, the ISA does not clearly outline the practices which

118 OSPAR Convention, Appendix 1, paragraph 6.

119 The IFC Performance Standards form an integrated part of the IFC Sustainability Framework. The former comprises eight standards that parties responsible for implementing and operating a project financed by the IFC need to meet throughout the life of the particular investment. IFC Performance Standards on Environmental and Social Sustainability (1 January 2012) <https://www.ifc.org/wps/wcm/connect/24e6bfc3-5de3-444d-be9b-226188c95454/PS_English_2012_Full-Document.pdf?MOD=AJPERES&CVID=jkV-X6h> accessed 5 August 2020.

120 ISO Standards <https://www.iso.org/standards.html> accessed 8 August 2020; regarding the possible application of the ISO in the Deep Seabed Mining Regime, see Makoto Seta, 'The Contribution of the International Organization for Standardization to Ocean Governance: The Contribution of the International Organization for Standardization to Ocean Governance' (2019) 28 *Review of European, Comparative & International Environmental Law* 304–313.

121 IMMS, Code for Environmental Management of Marine Mining (adopted on 2 November 2001, revised on 16 September 2011) <https://www.immsoc.org/IMMS_downloads/2011_SEPT_16_IMMS_Code.pdf> accessed 2 August 2020. It should be borne in mind that following and adhering to the principles and guidelines contained in the Code are voluntary in nature. The aim of the IMMS Code is to complement applicable binding national and international regulations for the protection of the marine environment with regard

contractors are required to adopt and implement. This, inevitably, causes ambiguities.[122] Identifying the best environmental practices may not always be clear. Because of the different social, economic, cultural, and ecological backgrounds of states and regions, the criteria for representing the best environmental practices in one area may differ from another.[123] Given the insufficient technical capacity of developing States, it is difficult for them to adopt the best environmental practices that meet the most stringent regulatory requirements in the world. Besides, the economic viability of the technology is also a critical factor in implementing the best environmental practices.[124] Nevertheless, it is undeniable that a restricted approach, which means that the ISA formally adopts, endorses, or issues the required guidelines and standards for best environmental practice and explicitly requires contractors to adhere to those guidelines, is beneficial to clarify and lessen the regulatory burden for both contractors and sponsoring States.[125]

At the national level, there is no doubt that a sponsoring State has the regulatory power to turn those international codes or guidelines into a legally binding norm. However, it is essential to note that many guidelines are primarily voluntary in nature. When deciding to do so, it is important for the sponsoring State "to consider whether such voluntary guidelines and standards are indeed capable of being applied in such as mandatory manner."[126]

### 3.2.5 Protection of Archaeological and Historical Objects

Under international environmental law, material assets, including archaeological and cultural heritage, are part of the environment, and thus environmental protection axiomatically includes protection of archaeological and cultural objects.[127] As ILC Draft Principles on the Allocation of Loss in the Case of Transboundary Harm Arising Out of Hazardous Activities, Principle 2 stipulates, "a narrow definition of environmental damage is limited to damage to

---

to marine mining where these regulations exist, and to provide environmental principles and guidelines for marine mining companies where these are absent or could be improved upon.

122 Gerber and Grogan (n 69) 4.

123 A Nollkaemper, 'Balancing the Protection of Marine Ecosystems with Economic Benefits from Land-Based Activities: The Quest for International Legal Barriers' (1996) 27 *Ocean Development and International Law* 153, 159.

124 Jonas Ebbesson, 'A Critical Assessment of the 1992 Baltic Sea Convention' (2000) 43 *GYIL* 38, 47.

125 Gerber and Grogan (n 69) 4.

126 ibid.

127 Sands and others (n 74) 700.

natural resources alone (air, water, soil, fauna and flora, and their interaction); a more extensive approach includes damage to natural resources and property that forms part of the cultural heritage; the most extensive definition includes landscape and environmental amenity". The LOSC also highlights the protection of archaeological and cultural objects in article 303 generally and in article 149 specifically referring to the activities in the Area. Article 303 also provides that "States have the duty to protect objects of an archaeological and historical nature found at sea and co-operate for this purpose". Article 149 stipulates that "All objects of an archaeological and historical nature found in the Area shall be preserved or disposed of for the benefit of mankind as a whole, particular regard being paid to the preferential rights of the State or country of origin, or the State of cultural origin, or the State of historical and archaeological origin."

Two observations are found from these provisions as to the protection of objects of an archaeological and historical nature. First, the term "archaeological and historical objects" is not defined in the LOSC. Moritaka Hayashi notes that it seems clear from the *travaux préparatoires* that they refer to all kinds of wrecks and related objects of archaeological and/or historical importance found at sea.[128] Tullio Scovazzi is of the view of that the article shall be interpreted in a broader sense, referring to "all traces of human existence having a cultural, historical or archaeological character",[129] as indicated in article 1(1)(a) of the Convention on the Protection of the Underwater Cultural Heritage (CPUCH).[130] In any case "archaeological and historical objects" which are man-made artifacts, cannot be considered as minerals and common heritage of mankind,[131] and thus the ISA has no competence to manage and control them.[132] Second, notwithstanding article 149, the LOSC "does not provide a means for implementing that objective [of the protection of archaeological

128 Moritaka Hayashi, 'Archaeological and Historical Objects under the United Nations Convention on the Law of the Sea' (1996) 20 *Marine Policy* 291, 291.

129 Alexander Proelss and others (eds), *United Nations Convention on the Law of the Sea: A Commentary* (CH Beck; Hart; Nomos 2017), 1055.

130 Convention on the Protection of the Underwater Cultural Heritage (CPUCH), adopted on 2 November 2001 within the framework of the United Nations Organization for Education, Science and Culture (UNESCO). The CPUCH entered into force on 2 January 2009 and, as of July 2013, there were forty-four States Parties.

131 In 1973, Turkey and Greece respectively submitted a draft article to the Sea-Bed Committee that extended the common heritage of mankind regime to 'archaeological and historical treasures', which reached no consensus. Regarding history on this account, see Satya N Nandan, Michael W Lodge and Shabtai Rosenne, *United Nations Convention on the Law of the Sea, 1982: A Commentary, Volume VI* (Martinus Nijhoff Publishers 2002), 227–232.

132 Hayashi (n 129) 293.

and historical objects]."[133] The ISA Exploration Regulations recommend several approaches, followed by the Draft Exploitation Regulations (March 2019) as well. It provides:

> The contractor shall immediately notify the Secretary-General in writing of any finding in the exploration area of any human remains of an archaeological or historical nature, or any object or site of a similar nature and its location, including the preservation and protection measures taken. The Secretary-General shall transmit such information to the Director General of the United Nations Educational, Scientific and Cultural Organization and any other competent international organization. Following the finding of any such human remains, objector site in the exploration area, and in order to avoid disturbing such human remains, object or site, no further prospecting or exploration shall take place, within a reasonable radius, until such time as the Council decides otherwise after taking account of the views of the Director General of the United Nations Educational, Scientific and Cultural Organization or any other competent international organization.[134]

This provision grants the contractor an obligation of notification of finding an archaeological or historical nature and gives the Council the power to take decisions on whether mining activities can be resumed after their suspension. The ISA has no further mandate in this regard. However, no information is provided as to "the preferential rights enjoyed by [the State or country of origin, or the State of cultural origin, or the State of historical and archaeological origin] under Art. 149 or the manner in which they should be harmonized with the benefit of mankind as a whole."[135]

It is worth mentioning that the provision of "human remains and objects and sites of an archaeological or historical nature" is explicitly set under the part of "rights and obligations of contractors" in the Draft Exploitation Regulations (March 2019). Therefore, a sponsoring State's national legislation must have a provision to require a contractor to comply with the LOSC and ISA

133 Sarah Dromgoole, 'Reflections on the Position of the Major Maritime Powers with Respect to the UNESCO Convention on the Protection of the Underwater Cultural Heritage 2001' (2013) 38 *Marine Policy* 116, 118.

134 Nodules Exploration Regulations, regulation 35; Sulphides Exploration Regulations, regulation 37; Crusts Exploration Regulations, regulation 37; Draft Exploitation Regulation (March 2019), regulation 35.

135 Proelss and others (n 130) 1057.

Regulations. It is suggested the national legislation incorporate the contents of the notification of finding and the necessary suspension of mining activities when such objects are found. Also, penalties attached to such a violation needs to be specified in the national legislation as well. Apart from this, neither the ISA nor the sponsoring State seems to have more authority.

### 3.2.6 Reasonable Regard for Other Activities

"Reasonable regard for other activities in the marine environment" appears in article 147 of the LOSC, which is under the section 2 "principles governing the Area", of Part XI. The Exploration Regulations contain this content in section 13.3 of the standard clauses for exploration contract, providing "the Contractor shall actively carry out the program of activities: (c) with reasonable regards for other activities in the marine environment."[136] This item is expressly described as an obligation of the contractor under the Draft Exploitation Regulation (March 2019).[137] It needs to be clarified that the "marine environment" in this context is different from that all other occurrences of the term in the LOSC. The meaning of "marine environment" in article 147(1) refers to the entire marine space across all jurisdictional zones, which is broader than the term in other occurrences.[138]

Two important elements of this obligation that are worth studying are the scope of "other activities" and "reasonableness". First, there is no definition of "other activities" in this context, but it would "encompass recognition of the right of all States to conduct activities in the marine environment"[139] and be naturally limited to lawful activities.[140] It should include "submarine cables or pipelines" since it is expressly stipulated by the Draft Exploitation Regulations (March 2019).[141] Fiji, Kiribati, Nauru, Tonga, and Tuvalu illustrate other existing or planned legitimate sea uses including, but not limited to, marine scientific research, navigation, submarine cables, fisheries, or conservation activities.[142]

---

136 Nodules Exploration Regulations, Annex IV, section 13.3(c); Sulphides Exploration Regulations, Annex IV, section 13.3(c); Crusts Exploration Regulations, Annex IV, section 13.3(c).
137 Draft Exploitation Regulations (March 2019), regulation 31.
138 Proelss and others (n 130) 1040.
139 Nandan, Lodge and Rosenne (n 132) 215.
140 Proelss and others (n 130) 1040.
141 Draft Exploitation Regulations (March 2019), regulation 31(1).
142 Comparative Study of the Existing National Legislation on Deep Seabed Mining (n 4), paragraph 79.

Second, the term "reasonable regard" appears only once in the LOSC, whereas the term "due regard" appears many times in the LOSC.[143] Indeed, the difference between these two terms is not in essence but in "semantics".[144] The use of the notion of reasonableness in law-making is not to reduce the effectiveness of the obligation but to render legal rules more flexible.[145] The ICJ seemed to support such flexibility and held that "[...] what is reasonable and equitable in any given case must depend on its particular circumstances."[146] Similarly, the European Court of Human Rights held that "reasonableness ...

---

143 "Due reasonable" appears in article 147 of Part XI, where "due regards" appears in article 142 and article 148 of Part XI. "Due regards" appears in other parts under the LOSC as follows: Preamble, 'with due regard for the sovereignty of all States'; Part II (territorial sea and contiguous zone), article 27(4) (criminal jurisdiction on board a foreign ship), 'in considering whether or in what manner an arrest should be made, the local authorities shall have due regard to the interests of navigation'; Part III (straits used for international navigation), article 39(3) (duties of ships and aircraft during transit passage), 'with due regard for the safety of navigation'; Part V (EEZ), article 56(2) (rights, jurisdiction and duties of the coastal State in the EEZ) and article 58(3) (rights and duties of other States in the EEZ); Part V (EEZ), article 60(3) (artificial islands, installations and structures in the EEZ), 'ensure the safety of navigation', 'Such removal shall also have due regard to fishing, the protection of the marine environment and the rights and duties of other States'; Part V (EEZ), article 66(3)(a) (anadromous stocks), 'States concerned shall maintain consultations with a view to achieving agreement on terms and conditions of such fishing giving due regard to the conservation requirements and the needs of the State of origin in respect of these stocks'; Part VI (CS), article 79(5), 'when laying submarine cables or pipelines, States shall have due regard to cables or pipelines already in position. In particular, possibilities of repairing existing cables or pipelines shall not be prejudiced.' Part VII (high seas), article 87(2), 'these freedoms shall be exercised by all States with due regard for the interests of other States in their exercise of the freedom of the high seas, and also with due regard for the rights under this Convention with respect to activities in the Area.' Part XII (protection and preservation of the marine environment), article 234 (ice-covered area), 'such laws and regulations shall have due regard to navigation and the protection and preservation of the marine environment based on the best available scientific evidence.'; Part XIII (MSR), article 245 (MSR conducting in the TS), article 246 (MSR conducting in the EEZ or on CS), 'due regard should be paid to the rights and interests of the coastal State is implied'; Part XIV (development and transfer of marine technology), article 267 (protection of legitimate interests), 'States, in promoting cooperation pursuant to article 266, shall have due regard for all legitimate interests including, inter alia, the rights and duties of holders, suppliers and recipients of marine technology'.

144 David Anderson, 'The Principle of Reasonableness in the Law of the Sea' in Holger P Hestermeyer and others (eds), *Coexistence, Cooperation and Solidarity, Vol. I* (Brill Nijhoff 2012), 662.

145 Olivier Corten, 'Reasonableness in International Law' in *Max Plank Encyclopedia of Public International Law* (2013).

146 *Interpretation of the Agreement of 25 March 1951 between the WHO and Egypt, Advisory Opinion, I.C.J Reports 1980, p. 73,* at 96, paragraph 49.

must be assessed in each case according to its special features".[147] However, this flexibility does not prevent the establishment of procedural standards. When envisaging a new regime for areas beyond national jurisdiction, Tullio Treves stated:

> It should state specific criteria for ensuring coexistence of different activities, and, if, necessary, establish priorities, or mechanisms for dealing with conflict. If a plurality of machineries is to be set up, each regime should make prevision for the possibility of efficient contacts and cooperation between them.[148]

There is currently no process to decide on the priority between competing interests. However, a mechanism could be established by a sponsoring State's national legislation to contact or adjust or qualify its activities. It could be operationalized by a compulsory negotiation procedure where the contractor is required to assess what other activities are planned or already conducted within the contracted area and analyze the mutual interference. Afterward, the contractor must come to a negotiation procedure with other sea users. Alternatively, it could also go to a compulsory negotiation procedure, as long as the contractor is requested by other sea users.

### 3.2.7 Respect for Indigenous People

Valuable deep seabed mineral resources are located primarily in the Pacific Ocean. Papua New Guinea, Fiji, Tonga, Vanuatu, and the Solomon Islands are all known to have significant quantities of polymetallic sulphides, whereas the waters of Kiribati, the Cook Islands, and, to a lesser extent, Niue and Tuvalu all contain polymetallic nodules.[149] The central equatorial Pacific region provides the best potential for crust mining, especially the exclusive economic zones around Johnston Island and Hawaii, the Marshall Islands, the Federated States of Micronesia, and international waters of the mid-Pacific.[150]

---

147 *Wemhoff v Germany*, Judgement of 27 June 1968, [1968] ECHR 2, paragraph 10.

148 Tullio Treves, 'Principles and Objectives of the Legal Regime Governing Areas Beyond National Jurisdiction' in Erik Jaap Molenaar and Alex G Oude Elferink (eds), *The International Legal Regime of Areas beyond National Jurisdiction: Current and Future Developments* (Martinus Nijhoff Publishers 2010), 22.

149 The World Bank, Precautionary Management of Deep Sea Mining Potential in Pacific Island Countries <http://pubdocs.worldbank.org/en/125321460949939983/Pacific-Possible-Deep-Sea-Mining.pdf> accessed 2 August 2020.

150 ISA, 'Cobalt-Rich Crusts' <https://isa.org.jm/files/files/documents/eng9.pdf> accessed 15 June 2019.

The Clarion-Clipperton Zone (CCZ), in which ISA approved sixteen plans of work for exploration, is located approximately five hundred miles southeast of Hawaii.[151] Indigenous peoples are widely distributed in these Pacific Islands States.[152] The term indigenous people usually refers to the descendants of those who inhabited a country or a geographical region at the time when people of different cultures or ethnic origins arrived and then those new arrivals later became dominant through conquest, occupation, settlement, or other means.[153] Although most legal definitions of the environment do not include people and their property,[154] indigenous people should be given special consideration due to their strong link to territories and surrounding natural resources. In the Pacific, some exploration licenses have already been granted by the Pacific Island States within their national jurisdiction.[155] The exploration activities within a national jurisdiction are already having adverse impacts on human communities. For example, there has been a steep decrease in the presence of sharks that affects the traditional fishing custom of "shark calling" carried out by indigenous peoples.[156]

Skeptics have argued that mining activities in the Area has no direct impact on indigenous people as it takes place in the deep ocean. However, "[t]his

151 An ecosystem-based approach to protect the deep sea from mining (EARSC, 9 December 2013) <http://earsc.org/news/an-ecosystem-based-approach-to-protect-the-deep-sea-from-mining> accessed 5 August 2020.

152 The term "indigenous" has prevailed as a generic term for many years. In some countries, there may be preference for other terms including tribes, first peoples/nations, aboriginals, ethnic groups, *adivasi, janajati*. Occupational and geographical terms like hunter-gatherers, nomads, peasants, hill people, etc., also exist and for all practical purposes can be used interchangeably with "indigenous peoples". <http://www.un.org/esa/socdev/unpfii/documents/5session_factsheet1.pdf> accessed 2 August 2020. Under the common UN understanding of indigenous peoples, at least some communities – and in many cases, a majority of citizens – in every Pacific Island nation qualify as indigenous and are extended protections as such. See 'Resource Roulette – How Deep Sea Mining and Inadequate Regulatory Frameworks Imperil the Pacific and Its Peoples', A Report by Blue Ocean Law and the Pacific Network on Globalisation <https://cer.org.za/wp-content/uploads/2016/08/Resource-Roulette-Deep-sea-Mining-and-Inadequate-Regulatory-Frameworks.pdf> accessed 2 August 2020, 9.

153 UN Permanent Forum on Indigenous Issues, 'Who are indigenous peoples?'<http://www.un.org/esa/socdev/unpfii/documents/5session_factsheet1.pdf> accessed 2 August 2020.

154 Sands and others (n 74) 700 and chapter 18.

155 Tonga, Fiji, Vanuatu, and the Cook Islands, among others, have issued exploration licenses for prospecting in their waters. See 'Resource Roulette' (n 153) 10–17.

156 'New Ireland Locals Fear Nautilus Destroying Shark Calling' (Deep Sea Mining Campaign, 18 October, 2012) <http://www.deepseaminingoutofourdepth.org/new-ireland-locals-fear-nautilus-destroying-shark-calling/> accessed 5 August 2020.

ignores the substantial stewardship [indigenous people] feel of the marine environment as a holistic entity, and one with considerable spiritual value."[157] It is further indicated that indigenous people "do not live at or directly utilize the offshore mine site should not be interpreted to mean that they do not value and/or exert ownership and tenure over such areas. [They] express a strong spiritual connection to all components of the ocean environment".[158] Furthermore, as indicated in section 2.3 of chapter 1, mining activities may have far-reaching impacts, which might have potentially negative impacts on indigenous peoples.

Indigenous people should be given special consideration, despite the fact no direct mention is made in Part XI of the LOSC. As Julie Hunter indicates, "[g]iven the documented impacts on numerous indigenous communities, indigenous concerns and rights must also be incorporated into any regime posting control over seabed resources."[159] Indeed, article 138 provides the legal basis for incorporating the consideration of indigenous peoples into the Deep Seabed Mining Regime. It provides:

> The general conduct of States in relation to the Area shall be in accordance with the provisions of this Part, the principles embodied in the Charter of the United Nations and *other rules of international law* in the interests of maintaining peace and security and promoting international cooperation and mutual understanding. [emphasis added]

"Other rules of international law" in this article includes international human rights law and customary international law, which establishes a direct link between the LOSC and international human rights law and customary international law.[160]

157 Richard Steiner, 'Independent Review of the Environmental Impact Statement for the Proposed Nautilus Minerals Solwara 1 Seabed Mining Project, Papua New Guinea' conducted for the Bismarck-Solomon Seas Indigenous Peoples Council (10 January 2009)<http://www.deepseaminingoutofourdepth.org/wp-content/uploads/Steiner-Independent-review-DSM1.pdf> accessed 23 July 2020, 6.

158 ibid.

159 Julie Hunter, Pradeep Singh and Julian Aguon, 'Broadening Common Heritage: Addressing Gaps in the Deep Sea Mining Regulatory Regime' (16 April 2018) *Harvard Environmental Law Review*, <https://harvardelr.com/2018/04/16/broadening-common-heritage/> accessed 18 April 2021.

160 Julian Aguon and Julie Hunter, 'Second Wave Due Diligence: The Case for Incorporating Free, Prior, and Informed Consent into the Deep Sea Mining Regulatory Regime' (2018) 38 *Stanford Environmental Law Journal* 3, 23.

Sponsoring States' national legislation should also be drafted and interpreted in a manner that expressly reaffirms their commitment to respect and protect indigenous peoples' rights as provided for and is consistent with human rights conventions and instruments, such as the United Nations Declaration on the Rights of Indigenous Peoples (UNDRIP).[161] Taking indigenous concerns and rights into consideration is also called "second wave" due diligence.[162] The due diligence of the sponsoring State "flow not because of where these activities occur, but rather where their effects are felt".[163] National legislation that ignore these other knowledge systems may lack legitimacy.

### 3.3 *Rights of a Contractor*

In addition to environmental duties and obligations, national legislation should also clearly document the rights of deep seabed mining contractors. A common mistake is that the focus is placed primarily on the obligations of the contractor, and rights are neglected. The national legislation should incorporate relevant provisions from the LOSC and related legal instruments as well as ISA regulations. Examples include giving express rights to the deep seabed mining operator for its activity in the designated area, such as security of tenure, along with other important rights.[164]

#### 3.3.1 Exclusive Right and Preferential Right

The LOSC accords the contractor the exclusive right for exploration and exploitation in Annex III, article 16 of the LOSC providing:

> [t]he Authority shall, ..., accord the operator the exclusive right to explore and exploit the area covered by the plan of work in respect of a specified category of resources and shall ensure that no other entity operates in the same area for a different category of resources in a manner which might interfere with the operations of the operator.

The exclusive right is one of the specific manifestations of the *security of tenure* stipulated by article 153(6) of the LOSC. That essential principle is repeated in the ISA Exploration Regulations[165] and in their standard clauses for exploration

161 SPC, *RLRF* (n 17), paragraph 6.16. United Nations Declaration on the Rights of Indigenous Peoples (adopted 12 September 2007, A/61/L.67/Annex) (UNDRIP).

162 Aguon and Hunter (n 161) 8.

163 ibid, 7.

164 LOSC, article 153(6).

165 Nodules Exploration Regulations, regulation 24(1); Sulphides Exploration Regulations, regulation 26(1); Crusts Exploration Regulations, regulation 26(1).

contracts.[166] Also, that right "will certainly be provided for in the Authority's future Regulations on exploitation".[167]

To ensure such a right, the ISA Exploration Regulations stipulate the LTC must not recommend approval if the proposed plan of work for polymetallic nodules/polymetallic sulphides/cobalt-rich crusts "might cause undue interference with activities under such approved plan of work for other resources."[168] This fundamental right should be reaffirmed in sponsoring States' national legislation. Also, the regulatory agency of the sponsoring State should follow the LTC's example to ensure the contractor's exclusive right, although the phrase "undue interference" is not defined and needs further explanation on a case-by-case basis by the LTC.[169] Indeed, the sponsoring State cannot guarantee the exclusive rights of the contractor absolutely, since activities in the Area is within the jurisdiction of the ISA. Nevertheless, the sponsoring State can at least guarantee that it does not approve such applications within its jurisdiction.

One right relating to the exclusive right is the preferential right which is stipulated by Annex III, article 10 of the LOSC. Under this article, a contractor who has an approved plan of work for exploration shall have a preference and a priority among applicants for a plan of work covering exploitation of the same area and resources. Such preference or priority may be withdrawn if the contractor's performance is not satisfactory.[170] This right is reiterated in the ISA Exploration Regulations and Draft Exploitation Regulations (March 2019). However, inconsistency exists in the organ that has the mandate to withdraw such preference or priority between these two categories of regulations. The ISA Exploration Regulations mandates the Council to withdraw such preference or priority with justifiable cause. Also, the contractor has a reasonable opportunity to be heard.[171] By contrast, the Draft Exploitation Regulations (March 2019) stipulate that the Secretary-General shall determine whether the applicant has such preference or priority with no further specification.[172] Nevertheless, this inconsistency has no material impact on the sponsoring

166 Nodules Exploration Regulations, Annex IV, section 2.2; Sulphides Exploration Regulations, Annex IV, section 2.2; Crusts Exploration Regulations, Annex IV, section 2.2.

167 Proelss and others) (n 130) 2225.

168 Nodules Exploration Regulations, regulation 21(6); Sulphides Exploration Regulations, regulation 23(6); Crusts Exploration Regulations, regulation 23(6).

169 Proelss and others (n 130) 2227.

170 LOSC, Annex III, article 10.

171 Nodules Exploration Regulations, regulation 24(2); Sulphides Exploration Regulations, regulation 26(2); Crusts Exploration Regulations, regulation 26(2).

172 Draft Exploitation Regulation (March 2019), regulation 10(1).

State's national legislation beyond the sponsoring State's jurisdiction. The sponsoring State only needs to incorporate the provision as to such preference and that priority is granted within its jurisdiction. Likewise, it is suggested to grant the opportunity for the contractor to respond as stipulated in ISA Exploration Regulations.

### 3.3.2 Transfer/Extension/Retention/Surrender of the License

Deep seabed mining is a long-term, capital-intensive, and high-technology activity. There have been cases where when mining activities start, the approved contractor may find that it does not have adequate financial capability or cannot meet new requirements of technology so is reluctant to continue mining activities. Another scenario may be that the contractor finds that it cannot finish the task at this stage although the legal period for exploration or exploitation is due. In face of those eventualities, the LOSC and 1994 Implementing Agreement has the option to grant the contractor rights of transfer[173] and extension[174] of its contract. Likewise, the sponsoring State's national legislation should reaffirm the contractor's right to transfer its contract to a third party or extend its contract upon approval of the regulatory agency. For instance, a sponsoring State's national legislation could shed light on requirements of the potential transferee. Alternatively, the potential transferee may be treated as a new applicant. Moreover, the license-holder shall have the right to apply for an extension before the end of the contract, and the extension may be determined by the regulatory body at its discretion, according to license-holder's application and its performance.

The experience from terrestrial mining demonstrates that when commercial exploitation is not a good option for some mines, given the overall market or for economic reasons, the usual solution is to reduce output or even shut down the mines over a period of time. Retention happens in the situation where the commercial value of minerals of a certain area is known by way of exploration, however, recovery is not currently economically viable. There is no doubt that preservation is the best protection for investors in the case of economic uncertainty, after all, investors would have already made major capital investment.[175] The Draft Exploitation Regulations (March 2019) incorporate the retention as "reduction or suspension in production due to market

173 LOSC, Annex III, article 20.

174 1994 Implementing Agreement, Annex, section 1(9).

175 Response of the China Ocean Mineral Resources Research and Development Association (COMRA) to the *First Working Draft of the Regulations and Standard Contract Terms on Exploitation for Mineral Resources in the Area (February 2016)*, submitted 2 November 2016.

conditions" under regulation 29, in which a maximum period of retention is five years.[176]

In addition, the terrestrial mining regime also provides for the license holder itself to be able to apply to the regulatory agency to request the surrender of the license. The Draft Exploitation Regulations (March 2019) also mention surrender of the contract, without further specification.[177] Based on the experience of terrestrial mining, in the case of a request to surrender, the license of the operator is released only after any outstanding liability or obligations have been met by the license holder and the State may require sign-off on a final report confirming this, before the surrender takes effect.[178]

These types of items should be included in the legislation of the sponsoring State for seabed mining and should be reviewed, accordingly, before the application is submitted to the ISA. Without such content, it is hard to believe that the sponsoring country has carried out the obligation of due diligence. It should be noted that under the Deep Seabed Mining Regime, the sponsoring State's regulatory agency is the secondary regulator, whose authority is subject to its jurisdiction. Indeed, the sponsoring State must be very cautious in provisions as to matters that require the ISA to make the final decision, such as retention. It is meaningless without the ISA's approval because the LOSC mandates the ISA to control and manage the Area and its resources on behalf of mankind as a whole, rather than any sovereign State.

### 3.3.3 Appeal

It should be noted that the Draft Regulations on Exploitation of Mineral Resources in the Area (August 2017) establishes a review mechanism to solve a contractor's dissatisfaction with the result concerning the interpretation or application of the exploitation contract, despite the existence of article 188(2)(a) of the LOSC.[179] Under this mechanism, where there is a dispute concerning the interpretation or application of the exploitation contract, the contractor could seek a review of the decision or action taken by or on behalf of the ISA. This is sometimes problematic as the appointment of a panel is a complex transaction.[180] However, the result of this review is final and binding.

176 Draft Exploitation Regulations (March 2019), regulation 29(3).

177 Draft Exploitation Regulations (March 2018), Annex X, standard clauses for exploitation contract, section 13.

178 SPC, *RLRF* (n 17), paragraph 14.39.

179 Draft Regulations on Exploitation of Mineral Resources in the Area (ISBA/23/LTC/CRP.3*, 8 August 2017), draft regulation 92.

180 ibid. A panel of experts shall be constituted as follows: the Contractor and the Secretary-General shall seek to agree upon the composition of the panel within thirty days of the

Unfortunately, this provision does not exist in the latest version of the ISA Draft Exploitation Regulations. Nevertheless, this is still a lesson that can be learnt by the sponsoring State's regulatory agency in dealing with appeals.

If the application of a license or the application of transfer, extension, or retention is objected to by the regulatory agency or a decision is made by the monitoring agency, the applicant should have a right to appeal in an administrative procedure. Sponsoring States should take appropriate measures to ensure that such appeal procedures are equitable, timely, not prohibitively expensive, and sufficiently comprehensive, so as to enable informed and timely responses that can be acted upon.[181]

The regulatory agency shall commence the hearing of opinions within a certain period. The applicant and other interested persons could participate in the hearing and present its evidence. Then, the regulatory agency could make a decision to retain or rescind its former decision. The Japan Mining Act has provisions as to appeal.[182] Its regulatory agency is the Ministry of Economy, Trade and Industry and it is required to commence the hearing of opinions within 30 days from the date of receipt of the application for examination or objection.[183] In addition to the applicant for the hearing, those who intend to participate in the hearing may participate as interested parties with the permission of the Minister of Economy, Trade and Industry and present evidence and statements.[184] With regard to a decision, it makes reference to its Administrative Appeal Act (Act No. 160 of 1962) which provides the procedure for decision making.[185]

National legislation should provide rights of judicial appeal against relevant decisions to a court with appellate jurisdiction or to other independent organs that may review the actions of the decision-maker.[186] Fiji, Kiribati, Nauru,

conclusion of the investigation under paragraph 3; if no agreement can be reached, the Contractor and the Secretary-General shall each nominate one member of the panel within a further thirty days; the two members so nominated shall agree upon the third member of the panel, who shall act as chairman; if the two members are unable so to agree within thirty days of the second of them being appointed, the President of the Seabed Disputes Chamber of the International Tribunal for the Law of the Sea shall nominate the third member of the panel.

181 SPC, *RLRF* (n 17), paragraph 17.3.

182 Japan Mining Act, articles 126–135.

183 Japan Mining Act, article 126.

184 Japan Mining Act, article 128.

185 Japan Mining Act, article 130.

186 Alberto Pecoraro, 'Deep Seabed Mining in the Area: is international investment law relevant?' (*EJIL: Talk!* 2019) <https://www.ejiltalk.org/deep-seabed-mining-in-the-area-is-international-investment-law-relevant/#more-17314> accessed 11 July 2020.

Tonga, and Tuvalu have provisions as to disputes between the sponsoring State and the applicant/sponsored contractor. These national legislations refer to the process of settlement by mutual agreement or mediation. In the event that this is not successful then it is referred to arbitration in accordance with its domestic law (Fiji, Kiribati, Nauru, Tuvalu)[187] or the Supreme Court (Tonga),[188] or ITLOS (Kiribati, Nauru).[189]

### 3.4 *Monitoring Oversight*

The LOSC clearly requires that appropriate environmental standards must not only be documented in domestic legislation but must also be implemented through monitoring and enforcement.[190] International legal requirements would not be met by a State merely by putting rules in place. As the ICJ notes in the discussion on the comprehensive nature of due diligence in the *Pulp Mills* judgement: "It is an obligation which entails not only the adoption of appropriate rules and measures, but also a certain level of vigilance in their enforcement and the exercise of administrative control … such as the monitoring of activities".[191] This calls for the robust monitoring of the performance of deep seabed mining operations in the Area, and their actual impact. According to the LOSC, the contractor is expected to prepare a monitoring program, based on the recommendations of the LTC, to observe, measure, evaluate, and analyze the risks or effects of pollution on the marine environment resulting from activities in the Area, from which the adequacy of existing regulations are examined as well.[192] Also, whether the contractor complies with these regulations can be monitored.[193] This provision is reiterated and developed by the ISA Exploration Regulations and Draft Exploitation Regulations (March 2019), from which the latter provide fulsome details.[194] Under the Draft Exploitation Regulations (March 2019), three methods are used to monitor the

187 Fiji Act, article 54(2); Kiribati Act, article 130(ii)(b); Nauru Act, article 54(2)(b); Tuvalu Act, article 126(2)(b).

188 Tonga Act, article 122(2).

189 Kiribati Act, article 130(ii)(c); Nauru Act, article 54(2)(c).

190 See eg LOSC, articles 214 and 215.

191 *Pulp Mills on the River Uruguay (Argentina v. Uruguay), Judgment, I.C.J. Reports 2010, p. 14*, at 79, paragraph 197.

192 LOSC, article 165(2)(h).

193 ibid.

194 Nodules Exploration Regulations, regulation 32 and Annex IV, section 5; Sulphides Exploration Regulations, regulation 34 and Annex IV, section 5; Crusts Exploration Regulations, regulation 34 and Annex IV, section 5. Draft Exploitation Regulations (March 2018), regulation 38(2)(9) and Annex VII, section 2(g).

environmental impacts of mining activities and the contractor's compliance, namely self-reporting, inspection, and remote monitoring. The following section will focus on the contents of the Draft Exploitation Regulations (March 2019) with a viewing to a sponsoring State's role in monitoring.

### 3.4.1 Self-Reporting

The main monitoring method is self-reporting. The contactor is required to submit annual reports with details of the exploitation work; quantity and quality of the resources recovered during the period and the volume of minerals and metals produced, marketed, and sold; details of the equipment used; annual financial statements; health and safety information; details of training carried out in accordance with the training plan; actual results obtained from environmental monitoring programs; a statement that all risk management systems and procedures have been followed and remain in place, together with a report on exceptions and the results of any verification and audit; evidence that insurance is maintained; details of any changes made in connection with subcontractors engaged by the contractor; and the results of any exploration activities. A statement that the contractor's financing plan is adequate for the following period and details of any proposed modification to the plan of work and the reasons for such modifications are also included.[195]

An applicant or contractor is requested to submit an EMMP, which will "set out commitments and procedures on how the mitigation measures will be implemented, how the effectiveness of such measures will be monitored, what the management responses will be to the monitoring results, and what reporting systems will be adopted and followed."[196] A performance assessment report must be compiled and submitted by the contractor.[197]

In both cases, if it appears to the Secretary-General, on reasonable grounds, that a contractor is in breach of the terms and conditions of its exploitation contract, he will issue a compliance notice describing the alleged breach and the factual basis for it. He will request that remedial action or other appropriate steps be taken within a specified time period. Failure to implement the measures set out in a compliance notice as to result in serious, persistent, and willful violation of the fundamental terms of the LOSC and ISA regulations may lead to the suspension or termination of the contract.[198]

195 Draft Exploitation Regulations (March 2019), regulation 38(1) and (2).
196 Draft Exploitation Regulations (March 2019), regulation 48(1).
197 Draft Exploitation Regulations (March 2019), regulation 52(3).
198 Draft Exploitation Regulations (March 2019), regulation 103.

Operational factors of mining activities require the contractor to "perform some degree of self-regulation" especially in monitoring, since "it would be almost impossible, and certainly cost prohibitive, for [the ISA] to analyze such a large amount of data in a meaningful way."[199] Regarding issues of reporting, the sponsoring State cannot do more than the ISA.

### 3.4.2 Inspection and Remote Monitoring

Self-reporting from the deep seabed mining operator should be supplemented with other methods of oversight, including a complaints/whistle-blower procedure, inspection by the monitoring agency, or remote monitoring.[200]

As indicated in section 3.4.4 of chapter 1, the LOSC indicated the "Authority shall have the right to inspect all installations in the Area used in connection with activities in the Area" and further indicated the Council to establish appropriate mechanisms for directing and supervising a staff of inspectors; the LTC is mandated to make such recommendations. Annex 4, section 14, of the ISA Exploration Regulations provides procedures of inspection. The Draft Exploitation Regulations (March 2019) provide a full description of the appointment and responsibilities of the inspector.[201] The sponsoring State is required to assist the Council, the Secretary-General, and inspectors to discharge their functions.[202] However, the above legal instruments do not specify how an inspection can be invoked. The sponsoring State can play a more significant role in this regard if the national legislation of the sponsoring State authorizes the monitoring body to conduct inspections regularly, or when it deems them necessary, or under complaint.

Moreover, the ISA utilizes an electronic monitoring system to monitor whether unapproved mining activities have occurred or are occurring. In this regard there is no need for the sponsoring State to duplicate the workload of the ISA.

## 3.5 *Liability of a Contractor and Enforcement*

Liability rules have many effects at both the domestic and international levels. They may be a form of an economic instrument that provides an incentive to encourage compliance with environmental obligations.[203] They may also be

199 Gerber and Grogan (n 69) 4.

200 SPC, *RLRF* (n 17), paragraph 14.42.

201 Draft Exploitation Regulations, regulations 96–100.

202 Draft Exploitation Regulations, regulation 96(2).

203 Sands and others (n 74) 228–229; see also, in this regard, C Murgatroyd, 'The World Bank: A Case for Lender Liability' (1992) 1 *Review of European Community and International Environmental Law* 436.

used to impose sanctions for wrongful conduct, or to require corrective measures to restore a given environmental asset to its pre-damage condition.[204] Finally, they may indicate the approach to get compensation for damage in implementing the polluter pays principle.[205]

In the context of deep seabed mining, apart from the aforementioned general rules of liability, specific rules of the Deep Seabed Mining Regime at the international level needs to be examined and incorporated into the sponsoring State's national legislation since the national legislation is the secondary regulation, which must follow relevant international convention and regulations. As mentioned in section 5.1 of chapter 2, the liability regime of the contractor is stipulated in the LOSC and ISA Regulations. Annex III, article 22 of the LOSC provides that:

> [t]he contractor shall have responsibility or liability for any damage arising out of wrongful acts in the conduct of its operations, accounting being taken of contributory acts or omissions by the Authority. … Liability in every case shall be for the actual amount of damage.

Furthermore, section 16.1 of the standard clauses for exploration contract of the ISA Exploration Regulations further provides that:

> [t]he Contractor shall be liable for the actual amount of any damage, including damage to the marine environment, arising out of its wrongful acts or omissions, and those of its employees, subcontractors, agents and all persons engaged in working or acting for them in the conduct of its operations under this contractor, including the costs for reasonable measures to prevent or limit damage to the marine environment, account being taken of any contributory acts or omissions by the Authority.[206]

It can be seen here that under the framework of the existing Deep Seabed Mining Regime, the contractor is liable only when it causes damage which can be attributed to its wrongful acts.

The liability regime relating to the exploitation phase is under development and has been identified as a priority component of the ongoing exploitation regulatory framework.[207] In any case, the national legislation of the sponsoring

204 ibid.

205 ibid.

206 Nodules Exploration Regulations, Annex IV, section 16.1.

207 Report of the Chair of the Legal and Technical Commission (ISBA/22/C/17, 13 July 2016), Annex II.

State can still play an important role in some aspects, for example, the standard of care, the corrective measures and sanctions, access to the domestic court, and the enforcement of decisions of the international courts and tribunals, on the basis of respect for the development of the international Deep Seabed Mining Regime.

### 3.5.1 Standard of Care

The costs of pollution should be borne by the person responsible for causing the pollution in observance of the "polluter pays principle", which purports that the person has an obligation to prevent the environmental damage beforehand and pay for the damage afterwards. The obligation to prevent environmental damage relates directly to the standard of care applicable to that obligation. Options of the standard of care include fault, strict liability, and absolute liability.[208] "There is probably no single basis of international responsibility, applicable in all circumstances, but rather several, the nature of which depends on the particular obligation in question."[209] The obligation in question may distinguish between dangerous activities which are likely to cause serious environmental damage and other activities. Activities which may result in oil pollution, transportation of hazardous and noxious substances, nuclear installations, and activities which may be conducted in the Antarctic usually attract a strict or absolute obligation and there are generally incentives for operators to adopt special precautions when engaging in such undertakings.

In the context of deep seabed mining, as mentioned in section 4 of chapter 1, the sponsoring State has the responsibility to carry out the fault-based liability, rather than strict liability. Due to the "inherent difficulties in establishing the direct liability of states, emphasis shifted to the development of civil liability regimes."[210] Discussion on the liability of the contractor addresses a

208 For general discussions of standards of liability in international environmental law, see Neil Craik, *Determining the Standard for Liability for Environmental Harm from Deep Seabed Mining Activities*, Liability Issues for Deep Seabed Mining Series, Paper No. 2 (October 2018); Louise de La Fayette, "International Liability for Damage to the Environment" in Malgosia Fitzmaurice, David M Ong & Panos Merkouris (eds), *Research Handbook on International Environmental Law* (Edward Elgar 2010); Robert Barnidge, 'The Due Diligence Principle Under International Law' (2006) 8 *International Community Law Review* 81.

209 R Jennings and A Watts (eds.), *Oppenheim's International Law*, vol. I (9th edn, Oxford University Press 1992), 509.

210 Tara Davenport, *Responsibility and Liability for Damage Arising out of Activities in the Area: Attribution of Liability*, Liability Issues for Deep Seabed Mining Series, Paper No.4 (January 2019), 2; see also Malgosia Fitzmaurice, 'International Responsibility and

completely different perspective, especially in the domain of standard of liability. Some commenters are of the view that the LOSC expressly indicates not a strict liability for the contractor;[211] others understand the provision to be much broader, indicating "[t]he use of the phrase 'wrongful act' in Annex III, article 22, should not be interpreted as necessarily requiring fault-based liability for contractors or the ISA".[212] Further, "[w]rongful in this context means that liability will flow from a breach of the requirements that the contractor ... is subject to under the deep seabed mining regime"[213] and "[i]mposing a strict liability (no fault) standard could be accomplished by clear indication that causation of serious environmental harm is itself a wrongful act, from which liability will flow."[214] Different opinions regarding the standard of liability of the contractor depend on the understanding of the interpretation of the term "wrongful act" by the LOSC. The author of this book disagrees with the overly-broad interpretation of "wrongful act" and agrees with the definition articulated in article 2 of the ARSIWA, although it refers to a State's wrongful act. It may be analogically applied to the contractor[215] whose "wrongful acts" might consist of an action or omission: (a) is attributable to the State under international law; and (b) constitutes a breach of an international obligation of the State.[216] It is noteworthy that the second element is "a breach of an international obligation".

Liability' in Daniel Bodansky, Jutta Brunnée and Ellen Hay (eds), *Oxford Handbook of International Environmental Law* (Oxford University Press 2007), 1012.

211 See eg Isabel Feichtner, 'Contractor Liability for Environmental Damage Resulting from Deep Seabed Mining Activities in the Area' (2020) 114 *Marine Policy* 103502.

212 Craik, *Determining the Standard for Liability for Environmental Harm from Deep Seabed Mining Activities* (n 209) 4.

213 ibid.

214 Neil Craik, 'Liability for Environmental Harm from Deep Seabed Mining: Towards a Hybrid Approach' (2019) 33 *Ocean Yearbook* 313, 327.

215 Linlin Sun, *International Environmental Obligations and Liabilities in Deep Seabed Mining* (dissertation Leiden) (Ipskamp Printing 2018), 189–191. When demonstrating the ILC's interpretation of internationally wrongful acts of the State can be applied to the contractor by analogy, Linlin Sun is of the view that when approaching the topic of State responsibility, the ILC made a critical distinction between primary and secondary rules, and the ILC restricted its task exclusively to the secondary rules, which are about the legal consequences of the breach of primary obligations. The distinction between primary and secondary rules is an analytical tool at a very abstract construction level. It can apply to different subjects, whether States or private entities. See also Keith MacMaster, 'Environmental Liability for Deep Seabed Mining in the Area: An Urgent Case for a Robust Strict Liability Regime' (2019) 33 *Ocean Yearbook* 339, 372.

216 For discussion on Responsibility of States for international wrongful acts, see Robert Barnidge, 'The Due Diligence Principle Under International Law' (2006) 8 *International Community Law Review* 81; James Crawford, 'The ILC's Articles on Responsibility of States for International Wrongful Acts: A Retrospect' (2002) 96 *American Journal of*

The commentary on the ARSIWA clarifies that "reference is made to the breach of an international obligation rather than a rule or a norm of international law".[217] Thus, simply taking "a breach of requirements" as a standard definition of "wrongful act" is not appropriate.

Nevertheless, the advantages of the application of strict liability to a contractor cannot be denied. The reasoning behind this option is, firstly, the fact that the contractor will be more meticulous in its operations under a strict liability, and thus it becomes more effective in preventing environmental damage. That being said, "strict liability may be justified as a means to promote deterrence of risky behavior by providing greater incentives for operators to take steps to prevent accidental damage".[218] Second, given that the strict liability requires no proof of fault for the finding of liability in relation to harm but only require causation, it will be quicker to identify who is responsible for the damage and subsequently for the compensation. That can be seen as a means for a sponsoring State to carry out its direct obligation "availability of recourse for compensation". Furthermore, although the contractor bears the financial liability burden of the accident under a strict liability, he has a right of recourse against others that may have been responsible, which could include suppliers and designers of equipment.[219] Strict liability may still allow certain exceptions to the imposition of liability, such as war and hostilities, intentional acts, governmental negligence and contributory negligence, "a natural phenomenon of exceptional, inevitable, unforeseeable and irresistible character", and compliance with a compulsory measure of a public authority.[220]

---

*International Law* 874; Riccardo Pisillo Mazzeschi, 'Forms of International Responsibility for Environmental Harm', in Francesco Francioni and Tullio Scovazzi (eds), *International Responsibility for Environmental Harm* (Graham & Trotman/ Martinus Nijhoff 1991); Mohammed Bedjaoui, 'Responsibility of States: Fault and Strict Liability' in *Encyclopedia of Disputes Installment 10* (Elsevier 1987); Rüdiger Wolfrum, 'Internationally Wrongful Acts' in *Encyclopedia of Disputes Installment 10* (Elsevier 1987).

217 ARSIWA, Commentary 13 to the article 2.

218 Craik, *Determining the Standard for Liability for Environmental Harm from Deep Seabed Mining Activities* (n 209) 2.

219 Legal Working Group on Liability, *Legal Liability for Environmental Harm: Synthesis and Overview*, Liability Issues for Deep Seabed Mining Series, Paper No.1 (July 2018), 12.

220 2010 HNS Convention (consolidated texts), article 7(2). The International Convention on Liability and Compensation for Damage in Connection with the Carriage of Hazardous and Noxious Substances by Sea, 1996 (1996 HNS Convention), was adopted by an International Conference organized by the International Maritime Organization (IMO) in London in May 1996. The convention has not entered into force due to signatory states not meeting the ratification requirements by 2009. A second International Conference, held in April 2010, adopted a Protocol to the HNS Convention (2010 HNS Protocol), that was designed to address practical problems that had prevented many States from ratifying the

As indicated in section 4.4.2 of chapter 2, a contractor may entail strict liability if the sponsoring State would like to be more stringent than the LOSC in this field. Indeed, national legislation is a platform, or the only platform, that has the authority to apply a strict liability to the contractor, since Annex III, article 21(3) of the LOSC provides the legal basis for a sponsoring State to apply a strict liability. Also, the Seabed Disputes Chamber expects the sponsoring State to "further deal with the issue of liability in future regulations on exploitation".[221] Thus, although the author of the book disagrees with the strict liability of contractor at the international level, since the LOSC should not be interpreted infinitely, she is in favour of granting the discretion to the Sponsoring State. Given obvious advantages of strict liability, the sponsoring State is encouraged to set strict liability in its national legislation according to its actual situation and legal traditions. It also provides strong evidence that the sponsoring State is executing its responsibility of due diligence.

However, quite a few contractors are state-owned entities or even state governments and would not be willing to place more liability on themselves. Additionally, contractors who are private companies may turn to other sponsoring States with lower standards or national law. Not surprisingly, none of the States with national legislation on activities in the Area apply strict liability in their domestic legislation. So, a tricky problem here may be how to incentivize a sponsoring State to use more stringent laws and regulations than those in the rules, regulations, and procedures of the Authority.

It must be appreciated that the introduction of more stringent laws would be challenging without a model law as the parameter. Indeed, the ISA's concerns about development of its member States' national legislation in relation to exploration and exploitation of mineral resources in the Area and thus the

original Convention. Once the 2010 HNS Protocol enters into force, the 1996 Convention, as amended by the 2010 Protocol, will be called the International Convention on Liability and Compensation for Damage in Connection with the Carriage of Hazardous and Noxious Substances by Sea, 2010 (2010 HNS Convention). Entry into force of 2010 HNS Protocol requires accession by at least 12 States, meeting certain criteria in relation to tonnage and reporting annually the quantity of HNS cargo received in a State. As of now, only Canada, Denmark, France, Germany, Greece, the Netherlands, Norway, and Turkey signed the 2010 HNS Protocol, subject to ratification. See Status of the HNS Convention and 2010 Protocol <http://www.hnsconvention.org/status/> accessed 5 August 2020.

221 Considering that the potential for damage, particularly to the marine environment, may increase during the exploitation phase, it is expected that member States of the ISA will further deal with the issue of liability in future regulations on exploitation. SDC Advisory Opinion, paragraph 168.

Council, in 2011, led the Authority to invite sponsoring States and other members of the ISA to provide information on relevant national laws, regulations, and administrative measures to the Secretariat of the ISA.[222] In 2014, the Chair of the Council indicated that to analyze common elements that may be contained in national legislation, the Secretariat of the ISA was undertaking a comparative study of such legislation.[223] In 2017, Secretary-General Michael Lodge also repeated this request. Also, at the ISA's 23rd Annual Session in 2017, Indonesian delegates, supported by the Netherlands and Tonga, proposed that the Council request that the Legal and Technical Commission (LTC) draft a model law to provide a template to assist States Parties in developing the necessary domestic legislation to implement the Convention.[224] However, it is not an easy task due to limited human recourses of the ISA and especially to obtain consensus that the ISA's priority at this stage is to draft the exploitation regulations.[225] It will be a tough and time-consuming task to adopt regulations for exploitation activities, and, thus, makes it difficult to give much consideration to other tasks. The eagerly-anticipated comparative study regarding the common elements of the existing legislation on deep seabed mining was finally released in 2019.[226] However, it cannot provide a modern law. As stated:

> While there are commonalities between the laws studied in this review, particularly between the Pacific Island States, there is also a divergence in specific content and approaches taken. Naturally, this will stem from drafting styles, the particular national regulatory and institutional contexts and differences in common law and civil law legal systems, and how the relationship between the relevant parties is determined for legal purposes.[227]

222 Decision of the Council of the International Seabed Authority (ISBA/17/C/20, 21 July 2011), paragraph 3.

223 Report of the Secretary-General on laws, regulations and administrative measures adopted by sponsoring States and other members of the International Seabed Authority with respect to the activities in the Area (ISBA/20/C/11, 28 May 2014), paragraph 8.

224 Report on laws, regulations and administrative measures adopted by sponsoring States and other members with respect to the activities in the Area (ISBA/23/C/6, 1 June 2017).

225 Summary report of the President of the Council of the International Seabed Authority on the work of the Council during its twenty-second session (ISBA/22/C/30, 29 July 2016), paragraph 19.

226 Comparative Study of the Existing National Legislation on Deep Seabed Mining (n 4).

227 ibid, paragraph 92.

As Mr. Lodge said, "it is not always easy to provide a one-size-fits-all model."[228] Nevertheless, it will be useful to review the common elements derived from the existing national legislation to provide a reference for sponsoring States or other potential sponsoring States to update or adopt legislation in respect to deep seabed mining activities.[229]

### 3.5.2 Corrective Measures and Sanctions for Non-compliance

In the face of a contractor's non-compliance, the sponsoring State needs corresponding mechanisms in the national legislation to adequately respond. The phrase "responsibility to ensure" can only be interpreted to mean to induce compliance of the contractor, which includes incentives to compliance and sanctions against non-compliance.[230] When the national monitoring agency finds that the contractor has breached the provisions of sponsoring States' legislation, it should submit a written warning to the contractor to correct its wrongful act which might include a request to undertake, or to cease, or to not undertake a specific activity within a certain period. Specified actions or outcomes, picked up by the reporting and monitoring measures or by a third-party complaint, are assessed as providing evidence of non-compliance, such as (a) waste and pollution not being properly managed, (b) exploration or exploitation activities being conducted outside of the boundaries of approval, (c) performance assessments or reports not being submitted, (d) environmental monitoring not being done, (e) unauthorized mining methods being used, or (f) other material and un-notified deviation from the plan of work or license terms.[231]

Where there is continued non-compliance or breaches are not remedied or there are new breaches of the action plan, sanctions would have to be imposed, namely, further and more serious enforcement action, such as, suspension, termination, or amendment of the license. Most States expressly illustrate situations that lead to suspension, revocation, and termination of a license or certificate of sponsorship. For example, the national legislation of Japan, Singapore, and the United Kingdom indicate that the violation of the conditions of the license or provisions of national laws leads to suspension

228 Earth Negotiations Bulletin, 'ISA-23 Highlights, Wednesday, 9 August 2017, Kingston, Jamaica' (Volume 25 Number 144, Thursday, 10 August 2017) <http://enb.iisd.org/vol25/enb25144e.html> accessed 9 June 2020.

229 Comparative Study of the Existing National Legislation on Deep Seabed Mining (n 4), paragraph 95.

230 SPC, *RLRF* (n 17), paragraph 14.46.

231 ibid, paragraph 14.48.

or revocation of license; Kiribati, Nauru, and Tonga indicate where there has been a serious, persistent, or willful breach by the rules of the ISA or national laws;[232] on another hand, the Czech Republic indicates where the contractor refuses to submit to an inspection, the regulatory agency shall revoke the certificate of sponsorship.[233] The author believes this is an effective incentive to encourage the sponsored contractor to comply with the relevant international and national regulations, since without certificate of sponsorship it is impossible to conduct activities in the Area. However, it should be noted that those actions will lead to serious results. Not only is the appeal process extremely complex and rigorous, and even though a license is withdrawn, the license-holder remains subject to any ongoing obligation or liability previously incurred.

Financial penalty mechanisms are used by almost all States, excluding France and Russia. The amounts of the fines can vary depending on the sponsoring State and type of offence. In addition, the failure to comply with an enforcement order made by the regulating agency may lead to the suing or prosecution of the operator's directors or other personnel (see Table 3). In any case, "the approach to sanctions is incremental … and is subject to the principle of proportionality (the fines are always given as a maximum amount)."[234]

### 3.5.3 Compensation

This section will focus on the specific issues relating to compensation by the contractor. The due diligence obligation requires the Sponsoring State to enact appropriate laws and regulations to effectively control persons under its jurisdiction and provide a means of securing compliance with those laws, including an obligation under article 235(2) of the LOSC to ensure "recourse is available under their legal systems for prompt and adequate compensation".[235] The Seabed Disputes Chamber denotes that that article ensures that the contractor can live up to its obligation to provide compensation for damages caused by its wrongful acts.[236] The ILC also states "[e]ach State should take all necessary

232 Comparative Study of the Existing National Legislation on Deep Seabed Mining (n 4), paragraph 49.

233 Czech Republic Act, article 17(1)(b).

234 Comparative Study of the Existing National Legislation on Deep Seabed Mining (n 4), paragraph 77.

235 LOSC, article 235(2).

236 SDC Advisory Opinion, paragraph 140.

TABLE 3 Sanctions in the states parties' national legislation

| States | Amounts of fines | Criminal punishment |
|---|---|---|
| **Belgium** | EUR 25 to 25,000 (around USD 28 to 28,020) | 15 days to 1 year |
| **China** | CNY 20,000 to 1,000,000 (around USD 2,909 to 145,427) | Subject to criminal liability |
| **Czech Republic** | CZK 1million to 100 million (around USD 43,945 to 4,394,550) | no |
| **Fiji** | FJD 10,000 (around USD 4,660) | 5 years |
| **Germany** | ≤ EUR 50,000 (around USD 56,047) | ≤ 5 years |
| **Japan** | ≤ JPY 1,000,000 (around USD 9,239) | ≤ 5 years |
| **Kiribati** | AUD 50,000 to 500,000 (around USD 35,054 to 350,545) | ≤ 10 years |
| **Nauru** | AUD 5,000 to 100,000 (around USD 3505 to 70,109) | ≤ 10 years |
| **New Zealand** | ≤ NZD 200,000 (around USD 134,559) + not exceeding 3 times the value of commercial gain | May be arrested |
| **Singapore** | ≤ SGD 500,000 (around USD 368,055) | ≤ 3 months |
| **Tonga** | TOP 100,000 to 1,000,000 (around USD 44,030 to 440,300) | ≤ 10 years |
| **Tuvalu** | ≤ AUD 250,000 (around USD 175,272) | ≤ 10 years |
| **United Kingdom** | GBP 1,000 (around USD 1,421) or another sum fixed by order | ≤ 2 years |

SOURCE: THE FORM IS CONCLUDED BASED ON INFORMATION FROM THE NATIONAL LEGISLATION DATABASE, AVAILABLE AT: HTTPS://WWW.ISA.ORG.JM/NATIONAL-LEGISLATION-DATABASE.

measures to ensure that prompt and adequate compensation is available for victims".[237] All these international instruments require the sponsoring State to

237 International Law Commission, *Principles on the Allocation of Loss in the Case of Transboundary Harm Arising Out of Hazardous Activities*, printed in 'Report of the

establish mechanisms to ensure promptness and adequacy of compensation within its domestic legal system.

#### 3.5.3.1 *Prompt Compensation: Access to Domestic Courts*

Promptness refers to "the procedures that would govern access to justice, and that would influence the time and duration for the rendering of decisions on compensation payable in a given case."[238] In general, damage claims may be brought in the courts of the place where damage occurs (i.e. the transboundary victim's own state); or in the place where harmful activity occurred, or in the place where the defendant is domiciled.[239] Although jurisdiction is the court of the defendant's residence, domicile or place of business,[240] the claim brought by foreigners may be declined in some legal systems due to the principle of *forum non conveniens.*[241] When claims are brought in the early stage of the deep seabed mining, it is not clear whether that situation will apply. In any case, in the context of deep seabed mining, the national court could be the court in the injured party's State or in contractor's State, namely, the sponsoring State.[242] Currently, only three sponsoring States, namely, Japan, Nauru, and Singapore, have provisions which give the claimant the right to access domestic courts for environmental damage in their national legislation.[243] They, respectively, empower a national court (Japan), the Supreme Court (Nauru) and the national high court (Singapore) to hear third-party claims made against its sponsored contractor.[244] Japan also stipulates the limitation of adjudication (three years of becoming aware of the damage or within twenty years of occurrence of damage). It also applies mediation as an approach to the settlement of disputes. An interesting observation on this point is that

---

International Law Commission on its Fifty-eight session', UN Doc A/61/10 (2006), principle 4(1).

238 Principles on the Allocation of Loss in the Case of Transboundary Harm Arising Out of Hazardous Activities, comment 7 to the principle 4.

239 Patricia Birnie, Alan Boyle and Catherine Redgwell, *International Law and the Environment* (3rd edn, Oxford University Press 2009), 312. See respectively *Handelskwekerij GJ Bier v Mines de Potasse d'Alsace, Case 21/76* [*1976*] *II ECJ Reports,* p. 1735; *Re Union Carbide Corporation,* 634 F Supp 842 (1986); *In re Oil Spill by Amoco Cadiz,* 954 F 2d 1279 (1992).

240 See generally McLachlan and Nygh (eds), *Transnational Tort Litigation* (Oxford University Press 1996), chapters 1, 4, 12.

241 Birnie, Boyle and Redgwell (n 240) 313.

242 Tara Davenport, *Responsibility and Liability for Damage Arising Out of Activities in the Area: Potential Claimants and Possible Fora,* Liability Issues for Deep Seabed Mining Series, Paper No. 5 (February 2019), 3.

243 Lily (n 13) 8.

244 Respectively, Japan Law, articles 27 and 28; Nauru Act, section 46; Singapore Act, section 17.

unlike Nauru and Singapore, Japan does not provide details in its legislation on activities in the Area. Rather, it refers to the relevant parts of the Mining Act.[245] For example, article 27(5) describes issues relating to adjudication thus, "[p]rovisions of Article 11 and Article 113 to Article 116 of the Mining Act (Act No. 289 of 1950) shall apply *mutatis mutandis* to compensation for damage ... deep seabed mining in Japan". For States with limited legislative capacity or limited practice (early stage of deep seabed mining activities), Japan's example provides a cost-effective approach that can be used as a model for other sponsoring States.

Furthermore, promptness can be achieved by a clear procedural arrangement. As ILC stated, given the often protracted nature of compensation claims in domestic courts, consideration ought to be given to the establishment of special national environmental courts.[246] The Law Commission of India made a very persuasive case for the establishment of national environmental courts in India.[247] Australia and New Zealand already have environmental courts.[248] Last, but not least, as Neil Craik mentioned, strict liability of the contractor can lead to prompt compensation, since "a strict standard relieves the claimant of the burden of proving fault".[249]

#### 3.5.3.2 *Adequate Compensation*

Regarding the adequacy of the compensation at the national level, article 235(3) of the LOSC provides that States shall develop "criteria and procedures for payment of adequate compensation, such as compulsory insurance or compensation funds". The ILC advises that these measures should include the imposition of liability on the operator, the requirement on the operator to establish and maintain financial security such as insurance, bonds, or other financial guarantees, and the requirement for the establishment of industry-wide funds

245 Japan Mining Act (Act No. 289 of 1950, adopted 20 December 1950, amended 22 July 2011).

246 Draft principles on the allocation of loss in the case of transboundary harm arising out of hazardous activities, commentary 7 to the principle 4.

247 See Law Commission of India, *One Hundred Eighty Sixty Report on Proposal to Constitute Environmental Courts* (September 2003).

248 For the introduction on the environmental court of Australia and New Zealand, see Elizabeth Fisher, 'Administrative Law, Pluralism and the Legal Construction of Merits Review in Australian Environmental Courts and Tribunals' in Linda Pearson, Carol Harlow and Michael Taggart (eds), *Administrative Law in a Changing State: Essays in Honour of Mark Aronson* (Hart 2008); Ceri Warnock, 'Reconceptualising the Role of the New Zealand Environment Court' (2014) 26 *Journal of Environmental Law* 507.

249 Craik, 'Liability for Environmental Harm from Deep Seabed Mining: Towards a Hybrid Approach' (n 215) 327.

at the national level.[250] The liability regime of existing hazardous activities echoes the ILC in practice.[251]

In fact, compulsory insurance is an imperative and necessary component in the existing compensation regime for hazardous activities to ensure adequate compensation.[252] In deep seabed mining activities, insurance is usually taken out by the contractor, not only to ensure that compensation is available and sufficient for damage but also to protect himself against harm to victims. During the exploration phase, due to the relatively low probability of environmental damage, despite the mention of insurance in the ISA Exploration Regulations, they did not provide details in this regard.[253] However, insurance is a significant criterion in the exploitation stage, where environmental risks are higher. Without the support of an insurance company, it, *de facto,* excludes most potential entities for deep seabed mining, especially those from developing States. Thus, the ISA Exploitation Regulations must provide more details regarding compulsory insurance. In fact, the provisions of "compulsory insurance" in international civil liability conventions not only require the persons involved to purchase an insurance policy and provide the evidence that they have done so, but also specify the insurance requirements relating to: (1) specified liabilities; (2) a certain amount; and (3) the liability insurer, who can be sued directly by claimants.[254] It can be seen here that the insurance system is closely linked to the liability system. No insurer is willing to take the business if the former two questions are not specified. For example, according to protection and indemnity (P&I) clubs,[255] in which most of the ship owners take out

250 Draft principles on the allocation of loss in the case of transboundary harm arising out of hazardous activities, principle 4.

251 Davenport, *Responsibility and Liability for Damage Arising out of Activities in the Area: Attribution of Liability* (n 211) 2–3.

252 See Chie Kojima, 'Compensation Fund' in *Max Plank Encyclopedia of Public International Law* (2009).

253 See eg insurance is stipulated in the Nodules Exploration Regulations, Annex IV, section 16.5 by one sentence: "The Contractor shall maintain appropriate insurance policies with internationally recognized carriers, in accordance with generally accepted international maritime practice."

254 Ling Zhu, 'Probing Compulsory Insurance for Maritime Liability' (2014) 45 *Journal of Maritime Law and Commerce* 63, 68; see also Ling Zhu, *Compulsory Insurance and Compensation for Bunker Oil Pollution Damage* (1st edn, Springer 2006).

255 Protection and Indemnity Associations, commonly called P&I Clubs, provide insurance for 90% of the world's merchant fleet against the inevitable risks it carries petroleum through narrow straits, and into crowded ports. With regard to the introduction of P&I Clubs, see NJJ Ronneberg, 'An Introduction to the Protection &(and) Indemnity Clubs and the Marine Insurance They Provide' (1990) 3 *University of San Francisco Maritime Law Journal* 1.

P&I insurance to meet their liabilities for oil-pollution risks, they are not willing to cover oil pollution without limitation. They have consistently stressed that they are unable to provide financial security for unlimited amounts and that a fixed limit is needed in any insurance certificate.

In view of the fact that the provisions of national legislation cannot be inconsistent with the regulations of the ISA, it is not appropriate for the sponsoring State to make provisions in this regard before the adoption of the regulations of the ISA. Fortunately, the Secretariat is reviewing the requirements of insurance and availability in the marketplace.[256] In any event, the sponsoring State should compel the contractor to purchase insurance in accordance with the regulations of the ISA in domestic legislation.

### 3.5.4 Enforcement of Decisions of the International Court or Tribunal

A domestic court may not have jurisdiction of some disputes arising from activities in the Area. Article 187 together with article 289(2) grant the Seabed Disputes Chamber a compulsory jurisdiction in some regard as indicated in section 3.2.3 of chapter 1. Furthermore, some cases could be delivered to commercial arbitration.[257] As far as cases before the international court or tribunal are concerned, the issue is related to the implementation of the decision of the international court or tribunal at the national level. In practice, the compliance record with decisions of international courts and tribunals is relatively good, and most non-compliance can be solved through an enforcement mechanism at the international level, mostly a political process.[258] Nevertheless, it is suggested that a sponsoring State should provide a legal basis for such enforcement in the relevant national legislation so that the decision can be enforced successfully. Among existing national legislation of sponsoring States on activities in the Area, the United Kingdom and Singapore expressly stipulate that the decision of the SDC and an arbitral award of the commercial arbitral tribunal referred to in article 188(2)(a) of the LOSC can be enforced internally.[259] New Zealand, a non-sponsoring-State, also stipulates that every decision of the SDC "shall be enforceable in New Zealand as if it were a decision of the High

256 Draft regulations on exploitation of mineral resources in the Area, Note by the Legal and Technical Commission (ISBA/25/C/18, 27 March 2019), paragraph 25.

257 LOSC, article 188(2)(a).

258 Thordis Ingadottir, 'Enforcement of Decisions of International Courts at the National Level' in Andre Nollkaemper and others (eds), *International Law in Domestic Courts: A Casebook* (Oxford University Press 2019), 349.

259 Singapore Act, articles 18–20; the United Kingdom Act, article 8A-C.

Court, and all the provisions of the law of New Zealand shall apply accordingly with any necessary modifications."[260]

## 4 Institutional Arrangement

The sole strategy of creating legislation is not sufficient for sponsoring States to achieve the desired result of ensuring contractors' compliance with its international environmental obligations. Implementation and enforcement of the regimes created are also crucial. A strong institutional structure, empowered by a "reasonably appropriate" national legislation is particularly important for the oversight of deep seabed mining activities and related environmental matters. There are two aspects to be noted when considering an institutional arrangement. First, in order to avoid a conflict of interests, administrative bodies that are responsible for granting licenses for the regulated activity, or that enjoy financial gain from it should be separate from those that have monitoring responsibility. Thus, different functions, such as legislative power, regulating power, and monitoring power should be assigned to different organs. Separation of powers calls for distinct legislative and executive branches. It will all require dedicated public administration capacity. It is recognized that this may be particularly challenging for small developing States with limited administrative and technical capabilities. Second, deep seabed mining in the Area is subject to dual-track management, i.e. the ISA and sponsoring State's regulating agency. Consequently, there is some degree of duplication in procedures between these two organs. The ISA and sponsoring States shall cooperate to avoid unnecessary duplication of procedures and compliance requirements under their respective rules, regulations, and procedures.

### 4.1 *Legislative Body*

Sponsoring States should utilize the services of legal professionals to review the laws, regulations, or administrative measures presented in sections 2 and 3 which outline the rights and obligations as well as procedures that all parties involved in seabed mining activities in the Area are required to honour. Since there are several different legal systems involved, the sponsoring State would have the right to determine the legal entity it would consult.

Furthermore, the legislative body should be responsible for the review of those legal texts. The legislative body should ensure the integrity of the

260 New Zealand Act, article 14(3).

national legislation by regularly reviewing: 1) ISA regulations to take note of any adjustments which will require the introduction of more stringent; and 2) improvement of national scientific and technological capacity so as to proactively and continuously adjust their legislation in order to meet the Good Industry Practice.

### 4.2 *Regulatory Agency*

The mere existence of the legislation for deep seabed mining in the Area is far from enough. Sponsoring States still require the creation or identification of a specialized body, department, statutory authority, or panel to implement the legislation, and to regulate contractors' performance on behalf of the sponsoring State.

The objectives of the regulatory agency are twofold. One is to maintain effective control of deep seabed mining activities in the Area by securing compliance by sponsored contractors with their obligations. The other is to protect and preserve the marine environment and protect the well-being of individuals and communities which may be impacted by seabed mining activities. Against this background, the functions of the regulating agency should include works relating to the granting of licenses and promoting deep seabed mining activities in the Area. In any case, adequate regulatory capacity is critical. Regulators must have sufficient knowledge, sufficient staff, and sufficient time to do a competent job, including evaluating different potential responses and implementing the chosen measures. The body must be adequately funded and properly qualified to assess the relevant information.

For the former function, it should include receiving and evaluating applications to conduct such seabed mining activities and reviewing EIAs in order to decide whether to grant or deny a license. For the latter functions, promoting deep seabed mining activities should include developing policies for the purpose of regulating mining activities and provide guideline or expert opinions with regard to the implementation of deep seabed mining legislation. To meet those functions, the regulatory agency should be empowered to take any action which is reasonably calculated to facilitate or is conducive or incidental to the performance of any functions abovementioned.[261] The following section discusses how to establish a competent regulatory agency to perform the functions and how it can use adaptive management as a tool to reach the objectives.

---

261 Tonga Act, article 14.

#### 4.2.1 The Competent Authority

At present, there are two ways for States to establish regulatory agencies: to establish a new national authority for deep-sea mining activities or to designate an existing ministry to undertake competency for regulating deep seabed mining activities.

Fiji, Kiribati, Nauru, Tonga, and Tuvalu have established new national authorities dedicated to seabed mining activities.[262] The regulatory agencies of Fiji and Nauru are corporate bodies with cross-governmental representation from different ministries and departments. The regulatory agencies of Kiribati, Tonga, and Tuvalu are operated by existing ministries which they renamed (respectively Kiribati Seabed Minerals Secretariat, Tonga Seabed Minerals Authority, and Tuvalu Seabed Minerals Authority).[263] States which do not have the relevant structures in place would be required to create new regulatory agencies, perhaps as stand-alone statutory bodies. This agency must be independent and able to make decisions in individual cases without undue influence from other responsible departments.

Some States designate an existing ministry to act as a regulatory agency; for example Belgium (ministry responsible for matters related to the economy), China (ministry responsible for oceanic administration), Czech Republic (Ministry of Industry and Trade), Germany (State Office for Mining, Energy and Geology), Japan (Ministry of Economy, Trade and Industry), and the United Kingdom (Secretary of State).[264] If this model is being adopted, it is important to ensure that these structures are fit for the purpose, taking into account the practical implications, environmental concerns, and enforcement challenges, which characterize deep seabed mining.[265] In any case, the regulatory agency should be mandated to establish an expert group, the members of which would have the capacity and specialized expertise to assess applications and EIAs and make recommendations to contractors in practice. Interdisciplinary integration is required in this group to ensure that legal, social, biology, geology, engineering, and biophysical science are included and integrated into the management recommendation at the plan, policy, and project proposal levels.[266]

262 Comparative Study of the Existing National Legislation on Deep Seabed Mining (n 4), paragraph 27.

263 ibid.

264 Comparative Study of the Existing National Legislation on Deep Seabed Mining (n 4), paragraph 25. The Comparative Study also mentions that New Zealand, Russian Federation and Singapore also refer to a Ministry or a Minister being responsible for administration of the Act without further specification.

265 SPC, *RLRF* (n 17), paragraph 14.12.

266 cf the LOSC, article 165(1).

It is worth noting that a small or developing State may lack such capacity. A working group suggested that delegating the function to a regional body or other third party would address this problem and also avoid the perception of bias and provide checks and balances against undue influence and conflicts of interest.[267] It further highlighted that articles 276 and 277 of the LOSC provides the legal basis for this initiative, which stipulates:

(1) States, in coordination with the competent international organizations, the Authority and national marine scientific and technological research institutions, shall promote the establishment of regional marine scientific and technological research centres, particularly in developing States, in order to stimulate and advance the conduct of marine scientific research by developing States and foster the transfer of marine technology.

(2) All States of a region shall cooperate with the regional centres therein to ensure the more effective achievement of their objectives.[268]

There is an obvious imperfection though. In case of the breach of a sponsoring State's "responsibility to ensure" due to an unwise or poor decision by the regional body, would the regional body assume the liability for the sponsoring State?[269] A possible solution is that such a regional body could act as an expert group or consultant. The small or developing State's regulatory agency makes the decision taking into account the recommendation of the regulatory agency. In this case, the State is still responsible for its decision but is guided by external professional opinion.

It is worth mentioning that some States also designate other ministries or entities to assist the regulatory agency in performing their functions, such as Belgium, the Czech Republic, China, France, Germany, and Japan.[270] In Singapore when a license is to be granted, the Minister informs Parliament that an inter-agency taskforce should be formed to oversee the decision-making process. This taskforce is comprised of the Ministry of Trade and Industry, the Ministry of the Environment and Water Resources, the Ministry of Foreign Affairs, the Ministry of Law, and the Attorney-General's Chambers. This taskforce can obtain consulting opinions from external, independent economic

267 ISA, Technical Study No. 10 (n 79), 31.

268 LOSC, article 276.

269 Sun (n 216) 306.

270 Comparative Study of the Existing National Legislation on Deep Seabed Mining (n 4), paragraph 26.

and environmental experts.[271] Yet, there is no express solution how and to what extent this taskforce can influence the decision-making process.

### 4.2.2 Application of Adaptive Management

Adaptive management, which refers to a structured process of learning by doing and adapting based on what's learned,[272] was formally proposed in the 1970s[273] and is a management approach to natural resources. It has been used in many aspects of management of natural resources, such as freshwater, forestry, and fisheries.[274] The rationale for this approach is that recourse managers are often required to manage activities in the face of scientific uncertainty and inscrutable, dynamic changes in ecosystems.[275] The presence of scientific uncertainty, in respect of the adverse impacts on marine environment of the deep seabed mining, "has led to increased interest in the use of adaptive management as part of the environmental regulatory structure for the mineral regime."[276] In July 2015, the Council of the ISA endorsed the decision by the LTC to develop an adaptive management approach as a matter of priority by late 2016.[277] Since 2018, the ISA Draft Exploitation Regulation (2018) has identified adaptive management as a tool of environmental management.[278] However, in the context of deep seabed mining in the Area, there are "considerable challenges" in implementing it at the

271 Rena Lee, 'Exploration and Exploitation of Ocean Mineral Resources: The Role of Sponsoring States' in Myron H Nordquist, John Norton Moore and Ronán Long (eds), *Legal Order in the World's Oceans* (Brill 2017), 158–159.

272 Byron K Williams, 'Adaptive Management of Natural Resources – Framework and Issues' (2011) 92 *Journal of Environmental Management* 1346, 1347.

273 CS Holling and United Nations Environment Programme (eds), *Adaptive Environmental Assessment and Management* (International Institute for Applied Systems Analysis; Wiley 1978).

274 Ministry for the Environment, *New Zealand's Experiences with Adaptive Management for Seabed Mining Projects* (n 96), 6.

275 Lucky Rist and others, 'A New Paradigm for Adaptive Management' (2013) 18 *Ecology and Society* 63, 63.

276 Neil Craik, 'Implementing Adaptive Management in Deep Seabed Mining: Legal and Institutional Challenges' (2020) 114 *Marine Policy* 103256.

277 Report of the Chair of the Legal and Technical Commission on the work of the Commission during the twenty-first session of the International Seabed Authority (ISBA/21/C/16, 15 July 2015), annex III; Decision of the Council of the International Seabed Authority relating to the summary report of the Chair of the Legal and Technical Commission (ISBA/21/C/20, 21 July 2015).

278 Draft Regulation on Exploitation of Mineral Resources in the Area (ISBA/24/LTC/WP.1, 30 April 2018), Annex VII, paragraph 2(g).

international level, such as in the institutional structure and procedure of the Deep Seabed Mining Regime.[279]

One valuable state practice for the application of adaptive management comes from New Zealand. New Zealand's Exclusive Economic Zone and Continental Shelf (Environmental Effects) Act 2012 (EEZ Act) expressly includes adaptive management.[280] In this regard, New Zealand also had two cases, namely Trans-Tasman Recourses Ltd marine consent decision (TTR case)[281] and Chatham Rock Phosphate Ltd marine consent decision (CRP case).[282] For both cases, the Decision-making Committee deemed that they would have particularly significant impacts on the biological productivity and energy input into the seabed ecosystem and considered applying the adaptive management approach.[283] The application of an adaptive approach could sufficiently reduce uncertainty and adequately manage any remaining risks, and would help the Decision-making Committee to make a final decision.[284] The Decision-making Committee considered a three-stage adaptive management approach: first, a data gathering stage ahead of actual mining; second, a trial mining stage (to validate the plume model over three blocks for a certain period); and third, fully operational mining. The first two stages would contain a go or no-go trigger.[285] Both applicants objected to this option because "staging of the activity was not commercially realistic."[286] Instead, TTR proposed

---

279 ibid; Aline Jaeckel, 'Deep Seabed Mining and Adaptive Management: The Procedural Challenges for the International Seabed Authority' (2016) 70 *Marine Policy* 205, 205.

280 Regarding the introduction of stipulation of adaptive management in New Zealand's Exclusive Economic Zone and Continental Shelf (Environmental Effects) Act 2012, see Ministry for the Environment, *New Zealand's Experiences with Adaptive Management for Seabed Mining Projects* (n 96) 10–11.

281 Environmental Protection Authority, 'Trans-Tasman Resources Ltd Marine Consent Decision', June 2014.

282 For CRP's full marine consent application, see Environmental Protection Authority, 'Decision on Marine Consent Application, Chatham Rock Phosphate Limited, to Mine Phosphorite Nodules on the Chatham Rise' <https://cer.org.za/wp-content/uploads/2016/08/EPA-New-Zealand-Chatham-Rock-Phosphate-Decision.pdf> accessed 5 August 2020.

283 Ministry for the Environment, *New Zealand's Experiences with Adaptive Management for Seabed Mining Projects* (n 96) 12 and 14.

284 Donald K Anton and Rakhyun E Kim, 'Current Legal Developments New Zealand: The Application of the Precautionary and Adaptive Management Approaches in the Seabed Mining Context: Trans-Tasman Resources Ltd Marine Consent Decision under New Zealand's Exclusive Economic Zone and Continental Shelf (Environmental Effects) Act 2012' (2015) 30 *The International Journal of Marine and Coastal Law* 175, 181.

285 Ministry for the Environment, *New Zealand's Experiences with Adaptive Management for Seabed Mining Projects* (n 96) 15–16.

286 Environmental Protection Authority, 'Trans-Tasman Resources Ltd Marine Consent Decision' (n 282) paragraph 795.

a "risk-based tiered approach", which means TTR "accept[ed] it may need to alter its operations in order to ensure it complies with whatever quantitative performance standards are eventually established."[287] The Decision-making Committee eventually objected to this proposal since it did "not provide sufficient certainty, clarity or robustness on which to form the foundation of an appropriate adaptive management approach."[288]

Some thoughts from this practice could be obtained for the sponsoring State's national legislation although they are applicable to distinct marine zones. First, there is no doubt that implementing an adaptive management approach in the application stage is most cost-effective for both regulator and applicant. But, it is worth noting that it is a paradox between adaptive management and security of tenure.[289] So it needs to justify the utilization of adaptive management once the license is granted. Second, the applicant has no objection to the application of adaptive management. The disagreement between the decision-making body and the applicants is in the way that adaptive management is implemented. Therefore, the sponsoring State has to strike a balance between legislative objectives and protection of the contractor's investments when applying adaptive management. Third, when using adaptive management in the national legislation, the sponsoring State must ensure that it is consistent with the ISA Regulations. It lacks legitimacy in theory, and it is meaningless in practice if the ISA does not recognize the approach. For instance, even though both the regulatory agency of the sponsoring State and applicant might agree to apply a scaled or staged approach, it makes no sense if the ISA does not approve this plan. In this sense, a regulatory agency of the sponsoring State has the right to deny an application, but only partial capacity to grant a license since it is subject to the approval of the ISA.

### 4.3 *Monitoring Body*

For most States, if not all, it will be necessary to introduce new laws to provide the requisite rules, regulations, and procedures. The SDC Advisory Opinion underscores what the Convention requires: passing laws is not, by itself, sufficient to satisfy a sponsoring State's obligations. Administrative implementation and oversight are also required: the Chamber quotes the ICJ judgement in its *Pulp Mills* case to explain that this consists of "not only the adoption of appropriate rules and measures, but also a certain level of vigilance in their

287 ibid, paragraph 145.

288 ibid, paragraph 850.

289 Craik, 'Implementing Adaptive Management in Deep Seabed Mining: Legal and Institutional Challenges' (n 277).

enforcement and the exercise of administrative control applicable to public and private operators, such as the monitoring of activities undertaken by such operators".[290] While the sponsoring State does not have an obligation to achieve the result that no incidents occur, it does have "to deploy adequate means, to exercise best possible efforts, to do the utmost" to achieve that result. The so called "adequate means" not only includes adopting provisions and measures regarding monitoring, but also includes establishing a monitoring agency to execute monitoring work stipulated in a sponsoring States' national legislation as in section 3.4 of this chapter. The functions of a monitoring agency should include: (i) to receive and assess reporting documents from licensed operators; (ii) to monitor their compliance with the terms of the license; and (iii) to take action to amend the terms of licenses or suspend activities if necessary, and to enforce sanctions for non-compliance. Such institutions must be given sufficient capacity and authority to perform these functions and to monitor compliance with the deep seabed mining legal framework.

It should be pointed out that the mandate of regulating and monitoring should be distributed to different agencies. In some cases, the agency which issues a license would not wish to withdraw it as it cannot receive fees or royalties from the license-holder after revocation. Therefore, in order to be just, the ideal scenario would be that there exists an independent monitoring agency. The monitoring agency is authorized to monitor objects and review the reports of the contractor. Also, it has power to inspect the operations of the contractor. The information received by the monitoring agency should be published to promote accountability and demonstrate transparency to the public, insofar as it is compatible with requisite commercial confidentiality. Another option is that the regulating agency could empower another agency to do the monitoring work. For example, the German Act provides that the Landesamt (regulatory agency in Germany) will appoint "supervisors", empowered to enter the operational facilities, business rooms, establishments, and airborne and waterborne vehicles of the contractor to obtain information or to carry out an inspection, and it may seize objects from these locations where it considers this to be necessary to its objective to prevent accidents and promote public safety.[291]

However, subject to administrative capability, most States probably cannot establish such an independent monitoring agency. Instead, they may prefer to grant the monitoring mandate to a regulating agency. On this occasion, there

290 SDC Advisory Opinion, paragraph 115; *Pulp Mills on the River Uruguay* (*Argentina v Uruguay*) (n 192), at 79, paragraph 197.

291 Germany Act, section 8(3).

should be an independent unit which is responsible for monitoring works under the regulating agency and its decision-making should be independent without interference from the outside.

## 5 Conclusion

Sponsoring States' environmental legislation for exploration and exploitation of deep seabed minerals in the Area is important. On the one hand, the ISA and international community need the sponsoring State's assistance to ensure contractors' compliance with its environmental obligations when conducting exploration and exploitation activities. On the other hand, a sponsoring State needs such legislation to exempt itself from unlimited liability from wrongful behaviors of its sponsored contractor. In practice, it needs indicators and parameters to instruct sponsoring States to establish "reasonably appropriate" national legislation. The present chapter attempts to provide those parameters for sponsoring States in guiding them on how to establish their national legislation and the relevant institutional arrangement for exploration and exploitation of the deep seabed minerals in the Area.

A prominent feature of the management of mining activities in the Area is that there are two regulators: the ISA is the primary regulator, whereas the sponsoring State is the secondary regulator. Given the characteristics of the two-track management of mining activities in the Area, the Deep Seabed Mining Regime must fully take the following two points into account. First, the division of the regulatory burden between the two managers must be clear, avoiding waste of administrative resources caused by duplicated regulatory burdens. Second, the ISA, as the primary regulator, should adopt adequate regulations and guidelines, under which the sponsoring State can develop specific rules according to its circumstances. The lack of guidelines and standards at the ISA-level will lead to legal variability at the national level and undermine the coherence of the international framework.[292]

That the sponsoring State is the secondary regulator determines that the sponsoring State has no absolute decision-making power. For instance, even if the sponsoring State approves the application, the application is invalid without the approval of the ISA. Similarly, even though the sponsoring State wants to add more to its domestic legislation, it is ineffective if it is inconsistent with the LOSC and the ISA Regulations. In other words, the legislation of

292 Rojas and Phillips (n 52) 9.

the sponsoring State must be carried out within the framework of the LOSC and the ISA Regulations. For example, in the Draft Exploitation Regulations (March 2019), there is no mechanism as to appeal for the cancellation of preference and priority of an applicant who has an approved exploration contract and wants to apply for an exploitation activity in the same area. If the sponsoring State is willing to set up such a mechanism, it can only have effect at the national level and cannot change the decision of the ISA. However, the objection of the sponsoring State is absolute if the objection means no sponsorship is provided. Without the sponsorship, the application cannot be approved since sponsorship is the necessary requirement of the application. From this point of view, the sponsoring State has absolute power over negative matters and only partial powers for affirmative matters and rights-giving matters (subject to the decision of the ISA).

There is a minimal and optimal level for a sponsoring State's national legislation. Reaching the minimal level requires a sponsoring State to abide by the basic requirements of the LOSC and SDC Advisory Opinion, whereas reaching the optimal level means the sponsoring State, according to its capabilities, tries its best to institute more stringent standards than required in the LOSC. The sponsoring State and its legislation can play a more significant role, at least in terms of application, monitoring, liability and enforcement.

Regarding the application, the sponsoring State should ensure that the applicant can be effectively controlled. Moreover, the legislation of the sponsoring State should make more specific provisions as to the applicant's financial and technical capabilities according to the actual situation in the country and be carefully examined by the regulatory body. Furthermore, the sponsoring State should ensure that the applicant pays compulsory insurance. Besides, the Environmental Performance Guarantee should be paid to the sponsoring State, rather than to the ISA, so that the goal of ensuring the contractor's compliance can be better achieved. Certainly, the last point is determined by the ISA Regulations, which the national legislation of sponsoring State must follow.

In terms of monitoring, the sponsoring State should establish an independent monitoring agency, or establish an independent monitoring unit in the regulatory body, or entrust an inspector without conflict of interest. Importantly, national legislation of the sponsoring State can specify the scope or circumstances of triggering the inspection, based on the provisions of the Convention and ISA Regulations. Specifically, national legislation can stipulate conducting inspections regularly, or when it deems necessary, or under complaint.

In terms of liability and enforcement, to guarantee prompt compensation, the sponsoring State should establish rules as to access to the domestic court or expressly refer to other domestic law in this regard. To guarantee adequate compensation, the sponsoring State can stipulate the strict liability of the contractor and the payment of compulsory insurance in national legislation. Besides, the sponsoring State can establish offences and impose civil and criminal sanctions if necessary.

CHAPTER 4

# China's Legislation in Relation to Deep Seabed Mining in the Area

## 1 Introduction

Chapter 1 presented the overarching picture of the ISA-centric Deep Seabed Mining Regime and pointed out the weakness of the existing international Deep Seabed Mining Regime in controlling the contractor. It concluded that the ISA needs the assistance of the sponsoring States to ensure the compliance of the contractor. Chapters 2 and 3 analyzed, respectively, from a theoretical and practical perspective, how and in what areas the sponsoring State can assist the ISA through its domestic legislation to ensure the contractor's compliance with its environmental obligations under the LOSC, the 1994 Implementing Agreement, and ISA Regulations. The book argues that the major problem is not the lack of a legal framework at the international level but the incomplete implementation and weak enforcement of relevant instruments among contractors. The relevant national legislation of sponsoring States could contribute to better implementation of international environmental obligations and stronger supervision and more rigorous penalties for contractors in cases of non-compliance. The legislation of the sponsoring State is an essential and necessary part of the entire Deep Seabed Mining Regime. It is advantageous for the validation and implementation of the international system at the domestic level and can also make up for the shortcomings of the international system in managing contractors.

Based on that discussion, this book will focus on one practical question: To what extent can those measures instruct state practice? Here, China will be used as an example for both particularity and universality. The selection of China's national legislation as a case study is based on three considerations.

First, China plays an increasingly important role in deep seabed mining. China started to invest in survey activities and research on polymetallic nodules in the 1970s,[1] and its sponsored contractor, China Ocean Mineral Resources R & D Association (COMRA), was registered as a pioneer investor in accordance

1 Wang Zhixiong, 'China and the Exploitation of Deep Seabed Polymetallic Nodules' (1991) 15 *Marine Policy* 132, 132–133.

 | DOI:10.1163/9789004472341_006

with Resolution II of UNCLOS III in 1991. Today, China stands as a key sponsoring State in the Area.[2] As of 2019, China has sponsored three contractors, including five exploration contracts, covering three mineral resources.[3] Also, China made contributions to the consultation process of Part XI of the LOSC and 1994 Implementing Agreement[4] and has increasing influence over the development of the Mining Code as a key member of the Council of the ISA.[5] It can be appreciated that Chinese legislation is critical to implementing the Deep Seabed Mining Regime at the national level to ensure the compliance of Chinese contractors. By perusing China's legislation on deep seabed mining in the Area, the international community can understand China's legislative attitude and understand how it will contribute to the development of the Mining Code. Research and improvement of Chinese legislation will help to promote the development of the entire deep-sea system. Second, it is difficult to deny that China is a special example due to its unique political and economic situation rooted in its ideology, which leads to the result that China may be at a particularly important juncture in global efforts in protecting the marine environment. Third, although there exists specialty, China's practice, as a whole, is a vivid reflection of the global situation as it presents the development and the problems every sponsoring State has encountered. China's practice mirrors the overall efforts of the international community in searching for a solution to address the problem.

---

2 Nengye Liu and Rakhyun E Kim, 'Current Legal Developments: China's New Law on Exploration and Exploitation of Resources in the International Seabed Area of 2016' (2016) 31 *The International Journal of Marine and Coastal Law* 691, 693.

3 COMRA has an exploration contract for polymetallic nodules (entry into force 22 May 2001, expiry 21 May 2016, extension to 21 May 2021), an exploration contract for Polymetallic Sulphides (entry into force 18 November 2011, expiry on 18 November 2026), and an exploration contract for cobalt-rich ferromanganese crusts (entry into force 27 January 2014, expiry on 26 January 2029); CMC has an exploration contract for Polymetallic Nodules (entry into force 12 May 2017, expiry 11 May 2032). Beijing Pioneer Hi-Tech Development Corporation (BPHDC), signed an exploration contract for polymetallic nodules with the ISA, which entered into force on 18 October 2019 and expires on 17 October 2034. Status of contracts for exploration and related matters, including information on the periodic review of the implementation of approved plans of work for exploration (ISBA/26/C/4, 17 December 2019), Annex I.

4 For an introduction on the account, see Keyuan Zou, *China's Marine Legal System and the Law of the Sea* (Martinus Nijhoff 2005), chapter 7; see also Keyuan Zou, 'State Practice in Deep Seabed Mining: The Case of the People's Republic of China' in Markus Kotzur and others (eds), *Sustainable Ocean Resource Governance* (Brill Nijhoff 2018).

5 China was part of Group B (largest investors) from 1996 to 2004 and Group A (largest consumers) from 2005 to 2020 <https://ran-s3.s3.amazonaws.com/isa.org.jm/s3fs-public/documents/EN/Council/Council1996-2020.pdf> accessed 12 August 2020.

It is against this background that this chapter will present a comprehensive overview of China's legislation on deep seabed mining. It will begin with a brief introduction to China's legal system, including its structure, hierarchy, legislative bodies, and their functions, thus making it easier to understand China's legislation. A substantial part of this chapter is devoted to describing the legal framework of deep seabed mining in the Area, including the Deep Seabed Area Resource Exploration and Exploitation Law of the People's Republic of China (hereinafter "China's Deep Seabed Law"), and three implementing regulations. That is followed by an examination of China's existing legislation on deep seabed mining within its jurisdiction, some of which formed the foundation for the legislation on deep seabed mining in the Area. Following will be a description of the institutional arrangement. Finally, the author will provide a list of proposals to improve the legislation.

## 2 Chinese Legal System

It is impossible to discuss deep seabed legislation outside of the context of the Chinese legal system. The modern Chinese legal system is unique, as it is difficult to characterize China's evolving legal system as belonging to either the civil or common law family.[6] Also, the Chinese legal system is different from the "socialist legal tradition", which dominated nations that embraced state socialism in much of the 20th century,[7] although China was and still is a socialist country.[8] Since the late Qing Dynasty, the Chinese legal system has been

6 It is submitted that, although China has extensively borrowed legal concepts, principles, terminologies, institutions, and procedures from Anglo-American jurisdictions (and most significantly the United States), it remains a civil jurisdiction, at least insofar as sources of law are concerned. As in countries in the Romano-Germanic civil law family, 'enacted law or legislation ... is apparently the primary, almost exclusive, source of law today' in China. Case law has never gained legitimacy in China, although more and more court decisions are published and studied by law students as persuasive legal materials. It is also worth noting that courts in China, especially the Supreme People's Court, often act like legislative bodies, making China distinguishable from other civil law countries at least with respect to law-making. See generally Jiangyu Wang, 'China: Legal Reform in an Emerging Socialist Market Economy', in EA Black, GF Bell (eds), *Law and Legal Institutions of Asia: Traditions, Adaptations and Innovations* (Cambridge University Press 2011), 33.

7 John Henry Merryman and Rogelio Pérez-Perdomo, *The Civil Law Tradition: An Introduction to the Legal Systems of Europe and Latin America* (Stanford University Press 2007), 1.

8 Mo Zhang, 'The Socialist Legal System with Chinese Characteristics: China's Discourse for the Rule of Law and a Bitter Experience' (2010) *Temple International & Comparative Law Journal* 1, 3.

shaped by three streams of influence: traditional Chinese legal thought, socialist ideology, and the Westernization of Chinese law, although "it is difficult to quantify the weight of each influence in shaping the legal system".[9] China has begun to re-establish its domestic legal system, which was to a large extent destroyed during the catastrophic Cultural Revolution (1966–1976), since China introduced economic reforms and the "open-up" policy in 1978.[10] As the Chinese Government vowed, the new Chinese legal system is "the socialist legal system with Chinese characteristics".[11]

## 2.1 *Legislative Bodies*

State organs at different levels embody distinct legislative powers with different designations and degrees of binding force by the Constitution[12] and the Legislation Law.[13] Under the modern Chinese legal system, the following organs have varying degrees of legislative power: 1) the National People's Congress (NPC) and its Standing Committee; 2) the State Council; 3) ministries and commissions under the State Council; 4) people's congresses and their Standing committees at the provincial level; and 5) executive branches at the provincial level.[14]

It is worth noting that apart from the aforementioned organs, administrations under ministries and commissions of the State Council also have mandates to adopt normative documents.[15]

---

9 Wang (n 6) 27. Regarding the historical antecedents and contemporary contexts, see Pitman Potter, *China's Legal System* (Polity 2013), 7–48.

10 Zou (n 4), 7.

11 "Socialist Legal System with Chinese Characteristics" was established as a goal by the ruling Communist Party of China (CPC) in 1997, which was from the Report at the 15th National Congress of the CPC: Hold High the Great Banner of Deng Xiaoping Theory for an All-round Advancement of the Cause of Building Socialism with Chinese Characteristic to the 21st Century (12 September 1997) by Jiang Zemin. See Zhang (n 8) 1.

12 The current Constitution of the PRC was adopted in 1982. It is a successor to three previous Constitutions, namely the 1954 Constitution, the 1975 Constitution and the 1978 Constitution. The Constitution (1982) was amended in 1988, 1993, 1999, 2004, and 2018.

13 Legislation Law of the People's Republic of China (adopted 15 March 2000, amended 15 March 2015).

14 Legislation Law, articles 7, 65, 72, 80 and 82.

15 State Council General Office Circular on Strengthening the Formulation and Supervision of the Management of Administrative Normative Documents (Guo Ban Fa [2018] No. 37, 31 May 2018) (in Chinese) <http://www.gov.cn/zhengce/content/2018-05/31/content_5295071.htm> accessed 15 August 2020.

### 2.2 *Structure and Hierarchy*

The modern Chinese legal system consists of seven branches and three levels of legislation. The seven branches of legislation are: 1) the Constitution and Constitution-related laws; 2) civil and commercial laws; 3) administrative laws; 4) economic laws; 5) laws on society; 6) criminal law; and 7) litigation and non-litigation procedural laws. The three levels are: 1) laws; 2) administrative regulations; and 3) local regulations, autonomous regulations, and separate regulations.[16]

It is important to understand that the Constitution is a "mother-law", from which other laws are derived as if they were its children.[17] Where there is a conflict between the Constitution and another law, the former prevails, because the Constitution forms the foundation of all other laws and has the supreme force.[18] Regarding the relationship between other instruments at different levels, the Constitution provides that laws should not conflict with the Constitution,[19] administrative regulations should not conflict with the Constitution and the laws,[20] and local regulations should not conflict with the Constitution, the laws, and administrative regulations.[21]

(a) The Laws (Falü)

The NPC is the highest state organ and the source of authority for all other state organs.[22] The NPC and its Standing Committee have the power to enact laws (the first level) covering all the abovementioned seven branches. It is worthy of note that only the legislation of the NPC and its Standing Committee can be called "law" (*Falü*) within China's legal system. The NPC has the authority to develop and amend the basic laws on criminal matters, civil matters, and state authorities, among others, while the Standing Committee of the NPC develops and amends laws other than those developed by the NPC. It also partially supplements and amends laws developed by the NPC when that body is not in session.

(b) The Administrative Regulations (Xingzheng Fagui)

---

16 State Council Information Office (SCIO), *China's Efforts and Achievements in Promoting the Rule of Law* (Information Office of the State Council of the People's Republic of China, 28 February 2008) <http://www.china.org.cn/government/whitepaper/node_7041733.htm> accessed 15 August 2020.

17 Albert Hung-yee Chen, *An Introduction to the Legal System of the People's Republic of China* (Butterworths Asia 1992), 45.

18 ibid.

19 Constitution, article 5.

20 Constitution, article 89(1).

21 Constitution, article 100.

22 Legislation Law, article 7.

The State Council, whose legislative power is just below that of the NPC and its Standing Committee, has the power to enact administrative regulations (*xingzheng fagui*). Likewise, only the enactments issued by the State Council can be named as administrative regulations (*xingzheng fagui*).

Under the Legislation Law, the State Council may formulate administrative regulations in the following situations: (a) when it is necessary to enact regulations to implement provisions of law; (b) when it is necessary to enact regulations to govern matters within the administrative functions and powers of the State Council as stipulated in the Constitution; and (c) when the State Council is delegated the law-making power by the NPC or its Standing Committee to enact regulations for matters originally within the national legislature's exclusive legislative jurisdiction.[23]

In terms of designation, enactments of the State Council may be titled *xize* or *tiaoli* (regulations), *guiding* (provisions) or *banfa* (measures), depending on the scope of the subject matter. When the State Council exercises the delegated law-making powers, its enactment will be called a *zanxing* (provisional), implying that formal statutes will eventually be made by the NPC or its Standing Committee in due course.

(c) Departmental Rules and Local Enactments

The departments under the State Council, the people's governments of the provinces, autonomous regions, municipalities directly under the central government, and the larger cities have also enacted numerous laws.

(i) Departmental Rules (*Bumen Guizhang*)

The departments under the State Council[24] are allowed to establish *bumen guizhang* (departmental rules) to implement law, State Council administrative regulations, decisions, or orders within the limit of their respective power. The rules, established by either a single ministry or several ministries jointly, should be made only pursuant to and for the purpose of enforcing laws or administrative regulations.[25] As a matter of fact, departmental rules, forming the largest

23 Legislation Law, article 56.

24 Pursuant to article 80(1) of the Legislation Law, the following organs are qualified to enact departmental rules: State Council departments, committees, the People's Bank of China, auditing offices, and directly controlled institutions with administrative regulatory functions may draft rules within the scope of that department's authority on the basis of laws, state council administrative regulations, decisions, or orders.

25 Legislation Law, article 80(2). The matters decided by departmental rules shall be within the scope of the law, State Council administrative regulation, decision, or order being enforced. Departmental rules not based on a law, State Council administrative regulation, decision, or order must not impair the rights of citizens, legal persons, or other organizations or increase the scope of their duties, and they must not increase the power of that department or reduce that department's legally provided duties.

group of normative legal documents, constitute the most relevant and practical body of law for the daily life of ordinary citizens and businesses.[26]

A set of departmental rules may have the generic designation of *guiding* (provisions) or *banfa* (measures). Apart from *guizhang*, the State Council and its ministries establishes, from time to time, other forms of official documents, including *mingling* (orders), *jueding* (decisions), *tongzhi* (notices), *tongbao* (communications), *pifu* (replies), *yijian* (opinions), *zhiyin* and *zhidao yijia* (guidelines).

(ii) Local Enactments

Local Enactments consist of local regulations and local rules. The governments of the provinces, autonomous regions, municipalities directly under the central government, and larger cities have also enacted numerous rules.

(d) Interpretation

It is inherent in the nature of a legal system that enacted written law or legislation cannot be the exclusive source of law applied by courts in deciding cases and thus rules of statutory interpretation and a doctrine of precedent are used as typical devices in this regard.[27] It is also what China utilizes. However, the system of "interpretation of laws" is rather "unique or peculiar" since the concept of "interpretation" adopted is quite different from that accepted in common law or even civil law jurisdiction.[28] According to the Constitution, the Legislation Law, and the resolution of the Standing Committee of the NPC in 1981 on the resolution of strengthening the work of legal interpretation,[29] and from the actual operation of legal interpretation, contemporary China has, initially, formed a kind of "Yiyuanduoji" (monistic pluralism) legal interpretation system.

"Yiyuan" can be understood as "the mandate to interpret the law belongs to the Standing Committee of the NPC". Article 67 of the Constitution gives the Standing Committee of the NPC the power to interpret the Constitution and the laws. Article 42 of the legislative law further stipulates that one of the following circumstances shall be explained by the Standing Committee of the NPC: (1) the specific meaning of a provision of such legislation requires further clarification; (2) a new situation arises after the enactment of such legislation, thereby requiring clarification of the basis of its application.

26 Wang (n 6) 36.

27 Chen (n 17) 95.

28 ibid.

29 Resolution of strengthening the work of legal interpretation (Adopted at the 19th meeting of the Standing Committee of the Fifth NPC on 10 June 1981).

"Duoji" shows that there are other types of statutory legal interpretations besides the legal interpretation of the NPC Standing Committee. According to the Standing Committee of the National People's Congress of 1981, the strengthening of legal interpretation of the resolution, China still has the following types of statutory interpretation:

(1) The question of the specific application of laws and decrees in the trial of a court shall be interpreted by the Supreme People's Court. Where the prosecution work in the specific application of laws and decrees, the Supreme People's Procuratorate to explain. The Supreme People's Court and the Supreme People's Procuratorate shall, if there are any differences of principle, report to the Standing Committee of the National People's Congress for interpretation or decision.
(2) Other laws and ordinances which do not belong to the trial and prosecution work, and how the specific application of the decree should be explained by the State Council and the competent department.
(3) Where the provisions of the local laws and regulations itself need to further clarify the boundaries or make supplementary provisions, by the enactment of regulations of the provinces, autonomous regions and municipalities directly under the Central People's Congress needs to explain or make provisions.[30]

Although China's legal system, generally, remains a civil jurisdiction and case law has never gained legitimacy in China, it is also worth noting that the mandate of the Supreme People's Court in interpretation makes China distinguishable from other civil law countries at least with respect to law-making.[31]

It is worth noting that apart from the aforementioned legal norms, there is also a type of legal norm called "normative documents" (*Guifanxing Wenjian*) that are issued by the government, including administrations under ministries and commissions of the State Council. They also impose binding obligations on individuals and legal entities, although they are not formal regulations as regulated by China's Legislation Law.[32] The nature of normative documents is administrative regulation as required by the LOSC, but the hierarchy of them is much lower than administrative regulations or rules promulgated by the State Council or relevant ministries.[33]

30 Zhiming Zhang, 'Research on the Legal Interpretation of Contemporary China' (in Chinese) <http://www.iolaw.org.cn/showNews.aspx?id=13739> accessed 15 August 2020.

31 See generally Wang (n 6) 37–38.

32 State Council General Office Circular on Strengthening the Formulation and Supervision of the Management of Administrative Normative Documents (n 15).

33 Hao Shen, 'Developing China's Legal Regime for International Deep Seabed Mining- The Present and Future' (2021) *Ocean Development and International Law*.

## 3 Legal System of Deep Seabed Mining in the Area and Relevant Policy

China's current legislation on deep seabed mining in the Area consists of one piece of law issued by the Standing Committee of the NPC and three normative documents issued by the State Oceanic Administration (SOA). The law is China's Deep Seabed Law.[34] The three documents are *Measures for the Administration of Licensing for the Exploration and Development of Resources in Deep Seabed Areas* (the Administration of Licensing Measures),[35] *Interim Measures for the Administration of Sample Management for the Exploration and Development of Resources in Deep Seabed Areas* (the Administration of Sample Management Measures)[36] and *Interim Measures for the Administration of Data Management for the Exploration and Development of Resources in Deep Seabed Areas* (the Administration of Data Management Measures).[37]

Preparatory work for China's deep seabed legislation started substantively in April 2013, when the Environment and Resources Committee of the National People's Congress (hereinafter "ERC")[38] held a symposium on ocean legislation, exploring legislation relating to deep seabed mining in the Area. Subsequently, the plan for deep seabed legislation was included in the secondary-class legislation plan of the NPC Standing Committee in October 2013.[39] In December 2013, the ERC set up a drafting and working group (hereinafter "the legislative drafting group") specializing in deep seabed legislative work which allowed for the substantive development of the area. The legislative drafting group

34 Deep Seabed Area Resource Exploration and Exploitation Law of the People's Republic of China (adopted 26 February 2016).

35 Measures for the Administration of Licensing for the Exploration and Development of Resources in Deep Seabed Areas (adopted 25 April 2017).

36 Interim Measures for the Administration of Sample Management for the Exploration and Development of Resources in Deep Seabed Areas (adopted 29 December 2017).

37 Interim Measures for the Administration of Data Management for the Exploration and Development of Resources in Deep Seabed Areas (adopted 29 December 2017).

38 Environment and Resources Protection Committee of the National People's Congress, is one of the special committees of the National People's Congress, led by the council of the National People's Congress; when the National People's Congress is not in session, it is under the leadership of the standing committee of the National People's Congress. Environment and Resources Protection Committee of National People's Congress is composed of one chairman of committee, several vice-chairman of committee and several committee members.

39 H Lu and others (eds), *Deep Seabed Area Resource Exploration and Exploitation Law of the People's Republic of China: A Commentary* (China Legal Publishing House 2017) (in Chinese), 9.

spent at least one year conducting legislative research and investigations at home and abroad. Members of the legislative drafting group visited quite a few prestigious domestic research institutes as well as many practitioners located in coastal cities such as Guangzhou, Xiamen, and Qingdao for high-level investigation and discussion. Moreover, in September 2014, the legislative drafting group visited the ITLOS headquarters in Hamburg and the ISA headquarters in Kingston, seeking their opinions.[40] After more than two years' prepartory work, the First Draft of China's Deep Seabed Law came out in June 2015. It sought views and opinions on the content and structure of the draft from the stakeholder base over the following month. After two reviews, the Standing Committee of the NPC adopted China's Deep Seabed Law by vote on 26 February 2016, and it came into force on 1 May 2016.[41]

Since the entry into force of China's Deep Seabed Law in 2016, there has been three normative documents regarding licensing measures, sample management, and data management, respectively, to complement China's Deep Seabed Law.[42] The latter two documents provide information on sample and data management and thus there are not too many details for marine environmental protection. Hence, this section focuses on China's Deep Seabed Law and the Administration of Licensing Measures.

## 3.1 *China's Deep Seabed Law*

### 3.1.1 Legal Framework

China's Deep Seabed Law contains 29 articles in seven chapters. The first chapter provides general provisions, including the legislative objective, legislative principles, applicable scope, administrative authority, etc. Supplementary provisions are given in chapter 7, incorporating terminologies mentioned in this law and their definitions, tax matters, and date of entry into force of the

---

40 See Permanent Mission of the People's Republic of China to the International Seabed Authority, 'Oceanic legislative study group of China visited the International Seabed Authority', <http://china-isa.jm.china-embassy.org/chn/xwdt/t1191407.htm> accessed 26 January 2020.

41 The NPC is responsible for legislating and amending the constitutional law, civil law, criminal law, national institutional law, and other basic laws, while the NPC's Standing Committee is responsible for legislating and amending all the other national laws. See Legislation Law Art. 7.

42 See the reply from the Permanent Mission of the People's Republic of China to the International Seabed Authority regarding 'The national laws, regulations and administrative measures adopted by China since 2017 with respect to the activities in the Area', text is available <https://www.isa.org.jm/files/documents/EN/NatLeg/China/China-1a.pdf> accessed 15 August 2020.

law. The main body of China's Deep Seabed Law consists of information relating to Exploration and Exploitation (chapter 2), Environmental Protection (chapter 3) and Scientific Research and Resource Survey (chapter 4), followed by provinsions of Supervision (chapter 5) and Liability (chapter 6), which will be concretely introduced in following sections (see Table 4).

The core contents of China's Deep Seabed Law can be divided into three areas: 1) Carrying out the primary obligations of the sponsoring State – "responsibility to ensure" – through accesssing, monitoring, and liability, which are respectively stipulated in chapter 2, chapter 5, and chapter 6 of China's Deep Seabed Law; 2) Protecting the marine environment and Chinese operators' legitimate rights and interests in the process of deep seabed mining in the Area, which are mainly stipulated in chapter 3; and 3) Improving China's own capacity for marine scientific research, resource investigation, and boosting overall capacity of exploration, exploitation, and environmental protection, which is presented in chapter 4.[43]

#### 3.1.2 Legislative Objective, Principles and Applicable Scope

China's Deep Seabed Law has two primary objectives. The first aims to safeguard China's national interests, i.e. regulating the exploration and exploitation of resources in deep seabed areas conducted by China-sponsored contractors as well as promoting deep sea scientific and technologicial research and resource investigation. The second focuses on maintaining the benefit for all mankind by means of protecting the marine environment and promoting the sustainable utilization of resources in the Area.[44] There are four key principles for activities in the Area: peaceful use, sharing and cooperation, marine environmental protection, as well as preserving the common interest of mankind.[45]

The applicable scope of China's Deep Seabed Law can be categorized into three areas: eligible subjects, applicable activities, and applicable area. The eligible subjects of China's Deep Seabed Law refer to citizens, juridical persons, or other organizations of the People's Republic of China.[46] China's Deep Seabed Law was enacted to regulate resource investigation, exploration, and exploitation of deep-sea resources and to boost marine scientific research and marine

43 H Lu, 'China's Deep Seabed Law: Theory and Practice' (in Chinese) (2016) 15 *The People's Congress of China* 10, 14.

44 China's Deep Seabed Law, article 1.

45 China's Deep Seabed Law, article 3. More discussion on this account, see Guobin Zhang and Pai Zheng, 'A New Step Forward: Review of China's 2016 Legislation on International Seabed Area Exploration and Exploitation' (2016) 73 *Marine Policy* 244, 247.

46 China's Deep Seabed Law, article 2(1).

environmental protection.[47] The applicable area is depicted as the "deep seabed area". It is further explained as the seabed, ocean floor and subsoil beyond the jurisdiction of the People's Republic of China and other countries.[48]

Four interesting observations are made on the terminology used in this part. First, "resource investigation" is used rather than "prospecting" although they are almost identical in meaning. Second, the term "resources" is maintained throughout the law. However, there is no explaination as to "resources". It is speculated that "resources" in this law not only refers to mineral resources but also other resources such as genetic resouces. Third, in this law, the term "deep seabed area" is used instead of "the Area" which is enshrined in LOSC. It is still uncertain as to whether there is any difference between the two.[49] Fourth, it is not clear whether foreign investments are accepted for mining activities in the Area under this law.[50]

### 3.1.3 The Main Contents of China's Deep Seabed Law

#### 3.1.3.1 *Exploration and Exploitation*

There are four main points in the chapter. First, China's Deep Seabed Law sets up a dual-track system for the application of exploration and exploitation in the Area, namely, licensing by China and granting a contract by the ISA. The former procedure is the prerequisite for the latter one. Moreover, licensing can also be seen as China's method of assessing the provision of sponsorship. The application process for engaging in resources exploration or exploitation activities in the Area involves the submission of supporting documents which the Marine Administrative Department under the State Council (hereinafter "MAD") has identified.[51] The MAD shall examine the materials submitted by the applicant. If the application is in the national interest and the applicant has sufficient funds, technology, equipment, and other capabilities and

47 China's Deep Seabed Law, article 2(1).

48 China's Deep Seabed Law, article 2(2).

49 Pursuant to China's Deep Seabed Law, article 2(2), "For the purpose of this Law, 'deep seabed areas' means seabed, ocean floor and their subsoil outside the jurisdiction of the People's Republic of China and other countries." Literally, the two terms should be identical. This article will use "the Area" referring to both.

50 Zhang and Zheng (n 45), 252.

51 "Marine Administrative Department under the State Council" is the exact wording in China's Deep Seabed Law. There is no specific reference of the administrative agency until the entry into force of the State Oceanic Administration's departmental rule *Measures for the Administration of Licensing for the Exploration and Development of Resources in Deep Seabed Areas,* on 27 April, 2017. For further information, see section 5 of this chapter.

conditions, the MAD shall grant a license to the applicant within 60 working days.[52]

Second, the contractor enjoys the corresponding exclusive rights of exploration or exploitation for specific resources in the contract area. China's Deep Seabed Law also specifies the obligations of contractors. Specifically, the contractors shall fulfill the contractual obligations of exploration or exploitation contracts. Besides, they must guarantee personal safety and protect the marine environment. Importantly, contractors engaging in exploration and exploitation activities in the Area shall protect objects of an archaeological or historical nature as well as submarine cables, etc. Finally, contractors engaging in exploration and exploitation activities shall also abide by the People's Republic of China's laws and administrative regulations in relation to production safety and labour protection.[53]

Third, the contractor may transfer the rights and obligation of exploration and exploitation contract, or change the contract, but must receive the approval of the MAD to do so.[54]

Fourth, the Deep Seabed Law stipulates the execution of an emergency system. If any accidents occur in the process of exploration or exploition of the international seabed resources that seriously damage the marine environment, the contractor must immediately start emergency plans and take effective amelioration measures.[55]

#### 3.1.3.2 *Marine Environmental Protection*

China's Deep Seabed Law attaches great importance to protection of the marine environment. This can be seen from the inclusion of the special chapter on environmental protection. This section draws on lessons from the international customary law and relevant regulations of the ISA on environmental protection, with the aim of attaining international standards and

52 China's Deep Seabed Law, articles 7 and 8. The following materials should be submitted: 1) Basic information on the applicant; 2) An explanation on the location, size, and categories of minerals that the applicant intends to explore and exploit; 3) Certificates of financial status and investment abilities as well as an explanation on technical capabilities; 4) An exploration and exploitation plan, including the materials on the possible impact of exploration and exploitation activities on the marine environment, and an emergency response plan for serious damage to marine environment; 5) Other materials required by the MAD.

53 China's Deep Seabed Law, article 9.

54 China's Deep Seabed Law, article 10.

55 China's Deep Seabed Law, article 11.

requirements.[56] It requires the contractors, within the reasonable and feasible scope, to utilize available advanced technologies and take the necessary measures to prevent, reduce, and control pollution and other hazards on the marine environment.[57] In particular, the contractor shall, in accordance with the provisions of the exploration and exploitation contract and requirements, and regulations of MAD, investigate and study the ocean conditions in the exploration and exploitation area, collect environmental baseline data, evaluate exploration and exploitation activities' impact on the marine environment; and formulate and implement an environmental monitoring plan on exploration and exploitation activities. Morever, the normal operation of monitoring equipments should be guaranteed to keep an original monitoring record.[58] Contractors engaged in exploration and exploitation activities shall take necessary measures to protect and preserve rare or fragile ecosystems, as well as exhausted, threatened, or endangered species and other marine creatures' living environments, protect the marine biodiversity, and maintain the sustainable utilization of marine resources.[59]

#### 3.1.3.3 *Scientific Research and Resources Investigation*

Chapter 4 of China's Deep Seabed Law addresses scientific and technological issues and sets out provisions to facilitate deep seabed research and resources investigation. China supports the training of professional talent and encourages cooperation in research among relevant industries. Specifically, China supports enterprises to conduct deep sea scientific and technological research as well as R&D of technical equipment.[60] The Deep Seabed Law stresses the construction and operation of the deep sea public platform, providing professional services for deep sea scientific and technological research and resource investigation activities, and promoting deep sea scientific and technological exchange, cooperation, and results-sharing.[61] Furthermore, the duplicates of relevant materials, and physical samples or catalogues of investigation of resources shall be submitted to the MAD and other relevant departments for public utilization.[62] Last, but not least, scientific publicity in deep seabed

56 Yu Jia, 'Exploitation of Resources in the Arena and the Sponsoring State Responsibility: New Developments in China's Legislative Work Concerning the Deep Sea' (2016) *China Oceans Law Review* 1, 23.
57 China's Deep Seabed Law, article 12.
58 China's Deep Seabed Law, article 13.
59 China's Deep Seabed Law, article 14.
60 China's Deep Seabed Law, article 15.
61 China's Deep Seabed Law, article 16.
62 China's Deep Seabed Law, article 18.

mining, such as opening vessels for scientific investigation, laboratories, exhibition rooms and other places and facilities, holding seminars, and providing consulting services are encouraged.[63]

#### 3.1.3.4 *Supervision and Legal Responsibility*

The state organ responsible for the supervision and inspection of contractors' exploration and exploitation activities is the MAD.[64] The MAD can inspect the contractor's ships, facilities, equipment used for exploration and exploitation activities, as well as logbooks, records, and data.[65] The contractors shall provide assistance and cooperation for supervision and inspection by the MAD.[66]

The Deep Seabed Law also stipulates that the liability is borne by the contractor for any violation of the law. If contractors submit false materials to obtain a license, or fail to perform their contractual obligations, or transfer the rights and obligations of the exploration and exploitation contract without the approval of MAD, or make significant changes to the exploration and exploitation contract, the MAD may revoke the license.[67]

If the contractor (1) fails to file a copy of the contract with the MAD for their record; (2) fails to file records with the MAD for reference in case of assignment, modification, or termination of the contract; (3) fails to submit data copies, material object samples or the catalogue coming from the resource survey on exploration and exploitation to the MAD; (4) fails to report the contract performance status to the MAD; or (5) rejects supervision and inspection or fails to coordinate with the MAD's supervision and inspection, the MAD shall order it to correct its action and impose a fine of CNY 20, 000 to 100, 000.[68]

If the contractor engages in deep seabed area resources exploration and exploitation activities without permission or fails to conclude a contract for the exploration and exploitation, the MAD shall order it to cease the illegal activities and impose a fine of CNY 100, 000 to 500, 000. If illegal income is discovered, it will be confiscated.[69] If the contractor causes pollution or damage to the marine environment or damage to objects of an archaeological or historical nature or to submarine cables, the MAD shall order it to stop the illegal activities and impose a fine of CNY 500, 000 to 1, 000, 000. If any crime is perpetrated, it shall be subject to criminal liability according to the relevant law.[70]

---

63 China's Deep Seabed Law, article 17.
64 China's Deep Seabed Law, article 19.
65 China's Deep Seabed Law, article 21.
66 China's Deep Seabed Law, article 22.
67 China's Deep Seabed Law, article 23.
68 China's Deep Seabed Law, article 24.
69 China's Deep Seabed Law, article 25.
70 China's Deep Seabed Law, article 26.

TABLE 4 The structure of the China's deep seabed law

| **General provisions (Chap. 1)** | | **Supplementary provisions (Chap. 7)** | |
|---|---|---|---|
| legislative objective | art. 1 | terms & definitions | art. 27 |
| legislative principles | art. 3 | tax issues | art. 28 |
| applicable scope | art. 2 | date of entry into force | art. 29 |
| supporting policies | arts. 4 & 6 | - | - |
| administrative authorities | art. 5 | - | - |

| **Explorations & exploitations (Chap. 2)** | | **Environmental protection (Chap. 3)** | | **Scientific research & resource survey (Chap. 4)** | |
|---|---|---|---|---|---|
| application & review procedure | arts. 7, 8 & 10 | pollution & hazard prevention | art. 12 | DSPP operation | art. 16 |
| contractor's rights & obligations | art. 9 | marine environment monitoring | art. 13 | data & sample management | art. 18 |
| contingency management | art. 11 | ecological sustainable development | art. 14 | incentive policies | arts. 15 & 17 |

| **Supervision & inspection (Chap. 5)** | |
|---|---|
| supervision authority | art. 19 |
| contractor's periodical reports & other obligations | arts. 20 & 22 |
| contents of inspection | art. 21 |

| Legal liability (Chap. 6) | |
|---|---|
| licence revocation & liability of compensation | art. 23 |
| fines & confiscation of illegal gains | arts. 24, 25 & 26 |
| criminal responsibility | art. 26 |

SOURCE: GUOBIN ZHANG AND PAI ZHENG, 'A NEW STEP FORWARD: REVIEW OF CHINA'S 2016 LEGISLATION ON INTERNATIONAL SEABED AREA EXPLORATION AND EXPLOITATION' (2016) 73 MARINE POLICY 244, TABLE 2.

### 3.2 *Measures for the Administration of Licensing for the Exploration and Exploitation of Resources in Deep Seabed Areas*

The SOA issued a normative document concerning the administration of licensing for the exploration and exploitation of resources in the Area in April 2017, namely the Administration of Licensing Measures, to complement China's Deep Seabed Law.[71] The Administration of Licensing Measures contains 29 articles in six chapters. The first chapter outlines general provisions, while supplementary provisions are given in chapter 6. The main body of the Administration of Licensing Measures, which is contained in chapter 2 (Exploration and Exploitation) and chapter 5 (Supervision) of China's Deep Seabed Law, provides futher details as to Application and Acceptance (chapter 2), Examination and Decision (chapter 3) and Extention and Change (chapter 4), followed by provisions of Supervision (chapter 5). The following will focus on new details provided in the Administration of Licensing Measures.

The preliminary section reiterates that the citizens, legal persons, or other organizations of the People's Republic of China who want to carry out exploration and exploitation activities in the Area shall obtain a license in advance. However, there are three important developments in this part. First, similar to article 5 of China's Deep Seabed Law which stipulates the Marine Administrative Department under the State Council (the MAD) shall be responsible for the supervision and administration of the exploration and exploitation of the resources in the Area, article 2 of the Administration of Licensing Measures specifically identifies the SOA as the agency with responsibility for the approval, supervision, and administration of exploration and exploitation activities in the Area. Second, the Administration of Licensing Measures has a provision, "the approval for the exploration and exploitation of the resources

71 An unofficial translation is available at <http://lawinfochina.com/display.aspx?id=23974&lib=law> accessed 13 August 2020.

in the Area shall be in the national interests and comply with the relevant plans of the state for the exploration and exploitation of the resources in the Area".[72] Here, national interests are emphasized as well as common interests. Third, article 6 of the Deep Seabed Law provides that "the state encourages and supports international cooperation in terms of the exploration and exploitation of resources in the Area, the relevant environmental protection, resource investigation, scientific and technological research, education and training, among others." And the Administration of Licensing Measures details that the state encourages and supports the aforementioned activities by taking "economic and technical policies and measures".[73]

With regard to supporting materials for application, the Administration of Licensing Measures specifies the requirements of financial and technological capabilities. With regard to financial capability, the applicant must prove that it has the appropriate financial and investment capacity as specified by the ISA. Documentation, such as the proof of funds, duplicates of the audited financial statements, project investment reports, financing programs or supporting documents on relevant financial resources, and a financial guarantee must be provided as proof. For technological capabilities, the applicant has to provide a summary of the experiences, technical equipment, knowledge, technical qualifications, etc. relevant to the exploration and exploitation work.[74]

After the SOA accepts an application, it has to examine all the materials received and, taking the national interests into account, decide whether to grant a license to the applicant within 60 working days.[75] If the SOA decides to grant a license, then it shall be valid from the issuing date to the contract's termination date.[76] However, the license shall be automatically invalidated if the licensee does not sign a contract with the ISA within three years of the date of the granting of the license.[77] If the SOA denies the application, the applicant has the right to appeal or litigate.[78] If the applicant requires an extension for the license it must submit an application for extension to the SOA before approaching the ISA for an extension. Also, the applicant could seek to appeal or litigate if the SOA denies the extension application.[79] The licensee can make minor changes to the license, by application. The licensee must also seek the

72 The Administration of Licensing Measures, article 3.
73 The Administration of Licensing Measures, article 4.
74 The Administration of Licensing Measures, article 6.
75 The Administration of Licensing Measures, articles 8 and 9.
76 The Administration of Licensing Measures, article 11.
77 ibid.
78 The Administration of Licensing Measures, article 9.
79 The Administration of Licensing Measures, article 15.

permission of the SOA in order to make material changes to the plan of work or contract, or fully or partially transfers the contract.[80]

Here the individual rights of the licensee are presented in regard to supervision. When the SOA is carrying out its responsibility of supervision and inspection, it must not hinder the normal production and business activities of the licensee, shall not claim or receive the property of the licensee, and shall not seek other benefits.[81] Moreover, the SOA has the authority to withdraw the license, in keeping with the provision of China's Deep Seabed Law. The Administration of Licensing Measures added a new provision concerning cancellation of the license in following situations: 1) the license expires and does not extend; 2) the licensee no longer has the ability to explore and exploit the resources in the Area; 3) the application by the licensee for suspension was approved; 4) the licensee is terminated due to dissolution, bankruptcy, and other reasons; 5) exploration and exploitation licenses for deep seabed mining in the Area are revoked according to law; or 6) other cases that should be canceled according to laws and regulations.[82]

## 4 Other Legislation That May Be Related to Deep Seabed Mining in the Area

In addition to legislation directly targeting deep seabed mining in the Area, China has some other laws and regulations regarding the exploitation of mineral resources and environmental protection. Although they are applicable only within China's national jurisdiction, they may provide a certain degree of reference for the improvement of China's Deep Seabed Law. Some legal mechanisms in the existing laws could be embodied in China's Deep Seabed Law.[83] For example article 27(5) of the Japan Act highlights issues relating to adjudication for mining activities in the Area by stating "[p]rovisions of Article 11 and Article 113 to Article 116 of the Mining Act (Act No. 289 of 1950) shall apply *mutatis mutandis* to compensation for damage ... deep seabed mining in Japan". China can make reference to that method. That is a cost-effective way of improving China's Deep Seabed Law in some respects. For this reason,

80 The Administration of Licensing Measures, article 16.

81 The Administration of Licensing Measures, articles 20 and 21.

82 The Administration of Licensing Measures, article 24.

83 Hao Shen, 'International Deep Seabed Mining and China's Legislative Commitment to Marine Environmental Protection Regional Focus and Controversies' (2017) 10 *Journal of East Asia and International Law* 489, 499.

two categories of legislation are worth reading. The first is the legislation on exploration and exploitation of the mineral resource, which is relatively mature after long-term development; the second category is the legislation on environmental protection, which is more thorough and better structured than relevant marine laws and regulations in China.[84] Although other branches of law, such as criminal law, are also closely related to laws for mining activities in the Area when prescribing criminal liability, they are not presented in this section. Also, this section does not systematically introduce the provisions of all of the legislation mentioned above but focuses on those provisions relevant to deep seabed mining or which will contribute to the improvement of China's Deep Seabed Law.

### 4.1 *Legislation on the Exploration and Exploitation of Mineral Resources*

There are two primary categories of legislation which address the exploration and exploitation of mineral resources: 1) Legislation on terrestrial mining, i.e. the Mineral Resources Law of the People's Republic of China (Mineral Resources Law) and Rules for the Implementation of the Mineral Resources Law,[85] the latter outlines the details of implementation of the former; and 2) Law of the People's Republic of China on the Administration of the Use of Sea Areas.[86]

(1) Mineral Resources Law

The Mineral Resources Law and Rules for the Implementation of the Mineral Resources Law together provide a general legal framework for mining activities intended to develop the mining industry, promote the exploration, exploitation, utilization, and protection of mineral resources, and to ensure the present and long-term requirements of the socialist modernization.[87] They are applicable to all the mineral resources within the territory of China,[88] certainly including deep seabed mineral resources. Pursuant to the Mineral Resources

84 Zou, China's Marine Legal System and the Law of the Sea (n 4) 10.

85 Mineral Resources Law of the People's Republic of China (adopted 19 March 1986, amended 29 August 1996 and 27 August 2009); Rules for the Implementation of the Mineral Resources Law of the People's Republic of China (adopted 26 March 1994).

86 Law of the People's Republic of China on the Administration of the Use of Sea Areas (adopted 27 October 2001).

87 Mineral Resources Law, article 1.

88 Rules for the Implementation of the Mineral Resources Law of the People's Republic of China, article 4. The exploration and exploitation of the mineral resources within the territory of the People's Republic of China and other sea areas under its jurisdiction must comply with the Mineral Resources Law and these Rules.

Law, mineral exploration must be registered, whereas mineral exploitation must be assessed and approved.[89] Regulatory agencies vary in keeping with distinct mineral resources.[90]

The Mineral Resources Law and Rules for the Implementation of the Mineral Resources Law pays some attention, although generally, to the environment. The exploitation of mineral resources must comply with the relevant environmental protection laws and regulations to prevent environmental pollution.[91] There are also some provisions mentioning specific aspects of environmental protection, albeit generally. For example, one of the requirements for the application for exploitation is that the applicant must have the capacity to implement the necessary measures for environmental protection.[92]

(2) Law on the Administration of the Use of Sea Areas

The Law of the People's Republic of China on the Administration of the Use of Sea Areas provides the regulation, in detail, on the administration of the use of sea areas including the procedures on how to apply for use, the period of use, and the approval process. Article 25 of that Law provides the various lengths of period for the use of sea areas. The maximum period for salt production and mineral exploitation is 30 years. There are two provisions as to environmental protection in this legal instrument. Article 11 states that the functional divisions of the sea shall be worked out under the following three principles: Protecting and improving the ecological environment, ensuring the sustained utilization of sea areas, and promoting the development of the maritime economy. Article 29 states, after the termination of the right to use sea areas, the original right holder shall dismantle all facilities and buildings for the use of the sea that may cause environmental pollution or that affect the use of the sea in other projects.

### 4.2 *Legislation on Marine Environmental Protection*

A series of four important environmental legislation relevant to deep seabed mining within Chinese jurisdiction exists: 1) Environmental Protection Law of the People's Republic of China;[93] 2) Marine Environmental Protection Law of the People's Republic of China;[94] 3) Law of the People's Republic of China on

89 Mineral Resources Law, articles 12 and 16.

90 Mineral Resources Law, article 16.

91 Mineral Resources Law, article 32.

92 Rules for the Implementation of the Mineral Resources Law, article 16.

93 Environmental Protection Law of the People's Republic of China (adopted 26 December 1989 and amended 24 April 2014).

94 Marine Environmental Protection Law of the People's Republic of China (adopted 25 December 1999 and amended 28 December 2013, 7 November 2016, 4 November 2017).

Environmental Impact Assessment;[95] and 4) Measures on the Management of Marine Nature Reserves (1995).[96]

(1) Environmental Protection Law

The Environmental Protection Law is the basic law for overall environmental protection in China. The General Provisions of the Environmental Protection Law state that "[e]nvironmental protection is a fundamental national policy of the state."[97] Moreover, "[e]nvironmental protection shall adhere to the principles of giving priority to protection, focusing on prevention, conducting comprehensive treatment, engaging the general public, and enforcing accountability for damage."[98] Although there is no mention of deep seabed mining, there are several provisions as to EIA, incentives, and liability, to which China's Deep Seabed Law and regulations can make reference.

Article 19 stipulates that an EIA shall be conducted, as legally required, in the preparation of a relevant development and utilization plan or the construction of a project impacting the environment. Article 65 further states that those environmental impact assessment agencies that resort to deception when providing environmental service, and are responsible for the environmental pollution and ecological damage as a result of their fraud shall bear joint liability with others responsible for pollution and damage, in addition to punishment pursuant to relevant laws and regulations.

Article 21 provides "[t]he state shall adopt policies and measures in finance, taxation, price, and government procurement, among others, to encourage and support the development of environmental protection industries such as technological equipment for environmental protection, comprehensive utilization of resources, and environmental services." Those incentives are also applicable to encourage and support the further reduction of pollutant discharge.[99]

Article 64 provides "those who cause damages due to environmental pollution and ecological destruction shall bear tort liability in accordance with provisions of Tort Liability Law of the People's Republic of China."

(2) Marine Environmental Protection Law

Marine environmental protection is generally governed by the Marine Environment Protection Law. Article 46 of the legislation provides general requirements on seabed mining: in building coastal construction projects,

95 Environmental Impacts Assessment Law (adopted 28 October 2002, amended 2 July 2016 and 29 December 2018).

96 Measures on the Management of Marine Nature Reserves (adopted 29 May 1995).

97 Environmental Protection Law, article 4.

98 Environmental Protection Law, article 5.

99 Environmental Protection Law, article 22.

effective measures must be taken to protect wild animals and plants and their habitats as well as marine aquatic resources under State and local special protection. It is strictly prohibited to mine sand and gravel along the shore. In conducting coastal opencast mining or shore-based well drilling to exploit seabed mineral resources, effective measures must be taken to prevent pollution to the marine environment.

(3) Environmental Impact Assessment Law

China's legal family of EIA includes the Environmental Impact Assessment Law of the People's Republic of China, the Chinese Plan Environmental Impact Assessment Regulations, and a series of EIA Guidelines.[100] Generally, China's EIA law and regulation are basic, but one article expressly provides that the EIA cannot end with the introduction of the project. Article 28 states the competent department of the ecological environment shall conduct follow-up inspections on the environmental impacts of the construction projects after they are put into production or after completion. If serious environmental pollution or ecological damage is caused, the causes and the responsibilities shall be ascertained. China's Deep Seabed Law can follow this example or at least make reference to it.

(4) Legislation on Marine Nature Reserves

The 1995 Measures on the Management of Marine Nature Reserves, which was adopted by the SOA, is the most important regulation to specifically address the management of marine nature reserves. It sets out the guiding principle of "conservation first, appropriate exploitation and sustainable development". The marine nature reserves are divided into two categories: national and local.[101] The marine nature reserves at the national level should be those which have great national and international importance and have great scientific and protective values.[102] Their establishment is subject to the approval of the State Council. A marine nature reserve may be divided into a core zone, a buffer zone, and an experimental zone in accordance with the natural environment, natural resource conditions, and requisite level of protection.[103] The Measures on the Management of Marine Nature Reserves also advise on the manner in which the marine nature reserves must be established[104] and on prohibited activities in the marine nature reserves.[105]

100 Regarding details of China's EIA law, regulations, and Guidelines, see <https://www.elaw.org/eialaw/china> accessed 14 August 2020.

101 Measures on the Management of Marine Nature Reserves, article 7.

102 ibid.

103 Measures on the Management of Marine Nature Reserves, article 17.

104 Measures on the Management of Marine Nature Reserves, article 6.

105 Measures on the Management of Marine Nature Reserves, article 15.

### 4.3 *Interim Conclusion*

Although the above laws and regulations apply to activities within China's national jurisdiction, they can still be borrowed or cited by China's Deep Seabed Law and regulations. In general, laws on exploration and exploitation of resource pays insufficient attention to environmental issues and relies mainly on environmental law. China's Deep Seabed Law can learn from the contents of those legislation. Additionally, there are many aspects of environmental legislation that are worth examining for the improvement of China's Deep Seabed Law and regulations, such as incentive measures and liability under the Environmental Protection Law, follow-up EIAs under the Environmental Impact Assessment Law, and provisions as to the establishment of marine nature reserves within contractor areas. Also, China's Deep Seabed Law can directly cite those laws and regulations, if necessary.

## 5 Institutional Arrangement for Mining Activities in the Area

It is not sufficient to achieve the desired result of ensuring contractors' compliance with its international environmental obligations merely by creating relevant legislation by sponsoring States. Implementation and enforcement of the regimes are also paramount. A strong institutional structure is critical to the implementation of legal, fiscal, and environmental matters and to oversee deep seabed mining activities in the Area. Accordingly, a "reasonably appropriate" national legislation needs to be carefully considered for the institutional arrangement from the perspectives of legislation, regulating, and supervision.

First, China has a clear legislative system.[106] With regard to China's deep seabed legislation, the NPC and its Standing Committee are the legislative bodies of "Law". In most cases, before its dissolution in 2018, the SOA was mandated to issue normative documents regarding ocean affairs with the lower hierarchy. Since 2018, all of the functions of the SOA, including existing adopted normative documents, have been transferred to Ministry of Natural Resources. These three normative documents can maintain their validity despite the transfer unless they expired.

Second, regarding a regulatory agency, there is a MAD in China's Deep Seabed Law and its function is presented in article 5:

> The MAD shall be responsible for the supervision and administration of the exploration, development and investigation of resources in deep

106 With regards to China's legal system, see Wang (n 6) 41–53.

seabed areas. Other relevant departments of the State Council shall be responsible for the relevant administration according to the functions prescribed by the State Council.

Since the MAD, namely, the Marine Administrative Department under the State Council, is not a specific organ, a question arises as to who is the MAD? Article 2 of the Administration of Licensing Measures specifically points to the SOA that was a subsidiary of the now-defunct Ministry of Land and Resources as the agency with responsibility for approval, supervision, and administration of the exploration and exploitation activities in the Area. This implies that the SOA could be the MAD. It is worth noting that the SOA did not excise the function of regulator for activities in the Area, but delegated it to its subsidiary COMRA in 2010.[107] It is important to highlight that the COMRA is also widely known as a contractor for three exploration contracts sponsored by China, leading to a scenario that it acts both as a contractor and a regulator.

In 2018, the institutional reform of the State Council became a turning point in the management of activities in the Area for China. In March 2018, the 13th National People's Congress announced that the newly formed Ministry of Natural Resources shall replace the functions of the Ministry of Land and Resources, SOA, and the State Bureau of Surveying and Mapping. Internally, SOA does not exist any longer. In dealing with international counterparts, however, SOA is reserved as the point of contact within the Ministry of Natural Resources. When SOA merged into the Ministry of Natural Resources, all of its functions were transferred to Ministry of Natural Resources. However, it is unclear, within the Ministry of Natural Resources, who will take over functions of the SOA to issue normative documents and to regulate mining activities in the Area. This is subject to a further reform plan.

Third, as far as the supervision is concerned, current maritime laws have problems in common, such as scattered enforcement power, repeated inspection, and duplication of construction problems.[108] Before 2013, more than ten agencies were mandated to deal with ocean-related affairs. Five important agencies constituted China's maritime enforcement capabilities, namely the China Maritime Police (CMP),[109] the Maritime Safety Administration of the Chinese

107 Jiancai Jin, 'Move Towards the Ocean and Build a Maritime Power' (2014) 4 *Institutional Reform and Management in China* 17 (in Chinese), 19.

108 Zou (n 4), 13.

109 The China Maritime Police is a part of the Border Control Department, which is an elite subcomponent of the People's Armed Police, under the Ministry of Public Security. The

Ministry of Transportation (MSA),[110] the Fisheries Law Enforcement Command (FLRC)[111] at the Chinese Ministry of Agriculture, General Administration of Customs (GAC)[112] and the State Oceanographic Administration (SOA)[113] of the Ministry of Land and Resources. They were subject to distinct central governments and all had local agencies in each province and city of China. Notwithstanding that, they had distinct mandates. It was difficult to avoid overlap in the functions and powers among the central government agencies, and between the central government and local governments. Thus, the extent of potential overlap raised issues over who should be responsible for what. This situation was creatively called "five dragons stirring up the sea".[114] In order to strengthen the overall planning and comprehensive coordination of marine affairs, in 2013, it was proposed to call a high-level meeting of the coordinating body of the National Oceanic Commission, which is responsible for the development of a national marine development strategy and coordination of major marine matters. The specific work of the National Oceanic Commission was to be undertaken by the State Oceanic Administration. Unfortunately, no further details regarding the National Oceanic Commission could be found afterward.

---

primary mission of the Maritime Police is crime fighting, but emergent threats of special concern include terrorism and piracy, although no cases of maritime terrorism have been reported in or against China to date.

110 MSA missions include inspection and registration of Chinese and foreign vessels in Chinese ports, investigation of maritime accidents, the training and certifying of seafarers, supervision of marine traffic control, maintenance of aids to navigation, implementation of domestic and international maritime laws, and maritime search and rescue. There are fourteen regional MSA offices, mainly in the coastal provinces but also at some inland river transport centers, such as along the Yangtze River. Each MSA regional office has a rescue coordination center, and several in coastal provinces have a variety of rescue subcenters.

111 FLEC is an organ of the Fisheries Management Bureau under the Ministry of Agriculture. It was responsible for the enforcement of laws concerning fishing and maritime resources in Chinese territorial waters and EEZ. It was charged with protecting Chinese fishing vessels and personnel, resolving disputes in fishing activities, preventing illegal fishing, and protecting maritime resources.

112 China's ports and on its coastal waters preordains the importance of the role of customs in maritime enforcement. Among the chief missions of China customs are the compilation of foreign trade statistics, revenue collection, customs control (declarations, etc.), counter smuggling, and port control.

113 SOA – specifically, its China Maritime Surveillance. Major missions for the SOA include environmental protection, scientific research, and enforcement of EEZ rights and interests.

114 Lyle Goldstein, *Five Dragons Stirring up the Sea: Challenges and Opportunities in China's Improving Maritime Enforcement Capabilities* (China Maritime Studies Institute, U.S. Naval War College 2010).

## 6 Proposals for Improvements to China's Deep Seabed Law

China's Deep Seabed Law is China's first piece of legislation on the activities in the Area, which filled a gap in the Chinese marine legal system, standardized the activities of domestic contractors in the Area and allowed China to fulfill its obligation of "responsibility to ensure".[115] Under China's Deep Seabed Law, there are chapters on accessing exploration and exploitation and supervision and liability, which demonstrates China's attempts to guide the activities of its sponsored contractors at all important stages and make efforts to lead them to the best results. From this point of view, China's Deep Seabed Law can be said to have reached the minimal level of the sponsoring State's national legislation presented in chapter 3.

China's Deep Seabed Law has two prominent advantages. First, China attaches great importance to marine scientific research and resource investigation, although it sometimes blurs the boundaries between resource investigation and prospecting. That can be seen from the inclusion of a specific chapter on scientific research and resource surveys.[116] China has also adopted two regulations on sample and data management, respectively. Based on the importance of marine scientific research and data collection for marine environmental protection, this approach is highly commendable. Second, China has made momentous efforts in environmental protection. A Chinese commentator calls it a "marine environmental protection-oriented legislation".[117] The word "environment" appears more than 20 times in the 29-article's law.[118] Protecting the marine environment and promoting the sustainable use of deep seabed area resources is also one of the objectives. In particular, China's Deep Sea Law has included a specific chapter on marine environmental protection, highlighting China's emphasis on environmental protection issues.[119]

Although China's Deep Seabed Law is a good starting point in its commitment to protect the marine environment in the process of mining in the Area, some improvement would further enhance its effectiveness. First, the relevant provisions in the chapter on environmental protection are quite vague and

115 Zhang and Zheng (n 45) 253; see also Yen-Chiang Chang, 'Chinese Legislation in the Exploration of Marine Mineral Resources and Its Adoption in the Arctic Ocean' (2019) 168 *Ocean & Coastal Management* 265, 266.

116 China's Deep Seabed Law, chapter 4.

117 Shen, 'International Deep Seabed Mining and China's Legislative Commitment to Marine Environmental Protection Regional Focus and Controversies' (n 83) 501.

118 ibid, 502–503.

119 China's Deep Seabed Law, chapter 3.

general, and thus difficult to operationalize.[120] Second, certain crucial components are missing from China's Deep Seabed Law. For instance, it does not provide provisions as to preferential rights.

This section explores strategies for improving China's national legislation in form and substance and should be looked at in conjunction with the contents of chapter 3. The proposal of this section is provided on the premise of fully appreciating the contents of chapter 3 in general and considering the actual situation of China specifically. It should be emphasized that proposals in this section do not deny China's efforts to carry out its "responsibility to ensure". On the contrary, the author believes that China's legislation has basically reached the minimal line of a sponsoring State's national legislation. The author's position is that China has an essential role in deep seabed mining activities in the Area and can do better. Consequently, this section aims to explore how and to what extent China could amend its legislation to produce the optimal sponsoring State's national legislation as discussed in chapter 3.

### 6.1 *Proposals for Objectives and Structure*

In section 2.1 of chapter 3, it is suggested that at least three objectives should be included in the national legislation. China's Deep Seabed Law already incorporates two of them, namely regulating the sponsored contractor's activities in the Area and protection of the marine environment. Furthermore, for national interests, China has also set objectives of "promoting deep sea scientific and technological research and resource investigation", "promoting the sustainable utilization of resources in deep seabed areas", and "protecting the common interests of mankind". It is suggested that China's Deep Seabed Law adds the first recommendation of section 2.1 of chapter 3, namely expressly indicating the objective of implementation of international obligations of contractors in the LOSC, the 1994 Implementing Agreement, the procedures, rules, and regulations of the ISA concerning activities in the Area, and the contract. It is also a sign of carrying out a sponsoring State's "responsibility to ensure".

As discussed in chapters 2 and 3, it is under a sponsoring State's discretion to decide what kind of legislative model it is willing to use, apart from a sponsorship agreement. China has chosen to adopt a high-level specific law and uses

120 Hao Shen, 'The Next Step of Devising China's Legal Regime for Deep Seabed Mining – The Environmental Regulation under China's Deep Seabed Mining Law' (2018) 46 *Coastal Management* 210, 217; see also Chang (n 113) 266; Jiancai Jin and Guobin Zhang, 'Chapter 9: The Forthcoming Breakthrough: China's Legislation on Activities in the Deep Seabed Area' in Myron H Nordquist, John Norton Moore and Ronan Long (eds), *International Marine Economy: Law and Policy* (Brill Nijhoff 2017), 245.

it as a framework, under which other subordinate legal instruments could be adopted to operationalize and refine it. As of now, there are three regulations operationalizing China's Deep Seabed Law. There is no doubt that adopting implementing regulations will be an effective way to improve the Chinese legal system on the Deep Seabed Mining Regime in the future. In addition, the importance of the function of the administrative measure or policy, especially in China's case, cannot be underestimated.

### 6.1.1 Utilizing Umbrella Legislative Pattern

China's Deep Seabed Law is just a skeleton which requires the addition of relevant details to flesh it out. There might be two main reasons why China prefers such a legislative method. First, ISA Exploitation Regulations are still under development, which may to large extent decide the contents of China's legislation, since the ISA legislation is the benchmark of a sponsoring States' national legislation. Thus, at this time, it is not appropriate to include too many details in China's Deep Seabed Law. Second, it is common practice in China to set such general legal texts and grant authority to certain professional agencies to provide details based on their expertise.[121] China's Deep Seabed Law has "delegation clauses" authorizing the "Oceanic Administrative Department of the State Council" (State Oceanic Administration, SOA) to promulgate rules and regulations on certain legal mechanisms.[122] Since the entry into force of China's Deep Seabed Law in 2016, three administrative measures, regarding licensing measures, sample management, and data management respectively have been introduced to complement China's Deep Seabed Law.[123]

Although significant efforts have been made to improve the legal system governing deep seabed mining in the Area, there is much room for further development, including the structure of the legislation. China is certainly willing to utilize the umbrella framework, which facilitates an overarching primary legislation and secondary rules and regulations to provide operational details, such as administrative regulations, departmental rules, or local enactments. Under the framework of China's Deep Seabed Law, complementary regulations and

---

121 Shen, 'International Deep Seabed Mining and China's Legislative Commitment to Marine Environmental Protection Regional Focus and Controversies' (n 83) 501.

122 Shen, 'The Next Step of Devising China's Legal Regime for Deep Seabed Mining' (n 120) 217–218.

123 See the reply from the Permanent Mission of the People's Republic of China to the International Seabed Authority regarding 'The national laws, regulations and administrative measures adopted by China since 2017 with respect to the activities in the Area' <https://www.isa.org.jm/files/documents/EN/NatLeg/China/China-1a.pdf> accessed 15 August 2020.

guidelines will provide relevant details, thus dealing with the current problem of inadequate operationalizing details. However, there are still two problems that need to be considered in regard to China's current legislation. First, the primary legislation also requires regular review and continuous amendment with the development of ISA Regulations, especially the ISA Exploitation Regulations. Second, the three administrative measures described above do not adequately instruct practice. Regulations covering areas such as an environmental baseline; pre-EIA; environmental impact monitoring and analysis during and after mining; emergency and emergency plans; and monitoring of the closure plan and post-closure activities are critical additions to be considered.[124] An optimal solution would be the revision of the primary legislation to include provisions that will mandate the more fulsome development of secondary legislation and administrative guidelines.

#### 6.1.2 Highlighting the Function of Policy and Guidelines

As the Seabed Disputes Chamber indicated in its Advisory Opinion that to fulfill its "responsibility to ensure", a sponsoring State is required not only to enact appropriate laws and regulations to properly oversee mining activities in the Area, but also to adopt administrative measures for effective implementation and enforcement of those rules. China is willing to follow this instruction, as China's Deep Seabed Law provides that "the State will make plans on the exploration and exploitation of resources in deep seabed areas and adopt economic and technical policies and measures to encourage deep sea scientific and technological research and resource investigation and enhance the capability of resource exploration and development and the protection of the marine environment".[125]

China is a policy-oriented State, which means the government discloses the direction of its development in policies. This allows an entity to take advantage of these. As a matter of fact, edicts, policy documents, and exhortations of the ruling party may have a better effect.[126] For this reason, it is suggested that binding clauses, such as penalties, should be included in the law and regulations, whereas exhortations of the ruling party, for instance, for utilization of new technology, could be more appropriately included in policies. Furthermore, in

124 Concluded based on ISA Draft Exploitation Regulations (March 2019).

125 China's Deep Seabed Law, article 4.

126 Chen noted that the principle of the supremacy of state law as against the edicts, policy documents, and exhortations of the ruling party of China and the orders, directions, and instructions of senior officially has not yet been firmly established in constitutional theory. See Chen (n 17) 77.

China's case, administrative measures or policy would be a more effective way to implement certain standards, which may be swiftly implemented, because there are no onerous procedures for the implementation of policy in China. In contrast, it is known that the law-making process – from drafting to entry into force – can take several years or even up to a decade. Consequently, guidelines would be the better option for technical issues than legislation, as technology is so dynamic and developing continuously, which means the law needs constant revisions to cope with new developments.

### 6.2 *Proposal for Granting a License: Procedural Requirements*

As presented in chapter 3, section 3.1.3, two plausible approaches, international tendering and application, may be used to engage potential operators who are interested in seabed mining in the Area to access a mining license. According to the Administration of Licensing Measures, the qualified person or entity who wants to apply to the ISA for carrying out the exploration and exploitation of the resources in the Area, shall submit an application to the regulatory agency before it submits an application to the ISA. That being said, China only adopts an *application* as an approach to access to mining activities in the Area in current legislation. In order to "standardize the procedures for the contractors engaged in deep seabed activities as well as provide the guidance for potential applicants interested in the exploration and exploitation activities in the Area",[127] China specifically adopted the Administration of Licensing Measures. Despite of this guidance, the following two points needs to be improved.

First, the category of the licensing should be differentiated. The ISA, depending on which mineral deposit type is being pursued by the applicant, has separate regulatory requirements for (i) prospecting; (ii) exploring; and (iii) exploiting of minerals. Some sponsoring States follow that example to differentiate distinct categories of licenses. China's Deep Seabed Law also covers both exploration and exploitation, which means there is no need to formulate a separate law concerning exploitation.[128] Nevertheless, it does not include prospecting, although there are provisions relating to resource investigation

127 Shen, 'International Deep Seabed Mining and China's Legislative Commitment to Marine Environmental Protection Regional Focus and Controversies' (n 83) 500.

128 COMRA, 'The Law of the People's Republic of China on the Exploration and Development of Resources in Deep Seabed Area Is a Significant Representation of China's Compliance with its International Obligations and Contribution on Promotion of International Law Development' (in Chinese) (COMRA, 21 March 2016) <http://www.comra.org/2016-03/21/content_8649472.htm> accessed 13 December 2020.

or marine scientific research.[129] The inclusion of additional details relating to prospecting, in keeping with the model of the ISA Exploration Regulations where prospecting and marine scientific research are subject to different regimes under the LOSC, respectively, is highly recommended.[130] Moreover, neither the Deep Seabed Law nor the Administration of Licensing Measures differentiates applications between exploration and exploitation. Considering the different environmental impacts of those two activities, "it is reasonable to assume that a more stringent standard of environmental measures is demanded for the application of the exploitation permit."[131] Hence, it is suggested to provide specific details of the application for exploration and exploitation respectively in the Administration of Licensing Measures.

Second, the scope of qualified applicants needs to be carefully considered. Article 153(2)(b) of the LOSC provides that qualified applicants are States Parties, state enterprises or natural or juridical persons which possess the nationality of States Parties or are effectively controlled by them or their nationals. China further specifies citizens, legal persons, or other organizations of the People's Republic of China are qualified applicants, which can include both state-owned and private companies. A related issue in this regard is whether foreign investment is acceptable for mining activities in China. Although its contents are revised yearly, the 2017 Guideline Catalogue of Industries for Foreign Investment within Chinese territory may provide a clue, which indicates foreign investment on prospecting, exploration, and exploitation of the rare earth elements within Chinese territory is clearly restricted.[132] This shows China's cautious attitude toward metal mining. It is hard to say that China will not adopt the same attitude in deep seabed mining.

### 6.3 *Proposal for Granting a License: Substantial Requirements*

As presented in section 3.1 of chapter 3, supporting documentation for applications should vary depending on the stage of mining activities. In this regard, the ISA Regulations have clearly listed the required documents, and thus applicants can submit application materials in accordance with ISA Regulations. Importantly, the ISA Council, rather than the sponsoring State, has the mandate to decide whether the application is approved with the recommendation

129 Zhang and Zheng (n 45) 252.

130 See chapter 1, section 3.3.1.

131 Shen, 'The Next Step of Devising China's Legal Regime for Deep Seabed Mining' (n 120) 218.

132 2017 Guideline Catalogue of Industries for Foreign Investment (adopted by National Development and Reform Commission and Ministry of Commerce on 28 July 2017).

from the LTC, whose members are recognized experts with distinct expertise. To avoid duplication of work, the regulatory agency of China does not need to conduct a substantive comprehensive review of the application materials. Instead, China shall play a role in ensuring the applicant's financial and technical capabilities and the payment of Environmental Performance Guarantees and insurance.

As indicated in section 3.1.4 of chapter 3, ensuring a contractor's financial and technical capability is an important job of the sponsoring State. In China's case, the current three contractors sponsored by China are all state enterprises, which means the financial capability could be guaranteed by the Chinese Government. It seems that there would be no need for concern on this point. Apart from the situation of capital and credibility of the applicant as stipulated in the Administration of Licensing Measures,[133] other certification of financial responsibility according to China's situation could also be added. In order to supervise the financial situations of the sponsored contractor, it is suggested to check the contractor's financial situation regularly or occasionally after issuing a license, by reviewing its audit reporting, to ensure a contractor's continued financial capability of carrying out mining activities. Even the monitoring agency can regularly check the financial situation of the contractors.

The parameters for the checking of technological standards include the experience, technical equipment, knowledge, technical qualifications, etc. relevant to the exploration and development work.[134] As indicated in chapter 3, personnel are also essential as people are operators of equipment and technology. All the staff should be trained systematically. Following the Czech Republic's example, as indicated in section 3.1.4.2 of chapter 3, it is suggested China specify what kinds of certificates of knowledge or skill are required.

The value of environmental bonds and insurance was already presented in section 3.1.4.3 of chapter 3. Since the application of environmental bonds is detailed in the ISA Regulations, there is no need to add more burden to contractors at the national level. It should be appreciated that deep seabed mining is a capital-intensive activity which means contractors have already contributed a significant amount of money at every stage. Thus, in order to protect a contractor's interests, minimizing repetitive financial burdens is also necessary. However, it is noteworthy to reiterate that environmental bonds should be fully or partially paid to sponsoring States because the sponsoring State plays an important role in controlling its sponsored contractor and paying

133 Administration of Licensing Measures, article 8(2) and (3).

134 Administration of Licensing Measures, article 6(4).

environmental bonds is an effective economic instrument to control contractors. This issue needs further consideration by the ISA.

Under China's Deep Seabed Law and relevant regulations, no provision as to compulsory insurance is mentioned. It is necessary to reiterate the importance of compulsory insurance in China's Deep Seabed Law and treat it as a requirement for application.

### 6.4 *Proposal for a Contractor's Environmental Obligations*

As analyzed in section 3.2 of chapter 3, obligations can be divided into two categories: general ones (such as duty to protect and preserve the marine environment and rare or fragile ecosystems) and specific ones (such as the precautionary approach and best environmental practice). The latter can be further categorized as either abstract or difficult to operationalize due to lack of specific standards. While, as indicated in chapter 3, the options available to a sponsoring State are limited in this regard, China can attempt to provide further guidance.

China's Deep Seabed Law refers to the utilization of the best available technology,[135] determination of the baseline[136] and conducting an EIA.[137] In addition, there is a provision implying utilization of the precautionary approach although there is no explicit wording as such.[138] Moreover, there is a provision as to the protection of cultural relics and submarine cables within the contract area,[139] but, there is no definitions and scopes of such terminologies.

China's Deep Seabed Law and regulations would be improved in the following areas. First, it is reasonable to add the missing international obligation of reasonable regard for other activities as it is an obligation required by the LOSC.[140] "Respect of indigenous peoples" might be considered due to its second wave of due diligence.[141] Second, guidelines for operationalization, such as for the EIA, is missing under the China's Deep Seabed Law and regulations. Third, China's Deep Seabed Law and regulations lack appropriate measures to incentivize the compliance of contractors with environmental obligations and other procedures.[142] Indeed, in China, incentive measures, including tax

135 China's Deep Seabed Law, article 12.

136 China's Deep Seabed Law, article 13.

137 ibid.

138 China's Deep Seabed Law, article 14.

139 China's Deep Seabed Law, article 9.

140 UNCLOS, article 147.

141 See section 3.2.7 of chapter 3.

142 Shen, 'International Deep Seabed Mining and China's Legislative Commitment to Marine Environmental Protection Regional Focus and Controversies' (n 83) 500–501; see also Zhang and Zheng (n 45) 252.

reductions, government subsidies, and government-sponsored debt are usually utilized in fields, such as cleaner production, energy saving, and renewable energy sources.[143] China's Deep Seabed Law and regulations can follow those examples.

### 6.5 *Proposal for a Contractor's Environmental Rights*

China's Deep Seabed Law explicitly indicates that a contractor shall enjoy exclusive rights to explore and exploit specific resources within the region specified in the contract.[144] However, it lacks the preferential right of the previous exploration contractor for an exploitation application. As mentioned in chapter 3, China should ensure such a right among its sponsored contractors, although it has no mandate to make the final decision in the international level.

The law is quite vague concerning the other rights of the contractor, as it only states that a contractor shall report to the SOA for approval before it transfers the rights and obligations under an exploration or exploitation contract or makes any major modification of such contract.[145] Furthermore, it also provides that the contractor shall report to the SOA if it transfers, modifies, or terminates the exploration or exploitation contract.[146] Here termination may refer to the completion of the contract rather than cessation in advance, since this "termination" only needs to be recorded rather than approved. Thus, it can be speculated that transfer and modification are accepted without details in China's Deep Seabed Law and regulations while there is no explicit provision regarding other rights, such as retention or surrender.

Under this situation, the legislation should grant the contractor the right to transfer its tenure to a third party upon approval of the regulatory agency and provides relevant details. Singapore, which is one of those countries with prescribed provisions regarding the Transfer of License, adopts an application-and-approval module. Both the licensee and the intended transferee are required to complete applications. The license only can be transferred to a Singapore company under approval.[147] The Cook Islands has a similar provision and further clarifies that the transferee is to be treated as an applicant.[148]

143 ibid.
144 China's Deep Seabed Law, article 9(1).
145 ibid, article 10(1).
146 ibid, article 10(2).
147 Deep Seabed Mining Act of Singapore, 2015, article 12.
148 Cook Islands, Seabed Minerals Act 2009, article 138.

The Administration of Licensing Measures grants the contractor the right to appeal the objection of an application and modification of a license through both administrative and judicial approaches.[149] But no further details are provided. It is suggested to refer to the specific applicable law.

### 6.6 *Proposal for Monitoring*

The sponsoring State has a role to play in monitoring. The information relating to monitoring and inspection are detailed in chapter 5 of China's Deep Seabed Law, presented in four provisions. The articles concerning the monitoring agency and self-reporting could be improved.

With regard to the monitoring agency, article 39 provides that the oceanic administration of the State Council is responsible for monitoring and inspecting the contractor's exploration and exploitation activities. What is puzzling is, what is this agency? This unclear mandate may lead to a confused scenario in which no agency actually has the responsibility for monitoring, or multiple agencies repeatedly monitoring one contractor, which may not only place more burdens on the contractor, but also lead to chaos of governance, reminiscent of the "five dragons stir up the sea" situation.

The two methods of monitoring that are frequently utilized in China are: 1) surveillance, including patrol by ships and aircraft and radar monitoring to see whether there may be some violation of law; 2) inspection of both ships and platforms.[150] Given the remoteness of the contract area, it is unrealistic to utilize patrols by ships and aircrafts to monitor the mining activities in the Area. The monitoring methods utilized by China's Deep Seabed Law are self-reporting and site visits by the monitoring agency. This area also needs to be improved. First, article 20 only requires annual reports, but there is no stipulation regarding reports triggered by specific serious incidents. Second, as indicated in section 3.4.2 of chapter 3, the LOSC and ISA Regulations do not specify how an inspection can be invoked. China can specify it by way of authorizing the monitoring body to conduct inspections regularly, or when deemed necessary, or under complaint.

### 6.7 *Proposal for Liability and Enforcement*

Liability is stipulated in chapter 6 of China's Deep Seabed Law, including four articles (article 23 to article 26). A proposal in this regard may be organized in the areas of liability, sanction, and compensation.

149 Administration of Licensing Measures, articles 9 and 15.

150 Zou (n 4), 13.

#### 6.7.1 Proposal for Contractor's Liability: Strict Liability?

Despite the opposing views,[151] it is an overwhelming view that the contractor's liability is not a strict liability under the Convention. Although there is no obvious wording, it is not difficult to conclude China follows the mainstream in its national legislation. As discussed in section 3.5.1 of chapter 3, the sponsoring State's national legislation may be the only platform to apply strict liability due to the mandate to a sponsoring State under the framework of the LOSC since the national legislation can be more stringent than that of the LOSC. It is undeniable that if the contractor assumes strict liability, it facilitates prompt compensation for the victim when damage occurs. There are at least two other benefits to implementing strict liability. First, when an accident occurs, there is no need for channeling, so the compensation process can be quickly realized. Second, "liability rules do not just have a compensatory effect, but also a preventive one."[152] Strict liability can increase the vigilance of the contractor.

So, is it possible to apply strict liability under China's deep seabed legislation? Before answering this question, it is necessary to examine provisions relating to environmental liability within China's legal system. As indicated in section 4 of this chapter, there are at least six laws relating to exploration and exploitation of marine resources and marine environmental protection. According to the Mineral Resources Law, in the case of destructive mining methods to exploit mineral resources, penalties may be imposed and mining licenses may be revoked; if mineral resources are severely damaged, criminal responsibility shall be pursued against those directly responsible.[153] According to the Environmental Protection Law, in case of damage caused by polluting the environment and destroying the ecology, it is liable for infringement in accordance with the relevant provisions of the Law of the People's Republic of China on Tort Liability, which stipulates the polluter shall bear the tort liability for damage caused by environmental pollution. The standard of care is strict.[154] Therefore, it is customary to establish strict liability for environmental

151 Neil Craik is of the view that a contractor shall assume strict liability under the LOSC. See section 3.5.1 of chapter 3; see also Neil Craik, *Determining the Standard for Liability for Environmental Harm from Deep Seabed Mining Activities*, Liability Issues for Deep Seabed Mining Series, Paper No. 2 (October 2018); Neil Craik, 'Liability for Environmental Harm from Deep Seabed Mining: Towards a Hybrid Approach' (2019) 33 *Ocean Yearbook* 313.

152 Michael G Faure and Ton Hartlief, 'Compensation Funds versus Liability and Insurance for Remedying Environmental Damage' (1996) 5 (4) *Review of European Community & International Environmental Law* 321.

153 Mineral Resources Law, article 39.

154 Environmental Protection Law, article 64; Law of the People's Republic of China on Tort Liability, article 7 and 65. See also Huixing Liang, 'Analysing the China Tort Liability

pollution within the Chinese legal system. Then, it is not entirely impossible to apply strict liability to legislation on mining activities in the Area. The tricky problem is how the ISA and international community can incentive sponsoring States, including China, to do so.

### 6.7.2 Proposal for Inducing the Compliance

As indicated in section 3.5.2 of chapter 3, there are two ideas promoting the compliance of the contractor: incentives encouraging compliance and sanctions against non-compliance. Under China's Deep Seabed Law and regulations, there are no provisions for incentives. As presented in section 4.2 of this chapter, articles 21 and 22 of the Environmental Protection Law provides some incentives, to which China's Deep Seabed Law can refer. Alternatively, China's Deep Seabed Law can incorporate those methods as well. With regard to sanctions, China adopts revocation of the license, corrective measures, and an order for the ceasing of wrongful act and fines as sanctions. Indeed, China can prescribe incremental sanctions from warning to revocation of the license in monitoring and enforcement if it wants to be more effective. For example, if the contractor does not submit the required annual report or performance report, he will get a warning and be ordered to submit one within a certain period. Persistent disobedience will lead to large monetary penalties or even revocation of the license. It is noteworthy that revocation of a license is a serious penalty. Indeed, the LOSC and the ISA Exploration Regulations strictly list three circumstance of suspension and termination of a contract.[155] China, as a sponsoring State, is empowered to go beyond it within its legal framework. But circumstances for the revocation of the license needs to be clearly and strictly listed and prudently decided, as it may result in a contractor's serious financial loss.

### 6.7.3 Proposal for Prompt and Adequate Compensation

In order to provide prompt and adequate compensation, it is suggested that China's legislation add the details regarding access to a Chinese domestic court, as well as local enforcement of decisions in international courts or tribunals. In tandem, the contractor should be required to pay a security deposit or contribute to a compensation fund to ensure that the victim receives prompt, effective, and adequate compensation. A compensation fund is primarily a solution for providing prompt, adequate, and effective remedies to those

---

Law' (in Chinese) <https://www.iolaw.org.cn/showArticle.aspx?id=2993> accessed 14 August 2020.

155 LOSC, Annex III, article 18(1); ISA Exploration Regulations, Annex IV, section 21.1.

who have suffered damages in the event of accidents or damages arising out of certain lawful activities. In China, there is already a national fund called the China Oceanic Development Foundation. It is a national public fund-raising foundation approved by the China's government in November 2015. Its department in charge is the Ministry of Natural Resources of the People's Republic of China. It is founded by the State Oceanic Administration of the People's Republic of China together with six state enterprises, which are China National Offshore Oil Corporation, China Petroleum & Chemical Corporation, China General Nuclear Power Group Co., Ltd., China Huaneng Group Co., Ltd., China Communications Construction Co., Ltd., China National Petroleum Corporation. It aims to provide funding to projects on oceanic development, such as the marine scientific research, marine space management and structural optimization, marine protection and restoration, marine disaster prevention and mitigation.[156] It is suggested for the Ministry of Natural Resources of the People's Republic of China expand the function of this fund to compensate for damage in the Area. To be specific, the contractors may make certain contributions to this fund, and, thus, that fund could be one of the resources to provide compensation when damages occur in the Area.

### 6.8 *Proposal for Institutional Arrangement*

Ideally, the institutional structure should at least include a legislative body, regulatory agency, and monitoring body. The ideal model is for each body to stand alone with clearly separated powers and functions to ensure its operationalization and independence. Alternatively, some bodies could be merged according to a sponsoring States' actual conditions and administrative capacities. Whatever model is followed, the institutional system should be complete with each body performing its duties.

More attention needs to be paid to regulatory and monitoring bodies. At present, COMRA, a subsidiary of the Ministry of Natural Resources after March 2018, still assumes the responsibility of the regulatory agency for activities in the Area. However, as circumstances change, the functions of COMRA should be reconsidered. In the past, COMRA was the only contractor sponsored by China. In 2018 and 2019, CMC and BPHDC, two Chinese state-owned companies, successfully signed contracts with the ISA. It is not difficult to expect that more diverse applicants will be involved in the deep seabed mining activities when it comes to the commercial exploitation stage. In this circumstance, it

156 Website of China Oceanic Development Foundation is available <http://www.cfocean.org.cn/index.php/index/about.html> accessed 15 December 2020.

will not be effective for COMRA to perform its functions if it is to act both as a contractor and a regulator. Notably, in the case of competing interests between Chinese contractors, it is difficult for COMRA to make a fair decision if it is a contractor as well. Moreover, after institutional reform in 2018, the responsibilities between national ministries have been re-divided; however, the internal responsibilities within ministries have not yet been clearly defined, which also affects the management of activities in the Area. Hence, it is time to reconsider the institutional arrangement for activities in the Area. In this regard, the emergence and development of COMRA is relevant.

The establishment of COMRA is closely linked to China's interest in the Area, which dates back to 1984. In that year, China initially established a strategeic plan through which it intended to apply for an exploration area relating to polymetallic nodules in the Area no later than 1990.[157] To this end, COMRA was established in 1990 with the function of developing new mineral resources for China, enhancing the development of cutting edge technology for deep seabed mining, and contributing to mankind's development and utilization of international seabed resources.[158] COMRA was registered as an international seabed pioneer investor in the United Nations in 1991[159] and was designated a state enterprise at that time.[160] In 2010, the SOA made it clear that COMRA was the regulatory agency for affairs relating to activities in the Area. Since 2012, the Chinese Government has intended to separate COMRA's role between a regulator and a contractor. To this end, COMRA internally became the Ocean Affair Administration (OAA), functioning as a regulator of deep-sea affairs.[161] However, such a plan cannot substantively function due to the lack of specific reform plan.

The Institutional reform in 2018 was an opportunity to redefine the functions between the OAA and COMRA. The OAA should assume the responsibility as a Chinese regulatory agency, specifically focusing on issues such as granting and withdrawing a license, and the implementation of the precautionary

157 Jin (n 107) 19.

158 COMRA was established on 9 April 1990 approved by the state council, its purpose was: through international seabed resources research and development activities, opened up new sources of resources in our country, promoted the formation and development of seabed high and new technology industry in China, safeguarded the rights and interests of China's developing international seabed resources, and made great contribution to human development and utilization of international seabed resources.

159 See COMRA, 'Brief Introduction' <http://www.comra.org/2013-09/23/content_6322477.htm> accessed 26 January 2020.

160 Wang, 'China and the Exploitation of Deep Seabed Polymetallic Nodules' (n 1) 133.

161 Jin (n 107) 19.

approach and adaptive management in the management process following instructions in chapter 3. For the approval of the application for mining activities in the Area submitted by Chinese enterprises, the Chinese regulatory agency is not authorized to directly or completely approve the application. Rather, it must wait for the ISA's approval, although the Chinese Government has already granted a license. That makes the license for mining activities in the Area different from other activities that needs a license as well. As Yu Jia noted "this kind or management is new to the competent authorities of China, who need to fully consider the relevant international rules when understanding the limits of their functions and powers and the pertinent procedures."[162] By contrast, COMRA should gradually complete the transition from the dual role to a "pure" contractor. As its name, it could be an "Association" of exploration and exploitation of deep-sea mineral resources, coordinating entities in this domain and making guidelines and standards for deep seabed mining.[163]

As far as supervision is concerned, in order to strengthen the protection and rational utilization of marine resources and safeguard the national maritime rights and interests, it is necessary to consolidate the enforcement powers at sea. China should expressly mandate a monitoring agency for mining activities in the Area. An independent and eligible inspector should be appointed, and sufficient authority should be given if it is impossible to separate the regulatory and monitoring power in practice.

## 7 Conclusion

China, the sponsor of more than one contractor covering all three categories of mineral deposit types, undoubtly plays a significant role in the exploration and exploitation of deep seabed minerals in the Area. There is no doubt that it is a challenge for China, a sponsoring State, to regulate its sponsored contractors and to ensure their compliance of international obligations arising from the LOSC and related international instruments within the Chinese legal system. The legal system for mining activities in the Area established by China through a law and three regulations almost meets the minimal standard of the sponsoring State meeting its "responsibility to ensure". Some missing contents, such as provisions on compulsory insurance, accessing national courts, and the enforcement of judgments of international courts, must be

162 Jia (n 56) 23.

163 Jin (n 107) 19.

supplemented. China can improve this system through an umbrella legislation and the introduction of relevant policies. Also, China can make some efforts to achieve the optimal level of a sponsoring State's national legislation in the following aspects. First, China can specify the scope of triggering an inspection based on the LOSC and ISA Regulations. Second, China's Deep Seabed Law can impose strict liability on its sponsored contractors. Third, in terms of punishment, China's national legislation can be more stringent than the ISA regulations. Fourth, it should have a national compensation fund. Moreover, that the institutional reform and how the regulator applies the adaptive management and precautionary approach should be China's main job in its institutional arrangement.

The function of a sponsoring State's national legislation is to regulate the sponsored contractor to ensure its compliance with environmental obligations in the LOSC and related legal instruments, clauses of the contract, and the ISA Mining Code. However, the sponsoring State's national legislation is not a panacea, and thus there are still some situations that cannot be incorporated in a sponsoring State's national legislation. Those include: 1) where one State sponsors more than one contractor, the sponsoring State needs a holistic management and coordination for all sponsored contractors; 2) where there is more than one department in charge of oversight of activities in the Area or regulating other activities in the high sea, those departments need to collaborate with each other. Besides, apart from deep seabed mining, China also has other concerns in the Area, such as the rules of the Diversity Beyond Areas of National Jurisdiction (BBNJ).[164] Hence, it is necessary for China to create a national ocean policy for activities in the Area to foster sustainable development of ocean areas, to protect marine biodiversity and vulnerable resources and ecosystems, and to coordinate the actions of different Chinese agencies and its sponsored contractors.[165] For a long time, China's marine management system was weak and decentralized and lacked a top-level design, although sector and local strategy existed in some areas, resulting in conflicts among those strategies.[166]

164 Xinmin Ma, 'China and the UNCLOS: Practices and Policies' (2019) 5 *The Chinese Journal of Global Governance* 1, 18–20.

165 Miriam C Balgos, Biliana Cicin-Sain, and David L VanderZwaag, 'A Comparative Analysis of Ocean Policies in Fifteen Nations and Four Regions', in Biliana Cicin-Sain, David L VanderZwaag, and Miriam C Balgos (eds), *Routledge Handbook of National and Regional Ocean Policies* (Routledge 2015), 5.

166 Zou (n 4) 244.

The Thirteenth Five-Year Plan for National Economic and Social Development of the People's Republic of China (13th Five-Year Plan), formulated by the People's Republic of China, outlines the development of the national economy from 2016 to 2020.[167] In this plan, two sections regarding the Area indicate that China will take an active role in formulating international rules in the Area, and strengthen the development of strategic, state-of-the-art deep sea technology.[168] In order to make overall plans and strengthen the top-level design of the deep-sea work, the 13th Five-Year Plan for Exploration and Exploitation for Deep Seabed Resources was jointly published by the State Oceanic Administration, the Ministry of Foreign Affairs, the National Development and Reform Commission, the Ministry of Science and Technology, the Ministry of Finance, and Ministry of Land and Resources[169] in 2017. The Thirteenth Five-Year Plan covers issues regarding resources investigation and exploration, technological innovation, basic scientific research, industrialization development, deep sea global governance, and supporting capacity building in the deep-sea area during the Five-Year Plan period. It is proposed that the work in the deep seabed during this period will be guided with the intention of "building a maritime power", adhering to the development concept of "innovation, coordination, green, openness, and sharing", and actively promoting significant projects, such as, "Jiaolong to explore the sea" to further enhance China's capabilities of investigation, exploration, exploitation of deep-sea resources, and environmental protection.

However, this plan is more concerned with marine scientific research and industrial development related to deep seabed mining activities. It would be more reasonable if it could cover more environmental concerns by promoting the precautionary approach and best environmental practices, overcoming fragmented sectoral approaches and taking cumulative environmental impacts into account, and utilizing the integrated environmental management approach. Besides, apart from deep-seabed-mining-related activities, investigating living resources and genetic resources needs to be incorporated as well. Moreover, although it is not an obligation in the LOSC, it is also important to recognize the particular situation of indigenous peoples and campaigns for the protection of their right to a free and self-determined life in their homeland.

167 Text of the 13th five-year plan is available at <https://en.ndrc.gov.cn/newsrelease_8232/201612/P020191101481868235378.pdf> accessed 15 December 2020.

168 ibid, chapter 6, section 1, and chapter 52, section 3.

169 In March 2018, the 13th National People's Congress announced that the newly formed Ministry of Natural Resources shall replace the functions of the Ministry of Land & Resources, State Oceanic Administration, and the State Bureau of Surveying and Mapping.

CHAPTER 5

# Conclusion

The past two decades witnessed the increasing global interest in deep seabed mining for political, scientific, and commercial reasons. It has been 19 years since the ISA granted the first six exploration contracts in 2001. With the continuous expansion of market demand and advances in science and technology, commercial mining will be possible in the near future. However, those activities will cause adverse impacts on the marine environment. In addition, there are also unknown impacts. While those negative impacts cannot be eliminated entirely, they certainly can be mitigated, through some methods such as *avoidance* and *minimization*.

The LOSC and 1994 Implementing Agreement, together, constructed the basic framework for the Deep Seabed Mining Regime, under which the ISA conducts its legislative mandate to set rules, regulations, and procedures to regulate contractors' activities in the Area. However, due to the lack of subjectivity under international law, non-State contractors are not obliged by the LOSC and 1994 Implementing Agreement. To solve this problem, the LOSC embodied a sponsorship mechanism, under which, a sponsoring State has the responsibility to ensure its sponsored contractor's compliance with provisions under the LOSC and to assist the ISA to ensure such compliance via the establishment of a regulatory system concerning activities within its domestic legal framework. In this sense, the sponsoring State's national legislation is an integrated part of the international DSM regime.

## 1 Carrying out "Responsibility to Ensure": Sponsoring State's Regulatory Role in Ensuring Its Sponsored Contractor's Compliance

As noted earlier, the sponsoring State has a responsibility to assist the ISA to regulate its sponsored contractor. Yet, one might well ask, what is the motivation for a sponsoring State to do so? The sponsored contractors are either state-owned entities or significant investors in the State. Regulating the contractor too rigorously could introduce the risk of a sponsoring State suffering economic losses in the event that the investor quits the sponsorship agreement due to rigorous or high standards and transfer to another sponsoring State.

 | DOI:10.1163/9789004472341_007

Hence, an important task is to examine the legal genesis that would motivate a State to do so. There are at least two points in this regard. First, according to the LOSC, the Area and its resources are the "common heritage of mankind". The concept is not only a statement of common ownership of resources by all States on a non-discriminatory basis, but it also includes an obligation of "protection of the natural environment". Therefore, the principle of common heritage of mankind requires a sponsoring States to make efforts to protect the marine environment. Second, a sponsoring State, under the LOSC, has "the obligation to ensure compliance by sponsored contractors with the terms of the contract and the obligations set out in the Convention and related instruments". The Seabed Disputes Chamber further directs that the "responsibility to ensure" is a sponsoring State's primary obligation. A violation of "responsibility to ensure" entails liability under the LOSC. Not only that, if a sponsoring State fails to carry out its legal responsibility and obligations under customary international law, whether damage occurs or not, the sponsoring State has to bear international responsibilities. These obligations and liabilities are the motivations for a sponsoring State to regulate its sponsored contractors. Then, it is time to conclude answers to three questions put up at the beginning of this book.

### 1.1 *What Role Does a Sponsoring State Play to Ensure Its Sponsored Contractor's Compliance?*

The responsibility of assisting the ISA decides a sponsoring State's role as the secondary regulator, which also determines that it has no absolute decision-making power. To be specific, the sponsoring State has absolute power over negative matters by way of objecting or withdrawing the sponsorship or license. By contrast, it only has partial powers for affirmative matters and rights-giving matters, because they are subject to the decision of the ISA. Thus, a sponsoring State's regulatory role is limited. Given the characteristics of the two-track management of mining activities in the Area, the Deep Seabed Mining Regime must fully take the following two points into account. First, the division of the regulatory burden between the two regulators must be clear, avoiding waste of administrative resources caused by duplicated regulatory burdens. National legislation should focus on assessing whether the applicant has the capability to comply and taking procedural measures to ensure such compliance. Second, national legislation in this regard should be neither a full copy of international Deep Seabed Mining Regime nor a pure domestic law without consideration of the international regime. Components of the national legislation can be concluded from the UNCLOS and related instruments, ISA regulations (including contract), other international conventions not incompatible with the UNCLOS and ITLOS SDC Advisory Opinion in 2011. Specifically, a sponsoring State should take appropriate measures in implementation, monitoring, and enforcement according to the State's situations and capabilities.

### 1.2 *What Should Be Included in the Sponsoring State's National Legislation?*

The questions then arise: what does carrying out the "responsibility to ensure" entail and how is it accomplished? Several measures can be identified for implementing "responsibility to ensure". First, it is an obligation to ensure that a contractor executes his task with due regard for the protection of the environment. This does not mean that a sponsoring State must closely monitor every action by its sponsored contractors. Rather, it requires a sponsoring State to institute processes and guidelines to direct the actions of the contractors to result in compliance. "Certain efforts" could be explained as taking "all necessary and appropriate measures". To be specific, it requires a sponsoring State to "adopt laws and regulations and take administrative measures". In the context of deep seabed mining, proof of a sponsoring State carrying its obligation of conduct is that it introduces legislation within its domestic legal system which mandates the actions to be observed by the contractor in complying with the practice of environmental protection. The legislative models and hierarchy are under the discretion of the sponsoring State. Furthermore, The Seabed Disputes Chamber indicates that "it is an obligation to deploy adequate means, to exercise best possible efforts, to do the utmost, to obtain this result." The words "adequate", "best possible efforts", and "utmost" all mean a high standard of conduct. Yet, a high standard does not mean infinitely high.

Second, "responsibility to ensure" is an obligation of due diligence. It is acknowledged that due diligence is a dynamic concept, the measure of which changes with the standard of the available technology. Consequently, the specifics of due diligence would need to be updated with the development of technology, distinct categories of mineral resources, and different stages. It is suggested, then, that a sponsoring State should keep its legislation under review and adopt adaptive management according to the development of technology and distinct categories of mineral resources. It is further suggested that a sponsoring State differentiate categories of licensing according to different mining stages. Furthermore, in order to avoid the phenomenon of "sponsoring States of convenience", "responsibility to ensure" should be applied equally to all developing States, as "sponsoring States of convenience" would "jeopardize the uniform application of the highest standards of protection of the marine environment, the safe development of activities in the Area and protection of the common heritage of mankind".[1]

In addition to the primary obligation, the Seabed Disputes Chamber also concludes direct obligations of sponsoring States, which can provide examples for implementation of due diligence, as the Seabed Disputes Chamber says, "compliance with these obligations can also be seen as a relevant factor in meeting the due diligence 'obligation to ensure' and that the said obligations are in most cases couched as obligations to ensure compliance with specific rules".[2] Those direct obligations include: implementing the precautionary approach; applying best environmental practice; conducting the EIA; ensuring financial and technical capacity; arranging for an emergency order; and ensuring availability of recourse for compensation. Those elements should be incorporated in the parts of the contractor's obligations in a sponsoring State's national legislation and be checked in different phases.

Third, a sponsoring State has to be "reasonably appropriate" in implementing the "responsibility to ensure". Three dimensions need to be considered to attain the requirement of being "reasonably appropriate". The first dimension requires a sponsoring State to "act in good faith, taking the various options into account in a manner that is reasonable, relevant and conducive to the benefit of mankind as a whole".[3] It is suggested that the sponsoring State incorporate provisions in relation to "due regards to other sea users", "respect to indigenous people", and protection of archaeological and historical objects in its legislation. The second dimension implicates that "sponsoring States may apply to the contractors they sponsor more stringent standards as far as the protection of the marine environment is concerned."[4] This actually suggests that sponsoring States should adopt higher or stricter standards than those mandated by international law. This method is usually applied to quantifiable indicators. In addition, sponsoring States could provide more detailed information in targeted legal instruments at the national level. Given that there are quite a few non-quantifiable indicators at the international level, providing details seems to be a necessity at the national level. The third dimension relates to the requirement of being "kept under review". "Kept under review" should be

1 SDC Advisory Opinion, paragraph 159.
2 SDC Advisory Opinion, paragraph 123.
3 SDC Advisory Opinion, paragraph 230.
4 LOSC, Annex III, article 21(3); SDC Advisory Opinion, paragraph 240.

understood from two perspectives. On the one hand, a sponsoring State should keep pace with the development of ISA's regulations. When the ISA adopts new regulations or amends existing regulations, a sponsoring State should react accordingly, at least meeting the minimum standard of ISA regulations. On the other hand, even where there is no update of ISA regulations, the sponsoring States should proactively and regularly (for example, every five years) review their national legislation. Sponsoring States should amend their legislation as new information becomes available in keeping with good industry practices and best environmental practices are updated, etc., which is also a requirement of the "due diligence" obligation.

Moreover, it is inherent in the "due diligence" obligation of the sponsoring State to ensure that the obligations of a sponsored contractor are made enforceable. Thus, it is suggested to establish mechanisms with regard to monitoring, liability, and enforcement in a sponsoring State's national legislation. Also, none of the aforementioned can be realised if there is no institutional arrangement.

### 1.3 *How Far a Sponsoring State Can Go to Ensure Its Sponsored Contractor's Compliance?*

There is a minimal and optimal level for a sponsoring State's national legislation. Reaching the minimal level is a "must" for a sponsoring State to assume its "responsibility to ensure", whereas reaching the optimal level is flexible, which means the sponsoring State, according to its capabilities, tries its best to institute more stringent standards than requirements in the LOSC. The optimal standard invites the sponsoring State, to explore in which aspects, apart from meeting the minimum requirements, it can also play a role, according to its national conditions and capabilities, to assist the ISA in achieving its objectives; or it can adopt more stringent requirements (higher standards or more details). The sponsoring State and its legislation can go further, at least, in terms of application, monitoring, and liability and enforcement.

In fact, chapter 2 outlines the theoretical basis of "responsibility to ensure", while chapter 3 attempts to provide concrete measures for performing "responsibility to ensure" in national legislation. The contents of the two chapters complement each other and contribute to the development of legislation for the sponsoring State. The table below shows the correspondence between theory and practice and provides the corresponding section in chapter 3 when a sponsoring State is implementing its "responsibility to ensure" (see Table 5):

TABLE 5 Index of the concrete measures for performing "responsibility to ensure" in national legislation

| Implications of "Responsibility to Ensure" (Chapter 2) | Specific measures in the sponsoring state's domestic legal framework | Reference to chapter 3 |
|---|---|---|
| **Implementing "Responsibility to Ensure" of conduct** | | |
| certain type of legislation within its domestic legal system | Objectives | section 2.1 |
| | Legislative models | section 2.2 |
| **Implementing "Responsibility to Ensure" of due diligence** | | |
| Variable concept-Development of technology | Best Environmental Practice | section 3.2.4 |
| | Adaptive management and | section 4.2.2 |
| | Precautionary approach | section 3.2.3 |
| Variable concept-Different mineral resources | | |
| Variable concept-Different stage | Different categories of Licensing | section 3.1.1 |
| Implementing the Precautionary Approach | Precautionary approach | section 3.2.3 |
| Apply Best Environmental Practice | Best Environmental Practice | section 3.2.4 |
| Conducting the EIA | Conducting EIA | section 3.2.2 |
| Ensure Financial and technical capacity | Financial capabilities (application) | section 3.1.4.1 |
| | Technological capability, equipment and personnel (application) | section 3.1.4.2 |
| Ensure Availability of recourse for compensation | Liability | section 3.5 |
| | Environmental bonds and insurance | section 3.1.4.3 |
| | Access to domestic courts | section 3.5.3.1 |
| | Enforcement of decisions of international courts or tribunals | section 3.5.4 |
| **"Reasonably Appropriate" Implementing "Responsibility to Ensure"** | | |
| Good faith | Protection of archaeological and historical objects | section 3.2.5 |
| | | section 3.2.6 |
| | Reasonable regard to other Activities | section 3.2.7 |
| | Respect to indigenous people | |

TABLE 5 Index of the concrete measures for performing "responsibility to ensure" in national legislation (*cont.*)

| Implications of "Responsibility to Ensure" (Chapter 2) | Specific measures in the sponsoring state's domestic legal framework | Reference to chapter 3 |
|---|---|---|
| Oversight | Self-reporting | section 3.4.1 |
| | Inspection and remote monitoring | section 3.4.2 |
| Liability and Enforcement | Standard of care | section 3.5 |
| | Corrective Measures and Sanctions | |
| | Compensation | |
| | Enforcement of decisions of international courts and tribunals | |
| **Institutional Arrangement for Implementing "Responsibility to Ensure"** | | |
| Legislative body | Legislative body | section 4.1 |
| Regulatory agency | Regulatory agency | section 4.2 |
| Monitoring arrangement | Monitoring arrangement | section 4.3 |

## 2 The Central Role of the ISA to Organise and Control Activities in the Area

Although the sponsoring State plays a significant role in regulating its sponsored contractor, it is important to note that the sponsoring State is neither the only nor the primary regulator. The ISA plays the leading and central role in terms of how "activities in the Area" may be carried out by contractors, and the sponsoring State plays the subordinate role. Sponsoring States are expected to assist the ISA by taking all "reasonably appropriate" measures to ensure the sponsored contractor's compliance with the relevant provisions of Part XI of the LOSC, Annex III, the 1994 Implementing Agreement, and the rules, regulations, and procedures of the ISA.

### 2.1 *ISA's Leading Legislative Role*

#### 2.1.1 Developing the Deep Seabed Mining Regime

The role of sponsorship is to achieve the goal that entities comply with the obligations set out in the LOSC and related instruments by way of transferring them from the international convention to States Parties' national legislation, which is based on the premise that the ISA has the regulations and standards in place. Moreover, a sponsoring State is advised to adopt even stricter standards than the LOSC. Without a benchmark, it is impossible to be more "stringent". The current focus of the ISA should be the development of the exploitation regulations. Deep seabed mining is entering a transition period from exploration to exploitation. Before commercial mining starts, the regulations on the exploitation of mineral resources in the Area should be in place, and, thus, developing regulations for exploitation of mineral resources in the Area is the priority of the ISA in the coming years. As presented in the chapter 1, which compared the prospecting and exploration phases, the exploitation phase has a higher possibility to cause environmental harm, which means the Exploitation Regulations have to deal with even more complicated situations. As of August 2020, there are six versions of the draft exploitation regulations.[5] The ISA is continuously improving the structure and contents of the draft exploitation regulations, which can be expected in the near future. Also, the ISA is developing a series of guidelines as a supplement to the exploitation regulations. Those instruments will, together, guide the sponsoring States to develop and improve their legislation. The legal instruments at the international and national levels, together, instruct the activities in the Area.

### 2.1.2 Capacity-Building for Sponsoring States' Legislative Skills

The ISA regulations, *per se,* cannot be automatically transplanted into the domestic legislation of the sponsoring State. That is because, first, international law and domestic law do not directly correspond on one-to-one, and thus the provisions of the international regulations cannot be directly and simply incorporated in the domestic law of the sponsoring State; second, due to the different domestic legal systems of sponsoring countries, the absorption of international law cannot be generalized. Due to these aforementioned two reasons, legislative expertise and skills are required to guide this process, especially for developing States. No matter which approach a developing State

---

5 First Working Draft of the Regulations and Standard Contract Terms on Exploitation for Mineral Resources in the Area (February 2016); A Discussion Paper on the Development and Drafting of Regulations on Exploitation for Mineral Resources in the Area- Environmental Matters (January 2017); Draft Regulations on Exploitation of Mineral Resources in the Area (ISBA/23/LTC/CRP.3*, 8 August 2017); Draft Regulations on Exploitation of Mineral Resources in the Area (ISBA/24/LTC/WP.1, 30 April 2018); Draft Regulations on Exploitation of Mineral Resources in the Area (ISBA/24/LTC/WP.1/Rev.1, 9 July 2018); Draft Regulations on Exploitation of Mineral Resources in the Area (ISBA/25/C/WP.1; 22 March 2019).

chooses to participate in the deep seabed mining activities in the Area – government as a contractor (such as Korea and India), sponsoring a state-owned enterprise (such as China), through transnational corporations (such as Nauru and Tonga),[6] or strategic alliances (such Bulgaria, Cuba, Czech Republic, Poland, Slovakia and Russia together sponsoring a consortium "IOM"),[7] adopting national legislation to fulfill its "responsibility to ensure" would constitute a major challenge for most developing States with any design to participate the deep seabed mining activities in the Area. To solve this issue, one plausible approach is that ISA establishes guidance for sponsoring States' national legislation, in which a legislative framework or even a template is provided, which a sponsoring State could follow to incorporate international regulations into its domestic legal framework. Unfortunately, there has not been guidance or a template in this regard. Moreover, it is helpful to provide a capacity-building to assist sponsoring States, especially developing States, to develop their legislative skills, and to develop "an effective regulatory/enforcement body composed of well-trained personnel to ensure that sponsored entities comply with minimum international standards".[8]

### 2.2 *ISA's Primary Regulative Role*

Although it is a two-track regulatory system for the Deep Seabed Mining Regime, the LOSC expressly grants the primary mandate to the ISA, controlling and managing the activities in the Area, which implicates the primary regulative role of the ISA. The mandate of the sponsoring State is to assist the ISA. This type of two-track regulatory system will undoubtedly result in the duplication of the regulatory burden and liability. This is a waste of administrative resources and an unfair double burden to the contractors. Sponsoring States and the ISA should cooperate to avoid unnecessary duplication of administrative procedures and compliance requirements. The problem of potential duplication could be solved by an arrangement between the ISA and the sponsoring

6 Such nominal participation by States in deep seabed mining through subsidiaries of a transnational corporation is arguable as it is not effective and direct participation of developing States in activities in the Area, which is opposite to the spirit and intention of the provisions of the LOSC. See Edwin Egede, 'African States and Participation in Deep Seabed Mining: Problems and Prospects' (2009) 24 *The International Journal of Marine and Coastal Law* 683, 695–697.

7 Regarding the analysis of participation in the deep seabed mining activities in the Area by developing States, see ibid.

8 Edwin Egede, 'The Area: Common Heritage of Mankind, Sponsoring States of Convenience and Developing States', in Markus Kotzur and others (eds), *Sustainable Ocean Resource Governance* (Brill Nijhoff 2018), 177–178.

State. Even in the situation of lacking a formal forum for dialogue, as a member of the ISA, a sponsoring State could communicate and work together with the ISA to reach a satisfactory solution of this issue.[9] By doing so, the ISA and the sponsoring State attempt to have a clear division of labors with respective focuses. The ISA still has the far-reaching mandate by the LOSC, but with a focus on administrative review or approval, such as assessing the proposed plan of work for exploration, technical support; providing guidelines and recommendations on technical and financial issues; and making policy and plans. Sponsoring States are expected to take on more burdens in fields in which it is difficult for the ISA to do more, for instance, monitoring and enforcement.

## 3 Collective Efforts in Promoting a Sponsoring State's National Legislation

It is anticipated that the situation will become even more complicated when deep seabed mining comes into the exploitation stage, since more actors, such as flag States, other international organizations, and other relevant bodies or even home States[10] will become involved in the deep seabed mining activities. That will require the sponsoring States to actively cooperate with those actors to exchange knowledge, information, and experience, and to use such knowledge and information to prepare and revise standards and operating guidelines to control mining activities in the Area. When a sponsored contractor conducts mining activities by ship or installation registered with a State other than the sponsoring State, both the flag State and the sponsoring State have jurisdiction, and the scope of their jurisdiction would very likely overlap. In this situation, it is suggested the sponsoring State and flag State cooperate to regulate the contractor.

The ISA Draft Exploitation Regulations indicate that sponsoring States shall cooperate with other States and competent international organizations to: 1) promote the health and safety of life and property at sea and the protection of

---

9 Rena Lee, 'Exploration and Exploitation of Ocean Mineral Resources: The Role of Sponsoring States' in Myron H Nordquist, John Norton Moore and Ronán Long (eds), *Legal Order in the World's Oceans* (Brill 2017), 162.

10 The concept of "home State" is not included in the provisions of the LOSC. It appears in the situation that contractors that are privately owned entities, are subsidiaries of parent corporations located in a different state. The State of a parent corporation is called the home State. See Tara Davenport, *Responsibility and Liability for Damage Arising out of Activities in the Area: Attribution of Liability*, Liability Issues for Deep Seabed Mining Series, Paper No.4 (January 2019), 15.

the marine environment; 2) exchange information and data to facilitate compliance with and enforcement of applicable international rules and standards; and 3) establish and implement programs to observe, measure, evaluate, and analyze the impacts of exploitation on the marine environment, to share the findings and results of such programs with the Authority for wider dissemination, and to extend such cooperation and collaboration to the implementation and further development of best environmental practices in connection with activities in the Area.[11]

11 Draft Exploitation Regulation (March 2019), regulation 3(d)(e).

# Bibliography

## Documents and Reports

### *International Seabed Authority*

#### Draft Exploitation Regulations


First Working Draft of the Regulations and Standard Contract Terms on Exploitation for Mineral Resources in the Area (February 2016).

A Discussion Paper on the Development and Drafting of Regulations on Exploitation for Mineral Resources in the Area- Environmental Matters (January 2017).

Draft Regulations on Exploitation of Mineral Resources in the Area (ISBA/23/LTC/CRP.3*, 8 August 2017).

Draft Regulations on Exploitation of Mineral Resources in the Area (ISBA/24/LTC/WP.1, 30 April 2018).

Draft Regulations on Exploitation of Mineral Resources in the Area (ISBA/24/LTC/WP.1/Rev.1, 9 July 2018).

Draft Regulations on Exploitation of Mineral Resources in the Area (ISBA/25/C/WP.1, 22 March 2019).


#### Exploration Regulations and Recommendations


Regulations on Prospecting and Exploration for Cobalt-rich Ferromanganese Crusts in the Area (ISBA/18/A/11, 27 July 2012), amended by (ISBA/19/A/12, 25 July 2013).

Regulations on Prospecting and Exploration for Polymetallic Nodules in the Area (ISBA/6/A/18, 13 July 2000).

Regulations on Prospecting and Exploration for Polymetallic Nodules in the Area (ISBA/6/A/18, 13 July 2000), amended by (ISBA/19/C/17, 22 July 2013), (ISBA/19/A/12, 25 July 2013), and (ISBA/20/A/9, 24 July 2014).

Regulations on Prospecting and Exploration for Polymetallic Sulphides in the Area (ISBA/16/A/12/Rev.1, 15 November 2010), amended by (ISBA/19/A/12, 25 July 2013) and (ISBA/20/A/10, 24 July 2014).

Recommendations for the guidance of contractors and sponsoring States relating to training programs under plans of work for exploration (ISBA/19/LTC/14).

Recommendations for the guidance of contractors for the assessment of the possible environmental impacts arising from exploration for marine minerals in the Area (ISBA/19/LTC/8), which is under review (ISBA/24/C/9).

Recommendations for the guidance of contractors for the reporting of actual and direct exploration expenditure (ISBA/21/LTC/11).

Recommendations for the guidance of contractors on the content, format and structure of annual reports (ISBA/21/LTC/15).

### The Assembly

Decision of the Assembly of the International Seabed Authority Regarding the Amendments to the Regulations on Prospecting and Exploration for Polymetallic Nodules in the Area (ISBA/19/A/9, 25 July 2013).

Decision of the Assembly of the International Seabed Authority Concerning the Appointment of the Secretary-General of the International Seabed Authority (ISBA/22/A/10, 21 July 2016).

Decision of the Assembly Relating to the Final Report on the First Periodic Review of the International Regime of the Area pursuant to article 154 of the United Nations Convention on the Law of the Sea (ISBA/23/A/13, 18 August 2017).

Letter dated 3 February 2017 from the Chair of the Committee Established by the Assembly to Carry out a Periodic Review of the International Regime of the Area pursuant to article 154 of the United Nations Convention on the Law of the Sea to the Secretary-General of the International Seabed Authority (ISBA/23/A/3, 8 February 2017).

Report of the Secretary-General of the International Seabed Authority under article 166, paragraph 4, of the United Nations Convention on the Law of the Sea (ISBA/21/A/2, 3 June 2015).

### The Council

Biodiversity, Species Range and Gene Flow in the Abyssal Pacific Nodule Province: Predicting and Managing the Impacts of Deep Seabed Mining (ISBA/14/C/2, 14 February 2008).

Decision of the Council of the International Seabed Authority (21 July 2011, ISBA/17/C/20).

Decision of the Council of the International Seabed Authority requesting an advisory opinion pursuant to Article 191 of the United Nations Convention on the Law of the Sea (ISBA/16/C/13, 6 May 2010).

Decision of the Council of the International Seabed Authority relating to the summary report of the Chair of the Legal and Technical Commission (ISBA/21/C/20, 21 July 2015).

Decision of the Council relating to an application for the approval of a plan of work for exploration for polymetallic nodules submitted by China Minmetals Corporation (ISBA/21/C/17, 20 July 2015).

Decision of the Council of the International Seabed Authority relating to an application by the China Ocean Mineral Resources Research and Development Association for extension of a contract for exploration for polymetallic nodules between the China Ocean Mineral Resources Research and Development Association and the Authority (ISBA/22/C/24, 18 July 2016).

Decision of the Council of the International Seabed Authority relating to an application for approval of a plan of work for exploration for polymetallic nodules submitted by the Beijing Pioneer Hi-Tech Development Corporation (ISBA/25/C/33, 15 July 2019).
Election of members of the Legal and Technical Commission, Report of the Secretary-General (ISBA/23/C/2, 11 November 2016).
Laws, regulations and administrative measures adopted by sponsoring States and other members of the International Seabed Authority with respect to the activities in the Area, and related matters, including a comparative study of existing national legislation (ISBA/26/C/19, 22 May 2020).
Regarding the legal, technical, and financial implications for the operation of the Enterprise, see Considerations relating to a proposal by Nautilus Minerals Inc. for a Joint Venture Operation with the Enterprise (ISBA/19/C/6, 4 April 2013).
Report of the Chair of the Legal and Technical Commission on the work of the Commission during the twenty-first session of the International Seabed Authority (ISBA/21/C/16, 15 July 2015).
Report of the Chair of the Legal and Technical Commission (ISBA/22/C/17, 13 July 2016).
Report of the Secretary-General on laws, regulations and administrative measures adopted by sponsoring States and other members of the International Seabed Authority with respect to the activities in the Area (ISBA/20/C/11, 28 May 2014).
Report on laws, regulations and administrative measures adopted by sponsoring States and other members with respect to the activities in the Area (ISBA/23/C/6, 1 June 2017).
Statement of the President of the Council of the International Seabed Authority on the work of the Council during the seventeenth session (ISBA/17/C/21, 21 July 2011).
Statement of the President of the Council of the International Seabed Authority on the work of the Council during the nineteenth session (ISBA/19/C/18, 24 July 2013).
Status of contracts for exploration and related matters, including information on the periodic review of the implementation of approved plans of work for exploration (ISBA/26/C/4, 17 December 2019).
Summary report of the Chair of the Legal and Technical Commission on the work of the Commission during the eighteenth session of the International Seabed Authority (ISBA/18/C/20, 20 July 2012).
Summary report of the Chair of the Legal and Technical Commission on the work of the Commission during the nineteenth session of the International Seabed Authority (ISBA/19/C/14, 9 July 2013).
Summary report of the President of the Council of the International Seabed Authority on the work of the Council during its twenty-second session (ISBA/22/C/30, 29 July 2016).
Proposal to seek an advisory opinion from the Seabed Disputes Chamber of the International Tribunal for the Law of the Sea on matters regarding sponsoring State

responsibility and liability. Submitted by the delegation of Nauru (ISBA/16/C/6, 5 March 2010).

Proposal for a Joint Venture Operation with the Enterprise. Report by the Interim Director-General of the Enterprise (ISBA/19/C/4, 20 March 2013).

### The Legal and Technical Commission

Analysis of regulation 11.2 of the Regulations on Prospecting and Exploration for Polymetallic Nodules and Polymetallic Sulphides in the Area (ISBA/20/LTC/10, 5 June 2014).

Application for approval of a plan of work for exploration for polymetallic nodules by the Beijing Pioneer Hi-Tech Development Corporation (ISBA/25/LTC/3, 11 January 2019).

Environmental Management Plan for the Clarion-Clipperton Zone (ISBA/17/LTC/7, 13 July 2011).

Issues related to the sponsorship of contracts for exploration in the Area, monopolization, effective control and related matters (ISBA/22/LTC/13, 21 June 2016).

### The ISA Technical Study

Clark AL and others, *Towards the Development of a Regulatory Framework for Polymetallic Nodule Exploitation in the Area* (ISA Technical Study: No. 11) (ISA 2013).

Herzig PM and others, *Polymetallic Massive Sulphide and Cobalt-Rich Ferromanganese Crusts: Status and Prospects* (ISA Technical Study: No. 2) (ISA 2002).

ISA, *A Geological Model of Polymetallic Nodule Deposits in the Clarion-Clipperton Fracture Zone* (ISA Technical Study: No. 6) (ISA 2010).

ISA, *Environmental Management Needs for Exploration and Exploitation of Deep Sea Minerals: Report of a Workshop held by The International Seabed Authority in collaboration with the Government of Fiji and the SOPAC Division of the Secretariat of the Pacific Community (SPC) in Nadi, Fiji, from 29 November to 2 December 2011* (ISA Technical Study: No. 10) (ISA 2012).

ISA, *Environmental Assessment and Management for Exploitation of Minerals in the Area: Report of an international Workshop convened by the Griffith University Law School in collaboration with the International Seabed Authority in Queensland, Australia, 23–26 May 2016* (ISA Technical Study: No. 16) (ISA 2017).

ISA, *Towards an ISA Environmental Management Strategy for the Area: Report of an International Workshop convened by the German Environment Agency (UBA), the German Federal Institute for Geosciences and Natural Resources (BGR), and the Secretariat of the International Seabed Authority (ISA) in Berlin, Germany, 20–24 March 2017* (ISA Technical Study: No. 17) (ISA 2017).

Smith CR and others, *Biodiversity, Species Ranges, and Gene Flow in the Abyssal Pacific Nodule Province: Predicting and Managing the Impacts of Deep Seabed Mining* (ISA Technical Study: No. 3) (ISA 2008).

### Miscellaneous

*Deep-Seabed Polymetallic Nodule Exploration: Development of Environmental Guidelines* (ISA, Sanya, 1998).

ISA, 'Comparative Study of the Existing National Legislation on Deep Seabed Mining', <https://isa.org.jm/files/files/documents/compstudy-nld.pdf> accessed 27 May 2020.

ISA, 'A Study Related to Issues on the Operationalization of the Enterprise-Legal, Technical and Financial Implications for the International Seabed Authority and for States Parties to the United Nations Convention on the Law of the Sea' (Technical Report 1/2019, 13 June 2019), Prepared By Edwin Egede, Mati Pal and Eden Charles, <https://isa.org.jm/files/files/documents/enterprise_study.pdf> accessed 29 December 2020.

Secretary-General Michael Lodge hosted his first inaugural reception since taking up office at his residence in Kingston, Jamaica on Friday 3 February 2017. https://www.isa.org.jm/sites/default/files/documents/EN/SG-Stats/reception_speech.pdf.

### *United Nations*

UNGA, 'Malta: Request for Inclusion of a Supplementary Item in the Agenda of the Twenty-Second Session' [18 August 1967] GAOR 22nd Session Annexes, Agenda Item 92.

UNGA, UN Doc A/C.1. /PV.1516 (1 November 1967).

UNGA, UN Doc A/Res/2340(XXII) (18 December 1967).

UNGA, UN Doc A/Res/2574(XXIV) (15 December 1969).

UNGA, UN Doc A/Res/2749(XXV) (17 December 1970).

UNEP, Training Manual on International Environmental Law (Division of Policy Development and Law, United Nations Environment Programme 2006).

UN DOALOS, 'The Law of the Sea, Baselines: An Examination of the Relevant Provisions of the United Nations Convention on the Law of the Sea' (1989) <https://www.un.org/depts/los/doalos_publications/publicationstexts/The%20Law%20of%20the%20Sea_Baselines.pdf> access 24 July 2019.

Decision taken by the Governing Council of the United Nations Compensation Commission during its third session, at 18th meeting, held on 28 November 1991, as revised at the 24th meeting held on 16 March 1992: Criteria for Additional Categories of Claims (S/AC.26/1991/7/Rev.1, 17 March 1992).

Guiding Principles on Business and Human Rights: Implementing the United Nations "Protect, Respect and Remedy" Framework (A/HRC/17/31, 21 March 2011).

Report of the United Nations Conference on the Human Environment, Stockholm (A/Conf.48/14/Corr. 1, 5–16 June 1972).

Use of the terms *best available techniques, best environmental practice* and related concepts in international environmental instrument, Expert Group on best available techniques, best environmental practice (UNEP/POPS/EGB.1/INF/3, 29 January 2003).

### *International Association for Impact Assessment*

IAIA and IEA, 'Principles of Environmental Impact Assessment Best Practice' (1999) <https://www.iaia.org/uploads/pdf/principlesEA_1.pdf> accessed 24 June 2020.

### *Secretariat of the Pacific Community*

SPC, *Deep Sea Minerals: Manganese Nodules, a Physical, Biological, Environmental and Technical Review.*, vol 1B (Secretariat of the Pacific Community 2013).

SPC, *Pacific-ACP States Regional Legislative and Regulatory Framework for Deep Sea Minerals Exploration and Exploitation (RLRF)*, Prepared under the SPC-EU EDF 10 Deep Sea Minerals Project (1st edn, July 2012).

### *International Law Commission*

ILC, *Articles on Responsibility of States for Internationally Wrongful Acts*, printed in 'Report of the International Law Commission on its Fifty-third session', UN Doc A/56/10 (2001), 26–143.

ILC, *Articles on Prevention of Transboundary Harm from Hazardous Activities*, printed in 'Report of the International Law Commission on its Fifty-third session', UN Doc A/56/10 (2001), 146–170.

ILC, *Principles on the Allocation of Loss in the Case of Transboundary Harm Arising Out of Hazardous Activities*, printed in 'Report of the International Law Commission on its Fifty-eight session', UN Doc A/61/10 (2006), 101–182.

### *National Governments Documents*

Ministry for the Environment, *New Zealand's Experiences with Adaptive Management for Seabed Mining Projects: A Submission to the International Seabed Authority to Support the Development of a Regulatory Framework for the Exploitation of Seabed Minerals* (Ministry for the Environment 2016).

NT EPA, *Interim Report: Seabed Mining in the Northern Territory* (NT EPA, November 2012).

### *National Laws and Regulations*

#### Belgium

Belgium Act on prospecting and exploration for and exploitation of, resources of the seabed and ocean floor and subsoil thereof, beyond the limits of national jurisdiction, adopted on 17 August 2013.

#### China

Constitution (1982) was amended in 1988, 1993, 1999, 2004, and 2018.

Deep Seabed Area Resource Exploration and Exploitation Law of the People's Republic of China (adopted 26 February 2016).

Environmental Protection Law of the People's Republic of China (adopted 26 December 1989 and amended 24 April 2014).
Environmental Impacts Assessment Law (adopted 28 October 2002, amended 2 July 2016 and 29 December 2018).
Interim Measures for the Administration of Sample Management for the Exploration and Development of Resources in Deep Seabed Areas (adopted 29 December 2017).
Interim Measures for the Administration of Data Management for the Exploration and Development of Resources in Deep Seabed Areas (adopted 29 December 2017).
Law of the People's Republic of China on the Administration of the Use of Sea Areas (adopted 27 October 2001).
Legislation Law of the People's Republic of China (adopted 15 March 2000, amended 15 March 2015).
Marine Environmental Protection Law of the People's Republic of China (adopted 25 December 1999 and amended 28 December 2013, 7 November 2016, 4 November 2017).
Mineral Resources Law of the People's Republic of China (adopted 19 March 1986, amended 29 August 1996 and 27 August 2009).
Measures for the Administration of Licensing for the Exploration and Development of Resources in Deep Seabed Areas (adopted 25 April 2017).
Measures on the Management of Marine Nature Reserves (adopted 29 May 1995).
Rules for the Implementation of the Mineral Resources Law of the People's Republic of China (adopted 26 March 1994).

### Czech Republic

Czech Republic Act No. 158/2000 of 18 May 2000 on Prospecting, Exploration for and Exploitation of Mineral Resources from the Seabed beyond the limits of National Jurisdiction.

### Fiji

Fiji International Seabed Mineral Management Decree 2013.

### France

Law on the Exploration and Exploitation of the Mineral Resources of the Deep Seabed 1981.
France Ordinance No. 2016–1687 of 8 December 2016 relating to the maritime areas under the sovereignty or jurisdiction of the Republic of France.

### Germany

Act of Interim Regulation of Deep Seabed Mining 1980; amended 1982.
Germany Seabed Mining Act of 6 June 1995, amended by article 74 of the Act of 8 December 2010.

### Italy

Regulations on the Exploration and Exploitation of the Mineral Resources of the Deep Sea-bed 1985.

### Japan

Law on Interim Measures for Deep Sea-Bed Mining 1982.

Mining Act (Act No. 289 of 1950, adopted 20 December 1950, amended 22 July 2011).

### Kiribati

Kiribati Seabed Mineral Act 2017.

### Micronesia

Seabed Resources Act of 2014.

### Nauru

Nauru International Seabed Minerals Act 2015.

### New Zealand

New Zealand United Nations Convention on the Law of the Sea Act 1996.

### Russian Federation

Russian Federation Decree of the President No. 2099 of 22 November 1994 on the activities of Russian physical and legal entities related to the exploration and development of the mineral resources of the seabed outside the continental shelf.

Government Decree No. 410 of 25 April 1995 on the procedure of activities of Russian physical and legal entities related to the development of mineral resources of the seabed outside the continental shelf.

### Singapore

Singapore Deep Seabed Mining Act 2015.

### Tonga

Tonga Seabed Minerals Act 2014.

### Tuvalu

Tuvalu Seabed Minerals Act 2014.

### United Kingdom

Deep Seabed Mining (Temporary Provisions) Act 1981.

United Kingdom Deep Sea Mining (Temporary Provision) Act 1981, as amended by the Deep Seabed Mining Act 2014, which entered into force on 14 July 2014 .

### *Research Institutes and Non-Governmental Organizations*

Allsopp, M and others, 'Review of the Current State of Development and the Potential for Environmental Impacts of Seabed Mining Operations' [2013] Greenpeace Research Laboratories Technical Report (Review) 3.

Cooney, R, *The Precautionary Principle in Biodiversity Conservation and Natural Resource Management: An Issue Paper for Policy-Makers, Researchers and Practitioners* (IUCN 2004).

ECORYS, 'Blue Growth: Scenarios and Drivers for Sustainable Growth from the Oceans, Seas and Coasts', Third Interim Report under MARE/2010/01 (13 March 2012) <https://ec.europa.eu/maritimeaffairs/sites/maritimeaffairs/files/docs/publications/blue_growth_third_interim_report_en.pdf>.

ECORYS, 'Study to Investigate the State of Knowledge of Deep-sea Ming', Final Report under FWC MARE/2012/06 – SC E1/2013/04 (19 November 2014).

Ekstrom J, Bennun L and Mitchell R, *A Cross-sector Guide for Implementing the Mitigation Hierarchy* prepared by the Biodiversity Consultancy (Cross Sector Biodiversity Initiative 2015) <http://www.csbi.org.uk/wp-content/uploads/2017/10/CSBI-Mitigation-Hierarchy-Guide.pdf> access 24 July 2019.

Global Ocean Commission, 'Policy Options Paper #5: Strengthening Deep Seabed Mining Regulation' (November 2013) <http://eu-midas.net/sites/default/files/publications/GOC-paper05-seabed-mining.pdf>.

Goldstein, L, *Five Dragons Stirring up the Sea: Challenges and Opportunities in China's Improving Maritime Enforcement Capabilities* (China Maritime Studies Institute, U.S. Naval War College 2010).

J Midgley and Associates, *Environmental Impact Assessment for the Proposed Dredging of Phosphate Enriched Sediments from Marine License Area No. 170*, Prepared for Namibian Marine Phosphate (Pty) Ltd. (January 2012).

MIDAS, 'Managing Impacts of Deep Sea Resource Exploitation: Research Highlights', <https://www.eu-midas.net/sites/default/files/downloads/MIDAS_research_highlights_low_res.pdf> accessed 24 December 2020.

MIDAS, 'Implications of MIDAS Results for Policy Makers: Recommendations for Future Regulations' <http://eu-midas.net/sites/default/files/downloads/MIDAS_recommendations_for_policy_lowres.pdf> accessed 24 December 2020.

Pew Charitable Trusts, First Report of the Code Project: Developing ISA Environmental Regulations (1st edn, 19 July 2017).

Resource Roulette – How Deep Sea Mining and Inadequate Regulatory Frameworks Imperil the Pacific and Its Peoples, A Report by Blue Ocean Law and the

Pacific Network on Globalisation <https://cer.org.za/wp-content/uploads/2016/08/Resource-Roulette-Deep-sea-Mining-and-Inadequate-Regulatory-Frameworks.pdf> accessed 2 August 2020.

Steiner, R, 'Independent Review of the Environmental Impact Statement for the Proposed Nautilus Minerals Solwara 1 Seabed Mining Project, Papua New Guinea' [2009] Madang, Papua New Guinea.

## Books and Articles

### *Books*

Birnie P, Boyle A and Redgwell C, *International Law and the Environment* (3rd edn, Oxford University Press 2009).

Bodansky D, Brunnée J and Hay E (eds), *Oxford Handbook of International Environmental Law* (Oxford University Press 2008).

Brown ED, *Sea-Bed Energy and Minerals: The International Legal Regime. Vol. 2: Sea-Bed Mining* (Nijhoff 2001).

Brownlie I, *Principles of Public International Law* (7th edn, Oxford University Press 2008).

Chen AH, *An Introduction to the Legal System of the People's Republic of China* (Butterworths Asia 1992).

Cheng B, *General Principles of Law as Applied by International Courts and Tribunals* (Cambridge University Press 2006).

Churchill RR and Lowe AV, *The Law of the Sea* (3rd edn, Manchester Universiisty Press 1999).

Craik N, *The International Law of Environmental Impact Assessment: Process, Substance and Integration* (Cambridge University Press 2008).

Crawford J, *State Responsibility: The General Part* (Cambridge University Press 2013).

Egede E, *Africa and the Deep Seabed Regime: Politics and International Law of the Common Heritage of Mankind* (Springer 2011).

Friedheim RL, *Negotiating the New Ocean Regime* (University of South Carolina Press 1993).

Harrison J, *Making the Law of the Sea: A Study in the Development of International Law* (Cambridge University Press 2011).

Herring PJ, *The Biology of the Deep Ocean* (Oxford University Press 2002).

Holling CS and United Nations Environment Programme (eds), *Adaptive Environmental Assessment and Management* (International Institute for Applied Systems Analysis; Wiley 1978).

Jaeckel A, *The International Seabed Authority and the Precautionary Principle - Balancing Deep Seabed Mineral Mining and Marine Environmental Protection* (Brill 2017).

Kesler SE, *Mineral Resources, Economics, and the Environment* (Macmillan; Maxwell Macmillan Canada; Maxwell Macmillan International 1994).

Kolb R, *Good Faith in International Law* (Hart Publishing 2017).

Lu H and others (eds), *Deep Seabed Area Resource Exploration and Exploitation Law of the People's Republic of China: A Commentary* (China Legal Publishing House 2017) (in Chinese).

Mareddy AR, *Environmental Impact Assessment: Theory and Practice* (Elsevier/BH, Butterworth-Heinemann, an imprint of Elsevier 2017).

Marr S, *The Precautionary Principle in the Law of the Sea: Modern Decision Making in International Law* (Brill Nijhoff 2003).

Merryman JH and Pérez-Perdomo R, *The Civil Law Tradition: An Introduction to the Legal Systems of Europe and Latin America* (Stanford University Press 2007).

Nandan SN, Lodge MW and Rosenne S, *The Development of the Regime for Deep Seabed Mining* (International Seabed Authority 2002).

Nandan SN, Lodge MW and Rosenne S, *United Nations Convention on the Law of the Sea, 1982: A Commentary, Volume VI* (Martinus Nijhoff Publishers 2002).

Potter P, *China's Legal System* (Polity 2013).

Proelss A and others (eds), *United Nations Convention on the Law of the Sea: A Commentary* (CH Beck; Hart; Nomos 2017).

Rao PC and Gautier P, *The International Tribunal for the Law of the Sea: Law, Practice and Procedure* (Edward Elgar Pub 2018).

Rayfuse R, *Non-Flag State Enforcement in High Seas Fisheries* (Brill Nijhoff 2004).

Rothwell D and others (eds), *The Oxford Handbook of the Law of the Sea* (Oxford University Press 2015).

Rothwell D and Stephens T, *The International Law of the Sea* (Hart 2010).

Schrijver N, *Development without Destruction: The UN and Global Resource Management* (Indiana University Press 2010).

Sands P and others, *Principles of International Environmental Law* (3rd edn, Cambridge University Press 2012).

Sun L, *International Environmental Obligations and Liabilities in Deep Seabed Mining* (dissertation Leiden) (Ipskamp Printing 2018).

Tanaka Y, *The International Law of the Sea* (Cambridge University Press 2012).

Trouwborst A, *Precautionary Rights and Duties of States* (Martinus Nijhoff 2006).

Walker GK (ed), *Definitions for the Law of the Sea: Terms Not Defined by the 1982 Convention* (Martinus Nijhoff Publishers 2012).

Wilde M, *Civil Liability for Environmental Damage: A Comparative Analysis of Law and Policy in Europe and the United States* (Kluwer Law International 2002).

Zhu L, Compulsory Insurance and Compensation for Bunker Oil Pollution Damage (Springer 2006).

Zou K, *China's Marine Legal System and the Law of the Sea* (Martinus Nijhoff 2005).

### *Journal Articles and Book Chapters*


Aguon J and Hunter J, 'Second Wave Due Diligence: The Case for Incorporating Free, Prior, and Informed Consent into the Deep Sea Mining Regulatory Regime' (2018) 38 *Stanford Environmental Law Journal* 3–55.

Alfredo C Robles, Jr, 'The 1994 Agreement on Deep Seabed Mining: Universality vs. the Common Heritage of Humanity' (1996) 12 *World Bulletin* 20–70.

Anderson DH, 'Efforts to Ensure Universal Participation in the UN Convention on the Law of the Sea' (1993) 42 *International and Comparative Law Quarterly* 654–664.

Anderson D, 'The Principle of Reasonableness in the Law of the Sea' in Holger P Hestermeyer and others (eds), *Coexistence, Cooperation and Solidarity, Vol. 1* (Brill Nijhoff 2012) 657–670.

Anton DK, Makgill RA and Payne CR, 'Seabed Mining: Advisory Opinion on Responsibility and Liability' (2011) 41(2) *Environmental Policy and Law* 60–65.

Anton DK and Kim RE, 'Current Legal Developments New Zealand: The Application of the Precautionary and Adaptive Management Approaches in the Seabed Mining Context: Trans-Tasman Resources Ltd Marine Consent Decision under New Zealand's Exclusive Economic Zone and Continental Shelf (Environmental Effects) Act 2012' (2015) 30 *The International Journal of Marine and Coastal Law* 175–188.

Ardron JA, Ruhl HA and Jones DOB, 'Incorporating Transparency into the Governance of Deep-Seabed Mining in the Area beyond National Jurisdiction' (2018) 89 *Marine Policy* 58–66.

Balgos MC, Cicin-Sain B, and VanderZwaag DL, 'A Comparative Analysis of Ocean Policies in Fifteen Nations and Four Regions', in Biliana Cicin-Sain, David L. VanderZwaag, and Miriam C. Balgos (eds), *Routledge Handbook of National and Regional Ocean Policies* (Routledge 2015) 3–48.

Bantekas I, 'Trust Funds' in *Max Planck Encyclopedia of Public International Law* (2010).

Barnidge R, 'The Due Diligence Principle Under International Law' (2006) 8 *International Community Law Review* 81–121.

Bedjaoui M, 'Responsibility of States: Fault and Strict Liability' in *Encyclopedia of Disputes Installment 10* (Elsevier, 1987) 358–362.

Bertram C and others, 'Metalliferous Sediments in the Atlantis II Deep-Assessing the Geological and Economic Resource Potential and Legal Constraints' (2011) 36 *Resources Policy* 315–329.

Blake DJ and Payton AL, 'Balancing Design Objectives: Analyzing New Data on Voting Rules in Intergovernmental Organizations' (2015) 10 *The Review of International Organizations* 377–402.

Bluhm H, 'Monitoring Megabenthic Communities in Abyssal Manganese Nodule Sites of the East Pacific Ocean in Association with Commercial Deep-sea Mining' (1994) 4 *Aquatic Conservation: Marine and Freshwater Ecosystems* 187–201.

Bourrel M, Thiele T and Currie D, 'The Common of Heritage of Mankind as a Means to Assess and Advance Equity in Deep Sea Mining' (2018) 95 *Marine Policy* 311–316.

Bowman M, 'Biodiversity, Intrinsic Value, and the Definition and Valuation of Environmental Harm' in Michael Bowman and Alan Boyle (eds), *Environmental Damage in International and Comparative Law: Problems of Definition and Valuation* (Oxford University Press 2002) 41–62.

Boyle A, 'The Environmental Jurisprudence of the International Tribunal for the Law of the Sea' (2007) 22 *The International Journal of Marine and Coastal Law* 369–381.

Boyle A, 'Liability for Injurious Consequences of Acts not Prohibited by International Law' in James Crawford, Alain Pellet, and Simon Olleson (eds), *The Law of International responsibility* (Oxford University Press 2010) 95–104.

Brown ED, '"Neither Necessary nor Prudent at This Stage": The Regime of Seabed Mining and Its Impact on the Universality of the UN Convention on the Law of the Sea' (1993) 17 *Marine Policy* 81–107.

Burlington LB, 'Valuing Natural Resource Damages: A Transatlantic Lesson' (2004) 6 *Environmental Law Review* 77–96.

Calvo G and others, 'Decreasing Ore Grades in Global Metallic Mining: A Theoretical Issue or a Global Reality?' (2016) 5 *Resources* 36–49.

Chang YC, 'Chinese Legislation in the Exploration of Marine Mineral Resources and Its Adoption in the Arctic Ocean' (2019) 168 *Ocean & Coastal Management* 265–273.

Churchill R, 'Dispute Settlement in the Law of the Sea: Survey for 2011' (2012) 27 *International Journal of Marine and Coastal Law* 517–551.

Corten O, 'Reasonableness in International Law' in *Max Plank Encyclopedia of Public International Law* (2013).

Craik N, 'Liability for Environmental Harm from Deep Seabed Mining: Towards a Hybrid Approach' (2019) 33 *Ocean Yearbook* 313–338.

Craik N, 'Implementing Adaptive Management in Deep Seabed Mining: Legal and Institutional Challenges' (2020) 114 *Marine Policy* 103–256.

Crawford J, 'The ILC's Articles on Responsibility of States for International Wrongful Acts: A Retrospect' (2002) 96 *American Journal of International Law* 874–890.

Davison-Vecchione D, "Beyond the Forms of Faith: Pacta Sunt Servanda and Loyalty" (2015) 16 *German Law Journal* 1163–1190.

De la Fayette L, 'ITLOS and the Saga of the Saiga: Peaceful Settlement of a Law of the Sea Dispute' (2000) 15 *The International Journal of Marine and Coastal Law* 355–392.

De la Fayette L, 'International Liability for Damage to the Environment' in Malgosia Fitzmaurice, David M Ong & Panos Merkouris (eds), *Research Handbook on International Environmental Law* (Edward Elgar 2010) 320–360.

Doeker G and Gehring T, 'Private or International Liability for Transnational Environmental Damage – The Precedent of Conventional Liability Regimes' (1990) 2 *Journal of Environmental Law* 1–16.

Dromgoole S, 'Reflections on the Position of the Major Maritime Powers with Respect to the UNESCO Convention on the Protection of the Underwater Cultural Heritage 2001' (2013) 38 *Marine Policy* 116–123.

Durden JM and others, 'Environmental Impact Assessment Process for Deep-Sea Mining in "the Area"' (2018) 87 *Marine Policy* 194–202.

Ebbesson J, 'A Critical Assessment of the 1992 Baltic Sea Convention' (2000) 43 *GYIL* 38–64.

Egede E, 'African States and Participation in Deep Seabed Mining: Problems and Prospects' (2009) 24 *The International Journal of Marine and Coastal Law* 683–712.

Egede E, 'The Area: Common Heritage of Mankind, Sponsoring States of Convenience and Developing States', in Markus Kotzur and others (eds), *Sustainable Ocean Resource Governance* (Brill Nijhoff 2018) 157–184.

Faure MG and Hartlief T, 'Compensation Funds versus Liability and Insurance for Remedying Environmental Damage' (1996) 5 *Review of European Community & International Environmental Law* 321–327.

Feichtner I, 'Contractor Liability for Environmental Damage Resulting from Deep Seabed Mining Activities in the Area' (2020) 114 *Marine Policy* 103–502.

Fisher E, 'Administrative Law, Pluralism and the Legal Construction of Merits Review in Australian Environmental Courts and Tribunals' in Linda Pearson, Carol Harlow and Michael Taggart (eds), *Administrative Law in a Changing State: Essays in Honour of Mark Aronson* (Hart 2008) 325–348.

Fitzmaurice M, ,International Responsibility and Liability' in Daniel Bodansky, Jutta Brunnée and Ellen Hay (eds), *Oxford Handbook of International Environmental Law* (Oxford University Press 2007) 1010–1035.

Freestone D, 'Responsibilities and Obligations of States Sponsoring Persons and Entities with Respect to Activities in the Area' (2011) 105 *The American Journal of International Law* 755–760.

French D, 'From the Depths: Rich Pickings of Principles of Sustainable Development and General International Law on the Ocean Floor – the Seabed Disputes Chamber's 2011 Advisory Opinion' (2011) 26 *The International Journal of Marine and Coastal Law* 525–568.

Gao J, 'The Responsibilities and Obligations of the Sponsoring States Advisory Opinion' (2013) 12 *Chinese Journal of International Law* 771–786.

Geddis E, 'The Due Diligence Obligation of a Sponsoring State: A Framework for Implementation' in Myron H. Nordquist, John Norton Moore and Ronan Long (eds), *International Marine Economy: Law and Policy* (Brill 2017) 246–268.

Gerber LJ and Grogan RL, 'Challenges of Operationalising Good Industry Practice and Best Environmental Practice in Deep Seabed Mining Regulation' (2020) 114 *Marine Policy* 103–257.

Glasby GP, 'Deep Seabed Mining: Past Failures and Future Prospects' (2002) 20 *Marine Georesources & Geotechnology* 161–176.

Glover AG and Smith CR, 'The Deep-Sea Floor Ecosystem: Current Status and Prospects of Anthropogenic Change by the Year 2025' (2003) 30 *Environmental Conservation* 219–241.

Godet L, Zelnio KA and Dover CLV, 'Scientists as Stakeholders in Conservation of Hydrothermal Vents' (2011) 25 *Conservation Biology* 214–222.

Halfar J and Fujita RM, 'Precautionary Management of Deep-Sea Mining' (2002) 26 *Marine Policy* 103–106.

Halfar J and Fujita RM, 'ECOLOGY: Danger of Deep-Sea Mining' (2007) 316 *Science* 987–987.

Hanley N, 'The Economic Value of Environmental Damage' in Michael Bowman and Alan Boyle (eds), *Environmental Damage in International and Comparative Law: Problems of Definition and Valuation* (Oxford University Press 2002) 27–40.

Hayashi M, 'Archaeological and Historical Objects under the United Nations Convention on the Law of the Sea' (1996) 20 *Marine Policy* 291–296.

Henley PH, 'Minerals and Mechanisms: The Legal Significance of the Notion of the Common Heritage of Mankind in the Advisory Opinion of the Seabed Disputes Chamber' (2011) 12 *Melbourne Journal of International Law* 373–395.

Herring PJ, Gaten E and Shelton PMJ, 'Are Vent Shrimps Blinded by Science?' (1999) 398 *Nature* 116–116.

Hey E, 'The Precautionary Concept in Environmental Policy and Law: Institutionalizing Caution' (1992) 4 *Georgetown International Environmental Law Review* 303–318.

Hunter J, Singh P and Aguon J, 'Broadening Common Heritage: Addressing Gaps in the Deep Sea Mining Regulatory Regime' (16 April 2018) *Harvard Environmental Law Review*.

Ingadottir T, 'Enforcement of Decisions of International Courts at the National Level' in Andre Nollkaemper and others (eds), *International Law in Domestic Courts: A Casebook* (Oxford University Press 2019) 349–386.

Jaeckel A, 'Deep Seabed Mining and Adaptive Management: The Procedural Challenges for the International Seabed Authority' (2016) 70 *Marine Policy* 205–211.

Jaeckel A, 'Current Legal Developments: International Seabed Authority' (2016) 31 *The International Journal of Marine and Coastal Law* 706–719.

Jayaraman KS, 'Deep-Sea Nuggets Prove Irresistible to Indian Miners' (2002) 417 *Nature* 212–212.

Jia Y, 'Exploitation of Resources in the Arena and the Sponsoring State Responsibility: New Developments in China's Legislative Work Concerning the Deep Sea' (2016) *China Oceans Law Review* 1–26.

Jin J and Zhang G, 'Chapter 9: The Forthcoming Breakthrough: China's Legislation on Activities in the Deep Seabed Area' in Myron H Nordquist, John Norton Moore, and Ronán Long (eds) *International Marine Economy* (Brill Nijhoff 2017) 235–245.

Kim RE, 'Should Deep Seabed Mining Be Allowed?' (2017) 82 *Marine Policy* 134–137.

Kiss A, 'Abuse of rights' in *Max Planck Encyclopedia of Public International Law* (2006).

Koh TB, 'A Constitution for the Oceans', in United Nations, *The Law of the Sea: United Nations Convention on the Law of the Sea with Index and Final Act of the Third United Nations Conference on the Law of the Sea* (United Nations 1983), xxxiii–xxxvii.

Koivurova T, 'Due Diligence' in *Max Planck Encyclopedia of Public International Law* (2010).

Kojima C, 'Compensation Fund' in *Max Plank Encyclopedia of Public International Law* (2009).

Kotzur M, 'Good Faith (Bona fide)' in *Max Planck Encyclopedia of Public International* (2009).

LaMotte KR, 'Introductory Note to the International Tribunal for the Law of the Sea: Responsibilities and Obligations of States Sponsoring Persons and Entities with Respect to Activities in the Area (Request for Advisory Opinion Submitted to the Seabed Disputes Chamber)' (2011) 50 *International Legal Materials* 455–493.

Lee R, 'Exploration and Exploitation of Ocean Mineral Resources: The Role of Sponsoring States' in Myron H Nordquist, John Norton Moore and Ronán Long (eds), *Legal Order in the World's Oceans* (Brill 2017) 153–164.

Levy P, 'The International Sea-Bed Area', in RJ Dupuy and D Vignes (eds), *A Handbook on the New Law of the Sea*, vol 1 (Martinus Nijhoff 1991) 587–633.

Liu N and Kim RE, 'Current Legal Developments: China's New Law on Exploration and Exploitation of Resources in the International Seabed Area of 2016' (2016) 31 *The International Journal of Marine and Coastal Law* 691–705.

Lodge MW, 'International Seabed Authority's Regulations on Prospecting and Exploration for Polymetallic Nodules in the Area' (2002) 20 *Journal of Energy & Natural Resources Law* 270–295.

Lodge MW, 'Collaborative Marine Scientific Research on the International Seabed' (2008) 3 *The Journal of Ocean Technology* 30–36.

Lodge MW, Segerson K and Squires D, 'Sharing and Preserving the Resources in the Deep Sea: Challenges for the International Seabed Authority' (2017) 32 *The International Journal of Marine and Coastal Law* 427–457.

Lodge MW, 'The Deep Seabed' in Donald Rothwell and others (eds), *The Oxford Handbook of the Law of the Sea* (Oxford University Press 2015) 226–253.

Lowe AV, 'The International Seabed: A Legacy of Mistrust' (1981) 5 *Marine Policy* 205–216.

Lu H, 'China's Deep Seabed Law: Theory and Practice' (in Chinese) (2016) 15 *The People's Congress of China* 10.

Lukashuk II, 'The Principle *Pacta Sunt Servanda* and the Nature of Obligation Under International Law' (1989) 83 *American Journal of International Law* 513–518.

Ma X, 'China and the UNCLOS: Practices and Policies' (2019) 5 *The Chinese Journal of Global Governance* 1–20.

MacMaster K, 'Environmental Liability for Deep Seabed Mining in the Area: An Urgent Case for a Robust Strict Liability Regime' (2019) 33 *Ocean Yearbook* 339–376.

Matz-Lück N and van Doorn E, 'Due diligence Obligations and the Protection of the Marine Environment' (2017) 42 *L'Observateur des Nations Unies* 169–187.

McConnell ML and Gold E, 'The Modern Law of the Sea: Framework for the Protection and Preservation of the Marine Environment' (1991) 23 *Case Western Reserve Journal of International Law* 83–105.

Morgan CL, Odunton NA and Jones AT, 'Synthesis of Environmental Impacts of Deep Seabed Mining' (1999) 17 *Marine Georesources & Geotechnology* 307–356.

Murgatroyd C, 'The World Bank: A Case for Lender Liability' (1992) 1 *Review of European Community and International Environmental Law* 436–442.

Nandan SN, 'Administering the Mineral Resource of the Deep Seabed' in David Freestone, Richard Barnes, and David Ong (eds), *The Law of the Sea: Progress and Prospects* (Oxford University Press 2006) 75–92.

Nelson LDM, 'The New Deep Sea-Bed Mining Regime' (1995) 10 *International Journal of Marine and Coastal Law* 189–204.

Nollkaemper A, 'Balancing the Protection of Marine Ecosystems with Economic Benefits from Land-Based Activities: The Quest for International Legal Barriers' (1996) 27 *Ocean Development and International Law* 153–179.

Noyes JE and Smith BD, 'State Responsibility and the Principle of Joint and Several Liability' (1988) 13 *Yale Journal of International Law* 225–267.

Noyes JE, 'The Common Heritage of Mankind: Past, Present, and Future' (2012) 40 *Denver Journal of International Law and Policy* 447–471.

Ogley RC, 'The Law of the Sea Draft Convention and the New International Economic Order' (1981) 5 *Marine Policy* 240–251.

Oyarce XH, 'Sponsoring States in the Area: Obligations, Liability and the Role of Developing States' (2018) 95 *Marine Policy* 317–323.

Paolillo FH, 'Institutional Arrangements', in RJ Dupuy and D Vignes (eds), *A Handbook on the New Law of the Sea*, vol 1 (Martinus Nijhoff 1991) 689–819.

Pisillo-Mazzeschi R, 'Forms of International Responsibility for Environmental Harm', in Francesco Francioni and Tullio Scovazzi (eds), *International Responsibility for Environmental Harm* (Graham & Trotman/ Martinus Nijhoff, 1991) 15–35.

Ramirez-Llodra E and others, 'Man and the Last Great Wilderness: Human Impact on the Deep Sea' (2011) 6 *PLoS ONE* e22588.

Rayfuse R, 'Differentiating the Common? The Responsibilities and Obligations of States Sponsoring Deep Seabed Mining Activities in the Area' (2011) 54 *GYIL* 459–488.

Rist L and others, 'A New Paradigm for Adaptive Management' (2013) 18 *Ecology and Society* 63–71.

Röben V, 'The Enforcement Authority of International Institutions' in Armin von Bogdandy and others (eds), *The Exercise of Public Authority by International Institutions* (Springer 2010) 819–842.

Ronneberg NJJ, 'An Introduction to the Protection &(and) Indemnity Clubs and the Marine Insurance They Provide' (1990) 3 *University of San Francisco Maritime Law Journal* 1–36.

Sands P and Stewart RB, 'Valuation of Environmental Damage – US and International Law Approaches' (1996) 5 *Review of European Community and International Environmental Law* 290–296.

Schrope M, 'UK Company Pursues Deep-Sea Bonanza' (2013) 495 *Nature* 294–294.

Seta M, 'The Contribution of the International Organization for Standardization to Ocean Governance: The Contribution of the International Organization for Standardization to Ocean Governance' (2019) 28 *Review of European, Comparative & International Environmental Law* 304–313.

Sharma R, 'Deep-Sea Impact Experiments and Their Future Requirements' (2005) 23 *Marine Georesources & Geotechnology* 331–338.

Sharma R, 'Deep-Sea Mining: Economic, Technical, Technological, and Environmental Considerations for Sustainable Development' (2011) 45 *Marine Technology Society Journal* 28–41.

Sharma R and Samantha Smith, 'Deep-Sea and the Environment: An Introduction' in Rahul Sharma (ed), *Environmental Issues of Deep-Sea Mining: Impacts, Consequences and Policy Perspectives* (Springer 2019) 3–22.

Shen H, 'International Deep Seabed Mining and China's Legislative Commitment to Marine Environmental Protection Regional Focus and Controversies' (2017) 10 *Journal of East Asia and International Law* 489–510.

Shen H, 'The Next Step of Devising China's Legal Regime for Deep Seabed Mining – The Environmental Regulation under China's Deep Seabed Mining Law' (2018) 46 *Coastal Management* 210–221.

Shibata A, 'A New Dimension in International Liability Regimes' in Akiho Shibata (ed), *International Liability Regime for Biodiversity Damage: The Nagoya-Kuala Lumpur Supplementary Protocol* (Routledge 2014) 17–51.

Scovazzi T, 'Mining, Protection of the Environment, Scientific Research and Bioprospecting; Some Considerations on the Role of the International Seabed Authority' (2004) 19 *The International Journal of Marine and Coastal Law* 383–410.

Scovazzi T, 'The Concept of Common Heritage of Mankind and the Genetic Resources of the Seabed beyond the Limits of National Jurisdiction' (2007) 14 *Agenda Internacional* 11–24.

Scovazzi T, 'The Seabed Beyond the Limits of National Jurisdiction: General and Institutional Aspects' in Alex G Oude Elferink and Erik J Molenaar (eds), *The International Legal Regime of Areas beyond National Jurisdiction: Current and Future Developments* (Brill 2010) 43–60.

Smith CR and others, 'The Near Future of the Deep-Sea Floor Ecosystems', in Nicholas VC Polunin (ed), *Aquatic Ecosystems: Trends and Global Prospects* (Cambridge University Press 2008) 334–350.

Tanaka Y, 'Obligations and Liability of Sponsoring States Concerning Activities in the Area: Reflections on the ITLOS Advisory Opinion of 1 February 2011' (2013) 60 *Netherlands International Law Review* 205–230.

Tanaka Y, 'Protection of Community Interests in International Law: The Case of the Law of the Sea' (2011) 15 *Max Planck Yearbook of United Nations Law Online* 329–375.

Taylor P, 'The Concept of the Common Heritage of Mankind' in Douglas Fisher (ed), *Research Handbook on Fundamental Concepts of Environmental Law* (Edward Elgar Publishing 2016) 306–334.

Thirlway H, "Advisory Opinions", in *Max Planck Encyclopedia of Public International Law* (2006).

Treves T, 'Principles and Objectives of the Legal Regime Governing Areas Beyond National Jurisdiction' in Erik Jaap Molenaar and Alex G Oude Elferink (eds), *The International Legal Regime of Areas beyond National Jurisdiction: Current and Future Developments* (Martinus Nijhoff Publishers 2010) 7–25.

Trouwborst A, 'The Precautionary Principle in General International Law: Combating the Babylonian Confusion' (2007) 16 *Review of European Community & International Environmental Law* 185–195.

Van Aaken A, 'Shared Responsibility in International Law: A Political Economy Analysis' in André Nollkaemper and Dov Jacobs (eds), *Distribution of Responsibilities in International Law* (Cambridge University Press 2015) 153–191.

Van Dover CL, 'Impacts of Anthropogenic Disturbances at Deep-Sea Hydrothermal Vent Ecosystems: A Review' (2014) 102 *Marine Environmental Research* 59–72.

Van Dover CL and others, 'Ecological Restoration in the Deep Sea: Desiderata' (2014) 44 *Marine Policy* 98–106.

Van Dover CL and others, 'Biodiversity Loss from Deep-Sea Mining' (2017) 10 *Nature Geoscience* 464–465.

Vitzthum WG, 'International Seabed Area' in *Max Plank Encyclopedia of Public International Law* (2008).

Walker WE and others, 'Defining Uncertainty: A Conceptual Basis for Uncertainty Management in Model-Based Decision Support' (2003) 4 *Integrated Assessment* 5–17.

Wang J, 'China: Legal Reform in an Emerging Socialist Market Economy', in EA Black, GF Bell (eds), *Law and Legal Institutions of Asia: Traditions, Adaptations and Innovations* (Cambridge University Press 2011) 24–61.

Wang Z, 'China and the Exploitation of Deep Seabed Polymetallic Nodules' (1991) 15 *Marine Policy* 132–135.

Warner R, 'International Environmental Law Principles Relevant to Exploitation Activity in the Area' (2020) 114 *Marine Policy* 103–503.

Warnock C, 'Reconceptualising the Role of the New Zealand Environment Court' (2014) 26 *Journal of Environmental Law* 507–518.

Williams BK, 'Adaptive Management of Natural Resources – Framework and Issues' (2011) 92 *Journal of Environmental Management* 1346–1353.

Williams BK, 'Passive and Active Adaptive Management: Approaches and an Example' (2011) 92 *Journal of Environmental Management* 1371–1378.

Wood MC, 'The International Seabed Authority: Fifth to Twelfth Sessions (1999–2006)' (2007) 11 *Max Planck Yearbook of United Nations Law* 47–98.

Woodwell GM, 'Curb Deep-Sea Mining Now' (2011) 471 *Nature* 36–36.

Walter C, 'Subjects of International Law' in *Max Plank Encyclopedia of Public International Law* (2007).

Weaver PPE and Billett D, 'Environmental Impacts of Nodule, Crust and Sulphide Mining: An Overview' in Rahul Sharma (ed) *Environmental Issues of Deep-Sea Mining: Impacts, Consequences and Policy Perspectives* (Springer 2019) 27–62.

Wolfrum R, 'Internationally Wrongful Acts' in *Encyclopedia of Disputes Installment 10* (Elsevier, 1987) 271–277.

Wolfrum R, 'Common Heritage of Mankind' in *Max Plank Encyclopedia of Public International Law* (2009).

Wolfrum R, 'Obligation of Result Versus Obligation of Conduct: Some Thoughts About the Implementation of International Obligations' in Mahnoush H Arsanjani, Jacob Cogan, Robert Sloane, and Siegfried Wiessner (eds), *Looking to the Future* (Brill 2010) 363–383.

Xu X, Zhang G and Xue GJ, 'China's Deep Seabed Law: Towards "Reasonably Appropriate" Environmental Legislation for Exploration and Exploitation of Deep Sea Minerals in the Area' (2017) *Asian Yearbook of International Law* 183–201.

Zhang G and Zheng P, 'A New Step Forward: Review of China's 2016 Legislation on International Seabed Area Exploration and Exploitation' (2016) 73 *Marine Policy* 244–255.

Zhang H, 'The Sponsoring State's "Obligation to Ensure" in the Development of the International Seabed Area' (2013) 28 *The International Journal of Marine and Coastal Law* 681–699.

Zhang M, 'The Socialist Legal System with Chinese Characteristics: China's Discourse for the Rule of Law and a Bitter Experience' (2010) *Temple International & Comparative Law Journal* 1–64.

Zhu L, 'Probing Compulsory Insurance for Maritime Liability' (2014) 45 *Journal of Maritime Law and Commerce* 63–76.

Ziegler AR and Baumgartner J, 'Good Faith as a General Principle of (International) Law' in Andrew D Mitchell, M Sornarajah, and Tania Voon (eds) *Good Faith and International Economic Law* (Oxford University Press 2015) 9–36.

Zou K, 'State Practice in Deep Seabed Mining: The Case of the People's Republic of China' in Markus Kotzur and others (eds), *Sustainable Ocean Resource Governance* (Brill Nijhoff 2018) 185–203.

### *Articles in Series (Liability Issues for Deep Seabed Mining Series)*

Legal Working Group on Liability, *Legal Liability for Environmental Harm: Synthesis and Overview*, Liability Issues for Deep Seabed Mining Series, Paper No. 1 (July 2018).

Craik N, *Determining the Standard for Liability for Environmental Harm from Deep Seabed Mining Activities*, Liability Issues for Deep Seabed Mining Series, Paper No. 2 (October 2018).

Lily H, *Sponsoring State Approaches to Liability Regimes for Environmental Damage Caused by Seabed Mining*, Liability Issues for Deep Seabed Mining Series, Paper No. 3 (December 2018).

Davenport T, *Responsibility and Liability for Damage Arising out of Activities in the Area: Attribution of Liability*, Liability Issues for Deep Seabed Mining Series, Paper No. 4 (January 2019).

Davenport T, *Responsibility and Liability for Damage Arising Out of Activities in the Area: Potential Claimants and Possible Fora*, Liability Issues for Deep Seabed Mining Series, Paper No. 5 (February 2019).

Xue GJ, *The Use of Compensation Funds, Insurance and Other Financial Security in Environmental Liability Schemes*, Liability Issues for Deep Seabed Mining Series, Paper No. 6 (February 2019).

Rojas AS and Phillips FK, *Effective Control and Deep Seabed Mining: Toward a Definition*, Liability Issues for Deep Seabed Mining Series, Paper No.7 (February 2019).

Mackenzie R, *Liability for Environmental Harm from Deep Seabed Mining Activities: Defining Environmental Damage*, Liability Issues for Deep Seabed Mining Series, Paper No.8 (February 2019).

### *Articles in Series (The ISA Discussion Paper)*

Discussion Paper 1- Dispute Resolution Considerations Arising Under the Proposed New Exploitation Regulations (April 2016).

Discussion Paper 2- Data and Information Management Considerations Arising Under the Proposed New Exploration Regulations (April 2016).

Discussion Paper 3- Developing a Communications and Engagement Strategy for the International Seabed Authority to Ensure Active Stakeholder Participation in the Development of a Minerals Exploitation Code (April 2016).

Discussion Paper 4- Enforcement and Liability Challenges for Environmental Regulation of Deep Seabed Mining (June 2016).

Discussion Paper 5- The Implementation of the Precautionary Approach by the International Seabed Authority (March 2017).

### *Miscellaneous*


Baecher G, 'The Nature of Risk in Geotechnical Engineering' (2005) *Post-Mining* 1 <https://www.researchgate.net/publication/255578059_THE_NATURE_OF_RISK_IN_GEOTECHNICAL_ENGINEERING_LA_NATURE_DU_RISQUE_EN_INGENIERIE_GEOTECHNIQUE> access 24 July 2020.

Cymie R. Payne, *Seminar on the Outcome of the Advisory Opinion Issued by the Seabed Disputes Chamber of the International Tribunal for the Law of the Sea on 1 February 2011 on the Responsibilities and Obligations of States Sponsoring Activities in the International Seabed Area* (Rochester, NY: Social Science Research Network, 7 April 2011).

Liang H, 'Analysing the China Tort Liability Law' (in Chinese) <https://www.iolaw.org.cn/showArticle.aspx?id=2993> accessed 14 August 2020.

Pecoraro A, 'Deep Seabed Mining in the Area: is international investment law relevant?' (*EJIL: Talk!* 2019) <https://www.ejiltalk.org/deep-seabed-mining-in-the-area-is-international-investment-law-relevant/#more-17314>accessed 11 July 2020.

Sommerer T and Tallberg J, *Decision-Making in International Organizations: Actors, Preferences, and Institutions*, Annual Convention of the International Studies Association, Atlanta, March 16–19 2016, <https://papers.ssrn.com/abstract=3059444>accessed 18 May 2020.

Tanielu T, 'Establishment of A National Regulatory Framework for the Exploration and Exploitation of Deep Sea Minerals: A Case Study for Kiribati' (United Nations-Nippon Foundation of Japan Fellowship Programme, December 2013).

Zhang Z, 'Research on the Legal Interpretation of Contemporary China' (in Chinese) <http://www.iolaw.org.cn/showNews.aspx?id=13739> accessed 15 August 2020.

# Index